MUSEUM ARCHIVES

AN INTRODUCTION

SECOND EDITION

SOCIETY OF AMERICAN ARCHIVISTS
MUSEUM ARCHIVES SECTION

Deborah Wythe, editor

THE SOCIETY OF AMERICAN ARCHIVISTS
SAA
ESTABLISHED 1936

Chicago

The Society of American Archivists
527 S. Wells Street, 5th Floor
Chicago, IL 60607 USA
312/922-0140   Fax 312/347-1452
www.archivists.org

Printed in the United States of America

Library of Congress Cataloging-in-Publication Data

Museum archives : an introduction / Society of American Archivists,
    Museum Archives Section ; Deborah Wythe, editor.
        p. cm.
    Includes bibliographical references and index.
    ISBN 1-931666-06-7
        1. Museum Archives. I. Wythe, Deborah. II. Society of American
        Archivists. Museum Archives Section.
    AM158.M88 2004
    069.5—dc22

                                                              2003067299

Cover image: The superstructure of the Brooklyn Museum of Art's Wing G and H
was erected in 1912–13 and not completed until 1925. BROOKLYN MUSEUM OF ART
ARCHIVES, PHOTOGRAPH COLLECTION. MUSEUM INTERIORS: CONSTRUCTION.

Graphic design: Matt Dufek, dufekdesign@yahoo.com.
Fonts: Minion (text and footnotes); Meta (secondary text and captions).

DEDICATED TO

ARTHUR BRETON

(1932–2000)

MUSEUM ARCHIVES PIONEER

TABLE *of* CONTENTS

FOREWORD

A museum's archives is its institutional memory. There we find the dreams of the founders and the pathways of ensuing generations that sought to make those dreams into realities. From soaring manifestos to long-range planning documents to daily meeting schedules to deeds of gifts and records of contributions, the archives retains for all time the raw, historical record of human beings working to build an institution in the service of humanity.

By preserving past records, the archives serves many needs, the most obvious being legal necessity. Documents and records that convey the spirit and intent of donors, artists, municipal bodies, and diverse expressions of the popular serve as guideposts to keep the museum within the law. Just as important is the guarantee that the work of past generations in the service of the institution, and by extension to broader communal benefit, will never be forgotten or "lost." This guarantee strengthens the resolve of present and future trustees, volunteers, donors, and the public-at-large to participate in an institution that will remember forever the sacrifices, visions, and successes of its constituents today.

The archives of the Museum of Fine Arts, Houston (MFAH), is a clear example. From the handwritten minutes of the first founders' meeting in 1900 to the computer-assisted drawings of the Audrey Jones Beck Building, the MFAH archives transcends the museum's history to chronicle both the emergence of Houston as an artistic and cultural center and developments in the art and architectural communities-at-large. Those architects, art historians, philanthropists, and artists whose contributions, designs, philosophies, faces, and even voices are preserved at the MFAH archives played roles that exceeded the confines of the museum. Whether they are interested in the architecture of Ludwig Mies van der Rohe or Rafael Moneo, the landscape designs of Isamu Noguchi or Ruth London, the installations of James Johnson Sweeney, or the civic activities of Will Hogg, Jesse Jones, or Alice Pratt Brown, present and future scholars from diverse disciplines are served by the MFAH archival collection. Within the worldwide art community, the MFAH archives consistently supports research for establishing provenance, compiling *catalogues raisonnés,* and publishing monographs.

In 1982, the trustees of the MFAH surveyed the institution's archival holdings. The nearly 700 linear feet of historic records that were to form the cornerstone of the MFAH archives were scattered among office spaces, closets, a storage vault, and—worst of all—an unairconditioned warehouse. Immediately, the trustees recognized both the records' value in developing and achieving the future goals of the museum, and their own custodial responsibility. By 1984, an Archives Advisory Committee had been formed, and a substantial grant from the National Historical Publications and Records Commission (NHPRC) had been obtained to build a formal museum archives. The museum undertook exhaustive efforts to gather, properly house, and catalog its historic records while deliberating on an appropriate permanent home for the archives. During these formative years, the archives grew dramatically as records stored in garages and attics appeared from myriad sources. An institutional records management program to distinguish between records of enduring value and those transitory in nature was developed to handle this near-avalanche of paper. In the fall of 1991, the museum archives moved into its present climate-controlled facility.

Since its establishment in 1984, the museum archives has become a tremendous resource for the MFAH in the same manner that all institutional archives serve their parent organizations. Its collections have been drawn upon to enhance design, fundraising, and marketing during extensive building and renovation projects and their corresponding capital campaigns. The MFAH archives has enabled prompt access to vital legal and financial records while decreasing liability by ensuring compliance with statutory retention requirements. Each year the archives is involved in the audit and budgeting procedures. It has navigated the organization through legal negotiations. In-house publications, whether brochures or monographs, draw upon the archives for both their information and graphics.

For these reasons alone I would endorse the establishment of an archives for any vibrant organization; in a museum setting the resource-building function of the archives is rendered all the more significant by its ability to provide contextual and interpretive information for the collection itself. Exhibition files, meeting minutes, and curatorial and administrative records provide information on the provenance, exhibition history, physical condition, and artistic significance of objects that have entered or will be considered for the permanent collection. Past collection policies guide future collecting and deaccessioning decisions. Checklists, label copy, lectures, and even comment sheets enhance exhibition, educational, and outreach programs. At the MFAH the personal papers of several major donors have been acquired, providing insight into collection strategies as well as documentation of provenance and the scholarly research of objects in or related to the museum collection.

The greatest endorsement that I can give to the establishment of a museum archives is the announcement that plans are underway to further expand the MFAH archives, which underwent a small expansion in 1996. Expansion plans will respond to the archives' special conservation and storage needs. Generous space will also allow for the more aggressive acquisition of manuscript collections that are closely related to the MFAH's history. A commitment to capture and deliver the historic electronic records of the MFAH will also be undertaken as part of the expansion. The staffing level has already been increased. Today more than ever, the trustees are committed to the concept of a vibrant archives inherently valuable and integral to the smooth operation of the museum.

As Mnemosyne, the goddess of memory, nurtured her mythological daughters—the nine Muses who preside over artistic creation and lend their name to the word "museum"—so do archives nourish the museums of which they are a part.

—*Peter C. Marzio,* Director
Museum of Fine Arts, Houston

PREFACE

*M*uch has happened in the archives world since the Society of American Archivists published William Deiss's *Museum Archives: An Introduction,* first edition, in 1984. The museum archives movement grew and flourished in both museums and the Society of American Archivists; many new museum archives were established; a strong core group of museum archivists emerged; and new archival techniques and issues arose. It became clear to members of the Museum Archives Section of SAA that a second edition was needed. It was also evident that the task of preparing one was too great for any one person and, more important, several members of the Section were excited by the prospect of contributing chapters and sharing their knowledge. The SAA provided funding for a planning weekend in February 1999, and the editorial committee (Ann Marie Przybyla, Sarah Demb, and Deborah Wythe) met and developed a prospectus, which was later accepted by SAA. The process since then has been intensely collaborative, with working group sessions at the SAA annual meeting; discussions at the Section meeting; information shared in *Museum Archivist,* the newsletter of the Museum Archives Section; and a final review by the entire authors' group.

Ludwig Mies van der Rohe with MFAH Director James Johnson Sweeney in Cullinan Hall, March 1964. Two additions to the MFAH were designed by Mies van der Rohe: Cullinan Hall, completed in 1958, and the Brown Pavilion, 1974. PHOTOGRAPH BY HICKEY & ROBERTSON; MUSEUM OF FINE ARTS, HOUSTON, ARCHIVES.

As editor, I have asked our authors to address their chapters directly to you, the reader. You may be an experienced archivist working in a museum for the first time, or you may be a museum staff member with newly assigned responsibility for the archives. This manual will introduce you to the tasks and issues you face and provide information about where to find more detailed resources. Curators, photo and film librarians, digitization project managers, and registrars who are interested in using archival techniques will also find much of interest here. Each chapter includes an overview of an archival function or topic and addresses specific issues relating its understanding within a museum context. We also include a brief history of the museum archives movement and information on museum functions and recordkeeping. The Resource Guide directs you to in-depth published materials and helpful Web sites, so that you can supplement your readings as necessary. Make special note of the Museum Archives Section listserv, where you can pose questions to other museum archivists directly.

Most museum archivists who came of age during the 1980s and 1990s, when many new museum archives were established, learned the details of our craft by talking to each other. We spent much time on the telephone and at the SAA annual meeting, bouncing ideas around, solving problems, giving support: an informal, continuous tutorial. We hope to bring some of that flavor to this manual. The authors speak both from personal experience and from their reading of the archival literature. You will hear different voices and experience different personalities; where there are different opinions or practice, we have tried to include them. As all elements of archival practice are interlocked with one another, you will find some overlap and necessary repetition among the chapters; preservation issues, for example, appear in a few different contexts, as well as in the preservation chapter.

And finally, a word about the illustrations. We chose not to illustrate the content of the chapters, but to include instead a wide variety of images drawn directly from the collections of many museum archives: people, buildings, galleries, events, and artifacts. We hope that you will enjoy these intriguing glimpses into the richness of our collections and the fascinating histories of our institutions.

We welcome you to the challenges and rewards of working in a museum archives and look forward to meeting you at the next meeting of the Museum Archives Section of the Society of American Archivists.

—*Deborah Wythe*, Editor

INTRODUCTION

1

THE MUSEUM ARCHIVES MOVEMENT

Ann Marie Przybyla

Archives and Museums

On the surface, archives and museums seem to be a good match. Both museums and archives are responsible for collecting and housing unique materials for study, display, and, more generally, "for the benefit of present and future generations."[1] Museum and archives employees work within theoretical and practical frameworks defined by their respective professions yet shaped by their own institutional needs. They share much of the same vocabulary, reflecting similar concerns and activities; they accession, manage collections, create classification systems, plan exhibitions, preserve cultural heritage, provide access, develop disaster plans, and rely on volunteers. In both fields, a small number of large, well-funded institutions overshadow smaller efforts struggling to survive financially and collect in an increasingly competitive arena.[2] Museums and archives even have in common the same sources of stress. Both have chronic space problems and, as with other cultural entities, tend to be among the first to face layoffs and closure during periods of fiscal shortages.

The division between museum and archival collections can be very indistinct, especially where nontextual materials are concerned. For example, archivists normally collect photographs that relate to their institution's primary collection and staff activities, but they may also actively pursue or commission original photographs with less direct associations.[3] Archives can assume custody of artworks, as demonstrated in a session titled "Art in the Archives," presented in 1999 at the sixty-third meeting of the Society of American Archivists (SAA) by archivists from the Amon Carter Museum and the Carnegie Museum of Art/Andy Warhol Museum. Architectural records in the custody of the archives have been used in general museum exhibitions, either to celebrate important anniversaries or to garner public support for future building projects. In addition, because of the difficulty of distinguishing between "documentary evidence," "artifact," and "object"—or fixing the line between archival and museum collections—institutional archives often contain commemorative plaques, buttons, pennants, ornamental seals, trophies, sculpted busts, and any other number of three-dimensional objects. Conversely, in a report on collecting issued by the American Association for State and Local History, sound recordings were listed as a "new category" for history museums to pursue along with "flat material: visual and/or written."[4]

Yet in spite of this apparent symbiosis, museums and archives developed as two distinct types of institution with separate histories and disciplines. As recently as 1986, John Fleckner lamented that archivists and museum employees worked in almost total isolation from each other, having their own professional literature, support organizations, and methodology, "even for describing or carrying out similar functions."[5] It has been argued that both groups have tended to focus inward as they struggle to define themselves and endure professionally, foregoing external ties in the interest of attaining self-confidence and maturity. One result of this longstanding nonrelationship has been that—until relatively recently—museum professionals, although avid collectors by nature and necessity, generally did not recognize the importance of documenting their own activities by collecting, maintaining, and making accessible the records of their institutions.

---

1 John A. Fleckner, "An Archivist Speaks to the Museum Profession," *Museum News* 65, no. 1 (October/November 1986): 17.

2 Richard H. Lytle, "Archival Information Exchange: A Report to the Museum Community," *Curator* 27, no. 4 (1984): 265.

3 Christraud M. Geary, Melissa A. N. Keiser, and Joan Stahl, "Museum Image Banks," *Museum News* 70: no. 6 (November/December 1991): 53.

---

4 John A. Fleckner, "Archives and Museums," *Midwestern Archivist* 15, no. 2 (1990): 71.

5 Fleckner, "An Archivist Speaks to the Museum Profession," 17.

Early Initiatives and the Belmont Conference

Alan Bain of the Smithsonian Institution Archives has observed that "museums have known about record-keeping problems and the need for preserving documents for years."[6] For much of that time, however, efforts to care for museum records occurred only intermittently. The Smithsonian Institution hired its first archivist in the 1890s, and the American Association of Museums (AAM) held a session on museum records at its second annual meeting in

Cornerstone-laying ceremony for new Corcoran Gallery of Art Building, May 10, 1894.
THE CORCORAN GALLERY OF ART ARCHIVES.

1907.[7] Employees of museums established at the turn of the twentieth century—the first great wave of museum construction[8]—were aware by mid-century of an alarming amount of precious space occupied by documents. In 1951, the controller of the Cleveland Museum of Art first investigated microfilming any records pertaining to the museum that predated its official opening in 1916. The museum's president and treasurer also compiled a list of "old records" to be destroyed after a specified period of time and others to be maintained permanently, essentially creating the museum's first records schedule. The board voted its approval of the schedule in 1956 but did not assign anyone the task of either destroying or preserving the records, which continued to languish—and grow—until the museum hired its first archivist/records

manager in the late 1980s.[9] Perhaps, as one historian has surmised, the relative absence of archival repositories in museums shows that museum administrators have traditionally been more concerned with "generating inspiration rather than knowledge about their cultural functions in a community."[10]

The tide began to turn in 1978, when the National Historical Publications and Records Commission (NHPRC) awarded a grant to the Detroit Institute of Arts to institute a comprehensive archival program, the first such award given to a museum. Over the next decade, the NHPRC funded twenty-four museum archives development projects for a total of $779,839 and an average award of $32,493.[11]

Museum archivists generally look to December 1979 as the true starting point of the "museum archives movement." In an organized effort to promote and support museum archives, twenty-two archivists and librarians from eighteen repositories in the United States and Canada met at the Smithsonian's Belmont Conference Center in Elkridge, Maryland. The meeting was organized by Arthur Breton of the Archives of American Art, with funding from the Smithsonian Institution's Educational Outreach Program. In his initial request for funds, Breton noted that several factors had coalesced to make such a meeting possible, including the employment of enough archivists and historians in museums to warrant a meeting of the minds to "mutually expand each other's knowledge of the matter." Breton subsequently explained that the conference was also intended to reduce the reliance that a growing number of art museums had placed on the Archives of American Art to provide microfilming services as well as advice on caring for their records.[12]

As originally planned, the conference was to include discussions of such topics as the advantages of

6 Alan L. Bain, "The Muses' Memory," *Museum News* 70, no. 6 (November/December 1991): 36.

7 Ibid.

8 Dillon Ripley, *The Sacred Grove: Essays on Museums* (New York: Simon and Schuster, 1969): 71–72.

9 Minutes of the Board of Trustees, January 25, 1956, Archives, The Cleveland Museum of Art, Cleveland, Ohio.

10 Robert W. Rydell, "The Historical Researcher," *Museum News* (April 1983): 42.

11 Laurie A. Baty, *Federal Funding for Museum Archives Development Programs: A Report to the Commission* (Washington, D.C.: NHPRC, 1988).

12 Arthur Breton, "Professionals Join in Bemont [*sic*] Conference," *Registrar's Report* 1, no. 9 (1980): 8.

having an archives program, how to initiate one, costs and funding, research use by staff and scholars, and appropriate measures for storage. On the second day, however, participants abandoned the agenda to spend two hours drafting a set of guidelines for museum archives. Directed primarily at museum administrators, the guidelines were eventually distributed in brochure form to hundreds of museums and published in several professional journals.[13] Immediately following the conference, the Smithsonian's Office of Museum Programs offered a five-day workshop on museum archives; Arthur Breton was invited to speak at meetings of the Art Libraries Society (ARLIS) and the Mid-Atlantic Archives Regional Conference (MARAC); the executive secretary of the Association of Art Museum Directors (AAMD) reported to his constituents on the Belmont Conference; and an entire issue of *Registrar's Report* was devoted to the subject of museum archives.

Because of the enthusiasm generated by the Belmont Conference and its aftermath, the Council of the Society of American Archivists created a Museum Archives Task Force[14] in January 1981. The task force established an ambitious series of nine goals, most of which involved educating museum administrators and other staff about the value of an archival program, defining the current status of archives in museums, and identifying needs and funding sources. It also intended to establish ties with other professional organizations, specifically striving to make the evaluation of archival programs a part of the museum accreditation process.[15]

To meet its goals, the task force distributed a survey along with the draft guidelines to 550 repositories. Half of the recipients responded, with 80 percent of the respondents asking for more information, and 40 percent requesting guidance on actually establishing an archives.[16] In 1984, the task force produced and distributed an information packet consisting of basic information for setting up an archives, a copy of the draft guidelines, and sample policies, procedures, and

forms from museums with newly established archival programs. The Society of American Archivists also published *Museum Archives: An Introduction,* by William A. Deiss, as part of its Basic Manual Series. In 1986, in recognition of the growing interest and acting on the task force's recommendations, SAA established a Museum Archives Roundtable, a forum for museum staff and archivists to meet annually and discuss their common concerns. To encourage communication among its members throughout the year, in December of 1986 the roundtable began publishing *Museum*

Exterior of Olmsted National Historic Site, Brookline, Massachusetts.
PHOTOGRAPH COURTESY OF THE NATIONAL PARK SERVICE, FREDERICK LAW OLMSTED NATIONAL HISTORIC SITE.

Archivist, a biannual newsletter that documented the emergence of new archives and their accomplishments in museums throughout the country and even around the world. The roundtable became an SAA section in January 1990. Thus, a decade after the Belmont Conference, museum archivists had successfully organized themselves into a unified—if still disparate—professional group with a common voice and vision.

The Growth of a Movement

The professionalization of museum archivists paralleled a very real increase in their number throughout the 1980s. A 1985 survey of archival repositories indicated that the greatest increase in institutional archives occurred in corporations and museums.[17] At the same time, archivists and researchers began

---

13 The Museum Archives Section of SAA revised the draft guidelines and issued them as an official SAA publication in 2003. See p. 234.

14 The task force consisted of eight to ten members from major museums and funding agencies; its number varied over the life of the task force as various members resigned.

15 Information about the Belmont Conference and the first goals of the task force came from Smithsonian Institution Archives, Record Unit 402, Archives of American Art, Records, c. 1954–1984.

16 Baty, *Federal Funding,* 9.

17 Paul Conway, "Perspective on Archival Resources: The 1985 Census of Archival Institutions," *American Archivist* 50 (1987): 179.

chronicling the benefits that these new museum archives were providing their parent institutions.[18] As was to be expected, curators found that institutional records are a valuable research tool for planning exhibitions, preparing publications, and caring for a collection. Beyond the demands of curatorial research, museum archivists were providing support to all segments of the institutional population, utilizing records for previously undiscovered purposes. They assisted development officers who were researching past donor relations, educators developing class materials for local schoolchildren, architects and contractors analyzing the construction and evolution of the physical plant, and much more. When scholars and other members of the public gained access to museum records, they found a surprisingly rich resource for understanding broader questions of social and cultural history, or the forces that "shape the cultural content of society."[19] Also, because so many archivists tended to function as records managers either by design or default, they proved to be vitally important to efficient and fiscally responsible administration.

The museum archives movement achieved its greatest momentum through cooperation with other professional groups. From the earliest days of the task force, archivists worked with Patricia Williams of the American Association of Museums to plan workshops and be a visible presence at AAM conferences. The task force met one of its original goals when, in 1987, questions about museum recordkeeping were included on the self-study for institutions seeking AAM accreditation. Moreover, "archivist" began appearing as a possibility in publications about careers in museums,[20] and courses on archives and records management are now featured in museum studies programs.

Various types of museums and professional groups—art, conservation, natural history, history, anthropology, zoology, and botany—joined in the effort to promote responsible recordkeeping. In 1980, Ann Abid, then librarian at the St. Louis Art Museum, surveyed seventy-five art museums to determine how many had an archives. She concluded that the responsibility for initiating a records program resided with the institution's librarian, a logical conclusion given the still fledgling effort of the archival community.[21] A decade later, museum archivists worked with the Association of Systematics Collections (ASC) to determine the number of archives in natural science repositories, subsequently adapting the draft guidelines from the

---

18 See especially the April 1983 and November/December 1991 issues of *Museum News.*

19 Rydell, "Historical Researcher," 30.

20 Jane R. Glaser and Artemis A. Zenetous, *Museums: A Place to Work—Planning Museum Careers* (London: Routledge, 1996), 70–72.

21 Ann Abid, "Archives in Art Museums: A Preliminary Survey," *ARLIS/NA Newsletter* 8, no. 2 (February 1980): 42–43.

THE VALUE OF A MUSEUM ARCHIVES

When I was Librarian at the St. Louis Art Museum, the museum acquired a gift of tapa cloth that was accompanied by a photograph album. I was called to look at the album, which contained photographs of Maoris in boats, holding artifacts—the usual sort of anthropological on-site views.

Each album page was identified with short descriptions of the mounted photographs. We took the album into the museum's archives, interleaved its pages with archival-quality tissue and generally cared for it. A few years later the museum hosted an exhibition of Maori art and artifacts, and several Maori people visited the museum to see the exhibition. We showed them the photographs, and they were actually able to identify some of the people and were very excited about seeing them.

At this point the museum administration thought that perhaps the photographs were too important to be left in the archives and should be moved to the photograph department and be treated as art. What this would have meant, of course, was that they would be separated from their original placement in the album and treated out of context as individual objects. The caption information might even be lost. I fought against the transfer and won, and as far as I know the photographs are still in the museum archives. It was a classic example of items being "too good" for the archives when they began to look interesting or important. It was also an example of a significant record that could have been lost if the archives hadn't preserved it in the first place.

—*Ann Abid*, Head Librarian
Ingalls Library, The Cleveland Museum of Art

Belmont Conference to meet the needs of ASC members.[22] At a joint meeting of the American and Canadian Associations of Zoological Parks and Aquariums, Steven P. Johnson explained the uses he had discovered for records as archivist of the New York Zoological Society, including researching the history of the animal trade and planning the reintroduction of endangered species.[23] Finally, it could be argued that the museum archives movement created an environment that made possible the establishment of affiliated groups such as the Council for the Preservation of Anthropological Records (COPAR), a nonprofit formed in 1995 to foster the care and use of records of anthropological research.

The Current State of Museum Archives

Currently, museum archivists seem to be taking stock, searching for ways to continue the forward advance of their predecessors. As we have seen, much of the history of museum archives is tied to the evolution and growth of SAA's museum archives section or to initiatives in large museums and professional organizations. The impression lingers that the daily experiences and needs of many archivists and nonprofessional staff who run archives in smaller collecting repositories remain unknown. Nor has the progress that we do know and can measure always been unimpeded. During the same decades of remarkable growth, some of the first and most significant recipients of NHPRC grants—the Corcoran Gallery of Art, Detroit Institute of Arts, and Philadelphia Museum of Art—dissolved their archives. Although the Corcoran and Philadelphia Museum of Art have since re-established full-time archives programs, the lapse indicates an administrative unwillingness to invest in and acknowledge the value of an ongoing program. Equally troubling, the absence of archival programs did not seem to constitute a "disabling deficiency" that endangered the accreditation status of any of the above institutions.[24]

Such challenges notwithstanding, noticeable strides have been made since John Fleckner's bleak

vision of just under two decades ago. When in September 1991 the Museum of Fine Arts, Boston, made the decision to close its archives due to financial constraints, the curatorial staff lobbied so heavily against the decision that management reopened the archives almost immediately.[25] Beginning in the late 1990s, many art museums have been faced with the daunting task of tracing the provenance of objects in their collections, sometimes numbering in the hundreds, in response to a renewed interest in identifying artworks that may have been seized by the Nazis.

View of Chinese Hall, 1933. Brooklyn Museum of Art Archives, Photograph Collection. Museum interiors: Asian Art (neg# 165).

While a tragic footnote to a tumultuous era, this issue of "Nazi-looted art" has given increased visibility and prominence to art museum archives.

In addition, some observers have suggested that changes in information technology provide opportunities for bringing the archival and museum fields closer than ever.[26] Curators charged with caring for "digital art" can benefit from working with archivists, who have been exploring methods of electronic records preservation for decades. Museum technology staff and registrars designing sophisticated collections management systems are finding that they can link object data with historical information culled from the institutional archives. Similarly, on-line catalogs available on institutional Web sites can provide unified description and access to archives and objects, even

---

22 *Museum Archivist*, February 1991, 14; February 1992, 3; September 1992, 6.

23 Steven P. Johnson, "Hornaday, Beeke, Crandall, and More: Archives at the New York Zoological Society," *Proceedings of the Aazpa/Cazpa Annual Conference*, September 1992, 13–17.

24 Baty, *Federal Funding*, 2; *Museum Archivist*, February 1989.

25 *Museum Archivist*, September 1991, 8.

26 For example, George Davis, "Unlocking Nature's Story—Archives and Archivists at the Academy of Natural Sciences, Philadelphia," *Museum News* 70, no. 6 (November/December 1991): 45.

though the collections remain physically distinct.[27] Whereas archivists in the past tended to highlight the inability of archivists and museum professionals to merge disciplines, today they tend to question the necessity of doing so, instead seeking to utilize new technologies to become complementary.

It is essential that museum archivists continue to demonstrate their value to their institutions and constituencies. Many of the museums that they serve are themselves being transformed into dynamic, highly competitive business ventures. Museum archivists must not only maintain established professional standards as they document these metamorphoses, but they must seek new ways to remain relevant in that changing world. They have managed to establish themselves as an identifiable subset within the context of two distinct professions, mostly because of the efforts of dedicated, energetic individuals who saw a need, and large institutions that had the ability and foresight to provide solid financial support. Their emergence was both the result and cause of greater communication across professional disciplines. Although they may still encounter occasional setbacks individually, a measure of their success as a whole is that they are no longer considered part of a "movement," which connotes something both innovative and novel, but are more frequently regarded as a standard feature of museum operations.

---

27 See, for example, the on-line catalog of the Western Reserve Historical Society at <www.wrhs.org>.

2

THE MUSEUM CONTEXT

Deborah Wythe

One of the basic principles of archival work is the importance of context: a document's significance and meaning is best understood within the broader scope of who created it and why, and what other records are associated with it. Context is also important to archives in an external sense. An archives within a larger institution is shaped by the mission of that organization. A museum archives, while sharing basic characteristics with other institutional archives, must work within an outline that is vastly different from, say, a university archives. A clear understanding of the institutional context is critical for developing a successful archival program.

This chapter addresses the ways in which the museum environment—the context—affects the operations of a museum archives. It provides an introduction to museum administration and recordkeeping and investigates how the archives fits into the picture of the museum as a whole. It looks at the organization and institutional culture of museums, defining the many administrative and curatorial functions found in museums; examines the functions of a museum archives as the keeper of institutional records and its broader role as a research center; and finally, explores the many types of records museum staff members generate.

While there are thousands of museums, small and large, in the world, one characteristic unites them all: the importance of the "object." Objects can be works of art, scientific specimens, historical artifacts, and documents. Even ideas, concepts, and events can be the driving force behind a museum; these more ephemeral "objects" may be interpreted via displays, diagrams, and models, or even presentations.[1] Botanical gardens and zoological parks, often classed among museums, treat live specimens as objects. Objects are collected, preserved, interpreted, and presented to the public. Museums exist because of objects; without them, their mission would be moot. Within the museum, the organizational structure mirrors this object orientation.

---

1 For example, a museum whose focus is performance or conceptual art may not hold any actual physical objects, but rather serve more as a venue than a collection. Children's museums may focus more on activities and displays than on collected objects.

"WHAT'S YOUR OBJECT?" A SAMPLING OF OBJECTS IN MUSEUMS

- Ceramic vessel
- Ball gown
- Battlefield
- Bible
- Silver tea service
- A "Happening"
- Conceptual installation
- Diorama of an Ice Age hunt
- A film and associated stills, posters, and ephemera
- Grove of gingko trees
- Historic house
- Lithograph

- Locomotive
- Model of DNA
- Model of the battle of Gettysburg
- Mounted eagle
- Netsuke
- Oil painting
- Panda
- *Peanuts* comic strip
- Photograph (art or documentary)
- Stone sculpture
- Teddy bear
- WWII airplane

Organization and Institutional Culture

Curatorial functions

Curators are the heart of the museum, selecting and acquiring objects and carrying broad intellectual responsibility for the objects and their interpretation. Curators select, acquire, and dispose of objects; describe and catalog them; do research; assist other researchers; write articles and books; and organize exhibitions and installations.

Registrars and collections managers manage the objects and information about them: their movements into, within, and outside of the museum; where they are stored; and their formal names, descriptions, and credit lines. All of these activities generate data, which is collected and managed by these professionals. The collections manager, a relatively new specialization, is responsible for the daily physical life of the object—storage, movements within the building, installation—and is often also strongly involved in automating access to object data. Collections managers are often assisted by skilled handlers or technicians who move, install, and mount collection materials.

Conservators evaluate, physically care for, stabilize, and restore objects. Conservation staff members, along with collections managers, are responsible for specifying and monitoring the environment (temperature, relative humidity, light levels) in galleries and storage areas; overseeing the materials used in the creation of object mounts, cases, displays; working with the registrar on monitoring the condition of loans moving into and out of the museum; and responding to damages and disasters.

Exhibition managers, designers, and preparators create the public manifestations of the museum's collections, working with curators and interpretation staff to install visually striking and intellectually engaging displays. The physical designing of exhibitions and installations goes hand in hand with the work done by curatorial and interpretation staff. Deciding how objects will be presented and in what contexts, and the production of those gallery environments, may be the responsibility of in-house staff or may be contracted out to specialized exhibition design firms.

Librarians and archivists collect, manage, and provide access to published and unpublished materials and provide reference service to researchers and members of the museum staff; gather and provide information in support of administrative functions; and manage rare book and manuscript collections, a curatorial activity.

Educators and editorial staff interpret the collections and bring them to life for children and adults through written materials, programs, and activities. The modern museum relies on an array of programs to make the collections engaging to a broad audience. Museum educators work with students and teachers in classrooms and the galleries; specialized staff members create didactics (wall text), labels, brochures, films, lectures, demonstrations, workshops, tours, and offerings of every kind to bring the public to the museum.

Administrative functions

The organizational chart of every institution reveals some form of governing body, which delegates authority for the day-to-day operations to an executive officer. The governing body, often a board of trustees, creates and updates the institution's mission statement, makes long-range plans, and oversees fiscal, legal, and administrative affairs. The museum's executive administration usually has a strong presence on the board, either as full members or *ex officio;* in the case of public institutions, elected officials or their representatives may also sit on the board.

The museum director provides leadership and works with the governing body to carry out the museum's mission. Led by the director, the executive administration plans, directs, and coordinates all the many activities going on in the institution; maintains relationships with outside organizations, including other museums, educational institutions, and governmental bodies; and acts as the museum's public face. In larger museums, the daily activities involved in these functions may be handled by separate offices, but close contact is likely to be maintained with the museum's director or president, whose name may well go on the materials generated by these other offices.

Public relations staff members represent the museum in the media world. Financial officers manage fiscal affairs and work with development personnel to raise money for museum programs. Many museums, as nonprofit institutions, depend heavily on raising funds to supplement the operating budget. Individual, corporate, and government donors are sought to support programs, building projects, endowments, and operating costs.

Membership and events staff members use the museum spaces and collections as outreach tools to entice and entertain members of the public. Museum spaces are used for fundraising and public relations events and are often rented to outside individuals and organizations for their own events. Marketing staff members often manage sales and reproduction rights activities, working in coordination with those responsible for the actual objects (curators, librarians, and archivists). Museum shops sell a wide variety of items and develop and market products related to the collections.

Information technology personnel support computer systems and bring the museum's programs and collections to the world outside its walls. Building and grounds operations and security employees maintain the building(s) and guard the collections.

While these administrative functions may seem to be generic, in reality they, too, are closely tied to the collections. Knowledge of the collections is critical to accomplishing all of these functions successfully. From the security officer who knows the objects in his or her gallery well enough to recognize damage, to the grant writer who makes an inspired pitch to a potential funder, to a product development person creating a new item to sell in the shop, all museum staff are involved with the collections.

The Museum Archives

The power of an institutional archives lies in its dual role. The museum archives is both a resource for the administration and for researchers: it is necessary for the day-to-day operation of the museum and it serves researchers of all kinds. Neither role should be overshadowed by the other.

As an active participant in the daily administrative life of the museum, the archives assists all departments by providing information and documents. This

CHANGING TIMES IN MUSEUMS

It is critical for archivists to understand not only the mission and functions of their own institution, but also the general purposes and goals of museums as a whole and, equally important, how the core nature of museums has changed over time. Such a broad knowledge base allows archivists to develop and define documentation strategies, collecting policies, appraisal decisions, and acquisitions that adequately capture the records that document what role(s) museums play in our society.

And museums *are* changing; what an exciting time to be a museum archivist! Museums increasingly are focused on educational objectives and audience development to plan a host of traditional and nontraditional outreach programs, including exhibitions. Museums have not stopped collecting objects—far from it—but many no longer view collecting and preserving objects as their main purpose, their *raison d'etre*. These activities are regarded as means to a higher purpose—public service and educational enrichment. The quality of visitor experiences has become of primary concern. In addition, reaching and retaining nontraditional museum audiences drives much of the current activity in museums. Such recent exhibitions as "The Art of the Motorcycle" (Guggenheim) and "Hip-Hop Nation" (Brooklyn Museum of Art) represent but two examples of museums deliberately seeking to alter and expand audience composition to include more representative, community-centered populations. Although there is ongoing debate in the museum community concerning these changes and what they mean, the trend is unmistakable.

From an archival perspective, it is important to understand the changing nature of museums and to regard them not as static places with set missions, functions, and perspectives, but as evolving entities. If and as museums change, either singly or universally, museum archives must succeed in understanding and capturing the nature of this change in meaningful ways. Study and capture the changing nature and purpose of your particular museum. Achieve a solid understanding of the primary functions that are undertaken at your museum—and ensure that the archives reflects all of them and if/how they change over time. Remain sensitive to any clues that an institution's mission (most tangibly defined by its offices, divisions, and departments) has expanded and/or altered—it is not always easily apparent or directly stated—and document such changes in the holdings maintained by the archives. Adopting a reflective and nonstatic approach to your museum acknowledges the complexity of its mission and ensures that the archives will capture a full accounting of its role in your community, the museum world, and society as a whole.

—Kathleen Williams
Smithsonian Institution Archives

may require finding materials in the archives, but it may also involve advising the person who inquires where to find information in another department. Archivists are often the best resource for "who has what" in the museum, as a result of records surveys and familiarity with both current and inactive records. The archivist may also be the museum's records manager, overseeing the life cycle of records from creation to disposal or permanent retention.

Archivists work with the museum administration, assisting staff members by supplying the documents needed to accomplish current work or place it in context. Creating an endowment campaign, for example, requires knowledge of past efforts. Contacts with potential donors are strengthened by information about prior contacts. The archives holds vital documents such as the museum's original constitution and articles of incorporation or legislative authority, often needed for governmental and grant reports. Public relations personnel use information and photographs from the archives to enhance the museum's public image. Membership and development publications may include images from the archives and draw on information such as lists of donors and trustees. The museum architects and engineers may require architectural plans, "as built" documentation, and information from prior contracts and specifications.

Curators and educators may consult the archives to provide historical context in labels or didactic text, to gain knowledge of specific objects or collections, to build on exhibition or installation history when planning an upcoming exhibition, or to investigate the work and opinions of their curatorial predecessors. Registrars are able to supplement the basic object information in their files with more detailed information from records in the archives, documenting credit lines, donor information, and exhibition history. Conservators need to document prior condition of objects, climatic conditions in the gallery, and early display and mounting methods.

The other, equally important, role of the institutional archives is as a research resource. By making inactive records available to researchers, both in-house and outside, the archivist contributes to research projects ranging from single, very specific questions to major scholarly efforts. Along with the museum library and other research programs, the archives functions as part of the research arm of the museum. The focus may be the object collection or the creators or collectors of the objects, or it may be the history of the institution itself. The purpose of the research may be a publication, a documentary, a simple note or citation, or personal projects such as family research. The researchers may be museum personnel or members of the general public. In many cases, a full answer requires access to the institution's primary source material—the holdings of the museum archives. The archivist works in concert with other reference personnel to guide researchers through published and unpublished sources.

Museum archivists have had frequent and impassioned discussions about the ideal place for a museum archives in the museum's organizational structure. Existing museum archives include independent departments answering to the chief executive, divisions of museum libraries, offices attached to the museum counsel, and components of collections divisions, to name just a few. The museum archives movement of the 1980s led to the establishment of many institutional archives programs that were often part of the museum's library.

The success or failure of the archives, however, depends not so much on its placement but on the support of supervisory staff and the ability of the archives to achieve the goals set out in its mission statement and to follow the standards set by the archives profession's ethical codes. Wherever it is situated in the organization, the museum archives must be able to serve all departments on an equal basis; provide equal access to researchers; have decision-making authority in archival and records management matters; and establish policies and procedures that follow archival principles.

Museum Records

In the following section, we will look at the records created in carrying out the many museum functions described above.[2] Depending on the institution, functions may be organized into a variety of departments or consolidated in the job of a single staff person, so the section is organized by function, not department. We will be working from the most centralized records— governance and executive administration, which often contain information that has been concentrated into reports—to the most localized records, which contain the details and document day-to-day activities. Understanding where information may be found will help the museum archivist develop documentation strategies and provide effective reference service.

---

2   Some discussion of the long-term value of records is included here; for further information please see the appraisal chapter.

Governance and executive administration

Minutes normally document the activities of the governing body; they may contain details of discussions or merely be a record of decisions made and actions taken. Audiotapes and transcripts may more fully document meetings. Reports from various museum departments often supplement the minutes; trustees may receive a packet of reports and supporting materials, which will be summarized in the actual minutes. Since museums are generally nonprofit organizations, governing body members often serve on a voluntary basis. As a result, their museum records are probably kept in their own business or home office. Correspondence files of trustees may contain valuable documentation of the inner workings of the board. In addition to forming an important part of an individual's personal papers, these records may also be a potential source for filling any gaps that exist in the official records: consider acquiring them for the archives.

Museums generally present acquisitions to the board for approval. The acquisition process generates records, such as accession lists, curatorial statements, deeds of gift, and bills of sale, that may include valuable information on the curatorial rationale for the acquisition, the purchase price and source of funds, and names and addresses of donors. Research institutions may have an approval process that requires staff to present proposals for and progress reports on projects, creating a central source of information on ongoing work.

The records of a museum director (the most common executive title) centralize and concentrate information about museum activities: acquisitions, exhibitions, projects, events, staff, budget, fundraising, governance, legal issues. Copies of correspondence from other departments are often sent to the director's office, resulting in a file that consolidates information from several areas. These subject or project files provide a broad overview of the topic and may document the activities of the director and his or her staff as well. Staff may send the director executive summaries, creating documents that bring together information in a brief, highly useful format. The director's files on individual departments contain correspondence, memos, reports, publications, and the like, providing a summary of that department's activities. In some cases, these files (often known as "reading files") will not document any actions taken by the executive administration; they are, however, the most important and most easily accessible record of the museum's work as a whole.

Materials that are museum related but do not have anything to do with the actual activities of the museum frequently come into the director's office and are filed along with records that are directly related to the museum. Other institutions send announcements of exhibitions, governmental agencies send reports and guidelines, and companies send promotional materials.

Depending on the size and organization of the museum, certain major projects may originate in the director's office. Records of special projects such as

First Lady Jacqueline Kennedy with Egyptian officials opening the exhibition *Tutankhamun Treasures* at the National Gallery of Art, November 3, 1961. NATIONAL GALLERY OF ART, GALLERY ARCHIVES, WASHINGTON, D.C.

mission statement re-evaluation, long-range planning, museum accreditation, audience studies, and capital projects may be found there, as may the voluminous final reports of these projects.

In addition, records of the personal and professional activities of the director are often preserved in the director's office files (although these might also be considered part of his or her personal papers and thus personal property[3]). Directors often serve on boards of other institutions, are active in professional organizations, and are consulted by their colleagues. These records may contain materials that are unavailable or restricted elsewhere (minutes, for example) or copies of confidential records such as recommendations and peer reviews.

---

3 A carefully written archives acquisition policy, as discussed in the appraisal chapter, will help you decide what actions to take when faced with personal papers among the museum's institutional records.

Collections

Records that document the object collection have a special place among the range of institutional records. These curatorial records focus on the object in greater depth and detail and have a chronological span that extends beyond daily activities. While administrative files deal with the day to day and become inactive within a few years, curatorial records represent a continuing, historical process: new information is added and older data refined year after year. Records relating to the collection are always permanent and logically a part of the museum archives, but many such records are permanently active and needed in the originating department on a daily basis.

The process of acquiring objects for the museum collections begins with initial contacts between the museum's curatorial staff and donors or vendors. Once an object is offered, negotiations ensue, an offer is made and accepted, the object is presented to and approved by the museum governing body, and it becomes a part of the collection. Each step generates records: correspondence, sales lists, provenance and background documentation, a deed of gift or sales contract, valuations, tax forms, purchase requisition, approval and payment voucher forms, receipts, shipping and arrival forms, listings in minutes and acquisitions records.

These records, perhaps the most mission-critical records of the museum, may be found together in a case file for the individual accession, or they may be filed with like documents (all arrival forms may be held in a single series, for example). They may reside in the curatorial department, in the registrar's office, in a cataloging department, in the legal counsel's office—or in any or all of the above. They may be in the originating office or in the archives. Procedures will have changed over the years, resulting in different forms and series of records (but containing much the same information). Where the records are found reveals much about the staff, organization, and workings of the museum: it is the archivist's job to understand these procedures and to be able to locate each part of the core documentation, wherever it is stored.

Relationships with donors and vendors often develop over decades, going far beyond the acquisition of a single object. While the actual donation or purchase of an object will be documented in the formal manner noted above, information about that object and other related materials may be foreshadowed in correspondence long before the actual transaction, and additional information may be exchanged later.

Unless the museum has a central file,[4] correspondence with these individuals may be dispersed in the correspondence files of several departments. Depending on their interests, donors and vendors frequently have separate relationships with more than one curator; important donors may also have a close relationship with the director or the board of trustees.

Many donors are themselves major collectors, with scholarly interests and highly developed collections. Their relationships with curators may involve a detailed give-and-take of information about exhibitions, objects available on the market, and potential purchases and donations. As the curator gives advice and shares information, his or her knowledge and opinions are documented in detail, and insights are revealed that may never be published.

The displays that form the central focus of most museums may be classified into two types: *exhibitions,* generally organized around a central theme and of limited duration, and *installations,* displays of the permanent collection. Installations may include entire galleries that are unchanged or changed incrementally during long periods of time, or they may simply consist of a single case that stays up for a month or two.[5]

The records of special exhibitions are some of the most voluminous and most heavily used materials in many museum archives. While the object documentation discussed above is highly valuable to in-house researchers and scholars with a detailed focus, a broad range of researchers, both outside and in-house, find a wide variety of information in exhibition files. These records reveal much about the objects included, the museum's philosophy and mission at the time, the curator's research efforts, and public reaction.

Exhibition records comprise object checklists, descriptions, appraisals, and conservation evaluations; correspondence with lenders (collectors, scientists, artists), scholars, and other museum professionals; documentation of object selection and rejection; background research; grant applications and fundraising correspondence; major and ephemeral publications; label and didactic texts; interpretive materials such as videos, slide shows and audio tours; installation design records; and reviews and press coverage. Exhibitions that tour may generate planning correspondence, additional loan and shipping records, and documentation of other installations and press coverage. Document types may include correspondence, memos, checklists,

---

4   A *central file* holds records from all departments in a single filing system.
5   The terms "to install" and "the installation" are also used more generically to describe the physical process of hanging or setting up an exhibition and the final results of that process.

insurance and appraisal documents, loan and shipping forms, drafts of texts, grant applications, catalogs, brochures, installation plans and models, invitations, press releases, reviews, clippings, photographs, negatives, transparencies, slides, videos, audiotapes, and interactive computer programs.

Since exhibitions are major productions, several museum departments are likely to participate, creating their own exhibition files. Copies of documents may well be circulated and appear in the files of several departments, creating complex appraisal questions. The curatorial file, containing a full set of copies, may be a convenience for researchers (though an increased storage problem for the archives). Curatorial research may generate large amounts of reference material photocopied from library sources. Once the project is completed, this material is no longer needed, though it may be wise to create a citation list of materials discarded. Some materials, such as loan forms, may be maintained permanently by the registrar.

Installations are much more difficult to document. Unlike special exhibitions, which are well-defined projects, installations are more process oriented. Objects from the permanent collection are grouped and placed into a gallery, labeled, and explained. Although the initial stages of major installation projects are sometimes well documented, the process is frequently informal, and the only documentation may be notations on location cards, a few memos requesting assistance moving and installing objects, drafts of labels and wall text, and (possibly) a photograph or two. Changes may take place incrementally over a period of years and the documentation is often buried in administrative and object files rather than segregated into an installations or gallery series. The initial installation may be described in a press release, but subsequent changes are almost surely not. Certain collections that are sensitive to light are "rotated" a few times a year, often without comment.

Other curatorial activities

Museum research, while often specifically pointed toward the production of a new exhibition or installation or toward documenting objects, may also be a more self-contained project. Surveys and studies of artworks in particular genres, scientific studies, archaeological digs, and the like are all carried out by museum staff with institutional or grant funding. These projects may generate voluminous data, background, and administrative files, as well as ongoing and final reports and publications. Records of

research projects document the history of the institution as a research center and are often of great value to scholars in related disciplines.

Curatorial staff members, much like university faculty, are also often involved in long-term scholarly projects and activities that are not funded by the institution but often revolve around the collections. They also correspond informally with colleagues and members of the public about the collections. The letters, memos, field reports, project descriptions, inventories, and notes found in these types of general correspon-

Hauling out block of fossil bones packed for shipment in "field bandages," 1926–1927, Folsom, New Mexico. Photograph by Harold J. Cook. Denver Museum of Nature & Science Image Archives, ME86-008.

dence or research files can be very valuable, as we noted in the discussion above about donor correspondence.

Curators also belong to professional organizations and serve active roles in their administration. They take on consulting jobs, serve on panels, review grants, write papers, and present lectures. The work—and records—involved with these activities are often so intermingled with their museum work that it is difficult to separate personal papers from institutional records.[6] Is a lecture about the collection to a professional group an institutional or personal activity? Is research for a book that includes information derived

---

6   Thoughtful acquisitions policies, discussed in the appraisal chapter, are key to unraveling these situations.

from study of the collections part of the institutional record, even if the museum did not directly fund the publication of the book?

All of the functions discussed above, exhibitions, installations, scholarly research, and special projects, may result in publications, both major and ephemeral. While the records documenting the production of these materials will be found in one or more administrative departments (editorial, design, production), the content-based records will often be found among curatorial files. Drafts and galleys frequently create a massive bulk of paper. The decision whether to keep multiple (or any) drafts of publications should be part of the archives appraisal policy. If a completed publication is available, it may be acceptable to discard drafts; any chapters or sections that were cut from the publication, however, should be retained. Museum publications frequently include essays by scholars from other institutions. Correspondence and contracts relating to these contributions may be important in addressing future copyright questions.

Registrar

Every object or collection acquired by a museum must be formally documented and accepted into the collection, resulting in a standard body of records that are generated and managed by the museum registrar. Input from curators, the director, and the board of trustees all funnels into formal documentation of the object. At the most basic level, this may consist of an object description, date of accession, and name of the donor or vendor; as more information is gathered, the object registration may expand to include extensive descriptive, background, and comparative information. Once the object is formally part of the collection, the registrar manages its movements within and outside of the museum, augmenting the record with details regarding loans to other organizations. Registrar's records are often based on a series of standard forms and, since access to information is critical to their mission, the records are generally well organized. Like some curatorial records, collections records in the registrar's office are permanently active, and the archivist will often find him- or herself working hand-in-hand with the registrar to answer collections questions.

The core collections documentation is considered "mission critical": without basic information about the collections, the museum would not be able to operate. Therefore, the archivist must ensure that these records are protected, whether in paper or electronic format. The registrar is also responsible for objects that reside in the museum temporarily, tracking their arrival, unpacking, condition, return, and shipment. Exhibitions may include both permanent collection objects and objects borrowed from other institutions; entire exhibitions may be circulated from and to other museums. These functions generate loan forms, condition reports, crating and shipping documentation, and insurance records. Unlike the records of the permanent collection, exhibition and loan records become inactive once the transaction is completed.

More and more museums are depending on databases to manage collections management functions, so electronic, rather than paper, records may be created. While most of the records are of immediate importance, some "audit records" created by the system or on paper may have permanent value. Thus, a computer system may be set up to reveal the current location of an object, but will store past locations to create an audit trail of who moved what when. This can be a valuable source of information on installations, which are frequently changed incrementally and with minimal documentation.

Conservation

Conservation records, documenting the physical care and restoration of the museum collections, also have both day-to-day and historical value. Every time an object is examined or treated, documentation of those actions is recorded in the object's file. This may take the form of textual notations (paper or electronic), photographs, slides, x-radiographs and results of other scientific studies, and information on and samples of materials. The goal today is to document all work so that it will be fully understood and reversible by future conservators. Prior to the establishment of scientific conservation/restoration laboratories in the 1930s, objects may have been treated by in-house or freelance restorers. Documentation of these activities may well be scattered among various series, especially curatorial, and ideally should be linked intellectually with ongoing conservation object records.

While most conservation records are valuable primarily for in-house use, their value to outside researchers must also be noted. Conservators evaluate and treat objects borrowed for exhibitions; museum objects may be deaccessioned; private individuals (often trustees and important donors) bring in objects for evaluation. In all these cases, the object documentation may be needed by current owners.

Programs and projects

Developing and producing the museum's many education, interpretation, and public programs results in voluminous files, which must be carefully evaluated to avoid being overwhelming. The records can be divided into three types: background research, production, and program materials. The latter are the most valuable: lesson plans or descriptions, actual didactic and label texts, printed programs, handouts, flyers, photographs, audio- and videotapes, and the like document that a program occurred and provide compact and reliable information about the actual event. Production materials are less useful. Correspondence files may include valuable documentation such as contracts with participants and possibly even texts of lectures, but may also contain memos and letters related to logistics that are of little value once the event is over. Background research and reference files are frequently derivative, containing copies of articles and materials provided by curators that were used to inform the creation of programs.

Program evaluation records and audience surveys often present a similar dilemma of high volume and questionable value. Many institutions make a practice of polling in order to be more responsive and successful in future programs. Depending on the type of evaluation, the data collected may or may not be useful beyond this immediate goal. The raw evaluation forms may well be transferred to the archives, and a decision must be made whether to retain them. In some cases, it is clear that the data have been analyzed and some form of report created. At the very least, it is important to document that evaluations took place and what questions were asked; the archivist, in consultation with the office that instigated the evaluation process, should then decide whether to retain the raw data, set up a sampling process, or discard the forms.

Records documenting the exhibition design and installation process include memos and proposals circulated among designers and curatorial, interpretation, and administrative staff members; sketches, floor plans, computer-assisted design (CAD) materials, and models; color, type, and materials samples; and logistics paperwork to accomplish the final creation of the gallery. The finished installation may be documented in a series of photographs: if this is not done on a reg-

ular basis, the archivist would be well advised to instigate such a process.

Once again, the decision must be made whether to document the entire process or just the final product. Many of the records generated by design and fabrication staff may not be of value much beyond the active life of the project. For example, for a few years after the project is complete, vendor information is very useful to the department, since staff may want to use it again. Later, such records have little research value.

Painting & Sculpture "study storage gallery," late 1960s. BROOKLYN MUSEUM OF ART ARCHIVES, PHOTOGRAPH COLLECTION. MUSEUM INTERIORS: PAINTING & SCULPTURE.

(If someone wants to track vendors in the future, that information will probably be preserved in financial records such as the general ledger.) In contrast, a gallery floor plan with notations of where and in what context objects were displayed has permanent research value. Analyzing and appraising these records will allow the archivist to preserve those record types that contain the most, and the most valuable, information.

Development, outreach, and administration

As with other museum activities, the records documenting development, fundraising, and special events may be divided into program documentation and logistics. For example, grant applications, award documentation, and reports are valuable permanent records that contain not only information about the particular project, but also distill information about the museum as a whole. Producing the applications, however, generates many notes, memos, and drafts that have little long-term value.

Files on individual and corporate donors are a bit more difficult to analyze. As long as the donors are active contributors, the records will remain active and valuable to the department. Once they are inactive, however, a decision must be made on how much to save and for how long. Assuming the records of donations are preserved in the financial records of the museum, the archivist must decide whether to pre-

Two buffalo in a paddock in the South Yard behind the Smithsonian Institution Building. They were acquired by the Department of Living Animals, which became the National Zoological Park. This photograph was taken sometime between 1886 and 1889. SMITHSONIAN INSTITUTION ARCHIVES, NEG. MAH8008A (RU 95, BOX 30A, FOLDER 19).

serve the backup correspondence files. Frequently, the same or similar letter is sent out to many potential donors; a central appeals file may contain the form letters and document categories of donors to whom it was sent. Often this process is carried out in electronic format, so hard copy may not even be available and preserving (or not) this documentation will fall under the archives' electronic records program.

Events, much like the public programs discussed above, require documentation that they happened, but not necessarily of all the steps that it took to produce them. If the museum has an annual gala, for example, the invitation, program, honoree information, photographs, and final financial reports may be

sufficient documentation; retaining guest lists, seating information, and the myriad memos and proposals involved with choosing caterers and the like is probably unnecessary.

The records of a museum marketing program may be divided between operations and product development/marketing. The former is primarily an administrative function and the files will be scheduled along with similar financial records. Product development, licensing, and marketing is more connected to the collections and thus of greater interest. Contractual or legal obligations may be involved as well. The choices of objects to reproduce or interpret in cards, calendars, posters, scarves, mugs, and children's activity sets reveal something about the institutional and market climates. How to document this is more difficult, since these records are also dominated by the ubiquitous logistics files. Annual and quarterly reports may provide this information, as may published catalogs. Starting a collection of sample products may be of interest.

Museum objects are often reproduced in book and article illustrations, advertisements, and video productions. Ideally, this publication history is recorded as part of each object's permanent record in the curatorial or collections management records. If not, a method should be sought to preserve this information in a compact form, since the records produced by a rights and reproductions department may be overly voluminous for the actual content contained.

The museum's public face is documented by a variety of ephemeral publications such as press releases, statements, brochures, pamphlets, public service announcements (PSAs), and its Web site. The first categories on this list are fairly easily dealt with; the only difficulty may be in dating some publications if they are not collected as they are produced. Reaction to the museum in the media is also an obvious area to document: clippings, articles, and audio- and videotapes reveal how the institution is perceived. Maintaining an archival "copy" of the museum's Web site is more difficult, both because of the electronic, hyperlinked format and because of the constant incremental change that usually occurs in Web sites. As technology evolves, the archivist must continually seek the newest and best ways to preserve the record, from keeping hard copies of content materials, to creating CDs with copies of files and software, to maintaining materials on a server.

Depending on the size of the museum, overall administrative functions (financial, purchasing, personnel, building operations, systems management, for example) may be managed by a single office, or they may be divided among various departments. Every office will also generate administrative records that may relate only peripherally to their specific mission, a fact that should be carefully considered during the appraisal process. These administrative files—working budget files, all-staff communications, and housekeeping memos, to name a few—may well be duplicated in central administrative files and may not have a value beyond their active life.

Museum building

While not accessioned as an object *per se,* many museum buildings may be classed as a work of art on their own merits. Designed to be both a showcase for the collections as well as a showpiece for the community, commissions for museum buildings have been awarded to architects of the highest caliber. The records generated during the concept, design, and construction phases are of great importance to both museum staff and outside researchers. As museums grow and change, their built environment acts as the physical embodiment of the philosophical approach of the trustees and executive administration.

Often voluminous and oversized, architectural records are a special challenge to museum archivists, who would be well advised to consult an architectural records archivist for assistance. Contemporary architectural records create even greater difficulties, since incremental change may be reflected only in CAD systems. An electronic records archives program must address the challenges of preserving and providing access to this information.

In addition to traditional architectural records, construction projects generate many records. The museum archivist must work closely with those responsible for projects (whether in-house staff or an outside construction management firm) to understand the purposes and potential research value of these records. Change orders, shop drawings, engineering reports, requisitions, cost reports, specifications, and general and subcontractor files must all be evaluated for their administrative, research, and legal values.

Special collections

Until now, we have discussed only institutional archives: the records of the museum itself. As collecting institutions, however, museums have traditionally acquired collections of personal papers and archival records. Curators are fascinated by ancillary materials that support the objects under their care and frequently accept them for their documentary value. Depending on how your mission is defined, the museum archives may become an active collector of personal papers and records of related organizations.

Special collections are another example of the importance of context. Archival materials acquired in conjunction with objects in the collections must maintain that context by creating intellectual links between objects and related materials (and other objects). Preservation concerns and storage practicalities usually dictate that these collections cannot remain together physically.

In the past, special collections were often the "stepchildren" of departments that did not have archival expertise to handle them. They may have been described at the item level, or not at all. With the establishment of an archives program, special collections may become the responsibility of the museum archivist. Maintaining the link to the object should be as simple as placing object or collection identification in the archival record, and vice versa. It is important to keep in mind, however, that the value of special collections materials may go far beyond documentation of the object with which they are associated. The archivist's job is to describe these materials in such a way that researchers are aware of the full range of information found in each collection. (It may also be his or her job to unravel various prior systems of accessioning and describing archival materials.)

In conclusion, just as the museum's activities support its mission to collect and interpret objects, museum recordkeeping reflects that focus on the object. Departmental interrelationships create interesting complications in recordkeeping: to trace the paper trail of a single activity (an exhibition, for example) may require researchers to study records in series generated by several different departments. As we shall see in the chapters on arrangement and description, these record series reveal more about the museum than just their contents; they document not just a specific activity or topic, but how the museum functions in its internal and external context.

3

GETTING STARTED

Susan Klier Koutsky

A museum archives program, whether well established or just beginning, is dependent upon three basic elements for survival: institutional support and funding, space, and qualified staff.[1] The absence of any one element can cripple the program or even bring it to a halt. In this chapter, we will examine these components and then suggest some important first steps for new museum archivists.

Institutional Support and Funding

The very first step you must take in establishing a museum archives—before collecting records, before hiring an archivist, and even before writing start-up grants—is to obtain institutional support from the highest level of museum authority. Ensure that the inception of an archival program is documented in the minutes of a board meeting and obtain written support from the necessary authorities. The archives program requires this ongoing support so that funds are allocated in every budget year, the archives is recognized during strategic planning efforts, and the needs of a growing archives program are addressed and met. High-level institutional recognition encourages support from all levels in the hierarchy and gives the archives museum-wide credibility, even if the program is a division within another department or a small, autonomous department. Museum staff members are more likely to work with the archivist and use the archives program if they see the importance administrative authorities place on the program. Ongoing administrative support is therefore essential both to the beginning and continuing success of the archives program.

Once you obtain institutional backing for the archives program, you must find the necessary funds for operation. Ideally, the archives will have a separate budget line drawing on regular institutional operating funds or an endowment. This is a great way for the museum administration to show its support for the program, and a good way to make sure that future funding is not dependent on the fickle outside sources known as "soft money." It is not always possible, however. While the cost of establishing an archives need not be exorbitant, a small nonprofit museum may have difficulty finding the funds within its regular budget, particularly in the early days, before the program has proven its worth. Allocation of stable institutional funding is an important goal.

A popular way of funding a start-up archives program is through grant money. Luckily, many possible grantors are available to museums, from private individuals to public and government agencies. Many granting agencies require that receiving organizations be nonprofit, with 501(c)(3) status, and be involved in educational ventures; museums that are governmental agencies may not always be eligible.

Granting agencies, whether federally or privately funded, vary in their application rules, granting period, and resources available. Spend time looking for the grant programs that best match your mission, goals, needs, and timeline. You will expend a great deal of time writing a grant proposal—effort that can be wasted if your project is not a good fit. A good place to begin is the Foundation Center, a nonprofit organization with offices in many major cities.[2] The center provides a library of resources including publications about specific grants and information on writing successful grant proposals. Center staff can help sort

---

1 In many respects, starting a museum archives is no different than starting any other type, and authors and archivists from a variety of archives recognize the importance of the elements suggested here. See, for example, Elizabeth Yakel, *Starting an Archives* (Lanham, Md.: Society of American Archivists and Scarecrow Press, 1994) and Small Archives Committee of the Association of British Columbia Archivists, *A Manual for Small Archives* (Vancouver, B.C.: Association of British Columbia Archivists, 1988). There are, however, aspects of these elements, noted in this chapter, that are unique or pertain especially to museums and their archives.

2 See its Web site at <http://fndcenter.org> for locations and a description of its services.

through the resources, narrow the field of candidates, and, for a fee, perform the research for you.

Three federal agencies—the Institute for Museum and Library Services (IMLS), the National Endowment for the Humanities (NEH), and the National Historical Publications and Records Commission (NHPRC)—are of great importance to museum programs.[3] Although their grant programs differ, each has provided seed money for archival programs. Study the grant guidelines and discuss your project with program officers to determine which is most appropriate, then draft your proposal. Keep in mind that other departments in your museum may be approaching the same agencies or foundations and cooperate with your development staff to avoid unnecessary and unprofitable competition.

While grants are a viable way to obtain initial funding for a museum archives, they cannot be relied upon indefinitely, nor will they cover everything. Grants often require a significant proportion of cost sharing, so your institution may have to provide either a dollar or in-kind match for part of the award. Most grant

---

3 Institute for Museum and Library Services, Office of Museum Services, 1100 Pennsylvania Avenue NW, Room 609, Washington, D.C. 20506; phone: 202-606-8539, fax: 202-606-0010; <www.imls.gov>. National Endowment for the Humanities, 1100 Pennsylvania Avenue NW, Washington, D.C. 20506; phone: 800-NEH-1121; <www.neh.gov>. National Historical Publications and Records Commission (NHPRC), 700 Pennsylvania Avenue NW, Room 111, Washington, D.C. 20408-0001; phone: 202-501-5610; fax: 202-501-5601; <www.nara.gov/nhprc>.

BUDGET CHECKLIST

In addition to staff salaries and benefits and basic office equipment and supplies, consider the following in creating a budget for a new archives program:

Equipment and tools
- Large table(s)
- Shelving
- Ladder
- Cart
- Kick stool
- Map case (flat file)
- Hygrothermograph or datalogger
- Light box
- Copy stand and camera
- Scanner
- HEPA vacuum
- Photocopier with a large platen
- Scalpel for pulling staples
- Bone folding tool
- Document weight bags or cloth-covered weights
- Soft brush for cleaning
- Apron or lab coat
- Disaster response supply kit

Supplies
- Records cartons
- Document boxes (full and half size; letter and legal)
- Flat print boxes (small, medium, large)
- Specialized boxes (i.e. card file, glass negative)
- Archival-quality 3-ring binders

- Folders (regular and photographic; letter and legal)
- Folder stock (large sheets)
- Acid-free paper (20-pound and heavier stock)
- Buffered and unbuffered acid-free tissue paper
- Acid-free corrugated board
- Document box spacers
- Paper photo enclosures (4-flap, envelopes)
- Inert plastic sleeves (slide, 35mm negative, 4 x 5″, 8 x 10″)
- Inert plastic L-fold sheet protectors
- Inert plastic in large sheets or roll (i.e. Mylar or Melinex®)
- Inert double-sided tape for encapsulation
- Inert paper clips (plastic or stainless steel)
- Cotton tying tape
- Dust masks
- Lint-free, chemical-free dust cloths
- Cotton gloves
- Document cleaning powder (eraser grains)
- Pencils (#2 and #5B)
- Erasers

Other
- Travel and professional development (archival organization meetings, workshops)
- Computer equipment maintenance
- Software and hardware upgrades
- Printer supplies (toner, paper)
- Off-site storage, if needed
- Consultants for special projects

programs stipulate a time period during which the money must be used, usually from several months to two years. Though some grants can be renewed, the time it takes to apply and the time spent waiting make this an unattractive option. Museum archives programs should not be dependent on grants for survival. Once your program is established, begin working toward institutional funding as soon as practical. Plan to use future grant money for one-time special projects that are out of the scope of the regular budget line and have a definite starting and ending date.

The Archives of the Morgan Library in New York contains several thousand letters and invoices documenting the books, manuscripts, and art objects collected by American financier Pierpont Morgan (1837–1913). This cartoon satirizes Morgan's prodigious acquisition of works of art from the other side of the Atlantic. CARTOON FROM *PUCK* MAGAZINE, CA. 1912. ARCHIVES OF THE PIERPONT MORGAN LIBRARY, NEW YORK.

Space

The second crucial requirement for a museum archives program—space—involves not just storage, but also work, office, reference, and possibly exhibition space. Consider all of the above activities and allocate room as needed. Familiarize yourself with the requirements of the Americans with Disabilities Act (ADA)[4] and make sure that your space conforms.

The most obvious space need is for adequate storage. In determining how much space is needed for archival storage, analyze the present extent of records and plan for future growth—a difficult task when the archives program is new, staff is not in place, and a records survey has not yet been undertaken. To help derive estimates,

talk to archivists in museums of a similar age and size to yours. Try to provide more space than you think you will need.[5]

Archival storage can be located either on the museum premises or off-site. Either is acceptable as long as the space meets preservation standards and is accessible to staff. Requirements include adequate floor loads, proper shelving, good security, and stable climate control.[6] In-house storage is usually more convenient, allowing quicker retrieval times and easier monitoring. When there is no acceptable storage area within the museum, however, obtaining off-site storage may be necessary. The cost of renting the space, controlling its environment, picking up records from the museum, retrieving records from storage, and delivering them back to the museum can add up to substantial sums of money. Because of the expense of off-site storage, it is all too inviting to relegate the archives to a substandard space within the museum. However, just as museum curators would cringe at this possibility for the permanent collections, do not consider this a solution for the archives unless the space can be upgraded to meet the preservation requirements of the records.

Storage spaces must accommodate sturdy shelving and heavy boxes. Consult your facilities personnel or engineering reports to establish allowable floor loads and make sure that you are not overloading the museum structure. This is especially important when considering compact shelving, and it is well worth hiring a consultant if expertise and information are not readily available in-house.

Security is another critical issue for storage and office areas. While archival collections may not initially seem to have high monetary value, most archival records are unique—and thus irreplaceable—so the loss of even some vital records can be devastating. All storage areas should be under lock and key, and patrons should not have access to them. Consult the museum's security staff for advice on designing secure

---

4   For information on the act, contact the Department of Justice at 800-514-0310 or <www.usdoj.gov/crt/ada/adahom1.htm>.

5   For example, many library renovations use providing for ten years of growth as a benchmark.

6   See the preservation chapter for more information.

spaces, monitoring access, and ensuring effective fire and flood protection.

Within the storage areas, consider the type and configuration of shelving used from the point of view of preservation, safety, and convenience. Purchase only high-quality shelving—avoid recycling old metal or wood shelving units, which may introduce preservation problems of their own into the archives. Compact shelving, while relatively expensive, is often an attractive shelving solution, as it allows for more records to be stored in a smaller amount of space. Select shelving sizes that match archival boxes, which should sit squarely on the shelf with no overhang. Avoid shelving sizes that will cause you to waste space. Aisles should be wide enough for safe, easy retrieval of records.

Maintaining a proper storage environment is the best, most cost-effective way to ensure the preservation of museum records. Storage areas must be clean, safe, protected from ultraviolet light, free of leaks, and free of insects, mold, and vermin. Temperature and humidity must remain as stable as possible, year-round. Since it may not be possible to achieve the optimal environment for every different type of media, you may have to compromise on environmental conditions that do the least damage to the most types of materials. Your conservation department personnel are an important resource in this area—take advantage of their expertise, or consult a preservation professional.

Besides storage space, the archives staff needs room for administrative tasks, processing records, and reference service. These may be contiguous or they may be separate, but each function should be supported with the proper furnishings and, ideally, all the spaces should be closely and conveniently located. Keep workplace safety and comfort in mind. Archivists lift and carry heavy boxes and work both seated and standing; they are at risk for both back and hand problems. Think about work-flow patterns, provide ergonomically sound furniture, and arrange the work space and its storage units for maximum convenience.

Typically, administrative work requires desks and chairs for archives staff, telephones, computers, storage cabinets for office supplies, bookshelves for reference works, and filing cabinets for administrative files. Many archivists prefer a separate, dedicated work surface for administrative work, segregating the archival collections they are working on from everyday paper-

work for safety's sake. The potential for losing, misfiling, or damaging records is a very real danger when administrative work and processing occupy the same work surface—no coffee in the archives!

The processing area should accommodate large worktables and shelves for incoming and in-progress collections. Keep the space as flexible as possible, to accommodate permanent staff as well as temporary interns and volunteers doing a wide variety of projects. Since this area may serve as a temporary storage space for records while they are being processed, the

The taxidermy laboratory at the Smithsonian Institution. William T. Hornaday and Andrew Forney, taxidermists, are pictured. Smithsonian Institution Archives, neg. 3662 (RU 95, Box 29, Folder 7).

environmental considerations discussed above apply. Archival supply storage space for boxes, folders, paper, and the like should be conveniently located. A separate quarantine area for incoming collections or dirty work can be helpful.

Reference service occurs in a public space, so the museum may want to provide furniture that reflects a less-utilitarian image than seen in the storage and work areas. Researchers require comfortable chairs and tables, ideally with power outlets and data connections for laptop computers. Access to a photocopy machine is important, although copying is usually done by archives staff, not patrons. Set up the room so that the sight lines allow a staff member to supervise readers at all times. If collections and readers must be in the same space (not an ideal situation), make sure that members of the public do not have easy access to the boxes; open stacks are not normal archival procedure. Since staff will be pulling boxes and bringing them to the reading room, easy access to storage areas and space to park carts are important. Sharing reference space with the library can be a natural way to cooperate and save staff time by sharing supervisory responsibilities.

A final consideration for museum archives is exhibition space. Exhibiting museum archival records is optional and up to the discretion of the archivist

Vladimir Fewkes (r) and John Tobler examining a season's yield from Czechoslovakia, 1937. PHOTOGRAPH BY REUBEN GOLDBERG. UNIVERSITY OF PENNSYLVANIA MUSEUM. NEG. 71158-61.

and the museum administration, but can be a valuable outreach effort. If exhibition space is allotted, even just a small display case, make sure this public space conveys a professional image, upholds preservation standards, and presents interesting and stimulating materials from your collection.

Staff

Archivist and educator Bruce Dearstyne states that "archival work is demanding and exacting and should be carried out by trained, experienced personnel."[7] The type and level of training and experience needed has been somewhat controversial, even among archivists. Generally, archivists have both undergraduate and master's degrees. The master's degree may be in

library science and/or history and should include archival coursework and a practicum. [8] For a museum archivist, it is very helpful to have some museum studies coursework and/or museum work experience. The Society of American Archivists[9] provides information on archival education, but does not certify programs, as the American Library Association does. Archivists may pursue individual certification through the Academy of Certified Archivists.[10]

Because of the complicated nature of archival records, you will certainly want the best person possible to look after the museum's records. Some museums appoint museum volunteers, clerical staff, or curators as archivists (all of whom are an important part of the audience for this book), but while these individuals may understand the workings of the institution, they need additional training in the areas of archival preservation, processing, access, and legal issues. If hiring a professional archivist is not within your means, provide archival training through workshops sponsored by national or regional archives associations and through mentoring provided by local archival institutions.[11] The museum should continue to support the archivist in any continuing educational opportunities that arise. This is especially important because the archival field is constantly changing in response to new technologies and best practices.

The number of staff members depends upon the size of the archival space, the amount of work, and the resources available. Once a professional is hired, he or she can train and direct additional personnel: associate archivists, assistants, technicians, interns, and volunteers. A full complement of archival personnel will allow for efficient records processing as well as prompt reference service.

7   Bruce Dearstyne, *The Archival Enterprise: Modern Archival Principles, Practices, and Management Techniques* (Chicago: American Library Association, 1993), 36.

8   For examples of job descriptions, see the employment section of the Society of American Archivists (SAA) Web site at <www.archivists.org/employment/index.asp>.

9   SAA is the national professional association for archivists in the United States. See the SAA Web site, <www.archivists.org>.

10 The Academy of Certified Archivists (ACA) offers certification to individuals who pass an exam and have the requisite education and experience. According to the ACA, the organization "takes a leadership role by defining the knowledge and abilities necessary to be an archivist." In doing so, the organization attempts to ensure professional archival standards and to promote the employment of professionals. See the ACA *Mission* at <www.certifiedarchivists.org>.

11 The Society of Southwest Archivists maintains information about meetings, workshops, and other events for archivists worldwide in the *Archivist's Daybook* on its Web site at <www.tulane.edu/~lmiller/daybook.html>.

First Steps

As the new museum archivist in a new or existing museum archives, the first few weeks on the job can be a bit overwhelming. Use this time to gather information and learn more about the institution and its records. As you probe and learn, a plan will start to emerge. Become familiar with the following areas of information as soon as possible:

- MISSION STATEMENT, POLICIES
  Does your institution have a mission statement and other policies? If so, familiarize yourself with them. Does the archives already have a mission statement and other policies in place? If not, begin thinking about the types of things to include in the policies. Begin collecting samples of policies from other comparable institutions.

- ORGANIZATIONAL STRUCTURE AND HISTORY
  What is the museum's organizational structure? Obtain copies of organizational flowcharts, phone lists, and histories. Learn the names of your coworkers and board members. Use these resources to help you understand the working structure of the museum. Search out past flowcharts and personnel lists. If no one has previously documented the names of personnel who held key positions (i.e., president of the board, chief curator, museum director), begin compiling such a list for easy reference. What are the names and dates of past museum exhibits? If this information has not yet been compiled, begin doing so. The resulting document will be a tremendous resource. [12]

- MUSEUM DEPARTMENTS
  What do the various museum departments do? Meet with each department head and learn about the kind of work they do and the types of records they create. This will help you understand the working structure of the institution and enable you to create logical record groups.

- INSTITUTIONAL RECORDS
  Where are they? Are inactive records already in one storage location or do you have to gather everything together from multiple offices or sites? Begin thinking about a strategy to survey the records.

- ARCHIVAL ENVIRONMENT
  Begin setting up environmental monitoring equipment to track the environmental conditions in storage and processing areas. Are the conditions acceptable?

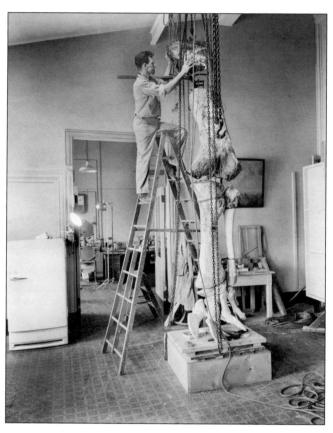

Fitting leg bones of *Haplocanthosaurus*. PHOTOGRAPH BY A. ROTA. AMERICAN MUSEUM OF NATURAL HISTORY LIBRARY, NEG. #335820.

- ARCHIVAL SUPPLIES AND EQUIPMENT
  Do you have a computer, telephone, and desk? Do the storage areas need shelving? Do you have supplies such as boxes, folders, pencils, and archival sleeves for processing? Begin to make lists of supplies and equipment needed and gather information on vendors. You may need to investigate outside grant or individual donor sources for big-ticket items.

During the information-gathering process, you will begin to formulate strategies to help you establish a presence in the museum, create policies and procedures, begin to identify and process archival records, and provide reference service. Then the real fun begins!

---

12 See the Art Institute of Chicago's Web site for an example of an exhibition history compiled by the archives: <www.artic.edu/aic/libraries/musarchives/archexhibit.html>.

ARCHIVAL FUNDAMENTALS

4

APPRAISAL

Deborah Wythe

Archivists face a huge challenge: *What should we keep?* Our repositories cannot and should not serve just as a central file for everything produced by our institutions: this is neither useful nor practical. Taking a passive approach and accepting whatever records are offered can lead both to serious gaps in documentation and to expending scarce resources on records with little enduring value. Evaluation and selection must be part of the process of creating and maintaining archives. This is *archival appraisal.*[2] Archivists must "determine if [records] have sufficient long-term research value to warrant the expense of preservation by an archival repository."[3]

Appraisal is one of our fundamental responsibilities, but it is often neglected in smaller institutions, at least in terms of establishing a formal appraisal process. Although many archivists make reasonable choices on an *ad hoc* basis, the best decisions grow out of a clearly defined and thoughtful appraisal policy, which is applied on a case-by-case basis as materials are offered to or selected by archival staff. "Let's keep it, just in case" is never a good collection-development or appraisal policy!

In this chapter, we will look at the ways in which appraisal interacts with other archival functions and discuss developing appraisal guidelines and establishing

> "Archivists have no graver responsibility than deciding what information they will preserve for society."[1]
> —Frank Boles

a program. We will also look at some of the types of records and appraisal challenges that are specific to museums.

As with most activities, appraisal starts with the mission of the archives. Establishing a clearly defined mission and collection-development statement is a critical prerequisite for your appraisal program. In the case of most institutional archives, the mission is quite simple: to document the history and activities of your institution. Some archives also extend beyond institutional records into special collections. Since mission statements are necessarily rather general, you will need to spend some time thinking about more detailed criteria to inform your appraisal work. Do you collect the papers of former staff members? How important must they be or how closely connected to the museum? Does this include all of their papers, or just those related to their museum activities? If a former scientific curator was also a novelist, would you accept her literary papers? Do you want to document community organizations or individuals that interact with your museum—artists, galleries, schools?

Appraisal also interacts with records management: it is the theoretical framework upon which your retention schedule is built. Once you have articulated what you want to document, decisions on which records to maintain and which to discard will be clearer. The resulting records retention schedule will help you to build a logical path to the archives for records and collections with permanent value and to divert less valuable records into records management, without having to rethink the process every time new materials appear. Appraisal thus becomes a seamless link in the life cycle of all records; many decisions are, in a sense, already built in. While policies, guidelines, and schedules may be revisited and revised from time to

---

1   *Archival Appraisal* (Chicago: Society of American Archivists, 1991), 1.

2   Contrary to its application in other fields, archival appraisal has nothing to do with establishing a monetary value for collections. If an individual donates a collection to the archives and needs a valuation for tax purposes, you may refer him or her to an independent appraiser, someone who follows and understands market values and can put a price tag on the materials.

3   F. Gerald Ham, *Selecting and Appraising Archives and Manuscripts* (Chicago: Society of American Archivists, 1993), 3. Much effort has been expended in the archival profession to develop appraisal theories and tools. A careful study of this literature and attendance at workshops led by the various proponents is certainly worthwhile. Ham summarizes the various theories in the above publication.

time, this kind of overarching structure should result in logical and understandable collection development and decision making, despite staff changes and shifting priorities.

Research and Study

As you begin to think about and flesh out your appraisal guidelines, certain information will inform your work. It will not be new to you—you have certainly been developing this basic knowledge from your first day on the job. This is a time to articulate and analyze what you know about your institution and identify and search out other information that you lack.

The first tool in every archivist's information kit is a thorough understanding of his or her institution's history, functions, and activities. How was it founded and by whom? Did it have relationships with other organizations? Has its mission changed? What programs have come and gone? Who were the important players over the years, both inside the museum and in its interactions with government or outside organizations? Supplementing this detailed knowledge, an understanding of local and national history and the changes in the general climate for cultural institutions can be critical. Your museum, for example, may have hosted WPA projects in the 1930s, provided programs for service personnel during wartime, or operated community outreach programs in the 1960s. A complete understanding of an institution's financial difficulties must include knowledge about the economic climate at the time. Understanding the history and context of your museum's records will lead to well-informed and lasting appraisal decisions.

The knowledge about the universe of extant records in the museum that you gained through a detailed records survey may reveal strengths—and weaknesses—that will lead you to appropriate decisions. If, for example, some records of the executive administration were lost over the years, you will need to look for other records to fill that information gap. Conversely, if your registrar's object records are pristine and complete, you may be able to avoid keeping duplicate records from a curatorial department. One department may gather and record data, another may evaluate it and produce useful summary reports. Does all

the paper still exist? Is there a complete, official set of minutes and reports?

Certain materials—publications, for example—may be the responsibility of another department, such as the library. Understanding who holds what and how strongly they feel about these collections can also be helpful—materials may have been collected in the years prior to establishing an archives, and responsibility may now change. Partnerships can help you avoid unnecessary duplication. Take into account existing collections outside of the archives, but also

James Brown trading stamps and the book in which to put them. Dr. Martin Luther King, Jr. encouraged economic empowerment for African Americans, and these stamps were issued by participating African American–owned businesses in the San Francisco Bay area in the 1960s. Just like Green Stamps, the filled books could be redeemed for merchandise. The promotion ended with Dr. King's assassination. GEORGIA MUSIC HALL OF FAME, MACON, GA.

consider long-term preservation and access concerns. If the publications in the library circulate, it would be wise to create a parallel archival collection. Or, if the treasurer's office holds the official set of minutes but they are not accessible to researchers, a set in the archives makes sense.

It can also be useful to investigate what records exist in other institutions and organizations. Museum employees are often members and officers of professional organizations. Staff members may also teach, do consulting, or have second jobs. Records of their activities and more general materials, such as minutes, mailings, and publications, may be preserved in their files. Do these organizations and institutions have archives programs? Could or should some or all of these records be transferred? Your institution may be a governmental or quasi-governmental organization. Are general directives and guidelines from the various governmental agencies preserved elsewhere?

Shelburne Museum founder Electra Havemeyer Webb at the Museum with her ever-present dogs, ca. 1957. SHELBURNE MUSEUM ARCHIVES, # PS 1/10: EHW 13.

As you study your institution and its records, you will learn about its organizational structure, both currently and over the years. Where did responsibility lie? Who answered to whom? What was the reporting structure? When did changes occur? What is the current structure? All of these criteria can be fluid and changeable, so a good understanding of institutional history is critical.

Based on your understanding of these interactions, establish an *office of record* for different types of records and information. In the appraisal process, the office of record becomes the primary source for documentation of a particular function. Knowing, for example, that your museum hired its first professional registrar in 1934 allows you to set that office as the office of record for collection documentation starting in that year and alerts you to look for other sources in earlier years. By creating various offices of record, you will be able to eliminate duplicate records that other offices maintain, assuming that the records of the primary office are complete. It is easier to establish an office of record and track various records series for current activities, since you can talk to the people who create and use the various files. Your records survey probably provides much of the information that you need, but if not, the answer is just a phone call or e-mail away.

Finally, your work with archives users, both staff and members of the public, will help you develop a sense of which records are already needed and useful, and a vision for potential new uses of your collections. Every appraisal decision must answer the question, "What is it good for?" Ultimately, a collection must be usable to justify its preservation.

Establishing an Appraisal Program

Once you have completed a detailed study of the topics outlined above and a thoughtful analysis of your results, you are ready to begin setting some appraisal policies and procedures. Write a detailed policy and document the rationale behind it. Answer the questions "What are we keeping?" and "Why are we keeping it?" If your archives has a staff, determine who will carry out appraisal and who will supervise the process.

Define the level or levels at which you will appraise. The appraisal process ideally approaches records at a fairly broad level—most archivists recommend the records series, a group of records that document a particular activity. If you plan to appraise at a more detailed level, create a written justification.

Establish guidelines and procedures. It may be helpful to develop a set of criteria and a decision-making grid. Using such a tool, the appraiser gathers information about the records, their creator, and interactions with other records series, and weights the answers. F. Gerald Ham provides a useful approach in the SAA Archival Fundamentals Series, as does Prudence Backman in a New York State Archives publication.[4] Each time you examine records that you are

---

4 Ham, *Selecting and Appraising,* 51–65; Prudence Backman, *Appraisal of Local Government Records for Historical Value,* Local Government Records Technical Information Series, no. 50 (Albany: State Education Dept., 1996). Other helpful readings on appraisal include: Frank Boles and Mark Greene, "Et Tu Schellenberg? Thoughts on the Dagger of American

considering accessing, test them against your appraisal policy.

As the archives and your appraisal program mature, refine your policies and procedures. Over the years, you will gain a broader understanding of your institution, the archives, and your users. Fine-tune the appraisal process, documenting the new aspects and the changed rationale. Create a paper trail so that future archivists and users will understand what you collected (or didn't) and why.

Appraisal is not always reactive. If you notice a gap or a potential problem in record-keeping, consider approaching the relevant department and suggesting changes to alleviate these difficulties.

The Museum Archives Section Working Group on Appraisal

Having just passed along the wisdom of the archival profession about appraisal at the series level, it is now time to relate some tales from the trenches. At the Museum Archives Section working groups in 1997 and 1998,[5] it became quite clear that most of the museum archivists who attended were engaged in what we called "microappraisal." Selecting or rejecting certain obvious records at the series level was the rule, but there was also a gray area where archivists were weeding records heavily prior to accessioning or as part of processing. Two examples follow.

Most museum development offices produce extensive grant files, which contain not only final proposals, award correspondence, and reports, but also multiple drafts, foundation research printouts, and memos. While your appraisal policy will probably call for documentation of grant activities, most archivists at the working group agreed that materials in the second category do not have permanent value.

In some cases, just identifying logical records series can be challenging. Many museums traditionally

use graduate students—not secretaries—in administrative positions, leading to inconsistent and sometimes inefficient filing systems. The single A-to-Z "series" favored by such staff members does not allow for effective appraisal. The run of records, often broken annually, may contain general correspondence, as well as files in consistent categories such as "donors," "gifts offered" . . . and "timesheets." What is the series? Is it the A–Z run of folders, or is it the various categories?

In both these cases, space constraints argue against accepting the series wholesale, but the infor-

Installation shot of exhibition "Handicrafts by Southern Mountaineers," on view October 14 through November 26, 1933. THE CORCORAN GALLERY OF ART ARCHIVES.

mational content calls for retaining at least some files and groups of documents. Your appraisal policy must recognize these challenges, and your procedures must provide a way to deal with them in the context of your resources.

Is this justifiable? As an analogy, I offer the city garden. If you have a tiny garden, you can be concerned with every square foot and every weed; a farmer or suburban gardener must take broader actions. Most museum archives are relatively small and the volume of incoming records is limited when compared to many other repositories, so this level of appraisal may be useful if the staff has time. As with the process outlined above, the critical step in any such action is consistency and documentation. Any microappraisal must be a subset of a general appraisal policy. Make sure that you write down not only exactly what you are doing, but also why you made the decision.

Appraisal Theory," *American Archivist* 59 (1996): 298–310; Mark Greene and Todd Daniels-Howell, "Documentation with an Attitude: A Pragmatist's Guide to the Selection and Acquisition of Modern Business Records" in *Records of American Business,* James O'Toole, ed. (Chicago: Society of American Archivists, 1997); and Mark Greene, "The Surest Proof: A Utilitarian Approach to Appraisal," *Archivaria* 45 (1998): 127–69.

5   Two issues of *Museum Archivist,* February 1998 and February 1999, contain reports on the working groups.

Museum Records and Appraisal[6]

Object records, which document the acquisition, cataloging, exhibition, movement, and conservation of the museum's collections, are considered mission critical documents; without these records, the museum is not able to function. As such, they are easily appraised: they must be kept. Since they are continuously active, however, object records are rarely transferred to the archives. In this case, appraisal must be done in cooperation with the staff members who care for these

Young sculpture class, 1950. BROOKLYN MUSEUM OF ART ARCHIVES, PHOTOGRAPH COLLECTION. PEOPLE: CHILDREN IN THE MUSEUM.

records. Once you have identified the various series of permanent records, make sure that the registrar's office and the curatorial staff are in agreement, and that they care for the records accordingly. Many object records are multipart—a form is created and copies circulated to several departments—so it should be possible to establish an office of record for each type and reduce duplication considerably.

Exhibition records probably constitute the most important, heavily used, voluminous, and complicated series in most museum archives. Nearly every department in a museum will have an exhibition series, since the various functions necessary to mount an exhibition are dispersed museumwide. Curators research and plan, administrators approve, registrars coordinate, development personnel raise funds, public affairs staff publicize, and education and events personnel produce programs, to name just a few steps in the process.

Exhibitions may be developed in-house, or may be developed and circulated by other institutions, in which case the process and the records generated can be quite different.

Files on each facet of exhibition planning and implementation document not only the work of the person who created the file, but also contain a variety of documents that are circulated among all participants.[7] As you confront the problems of appraising exhibition records, take into account this overlap. Using your knowledge of the process, consider establishing an office of record for each material type—checklists, labels and didactics, catalog text, installation layout, to name just a few— and use this record blueprint to inform your appraisal and processing decisions.

Documentation of permanent or long-term installations presents different challenges. While exhibitions generally have a definite end date and the files eventually become inactive, files relating to gallery installations may be ongoing, detailing incremental changes over a period of years. Like object files, they may never become inactive and may remain in curatorial offices. It is easy to overlook these files or to lose the connections between changes over a period of years. Point to the importance of documenting this museum function in your appraisal policy and consider implementing a plan to ensure that documentation of it is both created and preserved.

Research is also a central activity in most museums, both for specific programs such as exhibitions and for broad-based activities such as scholarly publication. Both your mission or collection development policy and your appraisal policy should present a way to differentiate between what belongs to the individual staff member and what is museum property. If you intend to collect the personal papers relating to staff members' research, develop clear guidelines noting what you collect and how it will be appraised. Such clarity will not only help you develop a well-rounded and logical collection, but will also assist you in negotiating with potential donors.

Research files frequently contain masses of photocopies of primary and secondary source material, whose continuing value is questionable once the project is

---

6   See also the museum context chapter for an in-depth discussion of museum records and their value.

7   While some institutions historically have created a central file of exhibition records, most archives follow the principle of provenance and retain exhibitions as a separate series within each of the various departments.

finished, particularly if a bibliography was produced. Copies of primary source materials from other repositories create difficult use and reproduction dilemmas. Offprints and articles may well be easily available in the museum library (many of the copies were probably made there). Consider how you want to handle these reference materials and include this in your appraisal guidelines.

Likewise, drafts of publications can form a huge proportion of research and exhibition files. Decide whether you want to retain these at all and, if you do, determine what constitutes a meaningful "version." You may also want to specify what drafts you do retain: first and last, perhaps, or any chapters not included in the final published work. As with all appraisal policy decisions, think about and articulate the long-term value or lack of value of these records. It may make sense to build in a procedure that avoids keeping the many pages of photocopies with minimal editorial changes that most writers produce but lets you make an exception for the papers of a world-class researcher and writer.

Museums produce a wide array of programs: educational offerings for children and school groups; classes and educational programs for adults; lectures and symposia for scholars and professional colleagues; special events for members; and films, talks, tours, and concerts for the public, to name just a few. All of these generate two types of records: program documentation and logistics. The routine records created by staff members as they plan and execute programs probably have little long-term research value, although they may be very useful as staff members develop similar programs from year to year. Documentation of the programs themselves—flyers and leaflets, program descriptions, programs, participant contracts, photographs, tapes and transcripts, reviews—is certainly valuable. In developing appraisal procedures for program files, consider routing some materials to records management, where they can be kept for a limited period, while other more valuable records remain in the archives. Again, depending on filing procedures, this may require some detailed sorting and weeding.

Development departments (or development staff within other administrative departments) interact with active donors; solicit new donors; and manage government, corporate, and foundation grant projects. Like program staff, development personnel generate masses of records, many of them logistical. In contrast, however, development staff members maintain important relationships with all types of donors over long periods of time. It is not unusual for the archives to receive a request to document the entire history of the museum's interaction with a particular donor, government agency, or foundation. The challenge is to retain enough documentation, without being buried under the notes, memos, drafts, and form letters that comprise a large part of development files.

Understanding extant development records as well as current recordkeeping activities in the department will assist you in developing an effective appraisal approach. Does the department maintain a "permanently active" file on each major donor? Is there a development officer responsible for government and foundation grants, or is grant paperwork handled by the staff member who conceived of the project—what is the office of record for grant records? How are broad funding appeals handled: does the office retain a single copy of an appeal letter with a mailing list or copies of all the letters sent? What kind of reporting does the department do? Do regular, detailed reports document incoming donations?

Financial records are, for the most part, handled under records management. The challenge of establishing an appraisal policy for financial records is identifying which records are concentrated enough *and* understandable enough to qualify for permanent retention. General ledgers, the standard "permanent" financial record, may seem obscure to people not schooled in accounting practices and, indeed, may require other documentation (such as an account code book) to be understandable. Enlist the aid of your accounting staff to explain current records to you and to help you understand older records. Older ledgers may require your own research.[8] Keep in mind that an important research need in museums is documenting the source of objects in the collection and that, when curatorial and registrar's records fail, the only place to look may be in old disbursements or funds ledgers.

Since only a small proportion of financial records actually deal directly with object purchases or collecting activities, it may be possible for these to be segregated (if they are not already) as they are created. Original invoices and cancelled checks for works of art, for

---

8   Useful resources for understanding older accounting records are Christopher Densmore, "Understanding and Using Early Nineteenth Century Account Books," *Midwestern Archivist* 5, no. 1 (1980), reprinted in *Archival Issues* 25 (2000); Dennis Meissner, "The Evaluation of Modern Business Accounting Records," *Midwestern Archivist* 5, no. 2 (1981); Joanne Yates, *Control through Communication: The Rise of System in American Management* (Baltimore: Johns Hopkins University Press, 1989); and John Armstrong and Stephanie Jones, *Business Documents: Their Origins, Sources, and Uses in Historical Research* (London: Mansell, 1987). See also "Secondary Sources" at <http://sca.lib.liv.ac.uk/collections/business.htm>.

example, can have considerable artifactual value and interest and should be retained if possible. The financial records of expeditions and digs, if not already preserved in curatorial files, can be valuable in documenting the people and places involved.[9] Once again, your knowledge of existing records will inform your appraisal decisions.

The records of museum operations—administration, building maintenance (inside and out), security, marketing, publicity, publications, outreach, information resources, and so on—must be carefully analyzed or you will be overwhelmed. Pay careful attention to the core mission of each department and how it can be documented. Consider the reporting structure of the museum and learn what documentation is created as part of the supervisory chain. If, for example, the admissions staff submits regular statistical reports to the director, you may not need to retain much else except for higher level policy and procedures decisions. Talk to staff members and discover what they need in both the short and long term. Ask them how they actually use inactive records. Use this information for appraisal purposes and to create appropriate records schedules for each department. Keep in mind the important public relations aspect of making the decision to keep only a tiny portion of a department's records and that you will have to explain why keeping records "just in case" isn't an effective policy.

Effective Appraisal

Several challenges face all archivists: massive volume, duplication, decentralization, and the proliferation of electronic formats. Appraisal provides a tool for dealing with all of these issues. Massive volume yields to the selection of particular series for deposit in the archives and the reasoned and organized short-term retention of the rest. Establishment of offices of record and processing procedures allows archivists to deal with the duplicate materials found throughout our collections. Likewise, understanding the structure of our institutions and how certain functions have been decentralized will lead to an effective documentation plan that is expressed in appraisal policies and procedures. Electronic records present their own problems, but as we will learn in that chapter, management of electronic records also rests on sound appraisal and records management programs.

Appraisal is a continuing process: research, analysis, policy development, and implementation. None of these facets is a one-time activity. Each time you accession a group of records, process a collection, or work with a researcher, think about your appraisal program and how well it is working. Reappraise collections based on new knowledge or change guidelines if you need to—even archivists make mistakes! Your institution will change and change again, and your appraisal policies must be flexible enough to reflect the new order. Follow developments in the archival profession and evaluate whether new techniques can help you.

While establishing a formal appraisal program may seem formidable, spending time thinking in global terms can be both interesting and liberating. It allows you to shift from the tunnel vision of looking at folders and documents to considering the records of your institution and the holdings of your repository in broad terms. Decisions based on thoughtful analysis and standards are more easily made and more likely to be accurate in the long term. Asked about collection development, your explanations will be understandable, well reasoned, and based on solid practices. The appraisal process can be as simple or as complex as you wish to make it, but it is an archival fundamental that is clearly necessary.

---

9   A recent researcher in the Brooklyn Museum of Art Archives, for example, was able to verify a curator's visit to a particular location from a list of expenses that included payment for mule transport to the site.

5

ARRANGEMENT

Polly Darnell

Archivists use the term *processing* to refer to all the steps that are taken to prepare archival materials for access and reference use. Arrangement and description, two of those steps, are closely linked, as each depends on the other. In its simplest sense, arrangement refers to the physical and intellectual order of archives: what papers are grouped together and the order in which papers, folders, boxes, and bound volumes are placed. Description, a topic more fully described in the next chapter, refers to creating finding aids for researchers to use in locating materials that will answer their questions. Processing also includes some preservation and appraisal.

Library, Archives, and Museum Perspectives

Because of the differing nature of the materials for which they are responsible, archivists, librarians, and museum registrars and curators treat material differently. While they all control collections that are made accessible through some form of descriptive cataloging, they come from professions that developed at different times from separate traditions. A museum archivist needs to understand these various perspectives.

Librarians, the longest-standing profession of the three, deal mainly with publications, which are focused, self-identifying, and usually exist in multiple copies. Archival materials are unique, frequently cover a wide range of topics, and do not introduce themselves. Publications usually have a title, author, publication data, and possibly preface, introduction, and dust jacket providing an explanation of what will be found within. The archivist must provide information on the context in which records were created, information essential to understanding them. The archivist gathers the necessary information from a variety of sources during processing and conveys it to the researcher in a finding aid, which can come in a variety of forms. As each archival collection is unique, so too is

the descriptive information about it; "copy cataloging" rarely occurs in archives. Librarians can share the catalog data for publications with few changes. Library materials are organized by discipline and subject, so that people browsing the shelves can find related publications easily. Archives, being unique, are kept in closed stacks where researchers are not allowed.

Both archivists and librarians create catalogs or other finding aids to get researchers to the materials they hold. Museum registrars and curators are primarily concerned with the physical nature of their collections and secondarily with their intellectual content. Their catalogs are not designed to provide members of the public with access to objects, but to gather information about them for control and interpretation, usually through exhibitions. Curators concentrate on the description of the physical object, bringing their knowledge of similar objects to bear; registrars are concerned with control of collections, tracking the ownership and movement of objects through storage, exhibitions, and loans.

Registrars handle objects singly, giving each item a unique number that can be used to track it. Archivists handle records collectively, because of both the quantities involved and the interrelated nature of the individual items. A single file drawer can contain thousands of pieces of paper (one source estimates 4,600), which can be described more effectively as a group in a sentence than item by item in a list, where researchers would be lost in the details. Imagine the difference between reading a description of the contents of a file drawer (e.g., "correspondence about museum programs, 1960–1970, filed alphabetically by program title") and reading a list of each document in the file.

While museums have ways of grouping information about related objects, no generally accepted method of categorizing objects works for all kinds of museums. Taxonomy, function, medium, style, or site may all be used as the primary organizing principle for information about the collections of different types of museums.

The importance of each type of information will vary with the type of museum. Varied as archival collections are, certain principles do work for all of them.

Principles

The foundations of archival work are known as *provenance, original order, collective description,* and *levels of control.* These are the ideas and principles that should guide you during processing.

The archival principle of *provenance* holds that

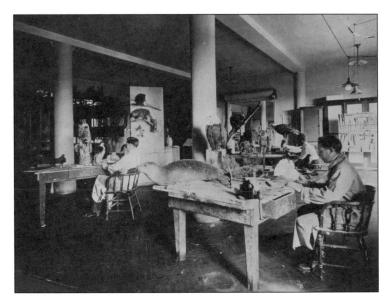

Taxidermy workshop, n.d. Brooklyn Museum of Art Archives, Photograph Collection. Museum interiors: Natural History.

records created or received by one recordkeeping unit (office, position, or department for institutional records; individual or family for personal papers) should not be intermixed with those of any other. For example, if the archives receives records from both the museum's board of trustees and the building and grounds department about construction of a new building, the fact that they are about the same subject does not mean that they can or should be interfiled. The records were created by people in positions with very different perspectives and functions: it is important to preserve that distinctiveness via provenance so that users know what perspective they're getting. Researchers looking for information about the new building are alerted by the archives' finding aids that both collections contain data on the same topic.

Artificial collections contain papers or records from different sources that are brought together by an individual whose papers the archives acquires, or occasionally by the archives itself for convenience in managing similar items acquired individually. For instance, the archives may acquire the papers of an individual who collected travelers' accounts of visits to Machu Picchu. This would be an artificial collection. Conversely, the documentation of an individual's own archaeological work and visits to Machu Picchu would form an organic set of personal papers. Following the principle of provenance, the archives would keep each collection together as acquired and *not* add the personal papers to the artificial Machu Picchu Collection.

Archivists may form artificial collections to deal efficiently with items that come in singly rather than as pieces in a collection. Provenance is maintained through the accession process, which makes it possible to distinguish the source of each item in such a collection. Museum publications, especially ephemeral ones, are often treated this way in the archives.

The principle of *original order* dictates that papers be kept in the order in which their creator used them. This order may be chronological, alphabetical (by name or subject, for instance), numerical (e.g., by accession number), or a combination of the above. As long as the records you receive are in some recognizable order, maintain that order if possible.

By maintaining original order you preserve as much information about the records as possible for researchers, letting them understand their original purpose and use. Not every researcher wants the same thing from the records and presenting them with the files as their creator used them comes closest to meeting everybody's information needs. It also preserves information about how the creator functioned. Of course, keeping records in their original order also saves on processing time and effort.

In some cases, the archives receives records whose original order has been completely lost. If you cannot determine this order, you'll have to impose one. Within the museum, various departments customarily use different filing systems, in addition to project and subject files of varying sizes. The same project may be given different file names by the various people involved. Registrars organize their records by object, using accession or catalog numbers. Curators may use those numbers for some of their files, but may also create exhibition, donor, or subject files. Conservation departments tend to use job numbers for treatment files, with a cross-reference to object numbers. Administrative files are more likely to be arranged chronologically or alphabetically by the names of people, organizations, or topics. No one system is inherently better than another—it just served the needs of that department better. Keep these differences in mind when you have to choose how to arrange a collection. The finding aids you create can provide cross-references to the filing schemes.

Collective description is the antithesis of museum cataloging, which aims to describe each object individually. Archivists describe records in hierarchical and interdependent groups—as record groups, series, boxes, and folders—before getting to the individual item. The value of most, though not all, records lies in their being part of a larger body of material. Describing each record individually would unnecessarily overwhelm a researcher with detail. Because groups of records share certain characteristics, finding aids can relate the salient facts without mind-numbing repetition. Collective description goes hand in hand with arrangement.

Control of collections—intellectual control through finding aids and physical control through organization and arrangement—is usually defined through the five following *levels:* institution, record group or collection, series, file unit, or item. In addition, some series may be broken down into subseries. Archivists work from the general to the specific, starting at the broadest level and working to the more specific as necessary and possible.

Whether they realize it or not, most archivists already have some control of their collections at the *institutional level.* Their collection policies are written at the institutional level and describe the focus of the archives' holdings, whether they include collected as well as institutional records, and the focus of any special collections within the archives.

Control at the *collection level* begins through the survey, transfer, and accessioning process (for records created by the museum) and through donation or purchase and accessioning (for collected records). Institutional records are typically organized into *record groups*—records from a particular office or department. Theoretically, the museum's organization chart can be your guide to creating and naming the groups, though in fact organizations change, departments merge and separate, and not every office will generate records that come to the archives.

The Shelburne Museum has both a record group (Presidents of Shelburne Museum) and an accessioned

collection (Webb Family Papers) that contain papers of museum founder Electra Havemeyer Webb. The record group is composed of institutional records generated by presidents, of whom Mrs. Webb was the first. The accessioned collection came from her son's estate and stays intact, in spite of the fact that it contains papers from two people who served as museum president. Keeping them together by origin maintains their provenance. Within institutional records and collections of personal papers, as well as in separately accessioned groups of materials, you may also find

Ass cart with expedition members, San Juan, Argentina, 1925.
Photograph by Frederic W. Miller. Denver Museum of Nature & Science Image Archives, MI25-178.

records of other organizations, often related in some way to the museum or individual.

Within a record group or collection, records are organized into *series,* comprising records maintained as a unit by the person or office that created them because they are related by a subject, function, activity, or form. Electra Webb's presidential records include series based on subject (collections of objects within the museum), function (receipts for purchased objects), activity (reports and speeches), and form (scrapbooks). The correspondence is divided into two subseries: one filed alphabetically by correspondent, and the other (letters of congratulations and "bread-and-butter" notes) filed chronologically. Office files are easily recognized as different series when a new file sequence starts. Archivists do much of their work at the series level.

A *file unit* is a folder or bound volume, the building block of the series. Folder titles on an incoming collection often provide essential clues to existing series and original order.

The individual documents make up the *item level*. Since most records don't have high individual value, archivists rarely do extensive work at this level. Having folders in a rational order may be sufficient without arranging each document within a folder.

At any of these levels, different arrangements may be used: chronological, alphabetical, numerical, or combinations of them. Traditionally, the order of series within collections runs from general to specific or from greater to lesser importance.

Processing Steps

In deciding processing priorities, take into account researcher demand (actual or anticipated), institu-tional priorities, and resources needed. One of those resources is time. Attempts have been made to determine how long it takes to process collections, but there are so many variables that archivists have found it may take anywhere from ten to forty hours per cubic foot of processed records. As you work, you'll have to keep your goal always in mind. Even at the institutional level, archivists work from the general to the specific, aiming first for overall control of their holdings—knowing what collections are where—and then for more complete control, collection by collection. Avoid getting bogged down in thorough processing of one series at the expense of having minimal control over an entire collection.

Once you've chosen a collection to process, begin

ITEM-LEVEL PROCESSING

While most processing is done at the series and folder levels, sometimes it must be done at the item level. This is frequently true at the Museum of Modern Art (MoMA), where collections contain correspondence with artists. More detailed processing is required for items of high interest, which need greater security. The significant items can be handled singly, without processing the whole series to the item level. Archives staff members are required to have a background in art history. Having a knowledge of the subject informs their processing priorities, so that they can recognize which items require special treatment.

Following are some samples of materials processed at the item level and comments from Michelle Elligott, MoMA's archivist:

Dorothy C. Miller Papers
Series I. Exhibitions. Sub-series 23. Calder: 19 *Gifts from the Artist,* 1967.
[Note: MoMA Exh. #819, Feb. 1—April 5, 1967]
Folder b. "Calder" ca. 1959—69
    ["re: Calder gift to MoMA in 1966 & exhibition of it Jan. 1967 on -." Incl. 1 ALS Alexander Calder—AHB, DCM (12/31/69); loan memos, DCM notes, and mimeographed sheets incl. 1 ALS (copy) Alexander Calder—JTS (6/4/42) [4 sheets] with DCM annotations.]

James Thrall Soby Papers
Series I. Subject Interest Material: Artists and Movements
Box 36. Folder 14. Shahn: Miscl., 1940's [27 items]

Incl. 9 printed matter; 2 ALS; 1 TL re: Shahn magazine; 1 TL Shahn—Walter Chrysler; 1 TL JTS—Shahn; 1 ALS Shahn—JTS

The *Alfred H. Barr, Jr. Papers* is MoMA's most important and most heavily consulted collection. For Series I. Correspondence, it was deemed essential to have a name index to the correspondence. Because it was such a big job (over 550 folders of material), a high school volunteer was used to complete the project over the course of three years. The result is neither a true index, nor an item description. It is simply a list of every correspondent within each file, with no attention given to the amount or type of documentation, nor its subject matter. So what follows may not be to the highest of archival standards, but I cannot tell you how useful it has been. Here is an excerpt from Barr's file titled simply "M":

Folder 282. M. (1955–1957) [microfilm reel: frame 2182:795]
    Mies van der Rohe, Ludwig; Millares, Manolo; Miller, Edgar; Missingham, Hal; Moholy-Nagy, Mrs. Sybil (incl. TLS); Moïse, Howard; Mongan, Agnes (Fogg Art Museum); Moore, Henry (incl. TLS); Moore, Marianne; Morey, Mrs. Rufus; Morot-Sir, Edouard (Ambassade de France); Morrison, Barb; Morse, John D. (Kent School); Moses, Robert (incl. typescript of 1957 October 24 interview)

—*Michelle Elligot*

by gathering all the information you have readily available about the papers and the person or office that created them. Review the accession or transfer records. Check published reference sources, institutional records, and individuals that are likely to provide background information.

For instance, if you have the field notes of a staff archaeologist, look at his or her publications. They'll provide context for the projects on which the archaeologist worked and may help you identify drafts of reports and articles. Annual reports of the museum will tell you about projects contemporary with the records you're processing. Tap into institutional memory! People who worked with the creator of the records, successors in the same office, and the donor may all be able to help you with records of fairly recent origin or older ones they've used.

You're looking for background that will help you answer the questions that you—like a newspaper reporter—will ask over and over again: who? what? when? where? why? and how? Who created the records? What kinds of records are they? When were they created? Where? For what purpose? What media are they: ink and paper, photographs, digital, or audio- or videotape? Some of your questions can only be answered by the records themselves, but background information readily available from other sources will help you identify what you're seeing and may save you considerable time. Think of the difference between getting an outline of someone's life from an obituary and piecing it together from personal papers—especially unorganized ones. Before you spend too much time on this step, however, remember that the obituary may be contained in the papers.

Next, survey the records. You'll need a big table devoted to this so that you can unpack boxes without danger of other material getting mixed in. You're still just looking for information, so don't rearrange anything. Go through each box or file drawer. Look at the contents, the forms of the material, and the existing arrangement. Take notes about what you see and put everything back as you found it. Do you have some clear filing sequences? Financial records? Meeting minutes? Lectures? Maps? What ranges of dates are you seeing for each type of material? Look for clues to filing sequences, such as folder labels, filing keywords penciled at the top of documents, numbering systems. Are the file sequences complete or do you just have folders labeled "A–M"? Are N through z in another box?

What kinds and quantities of supplies will you need to house the collection? Will you need letter- or legal-sized folders and boxes? Do the records show evidence of mold or mildew? Insects? Are there photograph formats you can't identify? Will you need to consult a conservator or photo historian?

Resist the temptation to put similar materials together. You need to know about the whole collection and have a plan for it before you start changing things.

When you've been through it all, sit down with your notes and think over what you learned about the collection. Consider ways the collection might be organized and whether it contains series of records. In some collections, the series are obvious because the creator already divided the records into series, identifiable from the filing sequences and file folder titles. For instance, one member of Shelburne Museum's staff

"MISCELLANEOUS"

When Sarah Demb was the archivist at Harvard's Peabody Museum, she confronted several boxes of unprocessed records left by her predecessors, labeled "Miscellaneous." Her method of handling them is instructive, as most of us will encounter such a collection. (Here's hoping we don't leave such collections for our successors!)

The boxes contained a wide variety of apparently unrelated documents. At first, they made no sense, so she left them and went on to other things. As she got to know the holdings of the archives and how they had been managed in the past, she found she understood some of the items in the boxes and what to do with them. She integrated an old accession file system into the current accession file system. Outdated reference materials could be discarded. Items that had been removed from collections were reunited with their source. Items that had been received singly were filed appropriately.

She did not discover what things were all at once, but gradually. Getting to know the "miscellaneous" collections of predecessors can take years. They should be reviewed periodically to see if you can identify more of the contents. At some point, when you've gone as far as you think you can, you may decide to deal with the rest as an artificial collection—one made up of materials from various sources—and make subseries based on the access points that are most significant: form, creator, or subject.

labeled his files "blacksmith research," "advertising," "correspondence with magazines," and "art file"—an easy transition to series.

In other cases, no series are necessary, because the collection is simple, small, or cohesive enough to be filed and described as a single unit. The papers of decoy collector Joel Barber consist of correspondence, clippings, catalogs of decoys and of decoy carving competitions, and photographs. There is no need to divide them into series, even though they occupy two document boxes. A single file sequence with folder

The reinstallation of a folk art exhibit in the Shelburne Museum's Stage Coach Inn was based on extensive research on Electra Havemeyer Webb's acquisition and early display of her collection and the relationship with Edith Halpert of the Downtown Gallery. SHELBURNE MUSEUM ARCHIVES.

titles that adequately describe the contents will provide sufficient access for a researcher, who can easily read through a list of the folder headings to find desired material.

In still other cases you must make sense of chaotic collections. Faced with this situation, look for groups of records that share some characteristics, making them easy to file together and describe as a group. The original organization may have been destroyed, so seek out like material. The papers of Shelburne Museum founder Electra Havemeyer Webb are an example of this kind of collection. Record-keeping at the museum changed from office-based files to a central file system twenty years after the museum was established. Some files created earlier were transferred to the central file, while others were simply boxed and stored. As later staff members discovered material relating to Electra Webb—written by, to, or about her—they removed it from storage or the central file

to a new file series. By the time archival processing of the collection began many years later, it was impossible to return them to the organization or order in which Mrs. Webb had used them. In cases like this, look for materials that share common characteristics: their function, form, or subject. Their physical properties may make it desirable to file some materials together. For instance, architectural drawings, because of their size, often form a separate series.

Some collections require considerable thought; in others the series are obvious. When you've come up with an organizational scheme, go back through your notes and see if it accommodates what you found. If it does, proceed. If not, think through how another scheme would work.

Decide to what level you're going to process each series. Will each series be rehoused in archival folders and boxes, or will some be left as they are, identified only at the series level? Gather the supplies you'll need: folders (letter or legal size, depending on what you found in your survey) and boxes (the most common sizes are cubic-foot records center cartons, five-inch document boxes, and two-and-a-half-inch document boxes). You may also need sleeves for photographs, permanent paper for photocopying deteriorating papers, oversized folders, drop-front boxes, and other more specialized storage containers depending upon the collection.

You'll need your big table again for the rehousing. Sort the collection into the series you've found or settled on. Then arrange each series in order and rehouse it as necessary. If there isn't already a coherent order to the records in a series, you'll have to decide how to arrange them. Your basic choices are chronological, alphabetical, or numerical. Even when your arrangement follows the original order, some papers may be moved, as you'll find some records misfiled and others not filed at all. Original order means that you follow the filing scheme in which the papers were found, instead of switching, for instance, from filing correspondence by name of correspondent to filing it by subject.

When people first start arranging archival collections, they are sometimes stymied by the dilemma of where to put papers that might reasonably be looked for in different places. There are two points to remember. The first is that the original order is preferable. If you change it, you must be able to explain what it was and why you changed it. The second is that the finding aid can direct researchers to the location of the papers and can put a pointer in the other places they might look. Don't double the size of a collection by photocopying records and putting copies everywhere you think might be logical.

While putting the papers in order, rehouse them in archival folders and boxes. As you do this, you'll take some basic conservation steps,[1] refine your appraisal, and prepare for creating finding aids.

- Remove foreign objects, such as paper clips (which are useful to hold papers together temporarily, but not permanently), rusty staples, rubber bands (which dry out and stick), sticky notes, and dried flowers.

- Sleeve photographs. Replace glassine envelopes with inert ones.

- Flatten folded and dog-eared items.

- Clean off surface dirt. Use a soft brush, a soft eraser like Magic Rub, or cleaning crumbs, working slowly and gently from the center to the outside, avoiding any pencil marks that might be erased if you're careless.

- Do not fill folders beyond what they can protect. See that when the folders are closed, all the papers are inside. Add as many folders as you need. Use folders that fit the boxes (e.g., do not use letter-sized folders in legal-sized boxes).

- Fill boxes full enough to hold folders upright without slumping. If necessary you can add filling (such as scrap archival matboard), use boxes that have a support bar, or place boxes on their sides so folders are flat.

- Photocopy highly acidic papers, such as crumbling newspaper clippings, onto permanent paper. Identify them as preservation copies that replace the original. You can do this by photocopying with them a strip of paper with a legend such as "Preservation photocopy of deteriorating original made on permanent paper" with the date. You'll have to decide whether to retain the original—not in the same folder—or discard it. In many cases the value of the original lies only in the information it contains, not in its format.

Make sure that you aren't losing any identifying information on the back.

- Put separation sheets in the place of items, such as large architectural drawings, that are kept in the archives but stored separately from the collection in which they were found. The separation sheet should note that the item was moved and where it can be found.

- Don't do anything when you don't know the consequences, such as using pressure-sensitive tape to mend tears. You can keep pieces of valuable torn originals together by putting them in a Mylar folder. Consult a conservator when you run into problems such as mold, mildew, insect infestations, or damaged bindings.

- Discard extra copies. These can be removed if they are truly duplicates, not annotated copies. You may also remove items that don't belong in the collection. While shoes and other equally odd items have turned up in some unorganized collections, you're more likely to find papers that got mixed in by mistake, such as a staff member's child's report card turning up in institutional records.

- Keep notes of what you learn about the creator and the records during arrangement for help in creating your finding aids.

Label boxes and folders as you work. Folders that are straight across the top give you space for the most information. Decide on a standard format. For example, starting at the left side, put the name of the collection, the series (or a roman numeral to designate the series), the folder title, dates, and—at the far right side—the number of the box and folder. Use the original folder title when available. If it doesn't clearly describe the contents, add to it. You may want to regularize the title format when a group of folders all have similar contents but slightly varied titles. File numbering may be saved until the end, when you know just what each box contains, but the rest of the labeling should be done as you work. Finally, label the boxes. You can label them in pencil as you work and create permanent labels as a final step.

Writing in pencil across the folder top allows you to make changes if necessary. For very large collections, some repositories have a rubber stamp made to save writing the same information repeatedly.

---

[1] See preservation chapter for further detail.

Adhesive labels eventually fall off—don't use them!

These are relatively detailed steps for processing. Practices vary among repositories, and among collections within a repository. Some collections receive minimal processing, while others are fully processed with each document arranged in order. Processing priorities are based on institutional priorities, the needs of the archives' users, and the resources available. As priorities change and resources expand, collections that received little initial attention can be revisited for more complete processing.

When you run into problems, revisit the concepts of provenance, original order, and working at the appropriate level. The same principles apply to all records, whatever their media. Always consider your dual objectives: to provide researchers with access to the materials they need and to preserve evidence of how and why the records were created.

6

DESCRIPTION
Deborah Wythe

Archivists describe; librarians and curators catalog. Archival description differs in several important ways from its two close relatives—the bibliographic records that libraries create and the object records found in museum catalogs:

- Archival materials are described in groups.
- Archival materials are placed in context by means of historical and biographical notes written by the archivist.
- Archival description is multilevel and hierarchical, ranging from a simple collection description, to series and subseries information, to folder lists and descriptions, and even to item-level description when needed.

Both the beauty and the challenge of archival description lie in its flexibility. No one method will be appropriate to every collection or item in the archives. Archivists must constantly study and evaluate the materials, the research audience's access needs, and the repository's capabilities.

Archival materials are acquired and accessioned in groups, remain in groups during arrangement, and are described in groups to maintain their history and context. A single document in an archival collection rarely tells a full story—it is part of a continuum of documents, activities, personalities, and outcomes. Our job as archivists is to protect the integrity of the group, which may be a collection, a series, a subseries, or a folder, and to describe the group in a way that expresses both the content and the interconnections among its parts.

Archival description is a "value-added" process. While arranging and processing a collection, you will gather information on the people and historical context of the records; you may even do research in other sources to gain a better understanding of the people and activities reflected in the collection. This knowledge is passed on to potential researchers, alerting them to the significance of the collection and essentially providing a head start in their research.

Description in Museums

Archivists are not the only staff members in a museum who describe things. An important part of your job in establishing a descriptive program for the archives will be explaining archival description to librarians, registrars, and curators; quantifying your needs; and justifying setting up specific tools for the archives, rather than (or in addition to) piggybacking on other departments' systems. The very understandable desire for institutionwide information resources must be balanced against the greater utility of tools that suit a specific task perfectly.

One of the greatest administrative challenges a museum archivist faces is the pressure toward item description. Museums thrive on item-level description. A ceremonial pot containing seventeen pebbles will be described as such, and the pebbles may even receive accession numbers so that they can be tracked. Even within the context of other, related vessels, it is most important as a single, unique item. You may be encouraged to "catalog" archival collections in this way, a method that does not exploit the full power of archival description. A cubic foot of correspondence files is not equivalent to one pot, or several hundred pots, and an important part of your job will be to explain and justify describing archival collections as groups, not items.[1]

A related challenge in museum archives is creating and/or retaining links between accessioned objects, manuscript materials associated with particular objects, and documentation created by museum personnel about the objects. Devising ways to accomplish this, while still creating broader archival descriptive tools, will

---

1 Which is not to say that archivists never do item-level description. See Michelle Elligott's sidebar in the arrangement chapter and the discussion of item-level description in the photographs chapter.

allow the museum archives to provide effective access to both museum staff, who are most likely to be seeking information about specific objects, and to scholarly researchers working on topics that have a broad scope.

Librarians and archivists share an important descriptive tool—MARC format (MAchine Readable Cataloging)—but again the focus differs. Library catalogers create a bibliographic record for each book in the collection, often copying cataloging data from records created by other libraries. Archivists may use the same on-line system and MARC format for one part of their descriptive program, but the records are unique and contain much more descriptive text in structured and elongated note fields.

No one descriptive tool fulfills all of an archives' needs. You will probably contribute information to more than one of your institution's databases: MARC records in the library system; accession records for archival collections in the collections management system; notes pointing to archival materials in the object records of the collections management system. You will also create repository guides, finding aids, and a wide variety of archival tools. This chapter provides an introduction to these tools, some thoughts on

---

TERMINOLOGY[i]

Finding aid: an access tool that describes an archival group, providing information on the contents and context of the records and a physical description of the materials.[ii] Some common elements follow:

- Biographical and historical note: narrative section of a finding aid that provides contextual information about the people and/or institutions represented in the collection.
- Scope and content: narrative section of a finding aid that provides a collective description of the collection, summarizing the contents and describing the types of records and information included.
- Extent: the physical size of the collection, usually expressed in cubic feet or linear feet;[iii] counts of items, boxes, or containers may supplement this measurement.
- Dates: the chronological extent of a collection from the earliest to latest materials (inclusive dates) and, if relevant, the years in which most materials fall (bulk dates).
- Container list: a list of the contents of each box, often a list of series and folder titles and dates, which may provide the most detailed information for access and retrieval.

Processing: the activities required to ready archival collections for use, including performing basic preservation measures, refining arrangement, and gathering information for description.

MARC (MAchine Readable Cataloging): a standard format, developed by the Library of Congress and endorsed by archival and library professional organizations, for exchanging information about archival materials via bibliographic networks.[iv] The format provides a wide variety of fields and subfields (many of which parallel the finding aid elements noted above) for entering structured information about the intellectual content and physical details of archival collections. The various MARC formats (books, archival materials, visual materials, etc.) have now been integrated, so all fields are available to catalogers of all types of materials.

Subject headings: standardized terms, most commonly those found in the Library of Congress Subject Headings (LCSH). A controlled vocabulary used to facilitate searching in bibliographic systems.

Authority control: use of standardized forms for names of people, institutions, organizations; for subject terms; and for form and genre terms.

Indexing: a detailed analysis of a collection or group of materials with the goal of providing access to information in individual documents or resources.

EAD (Encoded Archival Description): a document type definition (DTD) for archival finding aids encoded in SGML or XML.[v]

---

i   See also Lewis J. Bellardo and Lynn Lady Bellardo, *A Glossary for Archivists, Manuscript Curators and Records Managers* (Chicago: Society of American Archivists, 1993).

ii *Finding aid* is also used as a general term for any kind of descriptive tool, and *inventory* for this particular form.

iii Archival repositories can be divided into two groups: those that use cubic feet ("c.f." or container volume) and those that use linear feet ("l.f." or thickness of the materials). Thus a 10 x 12 x 15" records carton ("cubic foot box") would hold 1.25 l.f. of letter-sized files or 1 l.f. or legal-sized files. Either method can be useful for estimating collection size and storage needs.

iv See <www.loc.gov/marc>.

v   See <www.loc.gov/ead>; <www.iath/virginia.edu/ead>; and *Encoded Archival Description Tag Library*, version 2002 (Chicago: Society of American Archivists, 2002).

establishing a descriptive program, and a discussion of automation's role in description.

Finding Aids

The finding aid, a flexible, multifaceted document, includes both information directly derived from a collection's contents (folder lists, dates, collection size) and descriptive, contextual, and analytical material researched and written by the archivist. While they may look quite different, all finding aids draw from the same group of basic data elements.

Some of the basics are quite simple, and may even have been recorded as part of the accessioning process. Archivists assign a formal title to each collection, thereby providing a simple description of the contents (Jane C. Doe Papers; Records of the City Art Museum) and allowing readers to refer to the collection clearly. Inclusive and/or bulk dates place the collection in time. Extent (size of the collection) helps users evaluate how much time they are going to need for research and how much information they may find. A container list provides file-by-file information on the contents. Provenance and processing notes detail the history of the collection. This information is easily gathered and needs only to be placed in a structured, consistent format.

In contrast, the scope and content and biographical and historical notes are the heart and soul of a finding aid. Writing these sections, you will exercise

---

EXCERPT FROM A SERIES-LEVEL FINDING AID

BROOKLYN MUSEUM OF ART [record group]
RECORDS OF THE OFFICE OF THE DIRECTOR [sub-record group]
SERIES: Wills & Estates files
INCLUSIVE DATES: 1888–ongoing
EXTENT: 9 linear ft.
DATABASE ACCESS: INV/LEGAL
ACCESSION DATE: 10/15/1986 (survey; inventory)

Historical Note:
The Brooklyn Institute of Arts & Sciences maintained its Office of the Treasurer at the Brooklyn Museum of Art; one of the Treasurer's responsibilities was to attend to legal affairs for all the Institute departments. With the dissolution of the Institute, the legal files (known as "Wills & Estates") were adopted by the legal officer of the Office of the Director of the Museum.

The creators of this series were Institute Treasurers and Assistant Treasurers Gates D. Fahnestock (1904–1909), Clinton W. Ludlum (1910–1913), Daniel V. B. Hegeman (1914–1916), Herman Stutzer (Acting; 1917), J. Foster Smith (1918–1931), Edwin B. Maynard (1931–1949), Lloyd R. McDonald (1941–1958), Thomas A. Donnelly (1954–1978), Gloria Rosenblatt (1978–1984), and Museum Deputy Directors Roy R. Eddey (1981–1997) and Judith Frankfurt (1998–).

Scope & Content
The Wills & Estates files contain records relating to legal matters, particularly bequests, but also including grants, corporate donations, claims or actions for or against the Institute, gifts. Bequest files contain legal documents (Notices of Probate, Citations, Receipt & Release forms); wills and extracts, appraisals, affidavits; correspondence, legal opinions and letters of transmittal regarding estates; and financial statements from trusts in which the Institute or Museum had a residuary interest. Most of the correspondence is with the law firms that represented the Institute or Museum and with those representing the executors.

Access
The Wills & Estates series is a permanently active archival file that is held in the Office of the Director. Access is restricted to members of the Director's Office staff and the Archivist. Specific questions may be investigated by the Archivist for researchers. As a result of a survey undertaken in 1986, folder descriptions of the Wills & Estates files were entered into the Archives database (ARCH/LEGAL); new files are added as created.

Other Sources of Information
Files on bequests are also held in the Records of the Office of the Director; these may or may not overlap those held in the above series.

[Folder list]

your intellectual and creative skills to explain how the collection is organized, what it contains, what is most important or interesting, interrelationships with other collections, who the people and institutions are, and the historical context of the records. The text may be short and succinct or more expansive; regardless of their length, the notes must take readers into the collection in such a way that they are well prepared to use the records. The point is not to exercise your abilities as a historian (although some expertise is certainly helpful), but to use your archival understanding and

Promotional photograph for "Wonder and Horror of the Human Head" exhibition, 1960. UNIVERSITY OF PENNSYLVANIA MUSEUM. NO NEGATIVE.

skills to make the collection understandable. A finding aid must answer the question, "What do we have here?"

Just as archival collections are often arranged hierarchically, a finding aid may have a hierarchical and nested structure; the organization of a collection is often mirrored in the structure of the finding aid. Thus, a standard group of data elements—title, dates, extent, and descriptive notes—may recur at each level: the record group or collection, the subrecord group or subcollection, the series and subseries, each time providing more detailed information about a more limited selection of records. The records you are working on often dictate how far you need to go. A small collection with a simple structure may lead to a straightforward finding aid, while a complex collection requires that you find ways to present critical information in an organized and understandable fashion.

Finding aids may be produced and distributed in many formats. Hard copy is still useful and may be produced "on the fly" from a word-processed document, as needed. More and more, however, finding

aids are made available on institutional or collaborative Web sites. At this time, Web-based documents can be produced using several techniques, each having advantages and disadvantages that are hotly debated by proponents and opponents.[2] HTML (Hypertext Markup Language) is a formatting tool that is widely used and readable by all Web browsers; its simple structure supports formatting and searching at a very basic level. The EAD (Encoded Archival Description) document type definition was developed and endorsed as a standard by members of the archival profession for encoding archival finding aids in SGML (Standard Generalized Markup Language) or XML (eXtensible Markup Language) and mounting them on the Web. Using EAD, each element of a finding aid can be identified and encoded, or marked up, giving Web users access to standard output from system to system and, potentially, detailed search capabilities. EAD also allows users to reflect the nested and hierarchical structure of finding aids. Style sheets, used in conjunction with a marked-up document, allow repositories to define—and easily change—a standard appearance and organizational scheme for their finding aids.

The MARC Record

The development of MARC cataloging—a system with clearly defined fields and cataloging standards—allowed librarians and archivists to catalog materials ranging from books to archives to visual materials; to present these bibliographic records on local networked systems; and most importantly, to share information via regional, national, and international on-line bibliographic databases. MARC cataloging also provides some simple management tools such as recording donor information and tracking actions taken or anticipated. MARC-compliant databases can be found on shared systems such as RLIN (Research Libraries Information Network) and

---

2 See for example, *American Archivist* 60, nos. 3 and 4 (1997), for a series of articles on EAD, and search the archives of the Archives and Archivists listserv at <http://listserv.muohio.edu/archives/archives.html> on "HTML and EAD" for extended commentary on this issue.

000 03975cbd 2200565 a 450≠

001 23623

005 20011009112553.0

008 920825i18881992nyu eng

035 __ ‡9 NYBA92-A19

040 __ ‡a NBB ‡c NBB ‡e appm

090 __ ‡b DIR: W&E ‡i 09/22/92 N

110 2_ ‡a Brooklyn Museum. ‡b Office of the Director.

245 10 ‡a Wills & Estates files, ‡f 1888-[ongoing].

300 __ ‡a 9 linear ft.

351 __ ‡c Series ‡b arranged alphabetically.

545 __ ‡a The Brooklyn Institute of Arts and Sciences maintained its Office of the Treasurer at The Brooklyn Museum; one of the Treasurer's responsibilities was to attend to legal affairs for all the Institute departments (The Brooklyn Museum, Brooklyn Children's Museum, Brooklyn Botanic Garden, and Brooklyn Academy of Music). With the dissolution of the Institute in 1980, the Treasurer's legal files (known as "Wills & Estates") were adopted by the Deputy Director of The Brooklyn Museum, the member of the Director's staff responsible for legal affairs.

545 __ ‡b The creators of this series were Institute Treasurers and Assistant Treasurers Gates D. Fahnestock (1904-1909); Clinton W. Ludlum (1910-13); Daniel V.B. Hegeman (1914-16); Herman Stutzer (Acting, 1917); J. Foster Smith (1918-31); Edwin B. Maynard (1931-1949); Lloyd R. McDonald (1941-58); Thomas A. Donnelly (1954-78); Gloria Rosenblatt (1978-84); and Museum Deputy Director Roy R. Eddey (1981-).

520 __ ‡a The Wills & Estates files contain records relating to legal matters, particularly bequests, but also including grants, corporate donations, claims or actions for or against the Institute and Museum, and gifts. Bequest files contain legal documents (Notices of Probate, Citations, Receipt & Release forms); wills and extracts, appraisal, affidavits; correspondence, legal opinions, and letters of transmittal regarding estates; and financial statements from trusts in which the Institute or Museum had a residuary interest. Most of the correspondence is with the law firms that represented the Institute or Museum and with those representing the executors.

524 __ ‡a Records of the Office of the Director, Wills & Estates files, 1888-[ongoing], Brooklyn Museum of Art Archives.

555 8_ ‡a Unpublished finding aid available in repository.

555 8_ ‡a Folder-level descriptions available on-line in repository.

506 __ ‡a Permanently active archival file held in office, restricted to use of ‡d authorized staff members. ‡c Consult Archivist for details.

580 __ ‡a The Wills & Estates files form one of 12 series in the Records of the Office of the Director, The Brooklyn Museum.

583 __ ‡n 9 ‡o linear ft. ‡a inventoried ‡c 10/15/1986.

541 __ ‡3 Records of the Office of the Director, Wills & Estates, 1888-[ongoing] ‡a Director's Office ‡c Maintained in Director's Office

583 __ ‡3 Records of the Office of the Director, Wills & Estates, 1888-[ongoing] ‡a inventoried ‡c 10/15/1986 ‡k D. Wythe

541 __ ‡n 9 ‡o linear ft.

600 10 ‡a Buck, Robert T.

600 10 ‡a Buechner, Thomas S.

600 10 ‡a Cameron, Duncan

696 14 ‡a Fox, William Henry, ‡d 1858-1952.

600 10 ‡a Nagel, Charles

696 14 ‡a Roberts, Isabel Spaulding, ‡d 1911-

600 10 ‡a Roberts, Laurance P.

696 14 ‡a Schenck, Edgar Craig, ‡d 1909-1959.

600 10 ‡a Youtz, Philip Newell, ‡d 1895-1972.

696 14 ‡a Fahnestock, Gates D.

696 14 ‡a Ludlum, Clinton W.

696 14 ‡a Hegeman, Daniel V.B.

696 14 ‡a Stutzer, Herman

696 14 ‡a Smith J. Foster

696 14 ‡a Maynard, Edwin B.

696 14 ‡a McDonald, Lloyd R.

696 14 ‡a Donnelly, Thomas A.

696 14 ‡a Rosenblatt, Gloria

696 14 ‡a Eddey, Roy R.

773 0_ ‡7 c2bc ‡a Brooklyn Museum of Art. Office of the Director. ‡t Records, 1896-[ongoing] ‡w (NBBR-LIN)NYBA91-A1

856 [hotlink to an existing URL, if available]

OCLC (Online Computer Library Center), which require institutional membership (and fees); as part of integrated library systems and on-line public access catalogs (OPACs); and in smaller stand-alone database packages.[3]

MARC records allow archives to declare, "Here we are" and "This is what we've got." This is critical since, in many cases, there is no reason to suspect that a particular repository might hold a given collection. You must get researchers in the door, and MARC records remain an extremely important tool in this respect.

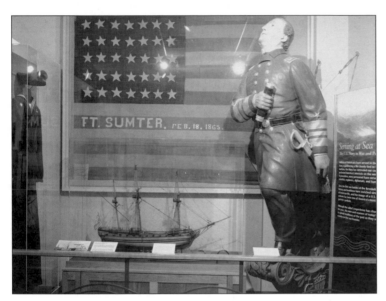

An imposing ship's figurehead representing Civil War admiral David G. Farragut anchors this portion of the Navy section in "Voyages: Stories of America & the Sea." This signature exhibition opened at Mystic Seaport in June 2000. COURTESY MYSTIC SEAPORT, MYSTIC, CONNECTICUT.

National and international MARC-based systems such as RLIN and OCLC serve thousands of repositories as a research gateway, although Internet resources are beginning to challenge and expand upon that role. Participating in the library OPAC at your institution will give the archives visibility as a component of the museum's research resources. Even if you do not have access to a local or national MARC bibliographic database at your institution, you can submit information to the National Union Catalogue of Manuscript Collections (NUCMC) at the Library of Congress. NUCMC creates MARC records on RLIN and provides access to them via a free RLIN gateway on the Library of Congress Web site.[4]

Although they share many of the same components, MARC records are not a substitute for formal finding aids. They often have system-defined size limitations, cannot reflect complicated collection hierarchies as clearly as a more flexible document, and generally are not used to record detailed contents or container lists. MARC's great strength is its standardization: data can be shared, transferred, and upgraded without great difficulty, and the use of name and subject authorities allows researchers to search and find materials across a wide variety of collections. In addition, a fully compliant MARC program also contains communication protocols that allow other MARC programs to recognize its records and exchange data.[5]

Each MARC "tag" (numbered field) consists of a standard set of subfields with clearly defined contents. These definitions are created and maintained by MARBI (MAchine Readable Bibliographic Information), a committee of librarians and other information professionals coordinated by the American Library Association and the Library of Congress.[6] Archivists and librarians depend on a variety of standards publications and other tools in creating and formatting the actual contents of each field.[7]

Other Tools

Archivists often develop more detailed, customized access tools to fulfill needs beyond those of the finding aid and MARC record.

York State may submit records to the New York State Archives for inclusion in the RLIN database.

5 While it is possible to create a MARC-like field structure and tags using off-the-shelf database software, such databases lack the ability to share information directly, without the use of additional software or programming.

6 <http://www.ala.org/Content/NavigationMenu/ALCTS/Division_groups/MARBI/MARBI.htm> and <www.loc.gov/marc>.

7 Most importantly, *Anglo-American Cataloging Rules*, 2nd. ed., 2002 revision (Ottawa: Canadian Library Association and Chicago: American Library Association, 2002), known as AACR2; and Steven L. Hensen, *Archives, Personal Papers and Manuscripts*, 2nd ed. (Chicago: Society of American Archivists, 1989), known as APPM. The next generation of archival descriptive standards, however, is underway with the CUSTARD project (Canadian-U.S. Task Force on Archival Description), which will reconcile APPM, the Canadian Rules for Archival Description (RAD), and the General International Standard Archival Description (ISAD(G)). A description of the project may be found on the SAA Web site at <www.archivists.org>. Sources of standardized terminology include the Library of Congress subject headings (LCSH), the Art and Architecture Thesaurus (AAT) at <www.getty.edu/research/tools/vocabulary/aat>; and the Thesaurus of Graphic Materials (TGM1 and TGM2) at <http://www.loc.gov/rr/print/tgm1/toc.html> and <http://www.loc.gov/rr/print/tgm2/toc.html>.

---

3 Software vendors often exhibit at the SAA annual meeting and advertise in archival publications. A search of the Archives and Archivists listserv will help identify vendors and point you to archivists who use their products.

4 See <www.loc.gov/coll/nucmc/nucmc.html>. Repositories in New

Indexes, inventories, chronologies, and item-level databases may all be appropriate in specific cases. Photograph collections, for example, frequently require item-level access and control: patrons wish to search for specific images, and archives staff members need to manage individual items in the digitization and rights and reproductions processes. Field notes may be extensive and rich, but without an index, may be much less useful. A large collection of "general correspondence" that is arranged chronologically may require description of the folder contents to provide adequate reference service.

Developing special tools has become much simpler in the age of computers and can be a useful, interesting, and creative part of your job, as well as an excellent way to involve volunteers and interns in your program. To be valuable, however, any such micro-access tools must be part of a well-thought-out and complete descriptive program.

Implementing a Descriptive Program

Descriptive techniques and tools achieve their greatest utility as part of a descriptive *program:* a well-planned sequence of activities, each one building upon and enhancing the others. Several steps are critical in setting such a program in motion:

- considering your resources for descriptive and reference work;
- understanding your users, both institutional and outside researchers;
- setting priorities for levels of description and which collections to attack first;
- designing procedures and implementing standards that will lead to consistent description collectionwide.

A descriptive program draws on and overlaps most other facets of archival work. It starts with your mission statement, grows out of the accessioning process, is accomplished concurrently with processing, and is a critical part of reference.

Once you have thought about and analyzed these topics, articulate your conclusions in written policies and procedures, begin to put them into effect, evaluate how well the program is working, and adjust as necessary. Approaching description in this way leads first to

an adequate level of access for *all* records under your care and then on to enhanced access to top priority materials. It will also help you avoid the pitfall of using scarce resources to create highly detailed access to certain collections and little or none to others.

Museum archives programs are generally small: most of us can't expect to have a description division! Planning a descriptive program must take into account both the resources available and other resources you may be able to obtain. As you work out audience needs, priorities, and procedures, consider

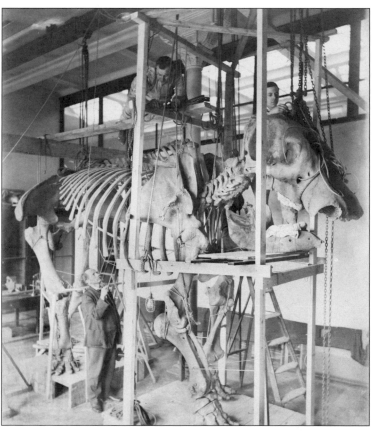

Warren Mastodon skeleton, 3/4 rear, front and figure. AMERICAN MUSEUM OF NATURAL HISTORY LIBRARY, NEG. #35356.

who will do the work and keep in mind that the basic framework *must* be created and maintained by permanent staff. Descriptive work done by interns and volunteers tends to be tightly focused on one collection; without professional oversight and supervision, you risk losing the broader overview and consistency that is critical to achieving descriptive control of your collections.

The primary audience for any institutional archives is likely to be the staff of the institution itself. If we ignore that fact and concentrate only on outside researchers, the archives may well be endangered as an institutional priority. On the other hand, outside researchers are often engaged in more in-depth studies that place the institution in a broader context, so we must keep their needs in mind as well. Analyzing collections and taking into account their context beyond your museum's walls can also help design and justify projects that are compelling enough to qualify for grant funding. The types of questions asked by these two classes of researchers and the tools needed to serve them may be quite different.

In-house reference requests (as well as many questions from members of the public) are often quite specific: the staff member or researcher is looking for facts, and it is very likely that archives staff will do the actual research and provide the answer. In many cases, *you* are the archives user, and it is critical that your descriptive tools serve you quickly and efficiently. As you work with staff, you will soon learn which types of questions are most common, which records are most useful, and which access points are necessary to find what you need to answer questions accurately and with ease. Curatorial staff members most often approach research on objects by accession or catalog number; archival records may be arranged by correspondent, topic, project, function, or date. Administrators may seek information on past activities or people, which may not be segregated out as

such in the records. Your descriptive tools must take these requirements into consideration, or you will spend all your time pulling down boxes and searching through folders, rather than going to the quickest, best source of information as directly as possible.

On the other hand, outside researchers are more likely to approach with a more general topic and to be willing to read through a range of materials that could potentially support their research. Some staff members working on scholarly projects, exhibitions and reinstallations, and provenance research have similar requirements for exhaustive study. They need the background and contextual information that will help them decide which records to study; they also need to be assured that you and your descriptive tools are directing them to *all* the potential resources for their work, not just the ones that happen to be most easily accessible. When providing this kind of reference service, supplying the most effective descriptive level in your finding aids can help cut down on the amount of work done by reference staff. At all costs, you must avoid having to bring out boxes of records that are inadequately described "just in case" there's something in them! While producing detailed descriptive tools

CASE STUDY

Stewart Culin, the Brooklyn Museum of Art's first curator of ethnology (1903–1929) was well known in his day, but rarely published, so even though his collections continued to be displayed in the museum, his work was largely forgotten. In the early 1980s, the museum unearthed his archives, organized portions of them, and used these series to inform an exhibition about Culin's Native American collections, "Objects of Myth and Memory" (1991). Five years later, an NEH grant led to a detailed finding aid, which was published, distributed to many museum and university libraries, and cataloged on RLIN.

A small but steady stream of researchers have always approached the archives to study Culin's papers, especially those related to Native Americans. Since publication of the finding aid, which covers his entire career, research use has expanded into more and more areas. We plan to mount an EAD version on the Web within the next year, thanks to a Mellon Foundation grant, and expect that that will lead to even more use. Using volunteers, we have created detailed database access to images and expedition reports, allowing researchers to mine the collection even more easily.

Descriptive tools:
Guide to the Culin Archival Collection
Collection and series-level MARC records in RLIN
Folder-level database
Item-level image database
Index to expedition reports

Culin reference requests

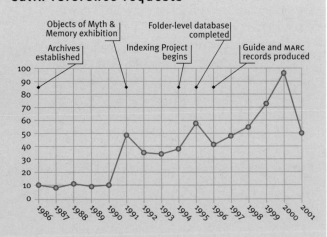

can be labor-intensive, it is work that must be done only once, effectively "front loading" your effort.[8]

Scholarly researchers often find their way to the museum archives in the hope that there is something there, based on prior knowledge, guesswork, and word of mouth. These researchers are often well prepared for work in your collections, even without finding aids or any effort to publicize the collection. For instance, they know that a particular scientist worked at the museum and that he or she was involved in an archaeological dig in a certain location and year, and they hope that you have his or her field notes. They may even help provide the context you need to understand them. Once a detailed finding aid is available and starts to circulate, however, new researchers are likely to appear and use the collection in new ways. Your understanding of both potential researchers and the materials themselves will aid in creating tools to provide appropriate access.

Priorities and Levels of Description

A fully realized descriptive program contains a hierarchy of levels:

- repository and/or institution
- record group or collection
- subrecord group
- series
- subseries
- folder
- group of items
- item

The following example follows one strand in the Brooklyn Museum of Art Archives:
- Records of the Brooklyn Museum of Art (institution);
  - Records of the Curatorial Departments (record group);
    - Records of the Department of Painting & Sculpture (subrecord group);
      - Objects (series);
        - Gifts (subseries);
          - Gifts received, 1945 (folder);
            - Jane C. Donor correspondence (group of items);
              - Letter re gift of Homer watercolor (item).

Depending on your priorities and resources, your descriptive program will fill in detail for some or all of these levels, *starting from the broadest*.[9] How far you travel down the road to detailed description will depend on the needs you identified by studying your users and the resources that you have available.

Keep in mind also that the level of description need not be consistent throughout your collection. Description at the record or subrecord group may be all you need in one case, while another part of the archives may require a folder list or even folder descriptions. It

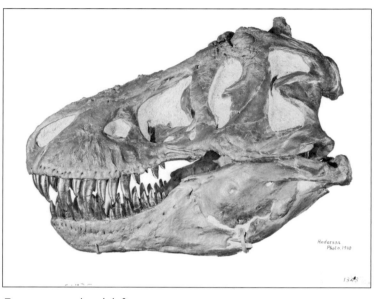

Tyrannosaurus head, left. Photograph by A. E. Anderson. American Museum of Natural History Library, neg. #35492.

may be most useful to complete some tasks up-front—creating preliminary box or container lists upon accessioning, for example—while others may have to wait until the records are processed. Articulate and justify these decisions to superiors and coworkers and document your procedures in a written manual or guidelines.

Some priorities are obvious and more or less universal. Every archives needs a repository description, for which you have probably already laid the groundwork in your mission statement or collection development policy: "What is it that we collect?" The next

---

8   In planning projects, you must often decide whether to invest a significant amount of time and effort at the beginning ("front loading") or to spend repeated small amounts of time over a period of many years. A container list is a simple example of front loading ("What is in this box?"). Indexing a valuable set of field notes is labor intensive, but saves great effort every time a question must be answered. Careful planning and design are essential in creating effective tools, however, so that the effort is not wasted.

9   Nonarchivists are often inclined to start with the narrowest description—a list of letters or correspondents, for example. This type of inventorying is frequently a waste of effort: it provides a dense level of detail with no overarching structure or context—a perfect example of "can't see the forest for the trees"—and often leaves more useful work unaccomplished.

level, defining your records groups or collections, is also critical, both in describing your holdings to administrators and grant agencies and in the decision-making process with each new accession: "How are the archives' holdings organized?" "How do the various pieces fit together?" This step is also fairly simple in an institutional archives, since the scheme usually mirrors the organizational structure of the museum, with the addition of some special and artificial collections. Once you have sketched out the basic structure, you can start filling in the details for records that are already accessioned: "What are the dates and extent of holdings?" "What types of records are included?" You may be able to define series and subseries at this point, though that may have to wait until you are ready to process the records.

The descriptive process is additive: you gather information and enhance description as you proceed. Once a structure is created and described in very broad terms, accessions can be plugged into the hierarchy and the description refined. This approach provides basic descriptive access from the moment materials are acquired. Simple MARC records in the museum's bibliographic database can make this level of description available to staff and researchers, even if it is some time until the records can be fully processed and a finding aid created.

Based on your priorities, records selected for full processing will receive more intensive descriptive treatment. Series and subseries will be defined and described, folder lists created or refined, and specialized access tools such as indexes created when needed. Standard final products include a finding aid and a bibliographic (MARC) record that include all the standard elements: creator, title, dates, extent, biographical and historical note, scope and contents note, details on the physical characteristics of the collections, and information on the contents at an appropriate level of description. You may also create databases or spreadsheets to record and manage repetitive information about the collection: folder lists, name authorities, indexes, and the like.

Procedures and Standards

Since it is very likely that at least some of the descriptive work done in your archives will be accomplished by interns, volunteers, and project staff, establish clear, written procedures and supervise descriptive work carefully. Everyone must collect the same information, express it with a consistent, controlled vocabulary, and use the same format. Bulleted guidelines and worksheets can be very helpful, as can working on description as processing goes on, rather than isolating it as a separate process. Review and edit descriptive work on a regular basis to avoid compounding errors. Most archivists have experienced or heard tales of collections that had to be entirely reprocessed and described due to ineffective earlier projects.

Simple techniques can go a long way in making description consistent and effective. Construct titles consistently at all levels: collection, record group, series, subseries, folder. Establish standard terminology for museum functions and departments. Start a name authority and always use the same format for names. Define a standard structure for folder titles, so that they will both make sense and sort properly. Decide if you are going to use linear feet or cubic feet to express extent and how each type of container should be calculated. If you are going to number series, subseries, and folders, decide on a standard format that is both logical and simple.

NUMBERING

Numbering schemes can become quite a headache; it is difficult to find ways to express all the possible levels.[vi] If well conceived, numbering can make it much easier for researchers to request and cite materials. Decide whether to number folders throughout an entire collection, a series, a subseries, or box by box. Consider what to do if (when) you find additional folders, have to add a new series, or decide to rehouse the collection. In general, simpler is better.
Some examples:
   Series: Roman numeral; subseries: capital letter; folder: integer (II.A.007)
   Series, subseries, folder: all numbers (2.1.007)
   Box and folder: numbers (box 124, folder 7)

---

vi On a personal note, this author avoids numbering schemes on anything except closed collections—groups of records where we're fairly certain there won't be accretions. At the Brooklyn Museum of Art Archives, we rely on standard series names and construct consistent folder titles that will sort properly in our folder-level database. For an example of a very complete and detailed scheme, see the system developed by Richard Pierce-Moses for the Heard Museum at <http://rpm.lib.az.us/hapm/index.html>.

Automation's Role in Description

Using and developing automated tools—that is, computer access to collections—greatly enhances the archivist's ability to both manage and provide in-depth access to the materials in his or her care. In the last three or four decades, automated techniques, including MARC cataloging with its attendant on-line public access catalogs and national bibliographic databases; relational and flat-file databases; spreadsheets; collections management packages; Encoded Archival Description; and word processing have moved from being available only to those with specialized computer science or programming training to becoming standard tools in every archival repository, from the smallest to the largest.

The emphasis must still be on the plural—tools—since no one technique or system will provide all the capabilities needed. We archivists need to lead researchers to our collections; find materials for them once they are there or find the resources to answer questions for them; share information with other repositories; develop techniques to produce both on-line and in-house descriptive tools; and manage our collections. We have already touched on MARC records and EAD above. In this section, we will discuss other automated tools and their uses, keeping in mind, however, that in the fast-paced computer world, flexibility and change are the most important watchwords.

Databases

Many archivists, because of the wide variety of materials and tasks that they deal with, find that an off-the-shelf database is an important tool. Databases, from simple flat-file to intricate relational varieties, allow archivists to tailor access and management tools to fit specific needs. In most cases, you can develop the skills needed to design and implement in-house databases that fulfill many needs.[10] The most essential requirement is the ability to think critically and analytically about information (i.e., data), skills that most archivists already use daily. Even if you choose to work with a systems professional to set up your database(s), you will have to do the intellectual planning, since the

---

10 The Microsoft Access for Archivists listserv is an excellent place to get advice. Send an email message to: <MSAccess4Archives-subscribe @topica.com>.

success of any database depends on a clear understanding of the data to be input; the types of users and their needs; and the desired output, whether on screen, in hard copy, or on the Web.

The characteristics of some sections of finding aids point us toward database techniques, rather than the more traditional word processing. Box and folder lists, for example, contain standard data elements (box number, series and folder titles, dates) and, while it is easy enough to format these in a word-processed document, setting up a database to handle such lists will

Schoolgirls view North American Indian exhibit, 1912. University of Pennsylvania Museum. Neg. 10991.

greatly increase the functionality of the data. A folder-level database can contain information that reaches beyond a single collection; allow searches that specify date ranges or folder title keywords; generate custom reports for researchers; include information that is important for management (shelf location and processing audit trails, for example); *and* output the data in a format that will plug into the finding aid. The beauty of databases is that the data is independent of format: it can be reorganized, viewed in many different ways, used to generate statistics and custom views, and linked to other data sets.

As you develop a descriptive program for your institution, you will discover areas in which providing access to more detailed information is desirable. In institutional archives, the archivist often does the research (and needs information quickly), so it can be to your advantage to "front load" the work and spend time creating access tools rather than going through box after box each time a reference query arises. In museums, reference queries often center around specific objects, donors, or vendors, and you may find that it is worth-while to expand the standard box and folder list to include a folder description with more detailed content information—a value-added action. Many document types could benefit from detailed access points or indexing, among them minutes, field notes, expedition reports, exhibition checklists, and staff and trustee lists. If criteria are clearly spelled out, the data can be gathered and entered by paraprofessional staff, interns, or volunteers.

Museum collections management databases assist staff with all activities surrounding museum objects—acquiring, accessioning, cataloging, storing, exhibiting, and lending them, to name a few—and also often provide tools for other activities such as exhibitions and donor relations. The approach generally centers around the individual object, which may make such systems difficult to adapt for archival collections, but if your museum accessions archival collections in the same way it does objects, you may need to find a way to represent your collections in the system. If this is indeed the case, spend as much time as possible studying the system and deciding how and in what depth to catalog archival collections, keeping in mind that other tools may provide additional or other functionalities that you need as well. For example, because the museum community has not agreed upon standards in the same way that the library and archives communities have, you may find that you need to create a MARC record so that you can share information on your holdings beyond your museum's network. You could also explore "crosswalks" developed by other institutions, such as the Getty's Metadata Standards Crosswalk, which enable you to map one descriptive standard to another.[11]

Finally, spreadsheets can also be useful in managing data, but keep in mind that, like word processing, their functionality is limited. They are primarily a very powerful tool for managing and manipulating numerical data, not the textual data that archives generate. In all cases, the task should match the tool and, when investing time and effort in collecting data, your goal should be to get the most out of that data.

In conclusion, keep in mind that you are not working in a vacuum. The archival profession has expended considerable effort on creating descriptive standards, not just to help individuals do their work, but to allow them to *share* their products. These standards and other helpful studies have been published by the Society of American Archivists and discussed at length in publications and at professional meetings. Archivists are almost always willing to provide advice, demonstrate their systems, and help colleagues solve knotty problems. While your collections may be unique, your solutions need not be: build upon the experience of the profession and customize as necessary.

---

11 See <www.getty.edu/research/institute/standards/intrometadata/3_crosswalks/index.html>.

7

RESEARCH USE: ETHICS, RESTRICTIONS, AND PRIVACY

Susan K. Anderson

The goal described in previous chapters is to make records readily accessible in a museum archives. However, it is sometimes necessary to restrict certain materials to protect a museum's proprietary interests and donors' privacy rights. Museum archivists need to work in accordance with legal statutes, professional standards, and ethical guidelines to ensure that appropriate actions are taken and controversial repercussions minimized.

Unfortunately, dealing with these issues can sometimes be problematic, and there is often a disparity between what is prescribed in the archival literature and what actually happens in an archives on a day-to-day basis.[1] To bridge this divide in my chapter, I have used a multifaceted approach, utilizing professional articles, ethical codes, policy statements, and personal observations from archivists themselves to provide a general perspective of ethics, privacy, and restrictions in museum archives. Throughout the sections below, I recommend having a written restrictions policy that is mandated by museum administration and imple-

mented throughout the institution. This is the strongest tool an archivist has to safeguard both access and privacy interests, and to avoid ethical dilemmas.

Ethics

It has been said that codes of ethics represent goals to strive for and provide a moral framework for a profession.[2] For years, archivists have looked to the Society of American Archivists' *Code of Ethics and Commentary*[3] for guidance, and its basic points apply to our specialization as well as any other. It should be noted, however, that it is easy for archivists to get caught in an ethical balancing act. Given the nature of our work as information professionals, we are often placed within library departments and taught the ideals of open access as embraced by the American Library Association.[4] Given the complex nature of archival collections, however, we are hard-pressed to exert the same degree of item-level control that librarians have. Compound this with rapidly changing attitudes toward freedom of information and more litigious attitudes toward privacy issues (both personal and institutional), and it is easy to feel pulled between the very different ethical needs of researchers, donors, and administrators.[5] Finally, certain members of the scholarly community are still very attached to the idea of having exclusive rights to particular groups of pri-

1   Mark Greene, "Moderation in Everything, Access in Nothing?: Opinions about Access Restrictions on Private Papers," *Archival Issues* 18, no. 1 (1993): 38. "(T)here seems to be a disquieting disjunction between our official manuals and broad archival practice."

"While museums are becoming more open about their archives, there is still reluctance to grant complete access to researchers. The museums are afraid of alienating benefactors by revealing privileged information and therefore disrupting the conduit of gifts (including both artworks and money). They are also afraid of "getting Swissed," as a State Department official put it—having embarrassing revelations of earlier conduct come to light. Finally, they are afraid of losing a work without compensation."
—*Jonathan Petropoulos*[i]

i   "Exposing 'Deep Files,'" *ARTnews* 98, no. 1 (January 1999): 143.

2   Karen Benedict, "Archival Ethics," in *Managing Archives and Archival Institutions*, James Gregory Bradsher, ed. (Chicago: University of Chicago Press, 1988), 175.

3   Society of American Archivists, *Code of Ethics for Archivists and Commentary* (Chicago: Society of American Archivists, 1992).

4   "The public library movement was founded on the principle of free and open access to information as a prerequisite for a free society. Archival repositories, on the other hand, evolved to meet the requirements of institutional or governmental executives, or in the case of manuscript repositories, an elite circle of gentlemen scholars." Elena Danielson, "Ethics and Reference Services," *Reference Librarian* 56 (1994): 112.

5   "The needs of donors . . . do not always coincide with those of researchers. . . . Archivists can inadvertently get caught in the crossfire." Elena Danielson, "The Ethics of Access," *American Archivist* 52 (Winter 1989): 53

mary source materials—which creates yet another constituency with which to negotiate ethical issues.[6]

A good way to think about ethics in relation to your own archives is to examine the mission statement of your museum. If no formal mission statement exists, talk to key administrators to determine whom your constituency is and how to best serve them. Museums receiving public funding have a responsibility to make their collections widely available to all, whereas private institutions primarily support in-house research and serious scholarly inquiry.[7] Quasipublic

A father shows his son the entry he wrote while awaiting his birth in a "Father's Book" kept in the maternity waiting room of Wesley Memorial Hospital. THE FLORENCE AND IKE SEWELL MUSEUM OF NORTHWESTERN MEMORIAL HOSPITAL.

institutions (which combine both public and private funding—this includes a great many of us) must balance both public and private interests; a museum's mission and institutional culture will largely determine which way the scales will tip. Discussions with staff members such as registrars and curators who have vested interests in your museum's records,[8] as well as colleagues from similar institutions, will also be helpful. Measure these examples against case studies in the literature and relevant sessions at professional meetings,[9] and it will be possible to piece together a unified approach that will be both tailored to your own particular program and ethically informed.

A logical extension of this process is to implement policies that provide a reasonable context within which you and researchers may operate. Provide registration forms with restriction information and other access guidelines for patrons to read and sign.[10] Such basic

tools, with administrative endorsement, will help flesh out finer points of the "moral compass" that ethical codes outline so well. Perhaps one of the most important contributions that you can make toward fair and equitable access[11] is to maintain an unbiased approach. Apply your access policy equally to all researchers and develop restrictions that are consistent, judicious, and have clearly defined parameters.

Restrictions

Types of restricted records

An informal survey of several museum archives[12] indicated that certain types of institutional records are frequently restricted because they contain proprietary information. These materials may be considered confidential because they impart too much information about the institution to the public, which could impair or compromise certain key functions or relationships within the museum community. Records relating to an executive body (such as a board of trustees) or individual (such as a director or CEO) usually contain privileged information concerning administrative affairs. In addition, they can include documentation of legal actions, which may also reside in the custody of a museum's legal counsel. Personal information is considered sensitive and is frequently found in personnel and donor files. Financial records—especially those concerning the price and valuation of art objects, artifacts, or specimens—are usually restricted for a period of time, as are insurance records, loan agreements, grant proposals, and portions of exhibition files that include any of the aforementioned records. Other record groups containing potentially sensitive material may be found in active collection files such as registrarial records and curatorial object or specimen files. These tend to be extremely valuable—and confidential—

6 "The landscape can be stormy. There are still scholars around who say, 'That's my territory, kid. Stay out.'" Milton Esterow, "Barnes Bars Barr," *ARTnews* 90, no. 10 (December 1991): 101.

7 William Deiss, *Museum Archives, an Introduction* (Chicago: Society of American Archivists, 1984), 24.

8 Katherine Kane, "Bridging the Gap," *Museum News* 70 (November/December 1991): 48.

9 Nancy Lankford, "Ethics and the Reference Archivist," *The Midwestern Archivist* 8, no. 1 (1983): 13.

10 Ruth Simmons, "The Public's Right to Know and the Individual's Right to be Private," *Provenance* 1, no. 1 (Spring 1983): 3.

11 "It is important to note that the SAA code provides for equitable access rather than equal access. The ideal is that each repository is open to all members of the public on equal terms. Equitable access gives a repository the right to define its primary clientele—an important consideration for private archives . . . that primarily contain proprietary information." Danielson, "Ethics and Reference Services," 111.

12 Several colleagues, as noted in the acknowledgments, consented to informal interviews, e-mail discussions, and requests for policy statements as I developed a restrictions policy for the Philadelphia Museum of Art in 1999 and performed specific research for this chapter in 2001. These individuals have provided informal advice and observations for this section and throughout the rest of the chapter, which are used with their kind permission.

THE PHILADELPHIA MUSEUM OF ART ARCHIVES

Restriction Policy

OVERVIEW

The ultimate goal of the Archivist is to provide access to the Museum's inactive records of enduring value on a fair and equitable basis. It is sometimes necessary, however, to restrict certain materials to protect individual privacy rights and legitimate proprietary rights of the Museum. The Archivist, in accordance with legal and ethical guidelines, will inform donors when it is appropriate or not to impose restrictions on incoming materials. Restrictions on access should be explicit and easy to enforce, and should be limited only to those materials that can be identified as sensitive. Unreasonable restrictions should be avoided, and all restricted materials should be assigned an expiration date at which time their sensitivity is no longer an issue, and the records may be safely accessed for research purposes.

PROCEDURE

1. The Archivist will work with donors to determine appropriate restrictions for sensitive or confidential materials, using legal guidelines, established business practices, the Society of American Archivists' *Code of Ethics,* as well as their "Standards for Access to Research Materials in Archival and Manuscript Repositories."

2. Restrictions will be imposed on access to certain materials, including but not limited to Board of Trustee minutes; Director's files; personnel files; financial information; recent transactions regarding art objects (especially valuations, loan agreements, and conservation treatments); legal actions; donor confidentiality; or anything that would compromise the Museum's security or operations.

3. Restrictions on donated materials will be clearly prescribed in the transfer documentation (see Inventory Worksheet, Deed of Gift Agreement, Accession Form, and Oral History Agreement). Terms for limited access (see steps 6, 7, 8, 9, and 10 below) should also be determined at this time, along with expiration dates for the restriction.

4. If restriction terms are not clearly prescribed, and it becomes apparent during processing that they need to be, the Archivist will attempt to contact the donor to establish the appropriate terms. In the absence of a donor's input, the Archivist may impose restrictions at his/her discretion.

5. A restricted file will be clearly marked "RESTRICTED" in red marker on the folder exterior, or a series will be so designated on both folders and container(s). Information regarding the nature of the restriction should also be included. Restriction of entire record groups or collections, however, should be avoided; limit access to only those materials that can be identified as sensitive.

6. Unless terms of limited access are noted (see below), only the donor, along with designated administrators, will have access to restricted files.

7. In determining limited access, the Archivist should consider a researcher's "need to know." For instance, a Museum employee needing to access materials in the course of doing his/her job demonstrates a high need to know, whereas an outside visitor making a casual inquiry does not. In general, the more serious and scholarly the nature of the inquiry, the more likely the researcher will be granted some degree of access.

8. In certain cases of limited access, the Archivist may use restricted files to answer questions for researchers, extracting out pertinent but non-sensitive information.

9. Another type of limited access would involve the Archivist consulting with the donor, receiving permission before allowing the researcher to look through certain groups of material.

10. Access to certain materials that are fragile or have high intrinsic value (such as the Museum's Charter) may also be limited, and the use of such materials will be supervised during examination.

11. Disputes regarding restricted materials will be settled in consultation with the Director/CEO of the Museum, who will be the ultimate authority in such matters.

aggregates of information. Even though they are of permanent value, they are often not transferred to the archives because of their direct and ongoing relationship to a museum's display collections.

Other restricted materials may include conservation records, because treatment information could be used adversely, such as using restoration techniques to create counterfeit objects. A museum's architectural records can be a concern, because they include details about the physical plant that could be used to compromise security or operations. Looting can become a danger if archaeological site maps fall into the wrong hands. Life science institutions restrict access to records documenting the whereabouts of endangered species or wildlife with a high market value. Finally, museums with technology-based collections sometimes limit access to plans for certain types of equipment or machinery, due to potential copyright issues.

Some museum records share qualities with a display collection and consequently share similar restrictions. For instance, artifacts sacred to Native Americans may require initiation into a particular group as a prerequisite for access. Tribes donating such artifacts may want to extend the same restriction to records that relate to the objects. Similarly, medical and anthropological museums can contain human specimens donated under the condition of anonymity. If there are related photographs and records, the condition of anonymous use may apply to them as well. Finally, some materials can be seen as both archival and artifactual (such as expedition notebooks) and should be restricted from routine handling because of their high intrinsic value.

The restrictions policy

Perhaps the best recourse for museum archivists is to develop a written restrictions policy. This policy can work within the constellation of other documents designed for archives management or be developed as part of a policy pertaining to a related activity such as accessioning or access. Ideally, this document should specify the types of restricted records; clearly state the conditions of restrictions; and relate to policies from

"When exposed to public scrutiny, there will be less chance that the profession can be accused of arbitrary or inequitable behavior if it has incorporated ethics in all levels of policy and performance."
—*Karen Benedict*[ii]

similar museums, standard archival texts,[13] the Society of American Archivists' code of ethics,[14] and the Society's *Standards for Access to Research Materials in Archival and Manuscript Repositories.*[15]

However, not all confidential material can be easily identified in a policy. Even if that were possible, very few archivists could scrutinize their collections to find every last sensitive document. Especially problematic are unwieldy backlogs of material, which may or may not contain restrictions set by donors. With this in mind, you can make general statements in a restrictions policy that apply to a broad variety of materials. It is common to impose a standard restriction on recently transferred records, varying from five to twenty-five years in length,[16] to allow confidential information to become less sensitive. Valuations are less relevant over time, and potentially scandalous information is less embarrassing after a staff member retires or a donor passes away. Some archivists restrict access to unprocessed records, which lack the beneficial scrutiny that comes with arrangement. Finally, you can consider including a general statement in the policy that states "records may be restricted at the discretion of the archivist," which allows you the flexibility of imposing a restriction if unforeseen circumstances arise. (Be prepared, however, to justify your decisions if and when you apply this aspect of the policy.)

A restrictions policy can also help ease interactions, whether you need to reassure nervous curators or explain clear guidelines to researchers sorting out which records they can actually use. Perhaps the most important reason for having a policy in place is to avoid the appearance of arbitrary decision making, which can damage both the archivist's and museum's credibility, since ad hoc decisions made at the research table can be construed as unreasonable or biased.[17]

ii "Archival Ethics," in *Managing Archives and Archival Institutions,* James Gregory Bradsher, ed. (Chicago: University of Chicago Press, 1988), 183.

13 Gary Peterson and Trudy Huskamp Peterson, *Archives and Manuscripts: Law* (Chicago: Society of American Archivists, 1985). Although long out of print, this is still a useful primer on a number of legal and ethical issues. See also SAA's Archival Fundamentals Series.

14 Society of American Archivists, *Code,* 1992.

15 Society of American Archivists, *Standards for Access to Research Materials in Archival and Manuscripts Repositories* (Chicago: Society of American Archivists, 1973).

16 Barbara Case and Ying Xu, "Access to Special Collections in the Humanities: Who's Guarding the Gates and Why?" *Reference Librarian* 47 (1994): 139.

17 Lankford, "Ethics and the Reference Archivist," 7–8.

Privacy

The best scenario for an archives is to have material transferred without any restrictions whatsoever. In lieu of this ideal situation, a restrictions policy is a particularly useful tool when dealing with donations. Make no mistake about it: the best time to consider restricting material is when a transfer agreement or deed of gift is filled out.[18] Donors usually have an intimate knowledge of their records and are often the best ones to determine confidentiality. If they cannot immediately identify sensitive material, they can at

---

18 Sara Hodson, "Private Lives: Confidentiality in Manuscripts Collections," *Rare Books and Manuscripts Librarianship* 6, no. 2 (1991): 112.

"The librarian or archivist should attempt to steer donors away from unnecessary or complicated restrictions and should refuse to accept discriminatory ones."

—*Helen Yoxall*[iii]

"Donors have been known to be cavalier about the release of information in their papers, particularly information relating to persons other than themselves. If the donor does not specifically protect the privacy rights of persons named in the donated materials, the archives should [do so] to avoid potential law suits."

—*Gary Peterson and Trudy Huskamp Peterson*[iv]

"Despite the fact that few states have privacy laws of their own, there is no national privacy legislation that covers non-federal records except for student records, national security information, and records generated as the result of federal grants and contracts. In the absence of specific legislation, most privacy issues are judged by common law principles and by court rulings in previous cases. In developing a uniform policy for dealing with privacy issues and the rights of the research public, the archivist should be guided by ethical concerns that normally will be confirmed in law and practice."

—*Donald Lennon*[v]

---

iii "Privacy and Personal Papers," *Archives and Manuscripts* 12, no. 1 (May 1984): 43.

iv *Archives and Manuscripts: Law* (Chicago: Society of American Archivists, 1985), 42.

v "Ethical Issues in Archival Management," *North Carolina Libraries* 51 (Spring 1993): 20.

---

least discuss potential problem areas with you. However, no degree of familiarity with the records can supercede your expertise and authority during this process. The archivist is in a unique position to educate donors as to when it is appropriate to impose restrictions—or not. You can also argue for limited access, providing a compromise between the differing priorities of donors and researchers.

As discussed previously, restrictions relating to departmental records in museums usually follow particular patterns. More problematic are personal papers, which can contain correspondence between donors and third-party correspondents. Such letters are usually considered privileged because they were written for a limited audience, and opening them to outside research puts personal privacy at risk. This is an especially tricky area, because even if a donor gives his or her complete consent, the correspondents have not and are probably unaware their intimate letters are being made available.[19] Some authors feel that archivists should exert conservative restrictions on such documents, as well as contacting and obtaining consent from third-party correspondents.[20] Some also recommend that archivists impose tighter restrictions than what was originally stipulated by the donor to protect third-party privacy rights. However, other writers point out that recent case law does not support such conservatism, and most archivists are hard-pressed to impose even modest restrictions.

It has also been observed that an archivist imposing additional restrictions beyond those prescribed by the donor betrays a lack of trust, which could be potentially damaging to their relationship. An alternative approach may be to design fairly open agreements and work with donors to provide varying degrees of access.[21] Whether you take a more conservative or liberal approach toward privacy issues, it is always a good rule of thumb to review any problematic situation with your museum's legal counsel. Showing him or her examples of donor agreements, collection samples, and typical reference inquiries will make his or her legal advice more pertinent to your particular situation.

Applying Restrictions

When determining degrees of access, the goal is to apply restrictions that are explicit, easy to enforce, and directed toward readily identifiable material.

---

19 Yoxall, "Privacy and Personal Papers," 40.

20 Hodson, "Private Lives," 116–17.

21 Greene, "Moderation in Everything," 35–38.

Unreasonable restrictions should be avoided whenever possible, such as barring access to entire record groups or collections.[22] You should also assign expiration dates for restrictions, when records can be fully opened to researchers and sensitivity is no longer an issue.[23] These are particularly important points for museum archives seeking grant funding. Funding agencies are usually hesitant to award processing grants to archives with extensive and/or permanent restrictions, because the primary reason for such support is to increase access to underused collections.

Archivists and curatorial staff review a manuscript collection together while working out interdepartmental access policies. PHOTOGRAPH BY GRAYDON WOOD. PHILADELPHIA MUSEUM OF ART.

After determining which restrictions should be applied, an archivist should identify problem areas to prevent researchers from stumbling across confidential material. There are various ways to designate materials as sensitive, which can be integrated into processing procedures. Beyond simply labeling a file folder as "RESTRICTED," you can separate confidential docu-

ments from the main folder and file them directly behind in either a specially marked folder or sealed envelope. This technique can also be used to protect confidentiality in active collection-related records such as accession, object, or specimen files if they are frequently accessed. Yet another method is to separate restricted material altogether in another container while preserving intellectual control. Information regarding the nature of restrictions should be included on separation notes and documents.

Limited access

There are varying degrees of restriction, and very few documents should be absolutely off-limits to everyone. Museum archivists frequently provide limited access, acting as intermediaries between researchers, on the one hand, and the director, curatorial departments, or donors on the other. Part of the process of determining limited access is considering a researcher's "need to know." For instance, museum employees needing access to materials in the course of doing their jobs have a high need to know, whereas casual visitors stopping by on a whim do not. In general, the more serious and scholarly the nature of the inquiry, the more likely you should grant some degree of access to records.

Another aspect of the "need to know" concept is determining possible negative intent if researchers seem to be going out of their way to find damaging information. Caution, as always, is a good rule of thumb. You do not want to alienate a researcher by dismissing him or her as a muckraker, nor do you want to encourage attacks on your institution or colleagues.

This situation will require you to examine problematic records to "tell a smoking gun from a water pistol,"[24] and consult with your museum's legal counsel. If there is real evidence of wrongdoing on the part of your institution (not just mere accusations), you are ethically bound to make the situation known to legal authorities. However, your superiors should be notified first, and your public relations department consulted for damage control. It is better to take charge of a situation by issuing a well-worded press release than to allow a scandal to erupt from prematurely leaked information.

In some cases of limited access, you can consult restricted files in the archives and extract information

22 Gerald Ham, *Selecting and Appraising Archives and Manuscripts* (Chicago: Society of American Archivists, 1993), 82.
23 Danielson, "The Ethics of Access," 54.

"Types of Projects Not Eligible for Grant Support . . . to process documents, most of which will be closed to researchers for more than 5 years, or not be accessible to all users on equal terms, or will be in a repository that denies public access . . ."

—NHPRC Grant Application Guidelines[vi]

vi National Historical Publications and Records Commission, NHPRC *Grant Application Guidelines* (Washington D.C.: National Archives and Records Administration, 2000), 3.

24 Peterson and Peterson, *Archives and Manuscripts*, 42.

on behalf of the researcher. This allows you to address specific questions without exposing users to sensitive details not relevant to their search. Another option would be to work with departments in extracting information from their active collection records (such as registrar's or curatorial files).[25] Other types of limited access would involve an archivist asking permission for a researcher to look through certain donor files. Or a researcher can ask on his or her own behalf through a "blind letter," which an archivist could mail, keeping a donor's address confidential.

Another way to make documents available when only a small portion is confidential (such as a name or a financial figure) is through redaction. This process involves making a copy of the original document and marking over any sensitive element. You must then make another copy, because some information might still be visible under close scrutiny, and give the final amended copy to the researcher. If a particular kind of record is frequently requested, such as a museum's architectural plans, it may be possible to eliminate certain sections (such as an electrical system layout) so the basic design can be shared without compromising security. Bear in mind that redaction should be done carefully and with some knowledge of the subject matter; if you have doubts, consult with a knowledgeable expert. Confidentiality is not preserved if a stray element accidentally remains on the reference copy.[26]

Another type of limited access is to review materials before delivering them to researchers, a compromise strategy for making unprocessed collections available. This type of spot-checking allows you to be selective

and restrict only what is necessary during particular reference interactions.[27] However, given the day-to-day demands of most museum archives, it may prove difficult to make extensive reviews on a regular basis. It is also possible for one staff member to restrict too much while another restricts too little from the same collection. This could result in researchers being exposed to different sets of material, despite the best of intentions, resulting nonetheless in unequal access.[28] As with other strategies presented here, there are pluses and minuses to each, largely determined by

Natives dragging bearded seals, Bering Strait, Alaska, May 1922.
PHOTOGRAPH BY A. M. BAILEY. DENVER MUSEUM OF NATURE & SCIENCE IMAGE ARCHIVES, BA21-395G.

the amount of intervention required to make limited access possible. It is ultimately up to the archivist in charge to determine which approach is most feasible, given the particular situation and his or her ethical "comfort level" with the risk involved. When strategies regarding such records are developed, they should be integrated into the departmental restrictions policy for consistent application.

Researcher Relationships

Museum archives (along with university and corporate archives) are set apart from other repositories because the primary research group is on staff. Not

---

25 Deiss, *Museum Archives*, 16.

26 Yoxall, "Privacy and Personal Papers," 39.

> "Once a value judgement is made, such as mentally labeling a researcher as a hack and thus less deserving of potentially invaluable assistance, the system is open to flagrant abuse. Charges of discrimination can badly damage a repository's reputation just as much as can neglecting the institution's principle benefactors."
> —*Elena Danielson* [vii]

vii "The Ethics of Access," *American Archivist* 52 (Winter 1989): 61.

27 Hodson, "Private Lives," 117.

28 "Lawyers rightly caution archivists about privacy and confidentiality laws. Staff members very commonly respond to such legal advice by screening papers and withdrawing on their own authority any letters or documents that reveal potentially embarrassing personal information. . . . In such an environment, the staff must be very realistic about the bad publicity engendered by prudish restrictions in the modern era. Biographers who learn that basic information about the lives of their subjects has been removed from their primary source material will feel cheated, and not without justification." Danielson, "The Ethics of Access," 56.

surprisingly, this creates a potential conflict of interest. It is no secret that archivists and curators approach records from different perspectives. Differences in training, professional priorities, and roles within an institution affect their respective philosophies concerning the treatment and use of archival collections.[29] While many records are transferred to a museum archives and come under an archivist's direct purview, sometimes departmental records are retained indefinitely by curators, or the curators may want to apply special conditions that go above and

The Prehistoric Archaeology exhibition in the Upper Main Hall of the Smithsonian Institution Building, ca. 1879–1903. SMITHSONIAN INSTITUTION ARCHIVES, NEG. 2962 (RU 95, BOX 41, FOLDER 4).

beyond reasonable limits set in a restrictions policy. Donors might also send manuscript collections to curatorial departments, especially if the records are considered part of an object or specimen collection, and/or have a direct relationship to one.[30] Although many curators manage small "pockets of papers" quite responsibly, some are inclined to use collections exclusively for their own research, especially if they belong to competitive disciplines that place an emphasis on new discoveries in primary source materials.[31] For an archivist already trying to balance the needs of donors and researchers, these situations can create yet another potential liability.

As with all issues relating to ethics, there are no hard-and-fast rules regarding scholastic monopolies. As was mentioned before, a restrictions policy can

work within the constellation of other documents designed for archives management. It is important to have a mission statement in place for a museum archives, to formally outline your responsibilities concerning all institutional records. This—along with administrative endorsement—can provide your strongest defense when approaching a curatorial department to try to establish a common dialogue regarding how records are handled.[32] Joint projects such as performing a records survey, developing interdepartmental access policies, writing a processing grant, or collaborating on a collection management system can also provide you with ample opportunities to interact with curatorial staff and introduce basic archival concepts, especially those concerning reasonable and equitable access.

It is also helpful to remember that codes of ethics exist for several professions. For instance, the College Art Association charges a scholar with "the moral obligation to share the discovery of primary source material with his colleagues and serious students."[33]

32 Kane, "Bridging the Gap," 48.

33 College Art Association, *Code of Ethics*, <http://www.collegeart.org/caa/ethics/art_hist_ethics.html>, 1995. In addition to this point, the *Code* also states: "He or she is not obligated to share anything of an interpretive nature that has been done with the source material. The recipients of documents or any other form of information from an art historian should in turn give the finder a reasonable opportunity to be the first to publish the material in question. The finder should seek to publish research as soon as possible, thereby showing respect and appreciation of art historians of the past and present who have contributed to the profession and from whom he or she has benefited. In the words of Aby Warburg: 'There are no reserved seats in scholarship.'"

"Scholastic monopolies occur when one or more scholars arrange with the owners of research materials to have exclusive access to the material for research purposes. . . . Research scandals arise when individuals or institutions purposefully restrict access to significant collections of research materials based on personal or institutional prejudice, ignorance, fear, greed or any one of a number of other natural human failings, including the desire to protect a treasured point of view."
—*Barbara Case and Ying Xu* [viii]

viii Barbara Case and Ying Xu, "Access to Special Collections in the Humanities: Who's Guarding the Gates and Why?" *Reference Librarian* 47 (1994): 135, 142.

29 Kane, "Bridging the Gap," 46–48.

30 Deiss, *Museum Archives*, 16, 27.

31 Case and Xu, "Access to Special Collections," 132, 135.

Knowledge of these and other professional standards can provide a certain degree of leverage when negotiating for increased access. Additional leverage can be gained through enlisting the support of a sympathetic administrator or curatorial colleague who can underline the points you are trying to make. There is also something to be said for demonstrating good ethics and collections management skills yourself, which can inspire trust, positive interactions, and perhaps even the eventual transfer of "satellite collections" to the archives. It is important to remember that when starting up a new archives program (or re-establishing one that has fallen by the wayside), a certain degree of public relations and education is a normal part of the process. Regardless of how large or small your museum is, one builds support for an archives program one relationship at a time.

Another possible solution regarding "scholastic monopolies" can be found in SAA's code of ethics itself: "Archivists endeavor to inform users of parallel research by others using the same materials, and, if the individuals agree, supply each name to the other party."[34] On the surface, this seems like an easy enough solution. However, there is an ethical dilemma inherent in the statement itself: the information provided to an archivist during a reference interview or on a call slip is considered privileged information—making this yet another privacy issue.[35] If you decide to introduce researchers, it's a good idea to include something (perhaps a check box) on your registration form so scholars can give their informed consent. An archivist can also contact the initial researcher first as a courtesy, to see if introductions should proceed further. You can also determine during the reference interview

how much a researcher already knows about "parallel research," or if he or she is interested in finding out more. It is possible that researchers are already acquainted with each other's work and intervention is not really needed on your part.[36]

Settling Disputes

Despite the best of intentions, sometimes disputes occur in this shaky realm of ethics, privacy, and restrictions. It might be that a researcher perceives that access has been unreasonably denied, or donors are upset when scandalous information is gleaned from their papers. Again, having established policies can provide some solid ground for you to stand on. It is also helpful to include in these policies some clause

A Dallas patron of the arts, ca. 1911. Courtesy of the Archives, Dallas Museum of Art.

regarding the resolution of disputes by a higher authority.[37] An administrator or archives committee can often de-escalate a situation by giving a disgruntled scholar a chance to vent his or her frustrations to a third party. It is recommended that an archivist brief the administrator(s) prior to the meeting, to ensure that all parties are informed and in agreement as to the best way to settle the dispute.

---

34 Society of American Archivists, *Code,* 1992.

35 Lennon, "Ethical Issues," 21.

36 Lankford, "Ethics and the Reference Archivist," 11. "(N)ews travels fast in scholarly circles. Scholars stake out certain areas of interest and that interest becomes known through publications, papers, and the grapevine. Why should archivists pretend not to know the research areas of their patrons? The scholars themselves pass the word."

37 Yoxall, "Privacy and Personal Papers," 41.

You should also measure the relative risks involved with a records-related controversy. Sometimes it is better for a museum to cooperate and open mildly sensitive records than to endure a protracted battle and be hurt by negative publicity.[38] Again, consultation with your legal counsel will prove valuable here, along with advice from a public relations department. Another source for sound judgment would include a trusted colleague who has dealt with a similar situation; chances are your situation is not completely unique.

---

38 Danielson, "Ethics and Reference Services," 113. "Previous generations of archivists have often taken shelter in legalisms and simply restricted materials that might invite controversy. Public opinion is shifting on this issue, and in the near future it may well become more of a liability to restrict controversial materials than to open them."

8

RESEARCH USE: OUTREACH

Marisa Bourgoin

Outreach activities such as public programs, exhibitions, and Web sites are all important ways to introduce audiences to the research topics, unique materials, and historical information available in an archives. Take advantage of them whenever possible! As is true with most archival repositories, museum archives hold materials that are of interest not only to specialized scholars but also to the museum staff, volunteers, and members of the community. Bringing attention to those holdings will increase research use, attract volunteers, establish the importance of the archives program to the overall mission of the museum, and, on occasion, facilitate donations or financial support. Acting as an advocate for the museum archives can be a richly rewarding and enjoyable experience with both tangible and intangible benefits.

Working in a museum environment offers some distinct advantages. Museums are themselves collecting and exhibiting institutions staffed by people who are sensitive to the special needs of unique objects. The museum archivist and the museum curator share a commitment to education, history, preservation, and access. Indeed, an upcoming anniversary, an important retrospective exhibition, or the opening of a renovated building and the desire of curatorial staff to gain access to archival materials for these events often provide the impetus for establishing an archival program. Collaboration between the two departments can take the form of adding archival materials to an exhibition being planned by a curator, or the museum archivist's participation in programs related to other projects. Many museums have installation and design departments that can facilitate planning and execution of exhibitions of archival materials. In addition, public programs such as lectures, tours, symposia, and the like are part of the daily rhythm of most, if not all, museums. Collect ideas for programs and exhibitions as you process and refer to collections—perhaps in a file with copies of interesting items or notes on upcoming anniversaries—and be prepared with a rich selection of ideas when an opportunity arises.

Keep in mind time and budgetary constraints when planning activities; programs do not have to be elaborate or expensive to be effective. Archivists who feel overwhelmed with just meeting the basic demands of their position sometimes view outreach programs as a luxury, but projects that are closely tied to the goals of the archives and the institution it supports are definitely not "frills." With creative planning and efficient use of available resources, the museum archives can make a contribution to any institution's program of outreach and education, no matter what its scale or budget.

Public Programs

Just as the museum archives serves two functions—it is a research center for outside scholars and an internal source of information for museum staff—the programs you devise should address the needs of both internal users and the public. Working effectively with the public is the best way to start: providing professional, helpful reference service to each patron. By facilitating access to the collections and responding in a timely and friendly manner to reference requests, you will demonstrate that the archives is an important and useful resource. Clear signage, easy-to-navigate registration systems, and appropriate accommodations for researchers all communicate the archives' commitment to public service.

As the archives program becomes more known in the community and within the museum, opportunities for you to participate in and initiate public programs should present themselves naturally. Establishing good working relationships with other museum departments is an important step. Hosting an open house for museum staff and volunteers provides a great introduction to the archives for those who may not be aware of the archives program, especially if the department is a recent addition to the institution. If possible, display archival materials for the open-house visitors to see. Early staff manuals or directories, photographs of staff members or museum installations, and other material related to the internal workings of the museum help connect museum staff members with their predecessors and the history of the institution. Be prepared to answer questions about the collections and make a point of engaging the interest of staff members whose work does not directly connect with the archives.

There may also be opportunities to participate in orientation sessions for new board members, employees, and/or volunteers. A few words about the history of the institution and the materials available for use in the archives will often be all that is required. It is helpful to have a short, set talk with slides, handouts, or other visual aids prepared for use in such situations. When possible, personalize your talks for each audience's interests. Board members will know that the problems they face aren't new if the roof has always leaked; auxiliary groups will be interested in how much money the group has raised during its history; volunteers will be happy to learn that their service to the institution is part of a long tradition of community involvement.

Internal newsletters and publications provide an excellent outlet for information on the archives in the form of news about new accessions or notes on the institution's history. Tidbits can be posted on staff bulletin boards or discussed at brown bag lunches with a special, perhaps fun, topic—or maybe a look at scandals at the institution or the weirdest item anyone tried to donate to the collections. Informal but informative programs can greatly contribute to the staff's quality of life and overall staff morale, as well as to the image of the archives as an interesting and worthwhile place.

As the archives' holdings and the archivist become better known to museum staff, you will probably be asked to participate in programs aimed at donors and prospects. In many institutions, membership and

REFERENCE POLICIES AND PROCEDURES CHECKLIST

Access policy
- ❐ Who can use the archives?
- ❐ Restrictions statement.
- ❐ What are your hours for staff? For members of the public?
- ❐ What services do you provide?
- ❐ What are your charges (photocopies, photographic prints, digital scans, reproduction rights)?
- ❐ How should your collections be cited?
- ❐ Procedure for reproduction requests.

Reference interview. Listen to the researcher's initial request, then ask questions to find out:
- ❐ the exact question, problem, or project;
- ❐ any relevant background;
- ❐ other resources consulted (published and archival);
- ❐ desired depth of inquiry (quick answer or thorough study).

Registration
- ❐ Record pertinent information (name, institution, address, e-mail, telephone, research topic).
- ❐ Consider copying a form of ID for security purposes.
- ❐ Provide a written list of procedures and rules for readers (handling, copying, reproduction).

Research
- ❐ Direct researcher to appropriate access tools.
- ❐ Pull materials selected.
- ❐ Record box/file list as part of the reference request (for security purposes and to assist with selection on future visits).
- ❐ Review handling, explain how to flag materials to be copied.
- ❐ Supervise, answer questions, provide additional guidance.

Follow up
- ❐ Make copies.
- ❐ Work with researchers requesting permission to cite or reproduce.

Administration
- ❐ Record and track reference requests (some will recur regularly).
- ❐ Record payments; provide receipts to patrons.
- ❐ Maintain statistics (staff/public; telephone/letter/visit; collections used).

development officers depend on the museum's curatorial staff to provide interesting programs for members and donors; the museum archivist should also be included in the roster of staff members available to give short talks and tours or longer programs when appropriate. In addition, you may be able to suggest or plan programs for off-site tours or excursions, often a favorite activity of membership groups.

While always keeping in mind the larger institutional fund-raising goals, take the opportunity to inform donors about the important work done in the archives and perhaps cultivate interest in supporting specific projects. Discuss any fund-raising leads that result from these programs (and indeed from any donor contact) with the development staff to ensure that potential donors are properly cultivated. If you distribute membership applications or other fund-raising materials, mark them in some way so that the membership or development office knows that you brought those members in.

Keep in mind also that membership groups such as "Friends of" organizations do, in some instances, maintain their own records, which may be of interest to the archivist. Participating in programs presented by these groups will introduce the work of the archives and perhaps facilitate transfer of any desired materials.

Complement programs aimed at internal and affiliated audiences with those for external constituents. As with other endeavors, developing relationships

ARCHIVES WEEK

As museum professionals, we are accustomed to showing our collections, but when it comes to getting the word out to the research community, we often depend on word of mouth, the Internet, or the old stand-by NUCMC. National Archives Week, held during the second week of October, gives us a chance to show off our collection materials in a lively public forum. Activities planned for Archives Week generally include lectures, fairs, and workshops. Museums are an excellent venue for such events, since they usually have meeting spaces that are open to the public—amenities that are increasingly difficult to find because of security issues in many cities.

Lectures are the most simple to organize. Find a researcher—perhaps a curator at your museum—who has done interesting work with your collections and ask him or her to talk about the project. A professor from a graduate program might address the future of the archival profession. An author could speak about the value of a newly processed collection. A small exhibition of materials from the collection or a series of slides adds interest to these events.

Coordinating an Archives Fair is more complicated—but a great deal of fun. At the fair, visitors see, discuss, and compare copies of collection materials, finding aids, databases, Web interfaces, and other means of collection access in a dynamic atmosphere. Fairs provide an avenue for the staff of archival repositories to get together and show collections to the public and each other as a cohesive professional group. They can raise public awareness of collections and develop and enhance collegial relationships. A good location will have a large open area with tables and chairs, space for visitors to look at the materials, and, ideally, places to hang posters, banners, and copies of interesting photographs and documents. Displays should not just sit there—be ready to interact with visitors and talk about your collections.

Archival workshops allow you to reach out to a variety of constituencies, limited only by your imagination and energy. Teachers are happy to learn how to help their students use archival resources, especially with the increasing popularity of National History Day, and they may be able to receive continuing education points for your workshop from their school district. Members of the public are always eager to learn about how to preserve their family treasures and will flock to a preservation basics workshop. They willingly bring along old photographs and papers, seeking advice from archivists and conservators. As you help them appraise the research value and condition of their materials—an archival *Antiques Road Show*—you will also make friends for your museum and meet potential donors to the archives.

Publicity is important for all these events. Post signs at your institution, local libraries, universities, and any place else you think may draw an interested crowd. Prepare a press release. Contact local newspapers, radio, and television stations. Look for local events listings on the Internet and consider specialty listservs, both good places for getting the word out.

—*Kristine L. Kaske,* National Air and Space Museum, Smithsonian Institution

with the staff members charged with public programs is of great assistance. As you participate in planning meetings, track exhibition schedules, note upcoming events, and become engaged in the daily life of the museum, your ideas about how the archives can contribute to the public programs schedule will come into focus. Archival presentations or programs can be planned in conjunction with other museum events and can also originate from the archives.

Consider scheduling an open house during a local meeting or conference of people who would

Girls looking at Chinese crystal sphere, ca. 1954. Photograph by Reuben Goldberg. University of Pennsylvania Museum. Neg. 139420.

have some interest in the museum's archival holdings: scholars, students, genealogists, librarians, archivists, museum professionals. It is possible to display relevant materials in an informal way with little or no expense—directly on worktables or existing shelves, in polyester envelopes or sleeves. If you expect to host such events frequently, facsimile copies of the highlights of the collection are useful to display in conjunction with a rotating group of original materials.

Workshops and seminars also bring people to the institution and to the archives. If a curatorial department is planning such an event, you might find ways for the archives to participate: be a speaker, contribute ideas for topics, or suggest scholars who have used the archives. It isn't necessary to wait for suggestions from other departments; the end of a big processing project or grant, or the opening of an exhibition are great times to hold events like these. Although seminars and workshops require more planning and organization, the first one is generally the most difficult. Experience

in coordinating these events will make planning future events less cumbersome.

Gallery talks or tours are often a repeating feature of a museum's public programs schedule. Museum staff, guest lecturers, and docents talk about particular objects or exhibitions in the museum's exhibition spaces, where the participant is able to view the objects in person. These programs may be planned as a series with different speakers or as individual, special-focus events. Announced through the museum's regular newsletters or other publications, gallery talks don't necessarily require tremendous publicity to be successful, just interesting and varied topics, and they can be inexpensive to present. In the same vein, slide lectures offer an opportunity to illustrate a topic with lots of great images and are portable to off-site locations like schools, senior centers, civic groups, and the like.

Exhibitions

Exhibiting archival materials is an excellent method of introducing audiences to the archives and its holdings. Either as a component of a larger exhibition or as the sole focus, an archival exhibition can present material that would not otherwise be available to the casual museum visitor. Visually interesting documents exist in every archival repository: maps, photographs, letters, publications, architectural drawings, and other types of documents can all be used to illustrate themes, document the institution's history, and inform the visitor. Stimulating materials, an enthusiasm for the topic, and some original thinking are critical elements to successful exhibitions.

Although many archival and curatorial exhibitions are planned well in advance, always be prepared to include archival materials in exhibitions. Don't be shy and don't expect curators to seek you out; if you have relevant and interesting materials, suggest including a case featuring them or adding them to didactic panels for upcoming exhibitions. Having an exhibition plan that is ready to be executed can allow you to take advantage of an unexpected gap in the schedule.

Creating an exhibition involves several key steps: selecting the theme and materials; designing and installing the exhibition; designing and composing labels and other publications; and planning related programs. In smaller museums, the archivist will probably be responsible for most of the tasks associated with exhibitions and may even need to become familiar with the proper methods of framing and label production. Archivists in mid-sized and large museums should be able to obtain assistance from in-house design and production departments, but understanding the entire process of planning and installing exhibitions certainly leads to a smoother project.[1]

Broadly outlined below, the steps to a successful exhibition can be a starting point for your efforts. However, consultation with museum colleagues is an excellent method of learning firsthand about the challenges of exhibition work. You might even consider volunteering to assist in the installation of an exhibition—archivists are, after all, familiar with handling fragile and rare materials—as a learning experience.

Determining the focus of an exhibition can be the result of extensive planning based on the museum's long-range goals or the serendipitous discovery of little-known materials. Archival materials may also supplement exhibitions designed by the museum's curatorial department or even add local interest to shows organized by other institutions. As you start to think about the content of archival exhibitions, examine the strengths of your holdings. Take into account conservation issues. Be informed about what exhibitions are planned for neighboring institutions, since there may be opportunities for complementary programming.

There are innumerable possibilities for exhibition themes, but archival exhibitions usually fit into one of two categories: exhibitions that have the archives and its work as the subject and exhibitions that illustrate a particular subject with archival materials.[2] Since a museum's archives is not the main focus of the institution—which has its own exhibition program—shows that relate to the museum's collections and exhibitions are probably more likely to be approved by the administration and placed on the schedule. This is not to say that "promotional" exhibitions that demonstrate the work and utility of the archives shouldn't be explored, but rather that it may be easier to place the latter type of exhibition on the museum's exhibition schedule.

Archival exhibitions celebrate institutional anniversaries, new accessions (either by the museum or the archives), or other milestones; complement exhibitions with related materials; highlight the achievements of a local figure or staff member; explore a broad theme in history or a narrow topic—possibilities abound. Developing collegial relationships with curators and an awareness of their research interests will generate possible topics. Maintain an idea file for exhibitions. A museum's archives will have numerous items of interest to

Queen Elizabeth II of England visiting the National Gallery of Art on October 18, 1957. NATIONAL GALLERY OF ART, GALLERY ARCHIVES, WASHINGTON, D.C.

exhibit and far too many ideas to fit into the museum's schedule.

Unless the archives has its own dedicated exhibition space, archival exhibition plans will need to be approved by the museum's administration and fit into the overall schedule. Developing a brief proposal is a good first step in organizing an exhibition—and selling it to the administration and to potential funders. It can be a short document with an abstract of the exhibition's themes and copies of representative materials or an oral presentation with slides. Exhibition sizes, budgets, and timelines vary widely and must be taken into account when planning.

Early in the process, discuss your ideas with the staff members responsible for public affairs, public programs, exhibition design, and graphics production.

---

1   Excellent texts on design, writing labels, fabrication, and other relevant topics are available through the American Association of Museums, the Society of American Archivists, and other professional organizations.

2   Gail Farr, *Archives and Manuscripts: Exhibits* (Chicago: Society of American Archivists, 1980), 11.

Long-range planning with these departments is critical: magazines have long lead times, program calendars are generally set well in advance, and the design and graphic departments often have busy, complicated work schedules. It is important to develop good working relationships with the departments and the relevant staff members on whom you will rely as the process continues.

One way to maintain those relationships is to create a timetable for exhibition planning, design, and installation. Schedules should be reasonable and flexible

Mrs. Dam with first grade class in North American Indian gallery, 1946.
PHOTOGRAPH BY REUBEN GOLDBERG. UNIVERSITY OF PENNSYLVANIA MUSEUM. NO NEGATIVE.

and take into account the unavoidable delays and pressures inherent in exhibition projects. Publication deadlines are of particular importance. If you are planning to produce a catalog to accompany the exhibition, be in touch with the publications department as soon as possible, so that reasonable deadlines can be defined. Because even the most modest exhibition generally has budget implications, the finance/accounting office and the fund-raising staff should be made aware of your plans and their costs. Keep in mind that securing money for your project could require meeting grant application deadlines months or years in advance.

Use the timetable as a planning document, enumerating the responsibilities of staff members involved in the project. Many museums have codified procedures (for requests for in-house services or for budget planning, for example) with which you should become familiar. If you don't already know the personnel who implement those procedures, make a point to introduce yourself and your project early on.

Interns and volunteers often can provide valuable expertise and help when planning and installing exhibitions, and the experience of working on an exhibition project can enhance their time in the archives.

As you begin to select materials that are in keeping with your theme or topic, take detailed notes regarding condition needs, framing issues, display requirements, items of particular interest, and information for labels and/or publications. It is far easier to compile these important bits of information early in the process than to go back later.

Obtaining a floor plan of the exhibition spaces as well as information on cases or other furniture that are available will help you make decisions about how much—and what type of—material can be included in the show. For example, certain exhibition spaces without natural light may be the only places where light levels can be restricted appropriately for archival materials. You may have to negotiate for space or display cases with the curator of a concurrent exhibition.

Look for items that convey the message or theme but are also visually interesting: photographs; architectural drawings; ephemeral material such as greeting cards; posters, postcards, or advertisements; unique bindings or materials; three-dimensional artifacts; or signatures of famous people. You might even want to plan a small installation around one particular item—an important accession, a photo of a VIP visit to the museum, a newspaper headline, a seminal exhibition—and search for items that complement it.

In compiling materials for the exhibition, you may need to supplement the original materials with surrogates, facsimiles,[3] or loans. If you have conservation concerns about the fragility of the materials or light levels in the exhibition, or if the original materials are simply unsuitable for exhibition (difficult to read or awkward to install), surrogate copies can provide a way to include the items. Also, consider including facsimiles of verso pages to preserve the flow of a letter or other manuscript. Facsimiles in the form of photomurals and collages can be design elements for the exhibition, used as section divisions or to highlight major points. Digital technologies make the production

---

3   *Surrogates* are copies of materials in another format (for example, a microfilm version of a diary), often used to reduce wear and tear on the original. *Facsimiles* reproduce the look and feel of an item, as well as its contents.

EXHIBITION BUDGET CHECKLIST

Salaries, wages, and fringe benefits
- Archivist
- Exhibition Curator
- Assistant Curator
- Exhibitions Manager
- Registrar
- Assistant Registrar
- Curator of Education
- Education Programs Coordinator
- Preparator
- Assistant Preparator
- Director of Public Relations
- Manager, Public Affairs

Exhibition development
- Travel
- Research materials

Consultants

Artist expenses
- Artist's fee
- Travel expenses

Exhibition preparation and installation
- Shipping, assembly of objects
- Shipping, dispersal of objects
- Contract art handlers
- Customs fees
- Loan fees
- Crating
- Matting and framing
- Conservation
- Insurance
- Painting of gallery (materials and labor)
- Construction of exhibition
- Crate storage
- Lighting (materials and labor)
- Maintenance (floors, windows, cleaning, etc.)
- Installation photography
- Video/audio (rental/purchase)
- Labels
- Wall text
- Header
- Special signage

Written materials — education and publicity
- Object photography for catalog, brochure, etc.
- Catalog design
- Catalog editing
- Catalog printing
- Brochure design
- Brochure printing
- Folder (for publicity and education packets) design
- Folder (for publicity and education packets) printing
- Photocopy/print education materials
- Photocopy/print publicity materials
- Slide/photo reproduction for education and publicity

Education and public programs
- Symposium
- Lecture series
- Minicourses
- Family day
- Film and video series
- Docent training
- Other

Media relations
- Photography for events
- Press preview breakfast
- Postage for press materials
- Catalogs for press distribution

Advertising
- Print advertising
- Other advertising

Events
- Opening

of surrogates or manipulated (enlarged or enhanced) images somewhat less cumbersome than older photographic processes. Surrogate copies can also make it possible to include items from other collections when the originals cannot be borrowed.

If you do choose to include original items from other repositories or other individuals, the museum's registrar or a curator should be able to help you prepare request letters and loan forms and to make the necessary arrangements for transporting, insuring, and returning the objects. Accredited museums have

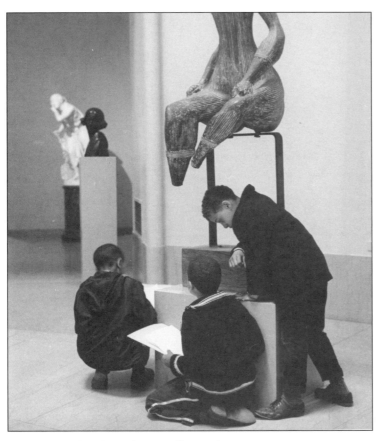

Students working in sculpture gallery, n.d. BROOKLYN MUSEUM OF ART ARCHIVES, PHOTOGRAPH COLLECTION. PEOPLE: CHILDREN IN THE MUSEUM.

facilities reports that detail the physical condition and administration of its buildings. Potential lenders (private and institutional) will generally wish to see it or a similar document before agreeing to lend. While requesting and administering outside loans does add another layer of complexity to the exhibition process, loans from other institutions (or from private individuals) can add depth or a different dimension to an exhibition. An added benefit of borrowing (and properly handling) material from private collectors is the relationship developed between the archives and the collector, which may facilitate future donations.

Design and installation should, ideally, be two separate processes. When at all possible, make decisions about case placement and layout before the exhibition is ready to be installed. Having to work in a hurry risks endangering fragile materials. Plan the use of the available space effectively by using floor plans or, if available, three-dimensional models. Some museums have computer-assisted design (CAD) drawings of galleries and can design exhibitions on-line, but many still rely on floor plans of exhibition rooms and use of scale models of cases or artwork. It can be helpful to make full-scale footprints of the cases with craft paper and move them around the exhibition rooms, getting a sense of how well their placement works. At the very least, make sketches or rough drawings before placing the actual furniture. Look carefully at the spaces the exhibition will occupy to identify issues relating to lighting, security, power supply, and the flow of visitors. And, as always, consult with your museum colleagues who have experience designing installations.

In general, uncluttered and straightforward designs are easier to execute, though complex and multilayered installations can be just as successful. Experience organizing exhibitions will help you develop an eye for exhibition design, but rely also on your own experience as a museum visitor and employee, and on your colleagues. The availability and costs of display cases, panel mounts, and matting/framing services, not to speak of conservation issues, may well dictate how the materials are displayed. Take advantage of whatever flexibility you do have to arrange the objects so that they tell the story in an attractive and comprehensible way. Plan case or frame layouts carefully—photocopies or digital copies of the materials laid out on those craft paper footprints can help you decide how objects will fit into cases or look on panels without handling the originals.

Handle the original materials to be included in the exhibition as safely—and as little—as possible. If your museum's installation staff does not have experience working with manuscript or archival materials, or if there are any items requiring particular attention, take time to explain how those objects should be handled and mounted. In smaller museums without an installation staff or the resources to engage outside contractors, it may be your responsibility to mount and frame the materials and install the exhibition.

Determine the condition of all materials before a display method is selected and aim to provide the most stable and safe environment possible. Are the materials clean? Creased? Fragile? Too heavy to be framed?

Perhaps the least expensive and least cumbersome method is to place items in cases without glazing and framing. Place items on backing materials—acid-free mat board or perhaps polyester film cut to size—to stabilize them and provide a buffer between the items and the case liners. To prevent things from shifting when you place items or replace the vitrine cover, use photo corners or a strip of polyester film to secure items to the backing materials. Original materials should never be permanently mounted to any material and all actions *must* be reversible. Strips of polyester film are also used to keep books open to particular pages. Although loose sheets, pamphlets, and other slim materials can in most instances lie flat in the exhibition case, you might consider propping up some materials, especially those placed in the rear of the case, for easier reading by the visitor and to add some visual interest. There are a variety of ways to elevate, highlight, and support materials: Plexiglas easels, pedestals, book-stands, and pyramids, to name a few.[4]

Correctly and safely matting, framing, and glazing items requires skill and experience. Although it is possible to acquire these skills through practice and reading, whenever possible have this work done by professionals in your institution or by contractors who work with unique and valuable materials. Be specific about the framing materials to be used; mat board, glazing materials, and frames should be appropriate for the objects and must meet museum and archival standards.

Labels and related publications communicate your ideas about the exhibition and its themes and concepts and thus must be carefully composed and produced. While the objects draw people into the exhibition, well-thought-out labels guide and inform the visitor. Notes taken during the process of selecting materials and organizing the exhibition will be useful at this stage, as will examples of labels written for your museum's installations. Museums generally have standard formats for object labels that include specific, standard elements to identify the items on display. Although archival materials may not be easily described in the same format as the object collections, conforming as much as possible to your institution's standards should simplify some of your work.

Exhibition labels should be clear, smart, scrupulously proofed, of an appropriate point size, and concise. The simplest label form contains the appropriate standard identification elements (title, date, maker, maker's dates, material, donor credit), depending on the type of object. You may also include interpretive text, explaining the history or significance of the object. Didactic

Northwestern Memorial Hospital's Florence and Ike Sewell Museum, opened in 1999, is an informative and welcoming destination for visitors, patients, and staff. THE FLORENCE AND IKE SEWELL MUSEUM OF NORTHWESTERN MEMORIAL HOSPITAL.

panels with a paragraph or two of text can be effective tools to guide visitors through the show.

Beverly Serrell's text, *Exhibit Labels: An Interpretive Approach*,[5] enumerates several types of interpretive labels, moving from the general to the specific: title, introduction, group or section labels, and captions. The simplest label form (sometimes called an identification label) includes at least some of the standard

4   For examples, see Farr, *Exhibits*, 38–39.

5   Beverly Serrell, *Exhibit Labels: An Interpretive Approach* (Walnut Creek, Calif.: Altamira Press, 1996), 21–29

elements (title, date, maker and dates if known, material, donor credit, etc.), which will themselves depend on the type of object. Compiling this information should be an easy matter if you have been maintaining an accurate working checklist. In general, each object will have such identifying information, and some objects may be highlighted or further explored in short caption text. For design purposes or if space is limited, you may consider listing information about several objects (in a case for example) on one label. Caption labels give short bursts on individual works and, as is the case with all interpretive text, should be clearly distinguished from the factual or descriptive information. Although each object in the show serves an important illustrative and instructive purpose, choose the most important, unique, or best examples for caption labels.

Single cases, or other modest exhibitions, may not require many additional labels, but you will probably want to have at least one panel with the title to the exhibition, introductory text explaining the purpose of the show and its main themes, and donor or sponsor acknowledgments, where appropriate. More complicated exhibitions, those that have distinct sections or themes or take place in more than one room, should

include additional section or group labels that discuss the important points or ideas presented in that part of the show. In these instances, the introductory panels might offer the visitor an overview of the exhibition's main sections and perhaps a floor plan or other information regarding the layout of the show.

Plan to submit drafts of your label text to the appropriate museum personnel (education department or curatorial staff) as the writing process continues. In some institutions, institutional approval of text to be displayed publicly is mandatory, but even if that's not the case, your colleagues will be able to offer another perspective on your labels as well as critical proofreading.

Much has been written about label design, typography, optimum length of label text, as well as evaluative techniques. A basic understanding of visitor behavior and the importance of well-written texts for public consumption can be gleaned from the literature, observation in your own exhibition spaces, and discussions with colleagues. You have probably noted, for example, that reverse type (light letters on dark backgrounds) can be difficult for some visitors to read, or that bullet points make for easier reading than long paragraphs. Your museum colleagues will also probably

SAMPLE LABELS (CORCORAN GALLERY OF ART)

Object label
William Wilson Corcoran, 1883
photograph
Matthew Brady, c. 1823–1896
William Wilson Corcoran (1798–1888), a prominent Washington banker and philanthropist, founded the Corcoran Gallery of Art in 1869. The American and European paintings and sculpture he had acquired formed the basis of the Gallery's collection, dedicated to the "encouragement of the American genius." His will left $100,000 for the formal establishment of a free school of art, which provided the impetus for the search for a new home for the institution.

Text label
"Simple and Monumental"
Ernest Flagg (1857–1947), a young architect trained at the École des Beaux–Arts in Paris, was one of several architects actively interested in the commission to build the new Corcoran Gallery. After a competition, Flagg's initial proposal received tentative approval from the Board of Trustees in 1892. The architect and

the Board worked together in refining the design until 1893.

Flagg's challenge was to develop a structure that dealt effectively with the unusually shaped lot created by the angled intersection of 17th Street and New York Avenue and conveyed the institution's importance to the city of Washington.

The final design has three parts: the main block on 17th Street which houses the gallery spaces, the hemicycle auditorium on the corner, and the art school on New York Avenue. Flagg's vision was of a building that would be both simple and monumental.

Label for a photograph
The Corcoran Gallery of Art has always had a cordial relationship with its neighbors in the White House. When Mrs. Kennedy visited the Corcoran on March 27, 1961, she was accompanied by the Chairman of the gallery's Women's Committee, Mrs. Edwin Graves. Mrs. Kennedy toured the exhibition "Easter Eggs and Other Precious Objects by Carl Faberge" and previewed a show featuring paintings by Albert Pinkham Ryder.

counsel you that the temptation to write long labels about each and every object must be resisted. Beverly Serrell suggests that 300 words is the maximum length for introductory labels and that group and caption labels be no longer than 150 words.[6] It can be difficult to write short labels at first, but the important skill of writing concise and informative labels can be acquired through reading and practice.

As for production, word processing and laser printers have made creating professional-looking labels and simple pamphlets possible for small repositories. A modest investment in good quality paper and printers and close attention to detail can result in clear and handsome labels. Typesetting, silk screening, and transfer or stick-on letters are other options. Whatever method is chosen, remember that the exhibition's labels are the aspect of the show directly created by its organizer and as such should serve to communicate the exhibition's main ideas. Overly designed, lengthy, cluttered labels detract from the content of the exhibition and discourage visitors. Well-designed, concise labels support the show's main purposes of education and elucidation.

Supplementary publications such as brochures or pamphlets, small books, or larger catalogs may be produced depending on time and budget resources available. As is true with labels, not every exhibition requires elaborate or expensive publications. At the very least, brochures or pamphlets should include a list of the works in the exhibition (the checklist), as well as some introductory text about the exhibition's main themes. Longer books offer the chance to preserve your hard work on the exhibition in a permanent form. If you do have the resources to produce full-scale books, the process of design and production will have to be undertaken well in advance of the exhibition's opening.

The final element of exhibition production, planning related programs, takes us back to the discussion in the first section of this chapter. Your own exhibition is now the focus of a gala opening, special tours, symposia, lectures, and other events drawn from your creative mind. Plan these activities carefully and begin early enough in the process so that they will run smoothly and provide an exciting extra facet to your installation and didactics.

Even modest exhibitions offer possibilities for public programs such as gallery talks, tours, school group visits, lectures, or workshops. Advanced publicity is critical—be sure your public affairs office knows of your exhibition plans. A well-crafted press release, a checklist of works to be included, and selected images are all that are needed to compile a basic press kit, but even a press release alone could suit your purposes. The release should include basic elements: a brief description of the exhibition, special mention of any extraordinary objects, donor credits, description of accompanying publications, information on the institution's location and hours, and the name and

A delegation from the People's Republic of China visits Northwestern Memorial Hospital's Florence and Ike Sewell Museum as part of an overall facilities tour. THE FLORENCE AND IKE SEWELL MUSEUM OF NORTHWESTERN MEMORIAL HOSPITAL.

telephone number of a contact person. Remember that local news outlets are inundated with press releases from institutions like yours and be sure to send the release in a timely fashion and make follow-up calls to those members of the press who seem most likely to carry a story. In many institutions, the public affairs office will be responsible for mailing and following up press releases, as well as coordinating press conferences and media visits. However, staff members in that office will rely on your expertise and enthusiasm for the exhibition—and most likely for the content of the press release.

News of your exhibition could also be sent to convention and visitor bureaus and tour directories in your area, as well as to any special interest groups with a connection to the exhibition's theme or contents. Invite your local professional group to tour the show with an announcement in the group's newsletter, or schedule a meeting around a tour and discussion of the

6   Ibid., 33.

exhibition planning process or other professional topic.

Public programs such as gallery talks and tours will enhance the value of the exhibition. Make plans with the museum's education department or public programs office to present at least one or two programs in connection with the exhibition. These programs can be directly related to the show's content but could also address closely related topics like exhibition preparation, conservation, or research opportunities. Programs could be designed to benefit school-age children—investigate whether the exhibition features a topic that could be tied to school curricula and follow up when appropriate.

Web Sites

It is obvious that the Internet can be an important outreach tool to introduce museum collections and institutional history to wider audiences. Technological advances and increasingly sophisticated sites designed for museums mean that the museum archives site can go beyond a brief introduction on a simple "brochure" page to become a comprehensive resource that provides access to finding aids, on-line database searches, or interactive timelines. Additional materials and information can be provided to supplement an archives exhibition, and the exhibition's life can be extended by reformulating it into a Web presentation. As with other outreach programs, sites do not have to be elaborate or comprehensive to be effective, and even the most straightforward site can have great value for researchers.

In most cases, the museum archives pages will be a part of a larger museumwide Web site. Develop a set of clear criteria for the archives section: its intended audience(s), the most important information to include, links to other related sites. Consider where you would like your Web site to reside within the institutional site. Your museum may have style guides, design templates, or other guidelines that will affect the look and location of the archives site.

Because a museum archives program does not always fit neatly within the overall structure of the institution, it may be difficult to find a sensible location for the archives Web site. Some museum Web sites have the archives site link on its home page, others have located the link in research, collections, or public affairs sections. Encourage the museum's Web designers to place the archives site where you feel it would be most easily found and also to include appropriate and helpful links in other places.

Be prepared to work closely with the museum's Web or graphic design staff, acting as an advocate for your corner of the museum but with realistic expectations. Providing visual images for the museum's site is a good way to introduce the information technology department to archives. Find out who maintains the site and work with him or her to ensure that the information you present is timely and accurate. If you will be responsible for any aspects of the design or coding of the archives site, make use of the on-line and off-line texts on Web site design, coding, evaluation, and other topics that are readily available.[7]

One way to approach design is to decide which questions the user should be able to answer on the archives pages. Start with the basics: hours, directions, researcher access, phone number, e-mail addresses, and other contact information. Once that is taken care of, begin to add information regarding specific holdings, policies, institutional history, and other relevant issues. Should researchers be able to peruse entire finding aids or just brief descriptions of your holdings? What images could illustrate the institution's history or the archives' photographic collections? Have you already created "content"—databases or electronic files with exhibition history, staff lists, a museum timeline—that might be helpful? How interactive would you like the site to be? Will it include search engines? E-mail reference forms?

As you begin to envision your ideal archives site, study Web sites related to yours by theme or institutional size for ideas. Visit other archives and museum archives sites to see how others have approached the problem. Make note of what you find helpful or distracting on Web sites and keep in mind that clear and easily navigable designs are well within the grasp of any designer.

Finally, talk to other archivists about how their work has changed because of the Internet and how they have responded to the challenges and opportunities. Like other outreach programs, Web sites repay the effort it takes to create and maintain them by enriching what we have to offer to museum staff and members of the public alike.

---

7 One such guide is Patrick J. Lynch and Sarah Horton, *Web Style Guide: Basic Design Principles for Creating Web Sites* (New Haven: Yale University Press, 2002).

9

ORAL HISTORY
Fred Calabretta

As we enter the new millennium, we leave behind a century marked by extraordinary events, trends, and personalities. The people who have lived during the twentieth century carry with them, in their collective memory, a vast and remarkable record of those times. Sadly, it seems likely that much of this collective experience will go unrecorded, and much of this knowledge of ordinary and extraordinary human activity will be lost. The oral history process affords a wonderful means of mining this body of information and preserving the results for posterity. Museums and historical societies are well positioned to carry out this important work.

Oral history offers many applications in a museum context. Documenting your institution's history is one option. Museums mirror society in their general policies, interpretation, and collecting trends. By choosing to document your institutional history, you are obviously documenting American culture as well. Museum-based oral history projects are also extremely valuable in documenting and interpreting historical themes and subjects of interest. Museum staff or outside researchers will find many uses for your oral history collection. Interview excerpts and content can be used

to support publications, exhibitions, education programs, Web sites, and press releases. Even if the oral histories do not see immediate use, they can be preserved, along with other primary source material, for future use. Oral history projects are also an excellent means of making friends and drawing support for your institution, or specifically, your archives.

Certain aspects of the oral history process distinguish it from informal or less structured methods of collecting information. Recording a conversation in a local restaurant or bar is probably not going to result in what would be considered a good oral history interview. A successful oral history experience requires more structure. One important characteristic of good oral history is that it should be executed with an emphasis on its long-term value versus its immediate use. It is not enough that the interview is meaningful to the interviewer; it should be of use to a researcher or other interested party well into the future. Take steps to ensure that a cohesive, well-documented interview recording is created.

Oral history should also comply with certain procedural guidelines. These include thorough organization and preparation for the interview, efforts to achieve the best possible sound quality, obtaining a signed release form, and taking steps to provide for the preservation of and access to the interview recording or resulting transcript. Oral history project managers and interviewers may also wish to consider the following three-part philosophical approach to their work: be prepared, be professional, and be nice.

The Value and Uses of Oral History

Several unique aspects of oral history contribute greatly both to the value and the appeal of the process. First, the interviewer is in a position to *create* a historical document. By the manner in which an oral historian prepares for and conducts the interview, he or she can shape its content and directly influence the nature

ORAL HISTORY DEFINED

Oral history may be defined as the process of conducting and recording an interview for the purpose of collecting historically significant information. The process is used to collect many types of information, including, but not limited to, folklore, biographical information, traditional music, the history of technology, and documentation of organizations and institutions. Additionally, it is used to document all types of group and individual human activity ranging from the playground to the workplace.

and extent of the information that will be preserved for the historical record. The interviewer is limited only by the age and experience of the narrators, and by the strength of their recollections. Some oral historians, myself included, occasionally fantasize about how wonderful it would be to interview individuals who lived during the mid-nineteenth century or earlier. While this is obviously impossible, it *is* possible to use oral history to document the lives of individuals who are long departed. A number of years ago I had an opportunity to interview a man whose grandfather was a whaling captain, Arctic explorer, and pioneering authority on the Inuit culture of Hudson Bay. The man I interviewed lived with his grandfather for twenty

years and could therefore provide valuable firsthand observations of someone who had been born in 1858. This illustrates the broad range of opportunities that exist for documentation using the oral history process.

There are other unique aspects of oral history. It provides a means of recording information that might otherwise be lost. For example, few people regularly write the long letters and extensive journal entries that were so common in the nineteenth century. Oral history can be used to help fill this gap. It also helps to humanize the historical record. Recollections recorded during oral history interviews are a wonderful complement to the dates, facts, and figures that are so prominent in other forms of historical documentation.

THE ROSENFELDS: MARITIME PHOTOGRAPHERS

The Rosenfeld Collection at Mystic Seaport is one of the world's largest single collections of maritime photographs, consisting of more than 800,000 images built on the inventory of Morris Rosenfeld & Sons, a photographic firm active in New York City from 1910 until the late 1970s. Morris Rosenfeld established the firm and was eventually joined by sons Stanley, David, and William. Though many maritime subjects are represented in the collection, the Rosenfelds are best known for their photographs of sailing yachts. In these excerpts from oral history interviews, William

Rosenfeld recounts the early days of his photographic career, and Stanley comments on creative aspects of the photographic process.[i]

William Rosenfeld: *It wasn't an individual in the business, it was a family involved in the business. Even as early as five or six years old, my father was taking me along on what he called, quote, a "job."*

And my earliest recollections, being small at that time, was being put in the corner of a stateroom [on a large yacht], with the old-fashioned flash powder trays, tall, with the big cap to set it off, and you'd wait for him to say, "shoot!", and you'd pull the string, and it would go "boom! boom!", and almost blow your head off. And you were involved in making the pictures, anywhere from five, to ten, to twelve years old.

And then you suddenly realize, years later, that you were carrying a tripod, and then later on a leather bag of plate holders, and then you realized that this lug of a bag of plate holders began at twenty-five pounds. And by the time you were eleven or twelve, it was sixty pounds of holders and glass plates.

It was a family joke. My father had been saying this many times. We'd be driving around or walking along, and he'd see an old man all bent over, and he'd say, "Ah ha! An

The Rosenfelds, celebrated marine photographers, occupy a rare position in *front* of a camera. Morris Rosenfeld, the founder of the family business, is second from the left. With him are sons David, Stanley, and William (l–r). DOUGLASS FRAPWELL, PHOTOGRAPHER. COURTESY MYSTIC SEAPORT, ROSENFELD COLLECTION, MYSTIC, CONNECTICUT.

i   William M. Rosenfeld, oral history interview, conducted February 21, 1990, by Fred Calabretta, Sound Archives, G.W. Blunt White Library, Mystic Seaport. Stanley Z. Rosenfeld, oral history interview, conducted March 17, 1988, by Fred Calabretta, Sound Archives, G.W. Blunt White Library, Mystic Seaport.

Oral history can be an effective tool for documenting underdocumented cultures and groups. Finally, one of the most unique and significant aspects of oral history is that if it is done properly, it is almost always a positive experience for *both* parties involved. The interviewer gains useful information, while the narrator appreciates the sincere interest in his or her life and experiences.

The past fifteen years have seen a dramatic increase in the use of oral history by museums and historical societies. Many institutions have discovered that oral history is a valuable tool, often providing substantial benefits without the burden of extensive financial strain. The oral history process has three primary applications in a museum context: documentation of collections and themes, interpretation of collections and themes, and documentation of the history of your institution. The latter may be the course most often pursued by museum archivists; however, all of these uses may be highly beneficial in supporting your institution's mission.

The first and possibly most obvious museum application of oral history is the documentation of collections and themes. Oral history can be used to learn more about human activity and the people and artifacts associated with that activity. The activity may be economic, such as industry, farming, fisheries, or mining. It may also reflect any other aspect of our culture or

---

ex-photographer!" And you'd ask him why. "From carrying the equipment around, he's all bent over!"

Stanley Rosenfeld: *I do enjoy dark room work. I did because the dark room work was always as significant to us, in many ways, as going outside. Because to go outside and take the original photograph, that was terribly boring. But each of us were actually in hand contact with the plates. From the time we loaded up the camera to go out on assignment, to the time we delivered the finished print, you had the opportunity all over again in the dark room, to re-create. And I think in many ways, the dark room required as much creativity and as much understanding of the materials, as any other part of photography.*

Nowadays, you can take a camera, go out with a 35mm camera, load it with Kodachrome, and you do your shooting, and then go back, and you didn't see it to the end until maybe an art director selected something, and you saw the print. But for most of my life, and through most of the lives of the Rosenfelds, you went out with a plate which was selected for its contrast, depending on the assignment, you came back and you developed it. And the developer, which was selected to create a certain contrast, found the detail, and you developed it with temperature, and with control, and with this strength of a solution to get that kind of control. You exposed it, knowing what was going to happen to it in the dark room.

You then went into the dark room with the negative, and then you could then create it all over again, by cropping, by enlarging. And then you could do shading, and then you could do burning in, and you could create new kinds of contrast, you could stencil the old composition, you could alter the old composition, and you'd come out with a different result . . . .

The photography was, I think, a much more significant art form when you dealt from the beginning to the end. And in many ways, I still feel that black and white photography is a significantly stronger art form than color photography.

This image of the racing yacht *Cotton Blossom II* reflects the artistic talents of marine photographers Morris Rosenfeld & Sons. Courtesy Mystic Seaport, Rosenfeld Collection, Mystic, Connecticut. Image acquired in honor of Hudson H. Bubar.

social institutions, such as art, popular culture, religion, recreation, sport, government, or the military, to name just a few examples. Interviews can document not just the activity, but also the people, both individuals and groups, and the artifacts or material culture associated with it. Oral history provides museums with an excellent means of enriching object catalog records and documentation files. All types of material, from manuscript collections, ships, tools, toys, and photographs, as well as collections of mixed materials, may be the focus of interview questions. Oral history can provide context and provenance for a collection of papers, or details about the manufacture, function, and significance of objects.

A second potential area for museum use of oral history is interpretation. A number of institutions have drawn extensively from oral history collections in developing successful exhibitions, publications, and education programs. The use of oral history narrative, whether in audio form or in printed quotation, is a wonderful means of telling stories and interpreting a museum's collections and themes. Visitors and readers generally relate well to the firsthand experiences of other people. The use of oral history in exhibitions is an area of great potential for museums. In an age when electronic technology and media are increasingly becoming an integral part of museum exhibits, both video and audio oral history recordings are an excellent resource.

Museums are becoming increasingly interested in documenting and studying their own past. One result of this process is that a number of them have adopted a third important application of oral history, that is, to help document the history of the institution itself. Whether under the auspices of a well-structured museum archives program or the museum's library, curatorial, or administrative departments, an oral history project focusing on your museum's history is an excellent idea. Interviews with former directors, trustees, and staff members can provide fascinating insight into the development, operations, collecting activity, research, and other history of your institution.

Project Design

An oral history project requires careful thought and planning, therefore project design is the obvious first step. As you develop an oral history project, be aware of several primary areas of responsibility and concern. A solid ethical approach is a key element of the foundation of a successful project and should be integrated into your planning. Give considerable attention to the importance of thorough interviewer preparation and the importance of building and maintaining good relationships with narrators. This is a responsibility of both interviewers and project managers. Also, remember that there is much work to be done after the interview is conducted and factor this into your planning. Make provisions for the preservation of tapes and develop a plan to provide access to interviews and related materials. With these factors in mind, the process of project design can begin.

As a project organizer, you must first possess a basic understanding of the oral history process. Once you have accomplished this—by attending workshops, studying reference material such as publications or Web sites, or consulting with experienced oral historians—you are ready to develop a plan. It is a good idea to put the plan into writing as a formal statement of purpose. Depending upon the nature of your museum, you may be able to borrow language from existing documents such as collection or acquisition policies or mission statements. Creating a statement of purpose is a good exercise in identifying project goals, and it can also be useful in providing the press, potential interviewees, new staff members, and others with an overview of your project. However, regardless of whether or not you prepare a formal written document, you must formulate a plan as your first step.

There are a number of major points to consider in the project planning stage, and you may wish to begin with thematic aspects. What are the themes or subjects you wish to document? The textile industry,

Added Benefits

A museum's oral history collection is an important resource, but oral histories also have significant value beyond the historical documentation they contain. The project, and the oral history process itself, can provide other benefits. For example, community or other off-campus oral history projects are likely to result in an increased awareness of, and interest in, your archives or institution. This can make friends for your museum or historical society and may result in support in the form of financial contributions, donations of documents or artifacts, or volunteer help. Because of the positive nature of oral history interviews, they are also likely to generate goodwill and positive publicity. Interviewers working with individuals from outside of your museum can and should be goodwill ambassadors for your institution.

experiences of Vietnam veterans, the expansion of your museum, trout fishing, or the lives of your former trustees and directors? What will be the nature of the information you collect? For example, will you be collecting biographical information, technical information, or folklore? You will also need to establish certain parameters, such as a chronological period and geographical region. Will you be documenting the entire history of your museum, or just the past twenty-five years? Do you want to document commercial fishing in your state, or along the entire Atlantic, Pacific, or Gulf Coasts?

Practical concerns also need to be addressed. What is the scope or magnitude of your planned project?

Who will manage the project and conduct the interviews? Do you want to conduct twenty interviews in a two-year period, or do you plan to conduct hundreds of interviews over an indefinite period of time? How will you identify narrators? What type of equipment and what recording format will you use for conducting interviews? Will you use a different, more durable format for preservation master copies? What are your plans for the disposition of tapes and related materials? How will they be preserved? And what steps will be taken to make them accessible to your institution's staff and the public?

Finally, you need to consider two vastly important aspects of your project: expenses and staff time. What

THE *CHARLES W. MORGAN* ARRIVES AT MYSTIC SEAPORT

The *Charles W. Morgan* was built in 1841 and is now preserved at Mystic Seaport as one of the Museum's most prized artifacts. The *Morgan* is the last wooden whaleship and one of only a few survivors of the thousands of square-rigged American ships that sailed the seas in the nineteenth century. In December of 1941, the tired old ship arrived at a fledgling Mystic Seaport. Elizabeth Schiebler, a future employee of the Museum, was thirteen years old and remembers that day.[ii]

Elizabeth Schiebler: *It was a disappointment. I wanted it to sweep up like a grand old lady, bejeweled, and ermined, with a swooshing cape . . . . I was all*

full of romantic ideas about what a square-rigger looked like, and I don't know what I was expecting, that it would come sailing up, with all the sails unfurled, and flags flying, and instead it looked like a little dead creature. . . .

And it was being towed, and I thought, what a sort of dismal end for a ship that had been so many places, and supported the lives of so many people . . . it just seemed so forlorn. And the day was forlorn, it was a lead gray sky, and cold wind. The whole thing just seemed like, what a hopeless task was being taken on here!

My affection for the Morgan developed after it was here . . . we'd stop and go on the Morgan most Saturdays. And play on it! We'd play hide and seek on it, and we'd play the game in the captain's cabin, taking turns trying to tip each other out of the gimballed bed. . . . I felt sort of ownership of it. It was our thing.

And then it started getting precious, and more precious and more precious. When I worked here, it was a kick being the interpreter on the Morgan . . . I'm stunned. Fifty years, a half a century . . . I think it's grand, I think it's wonderful with all the restoration that they've been able to do.

A forlorn relic of the great days of sail. The whaleship *Charles W. Morgan*, built in 1841, arrives at her new home at Mystic Seaport in 1941. COURTESY MYSTIC SEAPORT, MYSTIC, CONNECTICUT.

ii Elizabeth W. Schiebler, oral history interview, conducted May 23, 1991, by Fred Calabretta, Sound Archives, G.W. Blunt White Library, Mystic Seaport.

is your budget for the project? Consider the costs of equipment and supplies, personnel, travel expenses, and post-interview expenses such as processing, cataloging, and transcribing. After you determine costs, consider how you will fund the project. If you must seek outside funding, make grant writing a priority, keeping in mind application deadlines and lead-time requirements. How much time will be required to manage the project, plan for and conduct interviews, process and manage the collection of recordings, and provide access to the collection? Who will do this work? Will you need volunteer assistance?

Once your plan is complete and your staff is organized, develop a reasonable time-line. Another detail to consider is publicity. Publicizing your project can help generate interest in both your collections and your institution. You will also need to create two essential documents—a release form and an interview worksheet or documentation form. The release form is mandatory. Legally, a tape may not be used in any way unless you have obtained copyright by having the narrator sign a release form. Sample release forms obtained from other institutions may be useful models,

but it is also wise to formulate a release form after carefully considering the requirements of your own institution and consulting with an attorney. A worksheet or documentation form, completed by the interviewer, will provide basic information about the interview, such as names and addresses of the narrator and interviewer, the date and location of the interview, and notes on special circumstances or details.

The selection of recording equipment, and more specifically, a recording format, is a major challenge for oral history interviewers and project planners in the digital age. The frequency with which new formats are introduced provides more options but complicates the selection process. The life expectancy of various media must be considered. Magnetic tape, such as DAT tape; standard analog cassettes; or ¼″ open reel tape may be expected to last for twenty to thirty years or more, while fifty years or more is a reasonable life expectancy for good quality compact discs (CDs).[1]

---

1   Koichi Sadashige, "Storage Media Environmental Durability and Stability," *Data Storage Technology Assessment 2000*, Part 2 (St. Paul: National Media Laboratory, 2000), [text distributed on CD-ROM], 74–78.

EQUIPMENT SELECTION

The digital revolution has made it increasingly difficult to recommend specific recording equipment for oral history use. Analog cassette recorders have long been standard equipment among oral historians, but their use is undeniably on the decline. Digital recorders in various formats, particularly minidiscs, are rapidly gaining in popularity.

I have been using Marantz cassette recorders for more than fifteen years, and I highly recommend them. These recorders, as well as those manufactured by Sony, have long been the standard for high-quality oral history field recording. As long as Marantz and Sony continue to manufacture cassette recorders, they remain a viable choice for collecting oral histories.

The analog cassettes may easily be transferred to digital formats, which in turn provide all of the familiar digital advantages, including improved access, duplication with minimal loss of sound quality, and support of streaming audio and other computer-based applications.

Problems arise in anticipating how much longer quality analog recorders will be produced. Minidisc recorders are now widely used for oral history recording. With the increased popularity of minidisc and other

digital formats, manufacturers are likely to lose interest in production of analog recorders.

While I continue to advocate the use of quality analog cassette recorders, I also recognize the advantages of minidisc recording. This technology offers a very effective means of capturing oral histories in a digital format, and I expect to acquire a couple of minidisc recorders in the near future. The obvious problem with minidiscs is that they are totally unsuitable as a preservation format. Minidiscs need to be reformatted to more durable media, usually 1/4″ analog tape or compact discs (or, ideally, both).

Oral history equipment selection is a complicated issue. It seems likely that new analog cassette *and* minidisc recorders will be difficult to locate in ten or fifteen years. Sound archivists should anticipate format obsolescence and consider acquiring and storing unused machines to guarantee future access to recordings in their collections. Preservation in multiple formats, such as 1/4″ analog tape and CD, is a good idea. And lastly, all digital sound recordings should be considered transitional. Reformatting and migration are now essential elements of sound archives management.

Actually, owing to the likelihood of format obsolescence, the life expectancy of tapes and other recording media may be a moot point if machines for playback (access) cannot be obtained and/or maintained. The now-obsolete eight-track tape format illustrates this problem. It enjoyed a wave of popularity in the late 1960s, yet machines that will play these tapes are extremely scarce. Which of today's formats are tomorrow's eight-track tapes? The problem is amplified in the digital world, as manufacturers regularly introduce new formats to generate more sales. Tapes and disks may survive, but twenty years from now, will you be able to find a machine capable of playing them?

Traditional analog formats such as cassette or reel-to-reel tape have considerable merit for oral history recordings. The tapes, particularly ¼″ reel-to-reel tapes, afford adequate longevity. Cassette tapes for original recording of interviews and ¼″ tape for creating preservation masters have long been the standards in the oral history field. While they remain viable options in 2003, the survival of these formats is threatened by the success of digital and optical media such as minidiscs and compact disks.

With millions of standard analog cassette machines in existence, they remain a valid choice for collecting oral histories. The other best option is the minidisc format, which is enjoying considerable popularity in the oral history field and provides an effective means of capturing sound in a portable, digital format. DAT (digital audio tape) has never been widely used in the oral history field and appears to be an endangered format. Avoid microcassettes, the tiny tapes used for many years in office transcription equipment.

None of the formats used for collecting oral histories—analog cassette, minidisc, DAT, or microcassette—is a suitable preservation format. For preservation or master recordings, ¼″ reel-to-reel tapes are a safe choice, although some key manufacturers have already stopped production of the machines, and it is possible that in twenty years it will be difficult to find technicians and parts to maintain them. The other option is to transfer oral histories to good quality compact discs. CDs provide the two primary advantages of all digital audio media: specifically fast and precise access to information and reproduction with a minimal loss in sound quality. Preserving recordings in multiple formats, such as ¼″ tape *and* CDs, is a wise approach, helping to ensure future access to the recordings. Regardless of the format selected, archivists should seriously consider "collecting" and saving machines as well as recordings. If you have hundreds of cassette tapes in your collection, it would be wise to store a machine to play them, ideally a new machine.

In this era of rapidly changing recording technology, decisions about recording and playback equipment are not easily made. You need to consider a number of factors: cost, complexity of the equipment (DAT machines have more moving parts than analog machines—therefore more things can go wrong), technical expertise of those who will use the equipment and manage the tapes, intended use of the recordings, and the status and projected longevity of the recording format(s) being considered. All digital media should be considered transitional; they are temporary storage devices. You must assume that the information they contain will eventually have to be migrated to a newer format.

Determine the specific needs of your project, research your options, and choose a recording format, then obtain a recorder. You will also need one or more microphones. You may choose clip-on microphones, such as those used in the broadcast industry, or the standard microphone placed in a holder or stand. In addition to the microphone type you use, consider its recording pattern or field as well. Omnidirectional microphones provide a kind of wide-angle recording approach, while unidirectional microphones have a very narrow, focused recording field. Select microphones based on features or characteristics best suited for your project. Bruce Jackson's *Fieldwork* is an excellent source for understanding the workings of microphones and recording equipment.[2]

Additional equipment requirements usually include a computer and printer for transcribing, a transcribing machine, and possibly a tape player and headphones so users can listen to copies of the tape.

The Interview

Once equipment has been selected, the focus of your project shifts to interviewing. This is the core of the oral history process, and the interviewer has an obligation to arrange and conduct the interview in a responsible and effective manner. A well-conducted interview results in the preservation of historically significant information. An added bonus is that it also often results in a very rewarding experience for the interviewer.

Interviewers must have a clear understanding of the fundamentals of the oral history process. They

---

2   Bruce Jackson, *Fieldwork* (Urbana: University of Illinois Press, 1987).

should consult one or more of several excellent "how-to" manuals and, if possible, attend an oral history workshop presented by an experienced individual or organization.[3] They should also be familiar with the *Oral History Evaluation Guidelines,* published by the Oral History Association (OHA) and available online.[4]

OHA is the national professional oral history organization in the United States and this publication is standard reading. Some suggestions for interviewers follow—this may be you, as the archivist and planner, or the role may be delegated to another member of the oral history project team.

As previously noted, consider a three-part approach to your work: be prepared, be professional, and be nice. Being prepared means being familiar with your subject or topics as *well* as your recording equipment.

3   See any of the following: Willa K. Baum, *Oral History for the Local Historical Society,* 3rd ed., revised (Nashville: American Association for State and Local History, 1995); Edward D. Ives, *The Tape-Recorded Interview: A Manual for Field Workers in Folklore and Oral History,* 2nd ed. (Knoxville: University of Tennessee Press, 1995); Donald Ritchie, *Doing Oral History* (New York: Twayne, 1995). Professional organizations such as the Society of American Archivists, the Oral History Association, and their regional affiliates frequently offer workshops.

4   Donald Ritchie, ed., *Oral History Evaluation Guidelines,* rev. 2000, Oral

History Association, Pamphlet Number 3 (Los Angeles: Oral History Association, 2000). See also on-line at <http://www.dickinson.edu/organizations/oha/EvaluationGuidelines.html>.

RECALLING THE *CHARLES W. MORGAN*

The *Charles W. Morgan,* built in 1841, is the world's last surviving wooden whaleship. Listed on the National Register and preserved at Mystic Seaport, the ship is the centerpiece of the museum's waterfront. The following excerpts are from an oral history interview with brothers Francis and James Bement of Connecticut. Their grandfather, Joseph Francis Bement, was born in 1867 and sailed on the *Morgan* from 1886 to 1887. The Bement brothers view the ship as an artifact with special significance.[iii]

Francis Bement: *I had some wonderful times with my grandfather. In his later years, when he lived upstairs of us, he had mellowed a lot. He was still a very stubborn man, but he had mellowed a lot. And I used to enjoy going up there, listening to him tell stories. You know, he used to tell stories about how they would get the whale, and bring him alongside the ship, and the men would actually stand on the whale. . . . He told me these stories, how it was done, and so forth. To me boy, I was a kid, I was in another world when I was listening to him talk.*

Interviewer: *How do you two feel about the* Morgan?

James Bement: *To me, the* Morgan *is my grandfather.*

Francis Bement: *That ship, I have a feeling, I don't know if this is going to make sense to you, that the* Morgan *had the same personality that my grandfather had.*

James Bement: *She has a stubborn personality just like he did. She had to, to last this long. As many times as I've been down here. . . . I wouldn't come down here without going aboard the* Morgan. . . . *My kids have all been aboard the* Morgan *many times. My grandchildren are beginning to understand now what it was all about. As they get older, I won't let them lose touch with the* Morgan.

The restored whaleship *Charles W. Morgan* graces the waterfront at Mystic Seaport. COURTESY MYSTIC SEAPORT, MYSTIC, CONNECTICUT, ACCESSION #41.761.

iii   Francis Bement and James Bement, oral history interview, conducted 1991 by Fred Calabretta and David Littlefield, Sound Archives, G.W. Blunt White Library, Mystic Seaport.

Interviewers should design a well-organized question list. It may be desirable to prepare the question list in a carefully scripted format, beginning with requests for basic background information, grouping questions by theme or topic, asking sensitive or emotional questions toward the end of the interview, and possibly ending on a high note by asking for the best or most rewarding aspects of a job or experience. While a carefully organized question list is often extremely helpful, flexibility in using it is also important. The conversation may move in unanticipated but valuable directions.

During the interview, be professional in your approach. This entails doing everything required to obtain the most productive recording possible. Look for a recording location free from background noise and interruption. For example, record indoors rather than outdoors and turn off noisy fans or radios. Always try to obtain the best possible sound quality. There are two factors that determine the sound quality: equipment selection and recording technique. I believe that technique is actually more important. Budget equipment can produce a good quality recording if you use good technique, such as obtaining good volume levels and little background noise. Technique can compensate to some degree for equipment limitations. On the other hand, recording an interview using high-priced equipment doesn't guarantee good results if the interview is conducted in a noisy room, with the narrator seated too far from the microphone. Good sound increases potential uses of the recording, such as broadcast or exhibition, and also benefits researchers, transcribers, and other listeners.

Good interviewing technique requires some practice. Generally, being a good listener is the highest priority. In fact, interviewers should be heard as little as possible on an interview recording. I sometimes worry that future users listening to interviews I've conducted may assume that I am unresponsive because I frequently do not respond verbally to emotional or amusing comments. I do respond, but I try to use facial expressions and other body language so that my own comments don't overly detract from the narrator's reminiscences.

While it may sound trivial, being nice is perhaps the most important point. Express your appreciation and treat your narrators with respect and consideration from the moment you first contact them. This enhances the relationship, resulting in a more productive interview session. Throughout the interview and during all contact with the narrator be respectful and considerate. A narrator who willingly shares his or her reminiscences and life experiences is doing you a favor. Be sure to show your appreciation. It's a good way to collect useful information *and* make a friend for your project, archives, or institution.

At the conclusion of the session, if not before, be certain to have the narrator sign a release form. Following the interview, it is also the interviewer's responsibility to complete a documentation sheet. This documentation sheet or worksheet should include all pertinent information about the interview and should also include, or be accompanied by, a list of explanations, name and other word spellings, and any other information that may be of use to the cataloger, transcriber, or researcher. A thank-you note to the narrator is also highly recommended. By expressing your appreciation after the interview, you reassure the person that he or she has been helpful to you.

Processing

Complete the necessary paperwork, then deposit the recording in the archives. This begins the processing phase, specifically, the steps that will ensure the preservation of the recording and access to its content. Use original recordings *only* to make copies or masters, never for transcribing, casual listening, or research use. Make a duplicate, and, if possible, copy the original tape or disk to a more durable format for preservation.

Storage and environmental requirements of sound recordings, regardless of format, are relatively consistent with those for other materials. Any storage environment suitable for paper-based collections is also suitable for sound recordings, therefore a separate storage area is not required. Constant temperature and humidity levels of about 70°F and 50% RH respectively are fine for magnetic and optical media. Recent research suggests that a cooler and drier environment is likely to increase the longevity of recordings.[5] As is the case with other materials, temperature and humidity levels may be slightly outside the ideal range,[6] provided they are constant. Avoid severe fluctuations. Other standard environmental practices, such as good housekeeping and minimization of dust, are applicable to sound recordings.

Once the original recording is secure and copied, additional steps should be taken to make the recording and contents accessible. Create a documentation folder for each interview. This may contain the release form, documentation sheet, a copy of the question

---

5 Sadashige, "Storage Media," 75–77.
6 Indeed, different reference sources recommend different optimum ranges.

list, research notes, and any other material related to the narrator or the subject of the interview.

If possible, prepare a verbatim transcription. While you should encourage users to listen to the recording, since sound adds a rich dimension to the content, a transcript is a valuable tool as well. A researcher can read the same content approximately three times faster than he or she can listen to it. Transcripts in digital form are a great access tool for users, facilitating keyword searches and quick access to specific content. The transcribing process is time

Visitor in Classical Sculpture gallery studies a seated Dionysos, ca. 1958. University of Pennsylvania Museum. No negative.

consuming and may be expensive. It can take six or more hours to transcribe one hour of tape, at a cost of roughly $100 to $300 if a commercial transcribing service is to be used. Still, in an ideal arrangement, both transcripts and recordings should be available for researchers.

Cataloging is the next essential step in processing and promoting access to oral history collections. The best source of information for this is the *Oral History Cataloging Manual,* compiled by Marion Matters.[7] Interviews may be cataloged on either an item level or collection level; a combination of the two is desirable. A standard catalog record may be prepared or a more detailed MARC-format record may be created. Multiple examples of both are found in the Matters book.

Basic cataloging information may be derived from several sources. The interview documentation sheet

(also often referred to as an interviewer's worksheet) and transcript are likely to be most useful. If an interview exists in multiple forms, such as a sound recording, transcript, and digital text document, create a single catalog record that provides information about all forms of the interview and describes any related material.

It is often helpful to also prepare a finding aid or guide to an oral history collection, providing item-level descriptions of individual oral history interviews. This may be a published work or a word-processed document, available on-line or in printed form. It need not be extensive or formal. Even a basic guide will be helpful for users if it provides such fundamental information as the catalog number, extent of the transcript or sound recording, names of the narrator and interviewer, the date and place of the interview, and a general content note. The utility of the guide can be further expanded by providing a list of narrators and a basic subject index.

Since most of us continue to be print oriented in seeking information, taking extra steps to promote oral history collections can be useful. The special value, uniqueness, and added dimension of sound recordings may need to be emphasized. Consider encouraging and facilitating the use of interview recordings as well as transcripts. Establish a research space equipped with listening equipment. Making headphones available will enable you to use public areas and reading rooms as listening rooms, without distracting other users. Finally, although it may not be appropriate for all collections, consider making copies of recordings available for off-site use.

Legal Issues

The best protection against legal problems is a solid ethical approach. A good working knowledge of key legal issues associated with oral histories, as discussed in John Neuenschwander's *Oral History and the Law,*[8] is certainly critical for project managers and interviewers. You can apply many of the same legal policy guidelines that relate to other materials in your collection, but you should supplement this approach by consulting oral history publications and discussing any specific questions you may have concerning oral histories with an attorney. Copyright, slander, libel, and privacy are

7 Marion Matters, *Oral History Cataloging Manual* (Chicago: Society of American Archivists, 1995).

8 John A. Neuenschwander, *Oral History and the Law,* 2nd ed., rev. and enlarged (Los Angeles: Oral History Association, 1993).

among the issues that need to be considered. Good ethics and judgment are by no means a substitute for proper attention to such issues, but in many cases they do provide an effective deterrent in warding off legal problems.

Treating your narrators with respect and consideration and dealing with them in an honest manner can also circumvent problems. I feel somewhat protective of the people I interview. They have often shared their most personal feelings and emotions with me, and I don't want to see them hurt or embarrassed through irresponsible use of their interview and its contents. At the same time, I recognize that as archivists and custodians of intellectually valuable historical documents, we have an obligation to make these documents as useful and accessible as possible. The solution is to find a balance, and I believe we can treat our narrators with respect and still satisfy our obligations as archivists, collections managers, and curators.

Several specific legal issues should be noted. As previously discussed, an essential step is obtaining a signed release form, transferring title of the recording content to your institution. Try to obtain unrestricted title, but if the narrator wants to limit access, be prepared to offer use limitations or restrictions. Additionally, be sure your narrators understand the various ways the recording will be used, both in the present and, to the fullest extent possible, in the future. If they believe their personal comments will sit quietly on a shelf to be disturbed only occasionally by a researcher, they may be dismayed to learn that you have shared their comments with millions of people around the world via the Internet. Assuming you have obtained a signed release form, you have a legal right to use the contents of an interview in any manner you choose. However, as a courtesy, try to anticipate those uses and share them with your narrator.

Depending upon the subjects or themes of your interviews, they may contain controversial or inflammatory comments. Interviewers should not avoid controversial issues while interviewing; they may be an integral part of your institution's history or the historical theme you wish to document. For this or unanticipated reasons, tapes may include controversial or sensitive remarks. You may find that the narrator has revealed something highly personal and potentially embarrassing about a relative or neighbor. Although

you may be within your legal rights to make controversial interview content accessible, it may not be in the best interest of the narrator or your institution to do so. If this bit of information has no direct connection to the themes or subject of the interview, why risk problems by making it accessible? Project managers need to factor in legal concerns *and* the best interests of all parties involved, as they evaluate "problem" recordings. The key is to exercise good judgment, then make decisions about use, or possibly limited or restricted use.

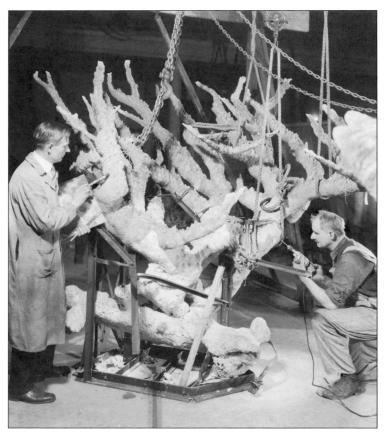

Coral Reef Group under construction. Chris E. Olsen and Louis the machinist tackling the large specimen, Feb. 1928. Photograph by Julius Kirschner. American Museum of Natural History Library, neg. #312488.

Regardless of the specific reason, and even if you obtain unrestricted title, it may be necessary to take one of several steps to limit access to sensitive recordings or comments. You may need to do some editing of recordings and/or transcripts for researcher or public use. If you do, keep a copy of the tape in its original, unedited format for posterity. A time lock is another option. This involves sealing the recording and prohibiting all access for a designated period of time, such as the life of the narrator. A last option is to choose not to accession a problem recording.

Several additional points regarding legal aspects of oral history should be noted. It may be useful to have scholars, researchers, and any other users sign a use agreement card or form. If you have such a form already in place for other collections, extend its use to your oral history collection. Make it clear to users that the contents of recordings or transcripts may not be used in any form, in whole or part, without permission. Another factor affecting use may be relevant if you work for a government institution. You may need to be aware of implications of the Freedom of Information Act as it relates to privacy issues or use restrictions and your oral history collection. You may not have the same flexibility as other institutions in your ability to restrict access to tapes, even if they contain controversial or embarrassing remarks.

Oral history project managers may at times ask themselves if their efforts are worthwhile. Archivists or interviewers may become discouraged as they realize that oral history projects require more than a casual commitment. Expenses and time demands may become significant concerns. Addressing legal issues may cause headaches, and the increasing complexity of recording technology may be daunting. And then there are the challenges regarding preservation of disks or tapes.

For those with such concerns, the most effective words of encouragement I can provide can be drawn from my own experience. Oral history interviews and projects have provided me with many extraordinary and rewarding moments. I have watched museum visitors with smiles on their faces or tears in their eyes as they read interview quotations in an exhibition based on an oral history project. I have documented the family life of a contemporary submarine sailor and have been nearly overcome with emotion as he offered to answer questions on tape, only moments after he was reunited with his family for the first time in six months. Upon completion of an interview with a woman who served in the u.s. Navy during World War II, she asked if she could give me a hug. All of these experiences were supplemental to the valuable information that had been collected and preserved.

In conclusion, there is no question that the advantages of oral history projects far outweigh the challenges. A well-planned and executed oral history project can be enormously beneficial. First and foremost, significant information is captured and preserved. This information will enrich the body of knowledge of your institution's history or any number of historical themes. It may also be very useful in support of various inside projects and programs and provide a rich resource for outside users. Your project may have other benefits as well. It is likely to generate increased interest in your archives and institution and may bring about the donation of collections of papers or other material. Oral history is a wonderful tool, and even if a project must be conducted on a limited budget, it will likely result in the creation of a valuable and unique resource. Finally, a successful oral history project may generate something else that museums can always use—new friends.

Managing Archival Collections

10

RECORDS SURVEYS

Deborah Wythe

A *records survey* is an office-by-office study and analysis of active and inactive records to identify and describe records series, creators, dates, extent, and how the records are used.[1] Surveys can be narrow or broad, ranging from a detailed records inventory to a more cursory box count, depending on your needs and resources. They can focus on records management issues or preservation,[2] or they can serve a more general purpose.

For an archivist starting a new museum archives program, taking over an established archives, or seeking to improve an existing program, a records survey is an important tool that can accomplish a number of critical goals. It lays the groundwork for establishing a records management program; helps determine the universe of records in the museum; provides background for defining the boundaries of the archives' collections; supplies information needed for informed decisions about space needs, growth, preservation, collection development, and appraisal; and brings the archivist into contact with the creators, managers, and institutional users of records. A well-conceived and executed survey project will build trust for the archives program and strengthen the program itself.

In this chapter, we will look first at the "why" and then the "how to" of records surveys.

Why Survey Records?

Records management

Before attempting to define what records to dispose of, what records to keep, and how long to keep them,

it is important to understand the inactive records that are already in existence and the active records that are being created every day. In the process of surveying, you will meet and talk with the staff members who create and manage administrative records; gather information on recordkeeping and how long the records are active; learn the names of various types of records in your institution; and discover the extent of inactive records. This information will provide the groundwork for developing an accurate and workable records schedule and a strong records management program that everyone can accept. It may also be useful when you assist departments to develop better filing systems.

Archival collection development

Until the archivist understands the universe of records in his or her institution, the development of the archival collection remains a somewhat haphazard process, dependent on what people offer or what the archivist happens to hear about. An understanding of all of the institution's records allows you to develop a documentation strategy, defining which records belong in the archives and lobbying for their transfer, if necessary. You can determine which records must remain in the departmental offices as permanently active files, provide advice on their care, and be in a position to provide access to them by directing users to the correct contact person. You can identify groups of inactive records with no permanent value and deal with them in an organized and timely manner. As part of the records survey, you will almost certainly find materials that were boxed up and fell victim to the "out-of-sight, out-of-mind" syndrome. These may be treasures—or trash—but knowing what they are, where they are stored, and how extensive they are will equip you to deal with them constructively.

---

1   For the purposes of this manual, we will be looking at the records found in a single institution. John Fleckner, in the SAA Basic Manual *Archives and Manuscripts: Surveys* (Chicago: Society of American Archivists, 1977), also discusses broader-based, multi-institutional, and topical surveys.

2   See those chapters for further discussion.

Administrative efficiency

In the course of your archival career—particularly in the early stages of developing a program—you will be called upon to present projections of collection growth and space needs. The data that are collected as part of a records survey can be an invaluable aid to developing estimates that are based on more than a hunch. If you have surveyed inactive financial records,[3] you will be able to create a reasonable graph of continued growth to support, for example, your request for an off-site records center. When an office move is scheduled and the call comes to remove all the inactive records—now!—you will have detailed measurements on hand, allowing you to specify how many records cartons and how many linear feet of shelving will be needed.

When the time comes for writing the archives budget or setting priorities for grant-funded projects, you will also have a sense of the preservation issues that your institution faces. If hundreds of videotapes are languishing in a storeroom, you could document the problem, present a plan, and seek funding to deal with it. You could inform your administration about boxes of valuable but endangered records in substandard storage areas, specifying exactly how much it would cost to save the materials. Or, you could identify and propose disposing of useless records that are taking up costly space.

Public relations (internal)

A records survey provides the archivist with a chance to circulate throughout the entire institution to meet—and help—everyone. The importance of this can't be overemphasized. An institutional archives that lacks visibility is in danger of being forgotten or cut when it comes to budget allocations, having records disposed of instead of being sent to the archives, and being "out of the loop" when historical projects are developed. By meeting and working with the staff members who create and manage the files, you become an acknowledged part of the life cycle of institutional records.

The survey process can also be seen as a kind of institutional oral history. Although it is possible to accomplish a basic records survey without talking to

---

3   Keep in mind, however, that electronic records are beginning to take the place of paper, particularly in the financial area. Be sure to stay in touch with changes in your institution.

anyone, a great deal of information will be missed in the process. The questions you ask about departmental files and procedures and the information that may be volunteered as staff members show you particular series will inform your understanding of the universe of inactive records and the records being created on a daily basis. You'll also build relationships by offering information and help as you go along. The staff member who shows you a file room may have some questions about managing records that you can answer on the spot, you may be able to authorize immediate disposal of some materials, or you may be able to arrange for transfer of other records to the archives. All of these things, diplomatically accomplished, will win friends and supporters for the archives.

The Survey

Planning

As with so many projects, the key to success is in careful planning. Articulate what a records survey is and what you hope to accomplish by undertaking it, since you will have to explain these two concepts to many people in your organization. Create a master list of departments and key personnel and think about priorities. Which departments need to be done first? Which present fewer challenges and can be scheduled later? Which are potential problems and should be saved until you have a proven track record? Set a reasonable time frame, leaving the survey neither rushed nor dragging on for months. Consider what information you need to gather and develop a survey worksheet (see samples in the Resource Guide). Decide whether to collect the data yourself or circulate a self-survey form for departmental staff to fill out (more on that issue follows). Decide how you are going to manage the data you collect (consider setting up a simple database) and make it most useful.

Authority

A survey is not a neutral undertaking: some staff members may resent or be suspicious of your interest in their files. (I was called a "professional snoop" once— in the nicest possible way—by an office assistant.) As a result, it is important for your institution's upper administration, not just your supervisor, to authorize the survey. You (or your supervisor) will need to sell

the project to the relevant administrator, an effort you should prepare for during the planning process.

The authorization can take the form of a memo, which you will probably write, to all department heads, explaining what a survey is, that you will be contacting them to set up an appointment, and that the survey is an important museumwide initiative approved by the administration. It can also be helpful, at this point, to arrange to speak to relevant staff members at one of their regular meetings. A special meeting is also a possibility but, frankly, attendance

Construction documents model (1/4″ scale) of the Getty Center, Los Angeles, designed by Richard Meier and Partners. Made of basswood, Malaysian birch, walnut, and ebony in 1993, the model measures 21 x 37′ and is part of the model collection of the J. Paul Getty Trust Institutional Archives. ©THE J. PAUL GETTY TRUST AND RICHARD MEIER AND PARTNERS. INSTITUTIONAL ARCHIVES, RESEARCH LIBRARY, THE GETTY RESEARCH INSTITUTE.

will probably be better at a meeting that is part of the regular monthly schedule. At such a meeting, you can once again pull out the explanations that you prepared during planning, present them to the group, answer questions, and start scheduling departmental visits.

Departmental visits

Once the initial steps are accomplished, consult your prioritized department list and begin scheduling visits. Ask the department head to appoint one staff member, ideally someone who is involved in managing the department's records, to be your liaison. Schedule a brief meeting with the department head, liaison, and any other staff members that they wish to include. Once again, explain the project, but this time also discuss specific goals for that department.[4] Both archives and departmental staff should be free to suggest goals. After the meeting, you may want to follow up with a brief memo articulating what was agreed upon.

Now the data gathering begins. A good first step is to ask the liaison to walk you through all parts of the department, pointing out where files are stored and giving a general description of the broad groups of files found in each location. Take notes! Once this has been accomplished, the liaison may go back to his or her work, leaving you to survey, with occasional check-ins to answer questions.

Sketch a plan of the room, noting where files are kept and assigning simple location identifiers. If you anticipate records being moved (they will be), consider assigning a survey ID to each group of records you survey. You can record this ID on a sheet of paper ("Archives Records Survey ID #223, 6/2000. Please keep this form with these records if they are moved.") and place it with the records, making your work immeasurably easier in the future and giving the survey results a much longer life.

Begin opening every drawer and box, proceeding in a logical order based on the information that you garnered from the tour with your liaison. Your goal is to be able to identify records series but, realistically, these will probably by somewhat scattered, especially among inactive records. Begin a new survey form for each new group or series you find and bring like records together intellectually into series later.

Spend the time to gather detailed information. It is worth your while to sample folders and record a date range for a series, to make sure that you have sufficient information to decide who created the records. You may even want to create a file list of disparate, but important files. The goal, however, is not to record every detail and simply make a folder list. As archivists, our strength is being able to look at the details and digest them into a description that tells the survey user "what are these records?" Many times, a folder list tells you very little: a statement such as "Records of Curator Jane C. Doe relating to Egyptian art educational programs" makes much more sense than "Brown, John C.; Visits; CSD #47; Images for Eternity; General correspondence A–Z; Board of Ed; Seminar; Teachers."

1856 broadside collected from the Peabody family by Charles Towne, unpublished George Peabody biographer. PEABODY MUSEUM, HARVARD UNIVERSITY (T2299), 970-22.

---

4   As discussed in the "Why?" section of this chapter, goals may include setting up a records schedule to relieve the department of inactive records; coming up with a documentation strategy to ensure that the archives preserves the department's history; or assisting staff with developing a more effective filing system.

BASIC DATA ELEMENTS

- department
- location
- record series name
- record creator
- description
- date range/bulk dates
- container(s)

- extent
- active/inactive
- ongoing/closed series
- use level
- survey date
- surveyor
- survey ID

Follow-up

As you complete segments of the physical survey, it is critical to process the information in a timely manner. A simple database will allow you to enter, manage, print out, and use the data. Keep in mind that for maximum long-term flexibility and effectiveness, a database should have a field for *each* data element. As you enter the data, you can draw on recent memory to fill in details, note elements that you missed or must follow up on, make connections between parts of series in disparate locations, and begin to formulate a plan for dealing with various records series. Create a final report for each department, with a summary of your findings, a list of records surveyed, and a plan of action, and discuss it with your supervisor and the relevant department head and records liaison.

Keep in mind that a records survey is not just a one-time, short-term exercise. Incorporate survey information into the daily work of the archives: develop a formal needs assessment that you can use in the budget and grant development process; create records schedules; accession important archival records; use the knowledge gained to inform long-range plans for preservation, processing, and storage; incorporate data into grant proposals; and locate and provide access to records that remain in departmental offices. A records survey is a labor-intensive project. The longer you can maintain and keep the data active and the more use you get out of the data, the more cost effective it will be—and the longer it will be before you need to repeat the process.

11

ACCESSIONING
Sarah R. Demb

Accessioning asserts intellectual and physical control over materials selected for permanent retention in the archives. Materials enter the archives in a variety of ways—transfer of institutional records, gift or purchase of special collections, or return of institutional records by gift or purchase—and may be treated differently depending on the type of accession. Upon receipt, archivists document ownership and rights; review any previous appraisals and perhaps weed the records; rehouse materials into archival boxes if necessary; and prepare a basic description.

Museum records—records created in the daily business of the institution and its departments—are already the legal property of the institution. The accession of museum records is a record of the *transfer* of materials from the department of origin or custody to the archives. They do not require a deed of gift, bill of sale, or transfer of copyright agreement upon accession into the archives. If the materials transferred are listed as permanent records under the museum's records schedule, they can be assigned an accession number[1] and prepared for processing (if not, they are assigned a disposal date and placed in records storage).

---

1   The classic accession number consists of two or three elements: the year, sequence in the year, and sometimes a subnumber to define

---

WHO ACCESSIONS ARCHIVAL RECORDS?

Since museums already have a department responsible for accessioning objects, museum archivists may face pressure to either conform to the registrar's procedures or even accession archival materials as part of the object accessioning system. There are, however, some significant differences between archival accessioning and museum accessioning that make this difficult.

- Museum registrars generally deal with objects at the item level; archivists handle materials in groups.
- Museum objects go through an intensive approval process for each accession and deaccession; archivists accession materials based on a pre-approved collection policy or records schedule and dispose of material based on appraisal guidelines and records schedules.
- Archival accessions may be joined with accretions of related records, and the resulting record group identification may be more important than any of the individual accession numbers for tracking materials.

- Archivists have different copyright, restrictions, and access concerns than do museum curators and registrars, and these need to be addressed in custom forms and procedures.

Deciding how to accession archives will involve significant negotiation among various staff members: the archivist, registrar, curator, librarian, and/or administrators. Find the method and the staffing that works best for your institution with the least complexity and compromise. Special collections accessioning is most akin to museum object accessioning, since it involves legal transfer, and such accessioning might best be handled as a special case by the registrar. Institutional records are less demanding—they require only a transfer of custody—so the archival accessioning process is an internal, administrative procedure and could easily remain in the hands of the archivist. Even if the museum registrar handles the formal accessioning process, create and maintain records for each accession in the archives, thus ensuring that all archival needs are met.

Whenever possible, institutional records transfers should be carried out according to authorized disposal schedules within the parameters of a records retention schedule designed by the archives staff. Unscheduled transfers or "irregular" accessions should be accompanied by an inventory list and memorandum of transfer identifying the records groups, series, and (possibly) folders included. Encourage departmental staff to contact you to discuss such transfers prior to boxing and sending them: a few minutes of appraisal in the department's office may save hours of work by staff and result in useful revisions to your records schedule.

Most institutional records are part of ongoing series that will be added to on a regular basis. Determine whether you want to accession these accretions separately and, if not, devise a method that allows you to track the intellectual and physical custody of the material over the years. Work with staff members in the office of origin on their records retention schedule and usage patterns to reveal how best to deal with continually growing archival record groups. Loan and exhibition files, for example, grow steadily and also receive high internal use, even after transfer to archives: they may demand detailed (folder-level) access tools even before they are processed. Your accession record and preliminary access tools must reflect these needs.

Materials such as personal papers and manuscript collections that form part of the museum archives but are not institutional records are often called *special collections*. Depending on your institution, the process of accessioning special collections may fall under the registrar's office or the archives. In either case, these materials are treated like objects or artifacts: they must be formally recorded as a purchase by or gift to the museum. Obtain a signed document from the donor (deed of gift) or seller (purchase agreement) detailing who holds the copyright, any access or use restrictions, and any other conditions that may be specified during the transfer, such as exhibition requirements or a specified time frame during which

processing must occur. A deed of gift should not be finalized without this type of information, whether in the body of the deed or detailed in a separate agreement or contract.

Ideally, there should be few or no restrictions on materials. However, when donors feel that some materials are too personal to be open, encourage them to limit any restrictions. A limited restriction might close a portion of the records until the death of the donor—avoid closing the whole collection when a portion will suffice. Discourage attempts by donors to

Allegorical figure of Manhattan by Daniel Chester French arrives at the Brooklyn Museum of Art after being removed from the Manhattan Bridge, 1964. Brooklyn Museum of Art Archives, Photograph Collection. Museum exteriors: French statues.

control access by researchers, particularly if you work for a public or publicly funded institution. If the donor requires researchers to obtain special permission for access, make sure that the process—and when it will end—is clearly spelled out. If permission is required in perpetuity, you may want to rethink how valuable the collection is to your repository when you consider the difficulty of tracking down the donor's heirs or executor for permission in a decade or two—or ten! On the whole, all collections should be made available according to the general archives access policy.

parts of the accession. Thus 2002.123.5 refers to the 5th item in the 123rd accession of 2002. Older systems often used a two-digit year (64.52), with the century understood; most are now being converted for obvious reasons. Other possible accession numbering systems—notable for their simplicity—are based on a sequential number (accession 532) or the date of accession (12/22/2000).

Although they fall under the care of the archives, special collections may be related to artifact or object accessions or may be separate museum accessions in their own right. As a result, these materials may have accession numbers that conform to the registrar's system. For example, when a museum acquires artifacts from an archaeological dig, the field records associated

Brooklyn Museum Art School sculpture instructor Toshio Odate works with a student, n.d. BROOKLYN MUSEUM OF ART ARCHIVES, PHOTOGRAPH COLLECTION. ART SCHOOL: INSTRUCTORS.

with that site may (and probably should) be part of the acquisition. In some museums, these paper records are accessioned as part of the artifact collection to which they are related and later transferred to the archives. In others, they may simply be transferred to the archives without being part of the formal accession. And, of course, special collections may have been maintained in the curatorial department as a "study collection" for many years before being transferred to the archives. Special collections records may thus be identified both by a museum accession number and an archives accession number. Retain any museum accession numbers to preserve the link between the records and the objects they describe and to put the records in context.

Museum (departmental) records that have left the museum in the past occasionally return to the museum as special collections donated by the families of the staff members who "took them home to work on." To prevent this situation, encourage museum staff to keep museum records at the institution and endeavor to make this recommendation a formal, institution-wide policy. However, when the inevitable donation of museum records appears on the doorstep, you must decide whether to accession the materials as a special collection to preserve this detour in provenance, or simply to consider them an accretion to departmental records, with appropriate documentation.

Practical Guidelines

The first step in accessioning is to accomplish legal or custodial transfer to the archives. Within the museum, transfers occur based on your records schedule and/or individual appraisal decisions, and are formalized by an internal procedure such as a sign-off by authorized departmental staff. In the case of gifts and purchases, donors and vendors also sign a deed of gift or purchase agreement.

Once the materials are the responsibility or property of the archives, either by transfer or through the deed of gift/purchase agreement discussed below, create an archives accession record.[2] This document records

- an accession number (or other identifier) for the incoming materials;
- date of transfer and/or accession;
- office of origin or custody, donor or vendor;
- title;
- date range;
- extent;
- brief description;
- types of media;
- provenance notes;
- restrictions;
- notes on preservation issues;
- documentation of relationships with museum artifacts and archival special collections.

Record all accessions in a centralized system that allows you to track departments or donors; collate accretions to collections; find specific materials acquired; and track the shelf locations of the collections. If your accession records are paper documents, this system—presumably a database—is a critical management tool. To the inevitable question, "Did we transfer exhibition x to the archives?" you must be able to reply, "I'll check!" and find the answer with ease. When you begin to process the records of a department, you will need to be able to locate the many accretions reliably and quickly. Some institutional archives create a MARC or similar bibliographic record upon accession to facilitate access to the collection, others wait until arrangement and description are completed before doing so.

Create a control file for each special collection or relevant group of institutional records (i.e., department) that contains documentation such as deeds of gift or transfer forms; preliminary inventories; correspondence related to accessions; research notes on the office of origin or biographical information on the records creator; appraisal, preservation, and processing notes; and the like.

In addition to the basic archives accession process discussed above, special collections materials require an extra step to document the legal transfer of materials to the museum. You may be able to base your special collections deed of gift or purchase agreement form on the one used by the museum registrar. This document should specify

- donor or vendor and the recipient (the museum);
- material conveyed to the repository;
- rights conveyed to the repository;
- restrictions on use and access;
- disposition of unwanted material;
- special provisions for administering the collection;
- provision for future accessions, if appropriate.

It is very important that copyright be assigned to the museum along with ownership of the materials themselves. Note, however, that the donor or vendor may not own the copyright to the materials he or she is placing in your archives. Simple possession of a letter, for example, does not constitute copyright: it must be transferred explicitly. This does not mean that the materials cannot be used by researchers, but simply that they cannot be reproduced beyond the legal "fair use" criteria. Be sure to consult a copyright expert when you have any questions.

LEGACY NUMBERING

Be sure to maintain a record of "legacy" numbers from previous archival, museum, or private collection systems. Changes in numbering systems often accompany changes in recordkeeping technology or media, such as ledgers to card files, card files to databases, "old" databases to "new" databases, and so on as data migrates.

Any number that is found with a collection, item, or object may be important in the future and should be documented as part of the accessioning process. Doing this, you will preserve the intellectual integrity of that system so that it can be re-created if necessary, identify related or "stray" objects, and track the provenance of items as they pass through superceded systems. On a very practical level, you may find that older "finding tools," such as card indexes, retain their usefulness when you preserve evidence of legacy numbers.

---

2 A sample accession record may be found in the Resource Guide.

Since most records will not be fully processed immediately, a number of tasks can be folded into the accessioning process to enhance your ability to provide access during the interim period:

• Reboxing materials into archival document boxes or records cartons regularizes your shelving needs (and improves the appearance of your storage area), preserves the materials, and allows you to standardize labeling.

• Creating a preliminary box and folder list, while time consuming, eliminates the need to pull multiple boxes and check their contents when reference questions arise.

• Establishing artificial collections or identifying categories of nonpermanent records as part of

your appraisal policy and removing these materials at the point of acquisition can conserve precious shelf space.

Consider creating an artificial collection of published materials—gallery guides, exhibition programs, annual reports, curatorial handbooks, and all types of published ephemera (press releases, brochures, invitations)—to facilitate the initial weeding process upon acquisition and accession.[3] These publications are often found with museum records, and, once the collection is established, multiple copies of publications and published ephemera can be "weeded," significantly cutting down on bulk within archival record groups. If your minutes series is well organized and complete, copies of minutes circulated to various staff members could be discarded. Likewise, you might want to remove drafts of grants or publications or other duplicate materials, based on your records schedule or appraisal policy. Consider these procedures carefully before implementing them, discuss them with the staff members who created and will use the files, document them with written procedures, and place a separation sheet in the folder or a memo in the control file.

Though a small and seemingly simple part of the archival life cycle, proper accessioning is important. If legal, custodial, copyright, and restrictions issues are ignored, future archivists may have to deal with uncertainty at best and legal problems at worst. Materials in storage can be managed more easily and located quickly when complete and consistent information is collected and recorded. The more attention and care given to accessioning, the smoother the process of arrangement and description will be: collecting relevant information at the point of acquisition, when it is fresh, will save considerable work later. Spend some time defining clear and usable procedures and then follow them consistently—the effort will pay off as your archival program runs more smoothly.

3   A reference library of your own museum publications is also a great help in determining office of origin when unclear and in identifying records related to a specific exhibition, space renovation, or other historic activity.

"Texas Centennial Exposition" exhibition catalog, Dallas Museum of Fine Arts, 1936. Courtesy of the Archives, Dallas Museum of Art.

12

PRESERVATION

Sarah R. Demb

Preservation—including preservation planning, preventative care, and treatment at the item level—forms a critical part of a museum archivist's job. The first two tasks, known as *preservation management*, are the responsibility of every archivist; the third, treatment, or *conservation*, is often delegated to specialists. As a preservation manager, you can ameliorate prior deterioration and ensure the long-term survival of your holdings by studying the condition of your collection; developing a preservation plan; and applying your knowledge of proper storage space, environmental controls, shelving characteristics, archival materials, and appropriate processing techniques. When problems arise that require special training—mold infestations, damage to valuable items, or deterioration of fragile media (to name just a few)—you will turn to professional conservators for guidance or to carry out the conservation treatment.

Preservation of the archival record can also be divided into two different categories: *physical* preservation and *intellectual* preservation. While this chapter deals primarily with physical preservation, it is important to note the difference. Archival materials are valued both for the information they contain (informational value) and as artifacts (intrinsic or artifactual value). A conflict between the two criteria may develop when the original is deteriorated: you may have to choose between preserving original documents (physical preservation) and preserving their contents (intellectual preservation). Due to the lack of records management and archival programs in institutions that may be more than a hundred years old, museum records are often highly degraded or damaged. If the records contain vital information, then reformatting or migration of data from the original document may supercede the intrinsic value of the original, physically compromised document.[1] In other cases, the value of the records as artifacts may lead you to devote time, effort, and funds to conservation treatment so that the original can be stabilized and retained.

While the preservation knowledge base and techniques of the archival profession apply fully to museum archives, several distinct characteristics link many museum archives: elderly buildings, access to museum conservators, object versus archival storage, and the pervasive use of pesticides in the past. These challenges and opportunities have a strong influence on both the problems that we face and the resources that we are able to bring to bear upon them.

This chapter often suggests the appropriate time to consult conservation personnel. Museum archivists have unprecedented access to conservation professionals: large and medium-sized museums ordinarily have in-house conservation staff; smaller ones may have a regular conservation consultant. When a problem arises, we can often call upon these fellow staff members for advice and action. While conservators usually think in terms of item treatment, they can provide valuable input when mass problems (an entire box of moldy documents, for example) arise. We also work in an environment where conservation (and by extension, preservation) is highly valued. Facilities personnel answer to conservators and collections managers in maintaining proper storage conditions, cleanliness, and security. It would be rare to find a museum where air conditioning is turned off over the weekend, as it is in many businesses and educational institutions. Disaster planning is understood and supported; conservation staff members assist archivists in responding to a disaster and vice versa.

In addition to assisting with physical preservation issues, doing conservation work at the item level, or advising you when your own preservation efforts are not sufficient, conservators can help you develop preservation policies, find consultants when you need

---

1 See F. Gerald Ham, *Selecting and Appraising Archives and Manuscripts* (Chicago: Society of American Archivists, 1993), 58-60, for a discussion of appraisal criteria and its impact on reformatting and intellectual preservation.

to outsource conservation work, and provide scientific expertise on preservation issues such as contaminated archival materials. Most conservators, whatever their specialty, have a good understanding of many different media and can suitably advise or refer you to appropriate colleagues.

You may also have access to preservation experts in your museum's library. Library preservation staff can be invaluable in helping you devise custom enclosures for nonstandard materials such as ledgers and notebooks, establish specifications for storage areas, write a disaster plan, and deal with issues such as binding, reformatting, and microfilming. Take advantage of all of the expert knowledge in your institution.

Planning

The first step in developing an effective preservation program is to assess the condition of your entire collec-

Agnes Lake washing a marble head of a Roman female found in the theater, Minturnae, Italy, ca. 1931. Photograph by Jotham Johnson. University of Pennsylvania Museum. Neg. S4-144003.

STANDARDS

From the standardization of paper sizes to the establishment of the Dublin Core metadata element set, standards assist the archival profession, particularly in the area of preservation. Keeping abreast of established and developing standards enables professional archivists, many of whom work in a solitary environment, to feel assured that they are operating within established procedures. Standards exist for microfilming, photographic and document storage, cataloging, records-management programs and even alphabetizing. While standards are being developed, the drafts and technical reports that are disseminated can provide guidelines and allow archivists to shape the final, adopted forms.

In the United States, standards are developed and promulgated by the American National Standards Institute (ANSI). Established in 1918, ANSI officially represents the U.S. at the International Organization for Standardization (ISO). Many ANSI standards are developed in conjunction with industry organizations, so that a standard may be published under their joint auspices, as indicated by the inclusion of a second acronym in the standard's title, such as ANSI/AIIM (American National Standards Institute/ Association for Information and Image Management). The National Information Standards Organization (NISO) is a nonprofit organization accredited by ANSI focusing upon technical standards for information

systems. NISO has approved thirty-three American standards, all available for download at ‹www.niso.org/ standards/index.html›. The International Organization for Standardization comprises nongovernmental standards organizations representing more than 140 countries. Unlike NISO standards, there is a charge to obtain copies of ANSI and ISO standards. (See ‹www.ansi.org/ public/search.asp›, ‹www.iso.ch/iso/en/CatalogueList Page.CatalogueList›, or ‹www.nssn.org/›.)

Some of the standards and technical reports most relevant to the archival profession include

- ISO 14523:1999 Photography, Processed Photographic Materials, Photographic Activity Test for Enclosure Materials;
- ANSI/NISO Z39.77-2001 Guidelines for Information About Preservation Products;
- NISO TR01-1995 Environmental Guidelines for the Storage of Paper Records;
- ANSI/NAPM IT9.1-1996 Imaging Materials, Processed Silver-Gelatin Type Black-and-White Film, Specifications for Stability (revision and redesignation of ANSI/NAPM IT9.1-1992) (same as ANSI/ISO 10602-1995).

—Lorraine Stuart

tion, gathering information that will be helpful in planning, prioritizing actions, and implementing best practices. If you have already undertaken a records survey, some of this information may already be in hand; if not, collect preservation data in the same organized, comprehensive way.

Which materials have the most problems? Which are stored improperly? Are some heavily used and need immediate attention? Are there dirty areas? Do you have sizable collections that are subject to deterioration (videotapes or nitrate film, for example)? Survey each storage area against a consistent checklist of physical, climatic, and materials storage conditions. Work with conservators and building facilities personnel to support your survey.

Most conservation departments monitor conditions in storage areas and galleries, tracking changes that occur over time. If your space has been monitored, study the hygrothermograph charts or printouts to assess the stability of your climate control. Discuss placing the archives under the monitoring program or purchase equipment and establish your own.

Preservation surveys facilitate careful planning and prioritizing of preservation projects and are an enormous help in securing grant funds. A survey shows that you know your collection's needs and are working toward the preservation health of the entire archives facility. You need not go it alone— and it can be very wise to bring in a specialist to help. Grants sponsored by regional nonprofit conservation centers (the Northeast Document Conservation Center, for example), as well as state and federal programs, can provide an experienced consultant who will conduct a survey and assist with preservation planning and implementation. Not only will you end up with a detailed report and plan, you will learn a great deal as well if you work side by side with the consultant. The success of future grant-funded initiatives can depend on this careful preparation.

Storage Areas, Environment, Shelving

Securing, outfitting, and maintaining an appropriate space for the museum archives can be difficult. Many museum buildings are old and lack a modern heating, ventilating, and air-conditioning (HVAC) system, making stable climate control difficult, if not impossible. Space is always at a premium and competition for prime space can be heavy. Facilities staff may have to be convinced that archival collections are collections and that they deserve the same level of care as art or artifacts. The negotiations can be a major challenge, but if you have a clear vision of what you require, the path may be easier. Most importantly, archival collections are not the same as object collections. They require different conditions, separate spaces, and appropriate shelving.

Archives stacks areas should be separate from artifact or art storage spaces: paper requires different

Barnum Brown (r) authenticating Folsom point *in situ* with Carl Schwachheim, Folsom, New Mexico, 1927. Photograph by J. D. Figgins. Denver Museum of Nature & Science Image Archives, 3210.2.

climate control and storage conditions than does art or artifacts, and it is likely that access will be required more frequently to archival storage areas than to other collections. Photographs and negatives are best stored in cool- and cold-storage rooms.[2] Guidelines for the various media are noted in the sidebar; you may need to work out compromises based on your particular situation. Involve your conservation staff to advise you and strive, at the very least, for stable temperature and humidity levels to prolong the life of your collections. Low humidity and stable temperature levels prevent mold growth and acid migration/transfer between items. Keep light levels low to minimize ultraviolet damage and to maintain a stable temperature.

---

2 Volatile nitrate negatives (usually old motion picture film) should be copied onto safety film even if they are kept in cold storage.

Ideally, stacks should have climate control and fire-suppression systems, and they should be protected by a fire, flood, and security alarm system. At the minimum, you will require a fire extinguisher, a dehumidifier/humidifier to keep humidity at a stable level regardless of the season, and a secure lock.

Full records cartons can weigh between thirty and fifty pounds each. Talk to your facilities staff or a structural engineer to make sure that the archives storage space has floor load levels that can support the weight.

Try to avoid archival storage in attics and basements, which are prone to leaks and flooding. If you must use a basement space, always store archival materials at least six inches above the floor to minimize potential damage from flooding. If the space has a sprinkler system or pipes in the ceiling, consider draping plastic over the tops of shelf ranges. Windows should be weather tight and fitted with UV filters or shades. Lighting fixtures should also incorporate UV filters.

All steel shelving and map cases should be powder-coated, if possible.[3] Wooden storage furniture should be sealed with moisture-borne polyurethanes to prevent

off-gassing of acids and lined with an effective barrier material (an inert metallic laminate, polyester film, or 100 percent ragboard).[4] With the exception of compact shelving, storage units should be bolted to the wall or appropriately braced. If your institution is in an earthquake-prone area, be sure to consult with your facilities and operations staff before installing shelving.

Remember to match the shelving to your boxes: 42″-wide shelves will hold three records cartons or seven document boxes. They are much more efficient than the standard 36″-wide shelves, which hold only two records cartons—with several inches of wasted space—or six document boxes. A shelving depth of 15″ accommodates records cartons as well as letter and legal document boxes.

---

3   Powder-coating furniture does not require volatile compounds that can off-gas into the storage area. If you are considering baked-enamel

furniture, consult your conservation staff, investigate the relevant standards and the vendor's application of them, and weigh the costs and benefits. "Questions . . . have been raised about the possibility that baked-enamel coated shelving may release formaldehyde and other volatiles harmful to collections if it has not been properly baked. Because of this concern about off-gassing, baked-enamel furniture is no longer widely recommended unless it has been properly baked. . . .Testing for baked-enamel coatings should comply with ASTM E-595." Sherelyn Ogden, *Library and Archival Materials: A Manual,* 3rd ed. (Andover, Mass.: Northeast Document Conservation Center, 1999) section 4, leaflet 2.

4   Ibid.

CLIMATE-CONTROL GUIDELINES

There are many resources—and some disagreement among them—for determining climate-control specifications. The following, from a variety of sources, provide guidance in evaluating current conditions and setting goals for long-term control. A *stable* environment within the general range of 65°F–70°F and 40%–50% relative humidity (RH) is generally considered an acceptable compromise. As always, call on your conservation department or conservation survey consultant for detailed assistance.

- Paper [i]
  Temperature: no higher than 70°F [ii]
  Relative humidity: [iii] 30%–45%

- Photographic materials [iv]
  Temperature: 68°F
  Relative humidity: 35%–40%

- Color and diacetate film ("cold storage") [v]
  Temperature: 23°F
  Relative humidity: 30%

- Magnetic tape/DAT ("cool storage")
  Temperature: 65°F–70°F
  Relative humidity: 20%–40%

- Floppy disk, CD, DVD: [vi]
  Temperature: 65°F
  Relative humidity: 35%

---

i   Sherelyn Ogden, ed., *Library and Archival Materials: A Manual,* 3rd ed. (Andover, Mass.: Northeast Document Conservation Center, 1999), section 2, leaflet 1.

ii   James M. Reilly, *Care and Identification of 19th-Century Photographic Prints* (Rochester, N.Y.: Kodak, 1986).

iii *Relative humidity* is the ratio (expressed as a percentage) of the actual amount of water vapor in the air compared to the maximum amount that the air can hold at a given temperature.

iv   Mary Lynn Ritzenthaler, Gerald J. Munoff, and Margery S. Long, *Archives and Manuscripts: Administration of Photographic Collections* (Chicago: Society of American Archivists, 1984), 96.

v   For cold- and cool-storage guidelines, see Eileen Bowser and John Kuiper, *A Handbook for Film Archives* (New York: Garland, 1991). For standards on preparing and handling cold-storage materials, see ANSI/NAPM 19.20-1996, Imaging Material: Processed Silver-Gelatin Type Black-and-White Film, Specifications for Stability.

vi   For a discussion of standards for electronic media, see the electronic records chapter.

Staff work areas and reading rooms are incompatible with archival storage and with object research areas for several reasons. "People" spaces need to be warmer than an ideal storage climate. It is very difficult to control eating and drinking in staff work spaces, which leads to pest problems. Artifact research can bring dirt and infestation into the picture.

If archives staff or patrons *must* share space with artifact researchers, design the space with appropriate flexibility in mind. Make sure that tables are large enough to accommodate all sizes of artifacts and/or

The superstructure of the Brooklyn Museum of Art's Wing G and H was erected in 1912–13 and not completed until 1925. BROOKLYN MUSEUM OF ART ARCHIVES, PHOTOGRAPH COLLECTION. MUSEUM INTERIORS: CONSTRUCTION.

archival materials. Cover research tables with ethafoam or acid-free paper to prevent detritus in collections from migrating to artifact or archival materials and vice versa and be sure to clean the tables after each use. Keep a supply of both cotton and latex gloves at the ready so that researchers use the most appropriate type according to the materials handled.

Housing and Handling Archival Materials

Once you have a reasonable storage area, you can begin to fill it with collections. It is good practice to rehouse all materials into standard, acid-free containers as soon as they arrive in the archives. Records cartons ("cubic foot boxes") are a good starting point: they are acid free, relatively inexpensive, easily labeled, and can be stored flat when not in use. This process not only preserves the collections, but the stacks will look organized, neat, and professional as well. As you process collections, you can gradually place materials into better-quality enclosures, appropriate to size and medium, for permanent storage.

Inspect each new accession as it arrives in the archives, monitoring materials for dirt, mold, and other contaminants. If possible, establish a separate "quarantine" area where records can be inspected and cleaned without endangering other collections. Museum records are notorious for being stored in inappropriate places—often alongside the

WHY ACID FREE?

Archivists and vendors frequently use the words "archival" and "acid free." Don't depend on the description "archival," which can be (and has been) used to identify anything. "Acid free" generally refers to paper products that have a pH of 7 or greater. Some papers (also called "buffered") are treated so that they have an alkaline reserve, which counteracts the acid in nearby materials, and recent advances have led to papers that are even more protective.

Acidic containers contribute to the transfer of acid to archival materials, which makes paper fragile and puts it at risk when handled. Transferring materials from acidic storage (cardboard boxes, old manila folders) slows deterioration and gives materials proper support. Fragile materials such as aging newsprint or carbon

copy paper—already highly deteriorated—require low-lignin or lignin-free enclosures, which do not produce damaging chemicals, resist deterioration themselves, and provide both physical protection and support.[vii]

Reputable archival vendors often provide detailed information in their catalogs, and a quick telephone call can usually yield information on exactly what types of materials (paper, board, adhesive) are used in any product. Make sure that your storage containers and enclosures are appropriate to the materials they will hold.

vii Sherelyn Ogden, ed., *Library and Archival Materials: A Manual*, 3rd ed. (Andover, Mass.: Northeast Document Conservation Center, 1999), section 4, leaflet 4.

objects they document—before transfer to archives. If the records were produced in the field or have remained with the artifacts since collections came from the field, exercise caution when rehousing. Check for dirt, mold, pest frass and casings, and other contaminants. Always clean records before transferring them to acid-free boxes.

Protect yourself. Use dust masks and ventilators if you suspect mold growth or if a smell irritates you; wear gloves (latex gloves for moving nonarchival and/or dirty boxes; cotton when handling dirty paper and photographs); and put on lab coats or full-coverage aprons to protect your clothes. A dental or HEPA vacuum with an old nylon stretched over the nozzle can be useful for cleaning collections. Regular dusting and vacuuming of storage areas, especially quarantine areas, is key.

Processing provides the opportunity to both stabilize and assess the future needs of collections. Several basic tasks are accomplished: foreign objects are removed, folded pages are flattened, materials are placed in proper storage folders and boxes, acidic or deteriorating paper is copied and/or isolated from other paper, and sensitive materials such as photographs are removed to storage areas with the correct level of climate control.[5] Consider photocopying or microfilming high-use collections or items to avoid degradation by continued handling.[6] Identify any document treatment projects that need to be added to your priority list.

As you process collections, store materials in appropriately sized boxes and folders. Although they offer some advantages (primarily ease of access), filing cabinets are not generally considered proper housing for archival collections. Disadvantages include stress and wear on folders and the materials in them, no provision for oversized materials, lack of flexibility for adding or moving collections, and low storage density per square foot of floor space.

Acid-free boxes and folders are available from manufacturers and distributors in a myriad of sizes, shapes, and materials. For routine use, select acid-free paper or board; long-term storage requires ph-neutral and/or buffered, depending on the materials; sensitive materials, such as photographs, call for lignin-free boxes.[7] Some of the basics include

- letter size (10⅜ x 12¼ x 5″);
- legal size (10⅜ x 15¼ x 5″);
- half-size (3″ deep);
- records cartons (10 x 15 x 12″);
- flat boxes in a variety of sizes.

Standard 8½-x-11″ pages fit in letter folders; 8½-x-14″ in legal. If possible, do not intermingle letter- and legal-sized folders, since the smaller folders will shift and the larger ones will become deformed. Anything bigger than legal is "oversize" and should be separated to appropriate storage. Groups of index cards can be separated and placed in appropriate boxes. Notebooks, albums, or other materials more than ¼″ thick or wider and taller than legal or letter sizes can be stored in custom-sized phase or clamshell boxes obtained from archival suppliers or made from acid-free board. Phase and clamshell boxes allow materials to be removed easily, avoiding abrasion of fragile edges and surfaces. If funds are short, use extra boxboard, ethafoam, or other acid-free materials to make spacers to fit outsized materials into your regular boxes, or make your own custom-sized boxes.

Oversized materials should be unfolded, folded, and stored separately in appropriate

---

5   A detailed discussion of processing steps can be found in the arrangement chapter.

Various fasteners removed from paper documents in the accession file envelopes. Collections Office. 1996/97 IMS Conservation Support Project, Peabody Museum, Harvard University. PEABODY MUSEUM, HARVARD UNIVERSITY (T. ROSE HOLDCRAFT).

6   Microfilm projects should yield a service copy for everyday use, a duplicate negative for reproduction purposes, and a master copy that can be stored for long-term preservation.

7   Extensive documentation of appropriate uses, specifications, and preservation rationale may be found in many catalogs.

enclosures and containers. Use flat boxes or map-case drawer units to relieve pressure on fragile materials, making sure not to over-stack materials within folders and/or drawers. Watch out for blueprints, which can react badly to the buffered paper often used for folders; use unbuffered, acid-free materials instead, unless they are in cold storage (below 35°F).

Inert plastic sleeves (polypropylene, polyester, or polyethylene) are useful for delicate or deteriorated paper. These should be preservation-grade quality and must be used in a climate-controlled environment to prevent trapping mold spores and moisture. Discard

The J. Paul Getty Museum's head painting conservator, Mark Leonard, works on one of two versions of *Sarah Siddons as the Tragic Muse* by Sir Joshua Reynolds. The paintings belong to Dulwich Picture Gallery and the Huntington Art Collections and were united for the first time for exhibition at the Getty in 1999. PHOTOGRAPH BY EDWARD CARREÓN. INSTITUTIONAL ARCHIVES, RESEARCH LIBRARY, THE GETTY RESEARCH INSTITUTE.

existing sleeves and rehouse the materials if the sleeves cannot be identified as archival: the plasticizers in nonarchival enclosures can be very damaging. Note that the static charge in polyester sleeves can lift certain pigments and graphite off the pages, so these sleeves should be used sparingly, if at all, with works of art on paper and materials written in pencil. Paper "4-flap" folders in various sizes and simple paper or tissue folders provide other options for enclosing items that need extra support or protection. Be creative!

Inert sleeves are also very useful for photographic materials (negatives, slides, and prints). These come in a myriad of sizes and styles and can be placed in acid-free binders or in boxes. If funds permit, you can sleeve negatives in Mylar and then in a paper sleeve for support and identification. Photographs require that we balance access issues and preservation concerns: their context within paper records is often important, but their format calls for different storage conditions. When removing photographs found in exhibition files and research records, maintain a paper (or electronic) trail of separated materials, but store them in your cool- or cold-storage area. (Or box them separately so that when you eventually do have specialized storage, you'll be ready to take advantage of it.)

Pesticides and Preservatives

Museum archivists risk contact with pesticides and preservatives. While contemporary methods of artifact preservation and insect control tend to be low impact, in the past many museums used dangerous substances,

---

TYPES OF PESTICIDES IN MUSEUMS[viii]

- **Botanical (not persistent):**
  pyrethrum

- **Inorganic (most widespread, hazardous, toxic, and persistent):**
  naphthalene
  paradichlorobenzine
  arsenic

- **Organic (toxic and persistent):**
  DDT
  Chlordane
  Lindane
  Parathion
  Malathion
  Diazinon
  Dichlorovos
  Vapona
  ethylene oxide
  methyl bromide
  sulfuryl fluoride/Vikane

viii James D. Nason, "Repatriated Materials and Pesticides," *Registrar's Quarterly* (Fall 1998): 5.

such as arsenic, on organic materials in storage and on collections brought in from the field. Museum records that were stored with or near artifacts may well have been treated with preservatives and pesticides; be aware of this and anticipate and mitigate any effects. Information on the chemicals used may be documented in object records and conservation or facilities department files. Spend some time doing research so that you will know about the materials used in your institution, when they were used, and which parts of the building or collection were treated. Museum conservators are well aware of hazards and know how best to deal with them; discuss your concerns if you suspect that archival materials have come into contact with these poisons.

Records can sometimes be cleaned and housed to prevent interaction with the substances, but you may have to reformat the records to preserve access to their intellectual content. If records cannot be cleaned, it may be possible to handle some materials without risk to staff or researchers if gloves and a respirator are used. However, it is crucial to consult with all appropriate personnel—pest-control management staff, conservators, curators, and occupational health and safety staff—before allowing access.[8] It is your responsibility to ensure that contaminated materials are not used in unsafe ways by museum staff and patrons.

---

8   Problems can arise with materials other than records. Exhibition cases of mounted animals and fossils in natural history collections, for example, can contain plastic cylinders of the preservative PDB (paradichlorobenzene). If the cases are not properly sealed, or if there is improper ventilation, dizzying toxic fumes may migrate to office and storage areas.

13

SECURITY

Paula Stewart

As museum archivists, we cannot afford to be complacent about ensuring the availability of our irreplaceable collections for future researchers. While there is no absolute way to prevent archival items from being damaged or stolen, proper planning can minimize the risks.[1]

Fortunately, many museum archives exist within organizations that already have a commitment to effective security. If such is the case with yours, work with your security professionals to evaluate and improve your procedures; set up secure work, research, and storage areas; and incorporate archives security needs into the larger institutional security plan. If your museum does not have a security department, it would be beneficial to work with administration and other department heads to develop and implement even a simple plan addressing security throughout the museum.

Physical Protection

Although security during use is most frequently associated with the phrase "archives security," museum records must be protected from the moment they enter the archival collections.[2] Your storage areas are critical in this effort. Design or retrofit all storage spaces—whether a room, a closet, or a shared space—with security in mind. Set up systems to prevent and detect hazards as well as to protect against theft. Although we will discuss storage areas in particular, most of these issues and suggestions apply as well to the archives office and work space—anywhere you work with collections.

At the least, storage areas must have smoke and fire detection systems, although detection coupled with suppression is preferable. Current standards for suppression favor a dry pipe water system.[3] Installing such equipment is expensive, of course. If your museum already has a detection and/or suppression system, discuss extending it to archival storage areas with the appropriate administrators. If a new or upgraded system is contemplated, make sure that archives spaces are included.

Get to know your storage areas with an eye to potential water damage. Are there pipes in the ceiling? Do roof drains or plumbing risers run through chases in the walls? If you are in the basement, do you have drains in the floor (which can either drain away water, or actually cause floods when they back up)? Is there evidence of prior leaks (stains on the wall or ceiling, bubbling plaster)? Take a tour of the spaces directly above the archives and look for the same clues. Talk to maintenance and conservation personnel about the history of your part of the building. Once you have assessed your flood and leak risk, take appropriate steps:

- work with building maintenance staff to solve ongoing problems;
- install water detectors on the floor;
- never store archival materials on the floor;[4]
- install the bottom shelf on all units an inch or two above the floor;

---

1 Some good resources are Gregor Trinkaus-Randall, *Protecting Your Collections: A Manual of Archival Security* (Chicago: Society of American Archivists, 1995) and Karen E. Brown and Beth Lindblom Patkus, *Collection Security: Planning and Prevention for Libraries and Archives,* Technical Leaflet, Emergency Management, Sect. 3, Leaflet 12 (Andover, Mass.: NEDCC, 1999), on-line at <http://www.nedcc.org/plam3/tleaf312.htm>.

2 Proper shelving, effective handling procedures, and use of archival-quality materials (discussed in the preservation chapter) are also important components of physical protection.

3 In a dry pipe system, water does not enter the sprinkler pipes until the system is triggered. This lessens the possibility of leaks over the collections.

4 When you have no choice but to place boxes on the floor *temporarily,* protect them from minor floods by raising them slightly. Cafeteria trays work well and cost only a few dollars each. Wooden or plastic skids, which you may be able to salvage with the help of your facilities department, can also be useful for raising large numbers of boxes above floor level.

- consider installing canopies or draping plastic sheeting above shelving units;[5]
- always store materials in closed boxes.[6]

Secure all storage areas with a lock[7] and limit access only to those staff members who truly need it. These restrictions should extend to temporary archives staff such as volunteers and interns. Base this decision on your institutional culture, the vulnerability of the collection, and the person in question. Collections are at risk not only from outside thieves, but, unfortu-

The office of the Smithsonian's International Exchange Service, established in 1848 to disseminate scientific publications to scholarly institutions in the u.s. and abroad. Smithsonian Institution Archives, neg. 15674 (RU 95, Box 31A, Folder 35).

nately, from insiders as well—staff, volunteers, and regular researchers given special privileges.

Know who has access to your storage area at all times. Control and record who has keys permanently and who uses keys on a temporary basis. Set up a sign-out system for shared keys. This also has a very practical purpose—you'll be able to tell who forgot to return the key and took it home by accident! Some institutions limit collections storage keys severely—one to the security department and one to the department, perhaps—and record all use of them. While inconvenient, this method has the advantage of requir-

ing that all staff members request access and be authorized to enter. Key-card systems can also record identification of all staff members entering an area.

Sometimes door locks are impossible and you must consider other alternatives. If you share a large storage area with other departments, meet with representatives to establish procedures and a joint security plan to control access. If archives collections are stored in compact shelving with materials from other departments (the library, for example), you can obtain a locking device that secures your shelving ranges. Filing cabinets in a passageway can be locked (inconvenient as this is). Keep in mind that archival collections are *collections,* not administrative materials. Try to avoid sharing space with empty vitrines, boxes of supplies, office furniture, the publications backstock, or the like. While these have value and may be in a locked space, a range of people are likely to parade through the room, moving materials in and out and compromising the safety of the archival collections. Maintain control of your collections space to the greatest degree possible.

Minimal labeling also can provide a measure of security that may be especially important in shared rooms or shelving. To prevent people from "browsing" box titles, assign a box number, print it on the container label, and maintain more detailed identifying information in a control document such as a database. Barcode technology is well suited for this application.

Cameras and motion detectors can add another layer of security in storage areas. Work with your security department to establish your needs and how to work with the existing systems. In the absence of a security department, talk to administration and facilities personnel to explore how a camera or motion-detection system could be installed and monitored. Finally, make sure that the archives offices and storage areas are part of the museum's regular night and weekend security patrols.

Security During Use

Archival collections are most at risk when out of the storage area: improper handling, exposure to light, temperature, humidity, and theft can all curtail the useful life of materials. A few precautions can reduce the risks.

Work with your conservation staff to devise handling and exhibition guidelines that minimize the

---

5   Monitor draped areas so that moisture from an undetected leak is not trapped inside; mold growth can result.

6   Boxes afford protection to their contents by shedding and absorbing water in the first minutes of a flood or leak. A box without a lid, however, holds water around its contents and can exacerbate water damage.

7   Card readers are becoming increasingly popular, but high-quality keyed locks are still acceptable.

risks associated with display. Use only people trained in handling, framing and matting, and displaying archival materials to set up exhibitions. Establish and follow guidelines for light levels, exposure times, temperature, and humidity in exhibition spaces. If any one factor fluctuates, adjust the other factors to compensate for the fluctuation.

During use by archives patrons, items are also at risk from exposure to light and from temperature and humidity fluctuation, but the greater dangers are mishandling and theft. As theft cases over the years have shown, no organization can consider itself immune.

Lay out your reading room with common sense and an eye to security. Always have a staff member monitor the room and make sure that he or she has good sight lines: all patrons and their work surfaces must be in clear view. The patrons should be able to see the reading room supervisor as well, so that they will know that they are being observed. Place any security cameras where they can survey the entire room. Pay attention to the placement of furniture, equipment, and book trucks so they do not obstruct supervision of patrons.

Knowing your users can also reduce risks. Practices such as limiting patrons to scholars and requiring letters of reference prior to making an appointment and then checking those references may be appropriate in some institutions. Check-in procedures also offer a measure of security. Register all patrons: record name, address, institution, and check a standard form of identification such as a driver's license or work ID. Have readers complete a researcher's agreement so that they learn—and sign off on—all rules and regulations. Although your check-in process may be less stringent for museum staff members, remember that they, too, may need to be reminded of proper handling procedures.

An archives or library staff member should be present to monitor the reading room at all times while patrons are using archival materials. In cases where staff is limited, arrange with other museum staff members to relieve the reference archivist for breaks or when he or she is required to pull additional materials. Consider scheduling a volunteer to work in the reading room during reference hours and serve as supervisor when you step out. In situations where no other staff members are available but a security camera exists, contact security to let them know you're leaving the

area and ask that they monitor the room more closely. *Never* leave the reading room unsecured.

Reading room procedures also can protect the collection. Control access to the reading room; staff must be involved both as patrons enter and as they leave. Provide a place to store all belongings except a pad or laptop computer. Many repositories prohibit use of pens for note taking and provide pencils instead. Develop and communicate handling guidelines and provide appropriate materials—gloves or book cradles, for example—to protect materials. Inform readers

The Corcoran Gallery of Art Ball, main stairs with flag sculpture by Mimi Herbert, 1976. THE CORCORAN GALLERY OF ART ARCHIVES.

that all items taken into the reading room are subject to search at the end of the day. A request form can help track the materials requested and used. Although few museum archives have the resources to track individual items, it may be beneficial for you to be aware of the most valuable records in the collections and take a few minutes after use to check them. Maintaining a folder-level listing of all materials consulted can be invaluable in reclaiming items if a theft occurs.

Ensuring security in the reading room can be a tricky proposition, as you balance patrons' needs against protecting the collection. You need not be excessive in this protection, but you do need to be diligent and enforce security measures equally with all patrons. Take the time to survey your existing situation, talk to other staff members with appropriate knowledge (security, conservation, and library personnel can be very helpful), and, most importantly, create and follow written policies and procedures.

14

RECORDS MANAGEMENT

Paula Stewart

An intrinsic connection exists between archives and records management programs. Records managers define *archival preservation* as the final stage in the life cycle of information, following creation, distribution and use; storage and maintenance; and retention and disposition. An effective records management program provides systematic control of each of these stages.

Museum archivists should be interested in records management for several reasons. Most importantly, a properly managed records management program ensures that the museum's archival records are retained and transferred to the archives at the appropriate time. However, a records management program benefits the museum in other ways as well. Such a program can control and even reduce costs associated with storing records, contribute to improved efficiency, and protect the institution during litigation.

The benefits of an efficient records management program are numerous. An efficient program controls creation, growth, and destruction of records through clearly defined policies and procedures. It reduces operating costs through the efficient use of space and equipment. It improves efficiency and productivity because inactive records are transferred into storage and valueless records are destroyed, making useful records more easily accessible. Well-organized and maintained records facilitate the assimilation of new technologies. Valuable resources are not needlessly spent solving problems such as file organization or ensuring that records are complete. An efficient program in which a retention schedule is established and adhered to rigorously ensures regulatory compliance and minimizes risks in litigation. It also identifies and protects vital information and supports better decision making by providing accurate and complete information to management. Acknowledging the value of an organization's information and providing adequately for the maintenance of a records management program also further fosters professionalism in running the museum. And, last but certainly not least

to the archivist, it protects the institutional memory by ensuring that the organization's historical records are identified, retained, and preserved.

Records managers are responsible for all records created, received, and used by an organization. Backed by management's full support and authorization, the records manager plans and implements an organizationwide records and information program with the objective of providing

- the right information
    - in the right format
        - to the right person
            - at the right time
                - at the lowest possible cost.

An organization's needs and resources determine how many records management staff members are employed. Staffing can range from a one-person program where records management is only one duty among many, to a large department headed by a vice president with a staff of supervisors, records analysts, and clerks. The first option is not particularly desirable, but is often the one faced by museum archivists.

Records managers work with a broad spectrum of people throughout the organization:

- with administration to ensure that records management issues receive the attention and support necessary to make the program effective;
- with managers to ensure that departmental needs are being met;
- with a network of departmental liaisons (administrative or personal assistants, secretaries, or others who understand departmental workings) to provide information and feedback and to ensure that procedures and guidelines are being followed in each department;
- with individual staff members to identify their specific records management needs.

In an ideal situation, a museum would employ both a records manager to manage the current and inactive records and an archivist to manage the institution's archival records. These professionals would work together to ensure that the institution's records are properly managed throughout the life cycle. Unfortunately, however, limited resources frequently force a museum to employ only a records manager or an archivist, if either is employed at all. In those cases, both must be willing to accept some responsibilities outside of their normal purview: to help maintain the institution's archival records or to accept responsibility for some records management duties, respectively.

It is crucial for an archivist with records management responsibilities—especially a novice to the field—to recognize his or her limitations. If archives demands are already pressing and resources limited, you may not be able to address as many records management issues as you would like in the beginning. You may have to balance duties, giving attention to the area of most benefit to the organization. Educational background and professional experience also may limit your endeavors. In such cases, turn to other archivists, especially those in similar organizations and with records management experience, for guidance. In matters regarding legal issues, it always is best to consult a lawyer. If your organization retains its own counsel, make use of this service. In its absence, you may be able to locate a local attorney who would be willing to assist *pro bono* or as a charitable gift to the museum.

THE BIRTH OF RECORDS MANAGEMENT

The field of records management developed from the practices of the National Archives and Records Administration, which was founded in 1934. The National Archives conducted a records survey as a way to deal with the abundance of records that had accumulated in the years since the government's establishment. It implemented its first records schedule under the authority of the Records Disposal Act of 1943. By 1949, the need for records management resulted in the establishment of a records management division within the National Archives. Three years later, nine federal records centers across the country were dealing with the government's inactive records.[i]

---

i Mary F. Robek, CRM; Gerald F. Brown, CRM; and David O. Stephens, CRM. *Information and Records Management: Document-Based Information Systems* (New York: Glencoe/McGraw-Hill, Inc., 1995), 20–21.

Education and Training

For archivists assuming records management responsibilities, continuing education is key. The information presented here covers only the basics. Professional associations such as ARMA International, the Society of American Archivists, and many regional organizations offer records management instruction at reasonable cost in seminars and hands-on workshops. In the 1990s, SAA and ARMA established a joint committee to foster cooperation between archivists and records managers. These two organizations now include records management and archives special interest groups, respectively, which sponsor educational sessions at their associations' annual meetings.

Credit and continuing education courses in records management offered by local universities are another important source of information. Many library graduate programs have expanded to include records management as well as archival training. Local colleges and universities may also offer continuing education courses, ranging from semester-length courses where topics are covered fully, to minicourses that provide a broad view of the basics or address just one aspect of records management.

The advent of Web-based distance learning programs promises to improve access to a wide array of records management instruction. As colleges, universities, and professional associations take advantage of burgeoning technology and increase the courses offered on-line, archivists desiring instruction will no longer be limited by geographical location. ARMA and a number of schools currently offer such courses, and indications are that this will only increase. If you plan to take advantage of these on-line courses, however, be cautious and take courses only from known professional associations or accredited colleges and universities.

If you wish to advance in records management, consider obtaining the Certified Records Manager (CRM) designation. The Institute of Certified Records Managers (ICRM), an international organization that serves as the official certifying body for ARMA International and the Nuclear Information Records Management Association, develops and administers the professional certification program, including certification examinations and a certification maintenance program. Benefits of certification include increased knowledge gained through examination preparation; enhanced professional status, including increased job responsibility with a commensurate salary; personal growth; and improved self-confidence.

The Importance of Communication

As with the archives program, communication plays a vital role in the development and maintenance of a records management program. Records management will be unfamiliar to many museum staff members: something new involving "their" records and having an impact on their jobs may naturally create suspicion and concern. Informing staff members of your activities, explaining new procedures, and soliciting their input will allay many of these concerns. Hold informal meetings prior to beginning a new project or implementing a new procedure and follow up with a written memo or other documentation. Regular newsletter or e-mail updates are also useful. Keeping the lines of communication open will require attention, but the goodwill and support you gain will be worth the extra effort.

Pay special attention to written materials, especially policies and procedures. To assure compliance, these official communications must be understood. A direct style of writing that aims for clarity, brevity, and simplicity is most effective. Use positive expressions, emphasizing what is to be done rather than what is not. Use terminology that can be understood by everyone. Each profession has its own jargon, so make sure to include clear definitions when using terminology specific to the archives or records management professions. Use command style: eliminate "should" and replace with "must." Be concise; use short sentences. Build each paragraph around a single point. Emphasize words through formatting. Use standard spelling, grammar, and punctuation.

For policies, procedures, and guidelines, pay attention to design elements. Do not crowd information onto pages and do allow sufficient white space. If the museum staff includes an editor or a designer, work with him or her to produce a document that can be read and understood with ease.

Regardless of the frequency and clarity of communication, don't be surprised when someone has a question. It is helpful to remember that records management is not a priority in other staff members' jobs and that they will look to you to provide guidance. Provide the requested information and then remind the person of where that and other information may be found. Work with human resources personnel to ensure that records management instruction is included in the orientation of new staff members and that taking on departmental records management responsibilities is reflected in job descriptions and salary differentials. Provide educational opportunities through regular training. Miniseminars or brown bag classes offered during lunch on a monthly or quarterly basis are excellent opportunities to provide instruction on specific topics and to create goodwill.

Establishing a Records Management Program

The first step in establishing a program is a self-study. Look at your archival resources and determine how much time and money you can devote to records management. Evaluate the status of recordkeeping in your institution: investigate whether records management issues have been addressed in the past; understand the current state of institutional recordkeeping; and, if possible at this stage, what records management activities might be most beneficial. Based on this knowledge, determine how deeply involved in records management you can become and whether a formal or informal program is required. If you run a one-person shop with limited funding and an active reference program, you may be able to manage only a very simple and basic records management program. If you already have a staff and a well-established archives program, you may be able to spend more time dealing with records management issues.

During this process, you will begin to make contacts throughout the museum. These interactions are essential to understanding the "big picture" and gaining support for the program. Consider assembling a strategic planning committee made up of managers from each department within the museum to help you identify the existing systems; determine and prioritize information needs throughout the museum; and support you in the development and refinement of the records management program. The planning group can evolve into a records management committee that provides feedback throughout the year.

Establish a network of departmental records coordinators or liaisons. Select an individual in each department who has an interest in developing a quality records management program and is willing to work directly with the records management staff. Because of their position in and knowledge of their departments, secretaries or administrative assistants frequently make the best coordinators. Stress that adding this responsibility can enhance career and promotion possibilities and advocate for recognition of records management work in the museum's salary scale.

Once you have a realistic view of what can be accomplished, obtain top management's support. Since a records management program doesn't generate income and usually is discretionary, you may be required to sell the program. Having a well-developed, clearly articulated strategic plan that states the short- and long-term goals of the program and addresses both its costs and benefits will assist in this.

The most effective arguments for addressing records management issues in a museum that has already made a commitment to its historical records involve illustrating how even a rudimentary program can reduce operating costs, improve efficiency and productivity, and preserve the institutional memory. Once you have convinced the administration of these benefits and the program has been approved, the appropriate official or administrator must issue a formal directive. This institutionwide document establishes the records management program and places it in the organizational structure. Most importantly, it gives the archivist the authority necessary for the program and requires staff compliance.

Records Management Tools

Once the directive has been distributed, you can begin addressing records management issues. Components of a comprehensive records management program include a records inventory, retention schedule, vital records protection and disaster recovery planning, active files management, electronic records manage-

Family Festival at the Getty Center, Los Angeles, December 16, 1997. Giant puppets designed by Michelle Berne of Celebration Arts.
PHOTOGRAPH BY MARCELO COELHO. ©THE J. PAUL GETTY TRUST.

ment, utilization of image technology, inactive records management, and archives management. It also may include related programs such as forms management, mail/message management, reprographics management, and records management procedures manuals. For the purposes of this manual, we'll only briefly touch on the components most likely to benefit a museum. More in-depth discussions of topics may be found in the publications listed in the Resource Guide.

The foundation for any records management program is one of the most useful records management tools for the archivist. The *records inventory,* a particular type of records survey,[1] identifies, quantifies, and describes the museum's records, providing a thorough account that assists the records manager in planning for their retention and disposal. A standardized form is used to collect basic information for each record series or group of related records. The basic informa-

---

1   See the surveys chapter.

tion gathered includes office or department, record series title, purpose, date range, linear measurement, physical description of records, housing of records, and information about the inventory itself (date, surveyor).

Depending on the other anticipated uses of the inventory, such as determining housing needs and planning future growth, you may decide to gather additional data. This may include alternate sources of the information contained in the documents, other records created from the data in the series, purposes for the records' creation, process by which the records were created, annual accumulation or growth, and the creator's suggested retention period.

By reviewing the records series identified in the inventory and consulting your appraisal policy, you will be able to identify the museum's archival records, differentiate them from nonpermanent records that will be under records management, and anticipate the quantity of records that will come to the archives and when they will be transferred.

Information gathered during the records inventory is incorporated into a *records retention schedule*. The retention schedule documents the organization's records series, records the retention period for each series, and provides authorization for the disposition of records. Records must be kept for an appropriate amount of time based on administrative, operational, fiscal, or legal requirements, but most of your organization's records should not be retained any longer than necessary.

While only a small percentage of records are archival, a museum archivist may find it necessary to schedule and retain items that normally would not be considered "records"

or "archival." Your appraisal policy should guide you in making these decisions. For example, staff members at most museums perform research and their files frequently include photocopies of published articles, which are not considered records and certainly not archival records. However, in the context of providing documentation on an object or event, these copies may take on added value. In such cases, you will have to determine how and where these copies are retained—whether in the archives as part of object, subject, or research files or in library vertical files—and for how long.

The actions that grow out of scheduling records—transferring inactive records to a records center and destroying records after their retention period expires—benefit the museum in a number of ways. Controlling the volume of records retained allows you to reduce costs. You will be able to devote the best "real

Dwight Franklin modeling lizard, April 1910. PHOTOGRAPH BY JULIUS KIRSCHNER. AMERICAN MUSEUM OF NATURAL HISTORY LIBRARY, NEG. #33401.

TERMINOLOGY[iii]

Record: recorded information in any media. This is a crucial concept, because an effective institutional program must address all records in all media, not just paper ones.

Records inventory: detailed information about existing records, including title, dates, creator, use, volume,

and rate of accumulation, compiled in preparation for creating a retention schedule.

Retention schedule: a document that identifies records series, defines how long each must be retained, and provides authorization for disposal.

Vital records: records containing information essential to re-establish or continue an organization after a disaster.

iii See also Lewis J. Bellardo and Lynn Lady Bellardo, *A Glossary for Archivists, Manuscript Curators, and Records Managers* (Chicago: Society of American Archivists, 1992).

estate" to active records and transfer inactive records to less-costly records center storage. When records reach the end of their retention periods, they are destroyed, thereby making room for the new records being created. Records management also increases productivity, because staff members are required to deal with only active and semi-active records, not with records that have outlived their usefulness.

Protecting the museum and minimizing risks during litigation are key benefits to retaining, transferring, and destroying records according to a retention schedule. Two issues are critical. First, for your schedule to be of maximum benefit in litigation, it must include viable retention periods. Ascertain any existing legal requirements for the retention of records and base the retention period on those requirements.[2] In the absence of legal requirements, base the retention period of museum records on your institutional needs. Consulting other museum archivists with more experience can be helpful. Regardless of how retention periods are set, document your reasoning and the resources used to make decisions and obtain written approval from the appropriate administrator.

Second, the retention schedule must be put together and used *in the normal course of business*. To be considered a valid program, you must be able to demonstrate that a retention schedule was in effect and that records were retained and destroyed according to it on a regular—not *ad hoc*—basis. This is particularly critical when records required for litigation

_____

2   The Resource Guide includes several publications helpful in this area.

OFF-SITE STORAGE

It is a truism in museums that the primary use of storage space is the care and preservation of objects, not records. Many museum archivists work in oddly shaped, cramped spaces in older museums or in newer buildings that were constructed without adequate records storage in mind. Still others have lost a portion of their valuable storage space to the encroachments of an expanding museum collection. When there simply is no more space left for records, off-site storage is a possible solution. Here are some things to keep in mind when engaging the services of an off-site storage vendor:

- **Investigate the vendor thoroughly.** Ask for a tour of the records facility to make sure that it is secure, clean, and environmentally suitable for storing your records. If there are several vendors from which to choose, conduct a careful cost comparison.
- **Understand all associated costs.** Ask for a fee chart. Monthly rental fees are usually fairly low; the real expense occurs when records off-site are needed on-site. A single request for a record can result in as many as four separate charges (i.e., to pull, deliver, pick up, and reshelve).
- **Know what the vendor means by "cubic foot."** Rental fees are usually based on the cost of renting space per cubic foot per month. Some vendors, however, do not consider standard archival storage cartons a cubic foot but may charge rental for 1.2 cubic feet per carton.

- **Carefully select appropriate records to store off-site.** Strive not to store historical records off-site but only nonpermanent records that can eventually be discarded. Most vendors will pull and destroy obsolete records, although they may also charge for retrieving, permanently withdrawing, and shredding them.
- **Have strict intellectual control of records stored off-site,** to be sure that when you request a record you receive the one that you need. Set up a database, at the file level when necessary. Conducting an extensive search of records stored off-site can be very costly.
- **Try, as much as possible, to have a backup plan.** If the vendor you've engaged doesn't meet with your satisfaction or service deteriorates over time, have an alternate option so that you're not trapped in an unhappy relationship.

Remember, contracting with a commercial storage vendor does not mean that you are abdicating responsibility for your institution's records. Off-site storage can be a great convenience and the answer to a chronic space shortage, but it also requires that you use an entirely different set of personal and professional resources to ensure the ongoing, appropriate care of your records.

—*Ann Marie Przybyla*

do not exist, since it may relieve an institution of the burden of producing those records. Keep in mind that at even the slightest suggestion of legal action, destruction of records must cease.

Once the retention schedule is complete, distribute it to the appropriate staff members. A records management manual can be an effective method for communicating the retention schedule, general policies and procedures, and forms for both the records management and archives programs. The manual must be easy to use and understand—or it will not be

Hauling collection to railroad from camp at mouth of Sand Creek on Red Deer River, 1914. PHOTOGRAPH BY BARNUM BROWN. AMERICAN MUSEUM OF NATURAL HISTORY LIBRARY, NEG. #19493.

used at all. You can issue the manual as hard copy in a three-ring binder or on-line. Both allow for relatively easy revision, but an on-line version maintained on the institution's intranet may be the best choice. Revisions to the manual are available immediately, paper copies need not be distributed, and departmental staff does not have to take the time to remove superceded pages and replace them with new ones.

Your work is not done with the creation of a schedule and a manual, though it will become more routine. Implementing a new records management program may involve considerable work in clearing out a backlog of records that should have been destroyed over the years. Your records inventory will help identify candidates for disposal. Some records (personnel and financial files, for example) may be sensitive and should be shredded rather than recycled intact. Consider the most cost-effective way to accomplish this: commercial services provide on-site shredding and removal, or heavy-duty shredders can be purchased or rented by

the week or month. (Light-duty office shredders are slow and will certainly waste staff time.)

After the initial records disposal blitz, implement regular and organized management of inactive records. Make sure that records transferred to your care are clearly and logically labeled; departmental staff should do this, but you must monitor their work to ensure that it is accurate and follows your standards. Develop a simple shelf-list database that allows you to identify and retrieve boxes easily and quickly. Dispose of records on an annual schedule, usually at the end of your museum's fiscal year. Encourage departmental staff to transfer inactive records to storage on a regular basis, ideally annually. If possible, handle transfer and disposal work in bulk no more than once or twice a year and provide records retrieval on a regular schedule based on your museum's needs. Compartmentalizing your work in this way can be particularly helpful when records management forms just one part of your job.

Finally, continue to refine your records management program and evaluate its effectiveness. Recordkeeping is not static, and your schedule will soon require revision. If a department is not transferring records, inquire why not and see if you can gain its cooperation. Maintain statistics. Tracking both the frequency of reference requests and which records are retrieved will help you assess your schedule and storage plan. Documenting how many cubic feet of inactive records were transferred to storage and how many were destroyed will assist with planning and may be vital facts in justifying your program, increasing your budget, and adding to your staff. One of the best results of a records management program on a shoestring could be the establishment of a position solely devoted to records management.

Beyond the Basics

As an information professional, you may be consulted on other issues related to the institution's records. Being familiar with other possible components of records management programs will therefore benefit both the museum and you. The museum receives an informed opinion, and you may be able to expand what you offer to the institution—increasing your value and that of your program. The following suggestions include services related to other areas of records management that you may want to offer.

Active files management pertains to the records that people use frequently and retain in their offices. You can offer staff members guidance on establishing or improving a filing system; on using standard alphabetic, chronological, and subject filing rules; and on improving efficiency and reducing costs through the use of the appropriate equipment. An added benefit of this outreach effort is that files will be in better order and condition if and when they are transferred to the archives.

Inactive records management refers to the records that people consult infrequently, but that must be retained for fiscal or legal purposes. You can assist staff by removing inactive records from offices where they take up costly space and interfere with the accessibility of active records. Providing and managing a storage area where records can be stored in record-center boxes and high-density shelving until their disposition date arrives is a useful and cost-effective service.

One of the fastest growing areas of concern in records management is the *management of electronic records.*[3] Electronic records are easily created and are more frequently considered personal items by staff members, making these records more difficult to manage than paper. It is this very ease of creation that makes management even more critical. Remember that a record is defined as recorded information regardless of medium; therefore, electronic records do come under the purview of the records manager and should be included in your retention schedule. While your resources may not allow you to become heavily involved in the management of electronic records, you still may be able to be of assistance. You can provide advice on creating, naming, and organizing directories so that their contents are conducive to retention and disposition; help develop standards for naming files (particularly in digital imaging projects); and define categories of files or e-mail messages that should be saved.

In a similar way, you may make recommendations on the use of *imaging technology.* With the organizational insight gained through your various records management endeavors, you will be in a unique position to know when and where imaging technology could be useful and which technology—microfilm or digital imaging—is appropriate to the application.

Finally, programs such as *forms management, mail/message management,* and *reprographics* management also may be part of a records management program and may require your input. E-mail, a rapidly growing concern, may be a part of message management. And if the files in your museum are cluttered with unnecessary photocopies, making access to true records difficult, employing controls provided by reprographics management may help solve the problem.

Keep in mind that the staff lists of today's museums often do not include professional secretaries and file

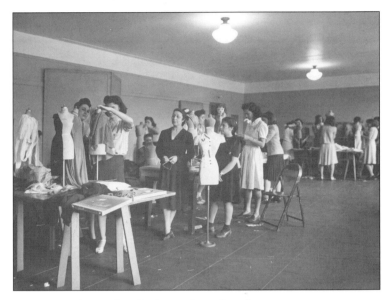

Madame Lyolene's class in the Design Lab, n.d. Brooklyn Museum of Art Archives, Photograph Collection. Design Lab: Madame Lyolene.

managers. While archivists would never want to claim either of those titles or be mistaken for a file clerk, we do have the knowledge and sensibilities that allow us to help paraprofessionals and graduate students set up and manage effective filing systems. View records management and its associated programs as an important part of your job; in the long run, everything that you can do to improve your museum's recordkeeping can only enhance the quality of the archives and increase your value to the institution.

---

3   See the electronic records chapter for further discussion.

15

DISASTER PLANNING

Paula Stewart

Disaster planning should be a priority for all departments of a museum; the museum archives has an additional focus on vital records protection. While a disaster may seem like a far-off and unlikely event, having a set of procedures, resource lists, and staff assignments[1] that are established in advance will allow you to respond smoothly to problems, both small and large.[2]

A first step in developing a disaster contingency plan is to determine the acceptable level of risk for your museum. Your goal is to balance the cost of protection with the cost of loss by performing a risk analysis to determine your organization's susceptibilities and determining how much security your institution wants and can afford. As you gather information about disaster response, you will begin to be able to assign an estimated price tag to each item—the time and money involved in reconstructing information, loss of revenue, uncollected accounts receivable, unproductive time, cost of hot and cold sites, and cost of furniture and equipment rental—and compare them with the costs involved in additional prevention and protection.

As with all initiatives, administrative support is an important prerequisite: the museum must allot sufficient time and money to this project to ensure its success. A committee composed of representatives from departments throughout the institution is also key to the development of a museumwide plan. These staff members will bring a variety of skills and viewpoints to the plan—thus producing a better plan—and will jump-start institutional acceptance. A disaster plan is only as good as the people who know it exists and are prepared to use it. The institutional priorities set by the committee will guide the development of the plan. Don't forget that, although the museum's collections and vital records are important, people must be the priority in any plan. Be sure to include procedures for both staff and museum visitors in your institutional plans.

As archivist and records manager, your primary area of concern will be the protection of the museum's information assets. Your training and organizational skills will allow you to make additional contributions, particularly in developing contact lists of suppliers, identifying urgent preservation issues, and even in writing the plan itself.

TERMINOLOGY

Disaster: a sudden, unplanned event that disrupts the operations of an organization. Disasters are classified into seven categories, ranging from a lost document (class 7), to the destruction of a building and its contents (class 3 or 4, depending on whether it occurs during work or nonwork hours), to a national disaster (class 1). Disasters include both natural and humanmade events.

Vital records: those records required for the institution to continue or resume business in the event of a disaster. Some museum record series normally identified as being vital are the charter, articles of incorporation, by-laws, directives, accession records, accounts receivable, and payroll.

---

1   Resources on disaster planning for libraries and archives, including copies of numerous plans, are available on-line at <http://palimpsest.stanford.edu/bytopic/disasters>. See also Beth Lindblom Patkus, *Disaster Planning*, Technical Leaflet, Emergency Management, Sect. 3, Leaflet 3 (Andover, Mass.: NEDCC, 1999), on-line at <http://www.nedcc.org/plam3/tleaf33.htm>; and Beth Lindblom and Karen Motylewski, *Disaster Planning for Cultural Institutions*, Technical Leaflet no. 183 (Nashville, Tenn.: AASLH, 1993).

2   Although you may be able to manage a small problem such as a leak or minor flood on an *ad hoc* basis, if you do have a formal disaster plan, the response will probably be smoother. Such an event is a valuable test of both the plan and your readiness.

Components of a Disaster Plan

A complete contingency plan addresses disaster prevention, preparedness, response, and recovery. Many institutions begin by focusing on disaster prevention and preparedness. Creating a departmental disaster plan can be a good first step (and learning opportunity), since you can probably accomplish this more quickly and easily than a museumwide project. Have a basic plan rather than no plan at all!

Disaster prevention addresses ways in which your museum can prevent disasters:
- safety guidelines;
- security procedures;
- art handling procedures.

Disaster preparedness details how your museum prepares for a disaster. Key components include:
- a summary of disasters that your museum is most likely to encounter;
- guidelines on how to respond to each;
- internal and external evacuation procedures;
- an explanation of the warning system used by the museum;
- a list of staff members and their assignments;
- a list of supplies and equipment and their locations;
- maps showing evacuation routes, emergency exits, and the location of fire extinguishers, wash stations, and other emergency equipment.

Disaster response outlines the museum's immediate response to a disaster. This includes various activities:
- meeting to develop and coordinate the efforts related to the specific disaster;
- contacting vendors;
- securing supplies;
- establishing alternate workplaces;
- dealing with the media.

Disaster preparedness and response procedures are frequently developed in tandem.

Disaster recovery addresses the museum's long-term recovery efforts, including procedures for the recovery of the affected areas:
- collections;
- records;
- office equipment and furniture;
- the building itself.

Vital Records Protection

No disaster contingency plan is complete without addressing the protection of vital records. Vital records must be protected against hazards such as theft, misplacement, and unauthorized access as well as against deterioration, fire, water, mildew, light, dust, pests, acids, fumes, natural disasters, explosions, nuclear fallout, and radiation. Both the medium and its legibility must be protected. Several steps are required in setting up an effective program:

- identify vital records;
- locate them as part of a records inventory;
- develop a departmental disaster plan;
- ensure that protection of vital records is incorporated into your institutional disaster contingency plan.

There are two main methods for protecting vital records: on-site protection and off-site protection. On-site protection may range from the establishment of a building devoted to vital records, to a records vault, to a file room, down to the use of fire-resistant safes and file cabinets. Of course, few museums would be capable of dedicating an entire building or vault to vital records protection. It is more likely that a file room would be outfitted for vital records protection, and the use of fire-resistant safes and file cabinets would be more common.

Off-site protection includes storing records or duplicates in any format in a different location. Such

National Gallery of Art staff members moving crated paintings in Biltmore House, Asheville, North Carolina, where the paintings had been evacuated for safekeeping during World War II. NATIONAL GALLERY OF ART, GALLERY ARCHIVES, WASHINGTON, D.C.

locations should be far enough away from the museum to avoid destruction in a class 1 or class 2 disaster (one that would affect a large area). Many vendors offer remote vault storage.

Disaster prevention procedures for records include establishing guidelines for the proper storage, security, and use of records. Disaster preparedness, response, and recovery include the identification of the vital records and procedures for obtaining those records in the event of a disaster as well as procedures for the recovery of all records. Detailed maps showing the location of records, particularly vital records, can improve rescue efforts and are extremely important in recovery efforts.

Do not overlook the protection of vital electronic records. The most common method of electronic records protection is backing up the museum's computer systems. Work with your institution's information technology manager to ensure that regular backups are being performed and that the backups are stored properly either on- or off-site (preferably both). Physical protection of removable media such as diskettes, tapes, and CDs—proper storage away from dust, heat, and magnets—should also be addressed under disaster prevention.

For your museum's disaster contingency plan to be effective, staff must read and understand it. Each staff member should be familiar with the entire plan and understand his or her responsibilities so he or she can act immediately and with confidence in the event of disaster. Hold training sessions shortly after the distribution of the plan and on a regular basis thereafter; incorporate disaster preparedness into new staff orientation. Conduct announced and unannounced drills to determine how the plan works, identify areas for improvement, and increase the staff's comfort level with procedures.

Contingency planning does not end with the production and distribution of the disaster plan. The plan is a dynamic document: review and revise it periodically (annually, at a minimum) to ensure that it contains current information and meets the needs of the institution.

A toy boat exhibit at Mystic Seaport provided a hands-on experience for this young visitor in 1990. Courtesy Mystic Seaport, Mystic, Connecticut.

16

PHOTOGRAPHS

Bernadette Callery & Deborah Wythe

Photographs occupy a special place in museums and in museum archives: they are diverse in subject and format, useful to different people and in a variety of ways, and their uses change over time. Photographs may be museum records or special collections in and of themselves, or they may be related to materials in either of these groups. They may be part of the documentary evidence identifying objects in the museum's collection, visual documentation of the museum's history, or research tools for study of a broad variety of topics. Collections of photographs or individual images may be acquired for a variety of reasons: to support or enhance the museum's research, education and exhibition missions; as art or documentary photography in the museum's object collections; to complement particular objects in the collection; or to document museum constituencies, such as communities, organizations, and other groups.

Since photographs are important tools in many aspects of museum work, the management of photographs within a museum may be the most complex an institutional archivist might encounter. Many different individuals and departments have a stake in these various kinds of photographic collections: curators, registrars, museum photographers, public relations officers, librarians, photographic rights managers, editors, designers, development officers—and archivists. These staff members use photographs for different purposes and all have slightly different approaches and viewpoints. Outside researchers add yet another perspective to the mix. As photographs created and/or used by museum staff in the course of their work become less active, they may be less valuable to the initial stakeholder and more valuable for research purposes. Photographic collections in a museum are not static and often have a life cycle akin to paper records.

In this chapter, we will look first at the types of photographic collections[1] that may be found in muse-ums and then at their place within the context of the museum and the museum archives. We will also consider the archival fundamentals: appraisal, arrangement, description, access, and preservation, as they pertain to photographs.[2] Photographic collections are arguably the most immediately appealing—and possibly financially rewarding—of our collections, but they have the potential of being the greatest time-eaters as well. As we will discuss below, issues of collecting policy, appraisal, responsibility, and rights and reproductions procedures are critical to good and efficient management of these wonderful resources.

Types of Photographs and Photographic Collections

Photographs as documentation of the object collections

Photographs were recognized as valid documentation of museum collections as early as 1911, when Henry Watson Kent reported on the use of a card catalog system for collection management at the Metropolitan Museum of Art. This system, influenced by the library practices promoted by Melville Dewey, under whom Kent had studied at Columbia University, was based on the distribution of multiple copies of the accession card, which had the description of the object on its recto and a photograph on the verso.[3] Collection

---

1   The term "photographs," in the context of this chapter, includes all still images: photographic prints of all types, 35mm slides and other types of transparencies, negatives, and digital images. The chapter on audiovisual materials includes further discussion of transparent media.

2   The standard reference for these topics is Mary Lynn Ritzenthaler, Gerald J. Munoff, and Margery S. Long, *Archives and Manuscripts: Administration of Photographic Collections* (Chicago: Society of American Archivists, 1984).

3   Henry Watson Kent, *What I Am Pleased to Call My Education* (New York: Grolier Club, 1949), 142–43. Kent first published his methods for museum recordkeeping in his unsigned article "Business Methods in the Metropolitan Museum of Art," *Bulletin of the Metropolitan Museum of Art* 6 (August 1911): 169–70.

records, including associated photographs, serve as surrogates for the collections themselves and frequently remain in the curatorial departments, convenient for use with the objects.

Photographs supplement written descriptions of museum objects at all phases of their life cycle, beginning with acquisition and accessioning. They record changes in objects before, during, and after conservation treatment; document their use in long-term installations and in special exhibitions; and are even maintained as part of the permanent record after an object has been deaccessioned. They range from formal images created in the museum photographer's studio and carefully made record shots of installations, to Polaroids that document an object's condition at each stage of a move. Photographs of objects, both individual record shots and as installed in a gallery, are an important segment of exhibition files; they may include both objects in the museum's own collection and items borrowed for special exhibitions.

Photographs can also provide context for an object. In scientific museums, field photographs, images of archaeological excavations showing objects *in situ,* and photographic records of anthropological encounters provide valuable documentation of objects and may be considered part of the accession itself. History museums may use photographs in similar ways, to document an object's or a structure's original condition or site, or to show how it was used. Art collections may be shown within the context of a collector's home and in earlier installations. Works of art may be documented during the process of their creation. In each case the link between object and photograph adds value in both directions: the information in the photograph provides context and meaning to the objects themselves, and study of the object, gallery, or site may reveal more about the context and history of the photograph.

Museum history

The visual documentation of a museum's history finds parallels in many institutional archives. The museum's buildings, galleries, staff members, visitors, and activities have all been the subject of documentary photography over the years. These collections can be of great value in tracing your institution's history and can enhance and supplement textual records in many ways.

Gallery shots—and the background in photographs of events—can reveal which objects were on display, how they were contextualized, and how installation design evolved and changed. Permanent installations change incrementally. Photographs often reveal more about these changes—and more easily—than written documentation. Exhibition catalogs rarely reveal which galleries were used for a show, photographs do. Studying an image with a magnifying glass can provide valuable information on how objects were labeled and how didactic panels and other ancillary information were used. Color photographs and slides can reveal which colors were used and how they defined the various segments of a show or permanent installation.

Images of the building as it was used and changed over the years provide information both about architecture and program. What kind of signs and banners attracted visitors? Was the signage aimed at particular groups? Which exhibitions rated special on-building

WHEN IS AN ACCESSION RECORD LIKE A SCRAPBOOK?

Scrapbooks and photograph albums are frequently cited as examples of "warring" media in archival collections, because various photographic and paper materials are combined. The components are often nonarchival and unstable, causing damage to other items nearby. Manuscript notations further complicate the situation. Conservators and archivists struggle to retain the arrangement of the photographs and their association with other manuscript or printed material as removal of any of these elements substantially alters the context of the whole.

Accession records for ethnographic and anthropological collections at the Carnegie Museum of Natural History frequently include photographs, in accord with a policy requiring that photographs accompany collection records. The photographs take the form of contact prints stapled to the accession sheets, which are eventually bound into volumes. Because this is not an appropriate long-term solution for the preservation of either the accession records or the photographs, museum staff members are looking for options that will allow them to retain the relationship between the two, perhaps enclosing the photographs in conservation-quality sleeves and binding them following the accession record.

advertising? How were the museum's grounds altered to accommodate different uses? What parts of the building were used for events and programs, and how did this change over the years?

Photographs of people and events can be of interest for many purposes: identifying staff members and trustees and showing how and where they worked in the museum; illustrating the popularity of a show or program by showing the crowds (or not); showing how galleries and public spaces were used; providing a visual counterpart to a simple program listing in the museum bulletin. You might find, for example, images of a museum educator surrounded by entranced children as she demonstrates a shadow puppet, the children watching a shadow play, and a scene of a classroom where the children are creating their own puppets. This complex of visual materials provides a wealth of information and context for activities that often cannot be found in the paper records. Events and programs may have traveled to other venues around your area or around the world. Did the museum sponsor a "museum-mobile" in the 1960s, reaching out to impoverished neighborhoods? Did curators and educators travel to local schools, taking along "handling collections" for children to experience? Photographs may reveal much more about the philosophy and practical approaches of these programs than text does—if the written records even exist. Educational programs are even more transitory than exhibitions and lack the convention of exhibition catalogs as documentation.

Some photographic materials start out as tools for daily work in museum departments. Once a project is completed, however, this type of photograph becomes an important archival resource with many potential uses. Daily progress photographs of the construction of the museum building or the renovation of a space, for example, may be of considerable value as historical documents once the initial phase of their life cycle is completed. They show construction techniques, the personnel involved, and machinery; when walls are torn down, they reveal older construction and gallery details; they identify when architectural details were installed; and they can be used to create a time-line to date other photographs. A storeroom move or reorganization may be documented with record shots; later these images may be the only evidence you have of storeroom configuration and conditions at that time. Given the continuous reallocation of storage space in most museums, older

accession records may refer to long-gone storage rooms, and these seemingly routine photographs may be keys to mysterious object locations that would otherwise be undecipherable.

Your museum may have active scholarly research programs outside the building—archaeological digs, anthropological expeditions, paleontological exploration, and collecting trips in the life sciences, to name a few. Such activities often result in massive amounts of visual documentation, both as part of the research and in less formal snapshots taken by staff members

Scholars consult the Getty Research Institute's Photo Study Collection, which houses two million images. The collection was started at the J. Paul Getty Museum in 1983. ©THE J. PAUL GETTY TRUST.

of each other in action. Both types of documentation can be valuable and, like the documentation discussed above, can be "read" for information beyond their initial (and continuing) research purposes. Photographs of staff at work on a dig, for example, show the objects being excavated, thus providing valuable information on provenance, condition, and context. These images, however, also show the institutional culture of the dig—staff responsibilities, interactions with laborers, the involvement of officials and local museum personnel—and may reveal much about the culture and color of the area.

Photographs as a research tool

Museum staff members have a long history of creating and using photographs as a research tool, not just to illustrate their work. Photographs allow curatorial staff to preserve and use a visual memory of sites and objects. Comparisons, measurements, and analyses can be made of items and sites that are situated thousands of miles apart, which can lead to and support important scholarly discoveries. Scientists, archaeologists, anthropologists, historians, and art historians all use this technique and, as a result, museum records often contain important collections of research photographs. The photographs themselves may be annotated and marked up, details may be enlarged, related images may be paired or grouped and, most importantly, the images may be linked to extensive textual documentation and finished publications.

Keep in mind that, as in the museum history documentation discussed above, the value of an image (or group of images) does not lie only in its original purpose. Photographic collections that developed as part of a research project are often valuable far beyond their creator's conception.

Special collections

In addition to all of the photographs created and used in the course of the everyday business of the museum—photographic "records"—it is very likely that you will find other groups of photographs purchased, donated, and collected by museum staff members. In many archives and libraries, these (along with manuscript or other noninstitutional collections) are known as "special collections." Often—ideally—these materials are related in some way to the museum's mission or collecting policy, but you may find that over the years curators have been unable to resist

WILLIAM HENRY GOODYEAR

Ever since the nineteenth century, architects and photographers have documented building design by capturing architectural images in photographs. At the turn of the twentieth century, art historian and Brooklyn Museum of Art curator William Henry Goodyear advanced the relationship between photography and architecture for his own scholarly goals. Goodyear developed a theory, based on direct observations, that medieval churches throughout Europe displayed asymmetries that were not accidentally created by settling stone or poor construction, but were the original builders' deliberate inventions. Goodyear spent many years traveling throughout Europe, meticulously noting measurements and taking numerous photographs of these "architectural refinements." The photographs, which incorporate tools such as surveyor's rods and plumb lines, became important evidence in validating his thesis. His innovative use of the new technology of photography appealed to many in the press and to some members of the scholarly community.

Today, the more than two thousand extant photographs are useful not only as evidence of Goodyear's work and theories, but also because they provide a visual record of medieval churches and cathedrals before the world wars. Potential users include a wide range of professionals—architects and historical preservationists, filmmakers, students, urban historians, religious scholars, photograph historians, and, of course, architectural historians. Research topics could focus on themes such as the impact of Goodyear's work within the profession of architectural history, how the use of photography affected architectural trends throughout the twentieth century, how the areas around churches were used and what that reveals about the urban streetscape, and how church interiors were decorated and furnished.

—*Laura Peimer*

Campanile [Leaning Tower], Pisa, Italy, with plumb line, 1910 Survey Expedition. WILLIAM HENRY GOODYEAR PHOTOGRAPH. BROOKLYN MUSEUM OF ART ARCHIVES, GOODYEAR ARCHIVAL COLLECTION. VISUAL MATERIALS [6.1.008], IMAGE #1072.

acquiring a wide variety of "cool stuff," so special collections of photographs may range far beyond the rest of your collections and may be under the care of several different departments.

Special collections may include photographs that are art objects or social statements in themselves. Collections of local professional photographers, such as "One Shot" Charles "Teeny" Harris and documentary photographer W. Eugene Smith, for example, are found at the Carnegie Museum of Art in Pittsburgh. Though this type of collection often consists exclusively of visual materials, correspondence and other memorabilia may accompany the images. In this case, the interaction of image and text provides another layer of value. Such contextual materials may identify the location and circumstances of the photographs, detail the photographer's processing methods, or provide further documentation of unrealized plans for their use.

History museums, in particular, find special collections of photographs invaluable. A collection of the work of city photographers or images from a newspaper's morgue can record the local landscape of the past. Personal papers and family collections often include significant groups of family photographs and scrapbooks. Local buildings, exterior and interior, may be documented in the papers of an architect, historic preservation professional, or amateur photographer.

Museums with anthropological collections are likely to hold photographs of people and places related to the cultures in the collection. These views of villages, landscapes, ceremonies, individuals, and groups provide context for the objects in the collection, are important research resources in themselves, and may be extremely useful in the creative process of designing installations.

Most museums have constituents—local groups with related missions—whose photographic collections could find a logical place among that museum's special collections. Art museums may be interested in local artists or arts organizations; science museums may collect materials from researchers with related specialties; history museums and historic sites look for collections from historians, historical societies, and sites that lack their own archival program. You may have a large slide collection documenting the artwork of local artists—a "slide registry." Photographs of the renovation of a local historic house and of its prior uses may find their way into your museum. The papers of a medical researcher may contain slides of cells or operations. An archaeologist may donate photographs of a dig sponsored by a defunct organization.

Folklorists may select your institution as the repository for their slides and videotapes of events. The possibilities are endless.

Photographs as art

When dealing with photographs, we often find ourselves on an interesting cusp: are the images documentation or art? Photographs that were created as documentation in the past may now be considered art. Many art museums have a photography department under curatorial control, but the question of "placement" for photographs can still be up in the air, and valuable materials can be found embedded in archival collections.

Is an original Lewis Hine photographic print "art"? Probably. Is a collection of Lewis Hine prints made by one of his colleagues or as part of a more recent publication project "art"—or archives? Art museum archivists are in an enviable position when there is a curator responsible for photographs, since a quick inquiry will often answer the question. An archivist at a botanical garden, however, may encounter a collection of photographs of plants that on their face are merely excellent documentary images. Finding out that they were created by Edward Weston changes the equation. Likewise, an archivist in a New England museum who finds a few architectural photographs might have some original Paul Strand works in the collection. Photographs, particularly by known photographers, can have an intrinsic value as art, beyond their informational value. Keep this in mind and research any photographers whom you can identify.[4]

Institutional Context

As institutions, museums are highly oriented toward visual resources: they present and interpret things that people can see in the galleries as well as read about in books and catalogs. Museum staff members in all departments find photographs useful in their daily

4   George Eastman House has an excellent database and a series of published catalogs that can help in this effort. See <www.eastman.org> or <www.geh.org>, which goes directly to the database. Other useful resources include Gary Edwards, *International Guide to Nineteenth-century Photographers and Their Works* (Boston: G.K. Hall, 1988); Lee D. Witkin and Barbara London, *The Photograph Collector's Guide* (Boston: New York Graphic Society, 1979); Les Krantz, *American Photographers: An Illustrated Who's Who among Leading Contemporary Americans* (New York: Facts on File, 1989); George Walsh, Michael Held, and Colin Naylor, eds., *Contemporary Photographers* (New York: St. Martin's Press, 1982); and Carl Mautz, *Biographies of Western Photographers* (Nevada City, Calif.: Carl Mautz Publishing, 1997).

work and as a result have a stake in their creation, use, and preservation. This interest and involvement creates interesting dilemmas for a museum archivist, most obviously in the area of dispersed responsibility and massive duplication. Which images and collections belong in the archives? Where do special collections belong? Who is responsible for the "master" image? Who acquires photographs? Who catalogs them? Who handles rights and reproductions? Who provides access to researchers? Are the collections held by curatorial or administrative departments available to researchers on the same basis as those in the library or archives? When do photographs become inactive and move to the archives?

Answering all of these questions—and setting up a logical and smooth system for handling your museum's photograph collections—requires both an intimate knowledge of your institution and a great deal of thoughtful and diplomatic negotiation with all of the stakeholders. At the very least, you must understand who holds what and how they see their responsibilities, since you are likely to be one of the first stops for staff and researchers looking for images. Defining how photographic materials are handled is much like the public relations work necessary for setting up a records management program, but more delicate, since people are probably more likely to be personally attached to photographs than to inactive records.[5]

Ideally, though, agreement should be reached museumwide as to which photographic collections belong in the archives and who is responsible for those that remain outside of archival control. If all of the individuals responsible for photographs are willing to "sign on" and participate in a central database or registry, so much the better. Each department will have different management needs and description conventions, but establishing some sort of a central intellectual link will simplify finding what a researcher or

---

5   There is also often a (misplaced) notion that photographs can be a revenue stream, so holding departments may be loathe to lose that opportunity.

DISTRIBUTED ARCHIVAL MATERIALS

Visual and textual materials are often dispersed among different departments within a museum, creating complex retrieval and use issues and leading to opportunities for collaboration. The following case study of one such situation, though it starts and ends with a film, involves photographic, textual, and collection records and field materials as well.

The Carnegie Museum of Natural History Library received a call for a copy of a film that had been produced to document a 1941 expedition to British Columbia, led by CMNH mammals curator J. Kenneth Doutt, to collect specimens for a mountain caribou diorama. The requestor, a Canadian parks planner researching historical population patterns of the caribou in that area, had seen a mention of the film in a 1946 *Carnegie Magazine* article. The diorama is still on display in the museum's North American Wildlife Hall.

We found the original film in Anthropology Department collections storage. A recent survey of the centralized film collection made this possible—the project had been initiated by the museum's Anthropology and Library staff due to suspicion that some of the films in the collection might be on nitrate stock and therefore a potential hazard to the collections housed elsewhere in the building.

Based on preliminary work which attempted to link photographic collections—both still and moving images—with specimen collections and the expeditions on which they were collected, we asked the Mammals Department collection manager to check for field notes and other expedition records related to this expedition. She located and transcribed field notes, clarified location information, and copied correspondence and specimen information on material collected during that expedition.

We then contacted the film curator of the neighboring Carnegie Museum of Art, who eased the film through a videola and a projector, to allow us to review the content of the film and to provide a preliminary assessment of the film. It had not shrunk beyond hope of reformatting, so it was taken to WRS, noted for their reprocessing skills, who produced a VHS videotape, service copy, and Betacam master.

The parks planner reported that not only was the film valuable as a record of wildlife abundance at the time of its making, but it provided visual evidence in support of historical geography studies of changes in the area due to logging; images of old-timers who served as guides for this expedition; and historical views of the Jasper town site and of the Angel Glacier, which has since receded significantly.

staff member needs, whether it is an item-level record for an accessioned photograph in the collections management system, a MARC record for a group of photographs in the library, or a finding aid describing visual materials in an archival collection.

Once you have surveyed, discussed, negotiated, and decided who is responsible for each facet of your museum's photographic holdings, define the collections that "belong" to the archives in your mission statement so that you know exactly where your responsibilities begin and end. Try to avoid creating duplicate collections: if the photography studio has a large, well-managed collection of exhibition images, it may be better to arrange for access to those holdings than to house your own set of images in the archives. Keep in mind, though, that archivists exert close control over their collections, carefully monitoring who borrows what and refusing to lend unique items such as master negatives—be careful when placing your trust in other departments. As you care for these valuable resources, continue to work closely with staff members in other departments who are also responsible for managing photographs.

Individual photographs and groups of images— not separate "collections," *per se*—are found in many museum recordkeeping systems, including registrar's files, item-level catalog records, research and publications files, and publicity files, to name just a few. In many cases, the photographs are an adjunct to paper files and have a similar life cycle. When exhibition files are transferred to the archives, voluminous folders or binders of photographs, slides, negatives, and transparencies are likely to be included. This context is, as always, important. The photographs are a visual record of the exhibition, documenting exactly which objects were included; supplementing checklists and exhibition catalogs; showing condition; and preserving the best evidence of the exhibition installation. Almost every series of records transferred to the museum archives will include some level of visual materials, which must be treated as an integral part of that series.

Finally, just as with the "permanently active but archival" files we have discussed elsewhere in this manual, some photographic records may have to remain in files in the departmental offices, even though they would be a desirable addition to the archives. Curatorial staff, for example, may find installation views of galleries permanently useful and want them easily at hand. You may choose to manage these caches of photographs in an environment of "distributed custody," providing materials and suggestions for housing them, creating finding aids to locate photo-

graphs in departmental files, and mediating between departmental staff members and external users for their use. Conversely, you may decide that it is critical to preserve the original print and negative in the archives and provide a reference copy for use in the department.

Appraisal

Creating a clear collecting policy and setting appraisal criteria apply just as strongly—if not more so—to

Artist Allie Tennant, one of the founding members of the Dallas Art Association, with her sculpture, *Tejas Warrior*, mounted in the Hall of State at Fair Park, Dallas, Texas, 1936. COURTESY OF THE ARCHIVES, DALLAS MUSEUM OF ART.

photographic collections. Photographs that are museum records, created during the everyday course of museum business, and special collections of photographs are judged by different criteria: measure each type against your archives collecting policy and act accordingly. There are, however, some unique characteristics of visual materials collections that may color your appraisal decisions.

Photographic collections are much more labor intensive, and thus costly, to process. If you simply accept everything you are offered, you will soon be inundated. Weigh the value of the materials against what it will take to preserve and provide access to them. If you have constructed a decision-making grid, as we discussed in the appraisal chapter, you may need to adapt it to reflect this difference between paper and photographic materials.

Photographs present a problem that we do not usually encounter with paper records: they require identification. If they are not annotated in some way, they may be essentially unusable. Photographs collected by curators in the process of research are a good

Construction of skylight over Central Court, 1914. BROOKLYN MUSEUM OF ART ARCHIVES, PHOTOGRAPH COLLECTION. MUSEUM EXTERIORS: CONSTRUCTION.

example of this. If the images are identified, the owning institutions noted, and the photographer credited, they may have a secondary life for new research projects or understanding the curator's own work. If, however, they are unidentified and have little or no context, ask yourself whether they are worth keeping.

The easy duplication of photographs also adds to our appraisal dilemma. Which image is the "original"? Do we need to keep all the various copies of an image from files of several offices? Polly Darnell, of the Shelburne Museum, notes that "we used the same photographs of Electra Webb, of the Ticonderoga, and of certain objects, over and over for several years for publicity, slide talks, and brochures. They turn up in curator's files, in marketing, in administrator's files, in education, but not necessarily in the central photograph file." Your appraisal policy and processing procedures should address this issue; we will discuss some options in the arrangement section below.

Defining an "office of record" for certain types of photograph can help avoid problems with unnecessary

duplication. If your museum has a central photograph collection of all images of objects in the collection (whether in the registrar's office, the photo studio, curatorial office, or a photo rights department), all other copies are ephemeral and can potentially be disposed of once they're inactive and no longer useful. At the Brooklyn Museum of Art, we decided early in the archives' history *not* to collect photographs of objects in the collection, except within a context such as an exhibition or research file. This policy allows us to simply transfer extra copies of object images back to the curatorial departments (where duplication is considered a virtue, not a problem).

While appraisal decisions for photographs that are museum records can be hazy at times—you will be assessing their value within the context of other records—appraising special collections of photographs falls squarely under your mission statement and collecting policy. If a photographic collection doesn't fit under your policy, it should be elsewhere—possibly in another institution. Photographs come with a greater burden of effort in most of the archival fundamentals: arrangement can be difficult, description is often more detailed, preservation requirements are more stringent, and research use can be much more labor intensive. Consider these—and your ability to fulfill them—carefully, before accepting a special collection into the archives. It may be that your library has a broader mandate and will accept a wonderful but out-of-scope group of photographs, or that, with some helpful advice from the archives, a curatorial department may be able to maintain the photographs that a curator just couldn't pass up.

Arrangement

Photographs almost always present archivists with a difficult choice: provenance or artificial collection? Will you follow the principle of provenance and maintain photographs in context with other materials—as you do with paper records—or create a central photographic collection with its own topical series? The choice may have been made long before a professional archivist arrived on the scene, so you may well face large and unwieldy photographic collections where all semblance of provenance, context, and original order are long gone.

For example, the collection of gallery shots that turns up in most museum archives almost certainly did not originate as the "gallery shot collection." The images were created by staff for many different purposes: publicity, highlighting a new installation, or documenting an old one before renovation, for example. Over the years, well-meaning individuals decided that they were more useful as a group than as individual photographs in the folders documenting installations or in public relation files. In this case, the instinct may be correct. If the photographs are well labeled, it should be easy to make the intellectual link between the textual and visual image files, and a series of gallery shots can be a very useful tool in understanding changes in the museum.

The fact that artificial collections sometimes work well, however, does not justify wholesale dependence upon them. At the Brooklyn Museum of Art, we recently found a group of photographs simply labeled "Transylvanian Costumes" that had been placed in a "picture file" (a group of images related by subject) by a former curator. Something about the images jogged a visual memory, and we were able to link these images to correspondence, a publication, an exhibition, and objects collected by the museum's first curator of ethnology, Stewart Culin, thus making them immeasurably more valuable.

If your museum has a staff photographer, historic photographs may have found their way into the files of that department over the years, perhaps during the course of copy photography for annual reports or other publications. Are they a "collection" or simply a group of disparate images that happen to be stored together?

The two approaches—provenance and artificial collection—are not mutually exclusive, but defining the parameters for "what goes where" requires some serious thought and planning. In general, most archivists follow provenance whenever possible, but deal with the rest of the images in a very practical manner by creating an artificial collection to manage them. Further, provenance may be maintained by means of intellectual links, not just physical location, which may allow you to select from the best of both worlds: context and accessibility.

Provenance

Archivists maintain provenance and context *because they are valuable tools for using and understanding materials.* This principle applies to nonpaper materials just as strongly—if not more so—as to standard tex-

tual files. Photographs, if not identified or connected to other explanatory materials, lose a significant portion of their informational value, as we discussed above.

In some cases, archivists sleeve photographs and leave them in place, with the textual materials. This may be prudent when collections are small or not professionally managed, since it reduces the risk of breaking the intellectual link or even mislaying the photograph. When photographs are physically separated from textual materials for preservation's sake, an intellectual link that goes *in both directions* can (and should) be

President Franklin D. Roosevelt speaking at the dedication of the National Gallery of Art, March 17, 1941. NATIONAL GALLERY OF ART, GALLERY ARCHIVES, WASHINGTON, D.C.

created to preserve context. Place a separation sheet in the paper file identifying the photograph that you removed and specifying its new location and devise a method so that the name and location of the source file travels with the photograph. Images that are removed from paper records may migrate to a parallel visual materials subseries within their record series or become part of a central photograph collection, depending upon which is more practical or logical. Creating a visual materials subseries is easier, since the photographs "belong" with the other records and the pointers in each direction are simple:

- In the file: "photograph removed [description]: see Series 10: Visual Materials"
- With the photo: "removed from Series 1: General Correspondence, folder 5"

As noted above, though, massive duplication may result from this method, and the photographs are not easily accessible for browsing—a request for images of the building itself, for example, might be difficult to fulfill without going to several record series. With a well-organized central photograph collection (as we discuss below), however, the destination may be specified, and the various sources recorded to maintain a link to the image's provenance and context:

- In the file: "photograph removed [description]: see Photograph Collection: Museum building, interiors, image #123"
- With the photograph: "removed from Records of the Director's Office, Series 1: General Correspondence, folder 5"

The central photograph collection

Not all images have an obvious context or provenance: it is very likely that your archives holds a large mass of images that lack any connection to paper records. Organizing a central photograph collection—an "artificial collection"—is a standard approach to this problem and is certainly a practical way to provide convenient access to images. First, follow the guidelines in the arrangement chapter and learn everything you can about the photographs in your care. Next, create a broad arrangement scheme that affords basic access, followed by more detailed schemes as needed. Do not simply start numbering images: devise an organizational scheme and arrange the collection before even considering item-level actions. Think like an archivist: in *groups*. A clear and simple intellectual framework, perhaps a series of topical or functional categories, can help you with the initial arrangement. For example:

- Museum building
- Galleries
- Exhibitions
- Staff and trustees
- Events and programs

As you refine the arrangement, define subgroups as you need them, keeping the system as simple and flexible as possible. Your goal is accessibility: the more transparent the arrangement is, the better it will work.

Negatives and prints

Collections of images present another arrangement dilemma. Different versions of the same image—negatives, slides, transparencies, and prints of various sizes and types—all have different requirements for proper housing and environment. In addition, it is very likely that all of these different formats of a single image are scattered throughout the archives: a transparency in a publication file, prints in three different paper files, slides in an educational program file and a curator's lecture file, and the negative in the photography studio's negative cabinet. Linking all of these disparate pieces into one intellectual whole is difficult and not always possible, considering the labor required to identify each one. (Unless your institution has had a well-thought-out and reliably executed numbering system since day one—an unlikely prospect. You will more likely be dealing with a number of disconnected systems.)

The key to gaining control of these various formats is an arrangement scheme that is logical and consistent across the board. Avoid setting up new and different arrangement schemes for each different format. Thus, if you have set up topical groups in your central photograph collection, create a parallel structure for slides, negatives, and transparencies. This will allow you to make matches between photographs of galleries and negatives of gallery images. The same is true for the photographs that remain as subseries within selected records series in the provenance model. If you find a group of slides from an exhibition, you can create or restore context by returning them to the exhibition visual materials subseries of the relevant curatorial department. As you work toward an eventual goal of linking each image to all of its component parts, a structure will grow that makes everyday access possible and provides the basis for the labor-intensive job of dealing with these multiple versions of the same image.

Description

Description of photographs follows the same principles as that of other archival materials: begin at the broadest level, think in groups, articulate the context, match the final level of description to your access requirements, and work within your resources. This is one area where item-level description is fully accepted—*but not on its own.* Multilevel description is especially important for photographs.

Describe photographs at the collection, series, and/or subseries levels just as you would describe paper records.[6] Who created the materials? When? For what purpose? What is the extent of the collection?

---

6 See the description chapter.

How is it arranged? What formats are included? What is the scope and content? This kind of collective description is critical, since the numbers of individual items can be overwhelming in photograph collections. Researchers will be able to focus on the most relevant groups of materials, and the photographs that they do find will be more meaningful because of their context.

Once you have established a descriptive framework, decide how much farther to go. Consider

- the size and scope of the collection;
- its historical importance;
- its potential research use;
- its artifactual value;
- its uniqueness;
- how its relates to the institutional profile or mission.[7]

Balance these criteria against your resources and proceed to item-level description *only* if the collection calls for it; broad, collection-level description is already accomplished for *all* photographic collections; and you can accomplish the task without compromising

---

7   Ritzenthaler et al., *Administration of Photographic Collections,* 86.

NUMBERING[i]

Legacy systems

Be attentive to numbering schemes provided by the original photographer or curator, as these may provide clues to the existence of and relationship between multiple formats. When rehousing or reformatting, be sure to transcribe notations found on the protective sleeve or the photograph itself, or valuable information identifying the subject or provenance of the photographs may be lost.

Creating a new system

As with arranging collections, simple and logical makes the most sense. Never design a system and then force materials into it—look at your collections, needs, and resources carefully when designing a new system. Avoid inventing elaborate numbering schemes that carry a lot of meaning; you're creating a location system, not a subject or condition classification system. Finally, to help future users, document the system *and* the logic behind it.

In the case of a special collection that is entirely photographs, the museum accession model works well: 1997.23.1-.35 gives you the ability to identify each of the thirty-five photographs in the twenty-third accession of the year 1997. If you later make a copy negative of one of those images, you might add a suffix: 1997.23.12.cn.

If you created an artificial collection with categories, subgroups, and folders, you may simply be able to tag an item number and format code onto the textual identification: "Museum building, interiors, 1936, #45n" specifies an individual negative in a particular group.

Items separated from museum records but maintained in the same records series can be identified by series, subseries, and item number: "Records of the Director's Office, Series 10: Visual materials, #22." If they are separated but not arranged into a visual materials subseries, you can use the same logic, but include the original folder title: "Records of the Director's Office, Annual Ball, 1987, #67."

Databases can be helpful, of course, in managing photographic collections, but your arrangement and your numbering system must make sense and be workable *before* automating them. All of the numbering systems above could be integrated into a database and the information entered at the appropriate level, whether an item description or a broad entry for a folder of images.

With the assistance of a database, it *is* possible to simply assign a unique number to each item and then use the database to locate and manage the various photographic collections. While this can be an attractive option, there are some disadvantages. Descriptive data must be entered for every image: is this within your resources? Items in a folder will have widely disparate ID numbers, based upon when they were added, which can be confusing when searching for or refiling an image. If you file by number, rather than in archival groups, it will be labor intensive to bring together related materials. Will you assign a unique number to each *image* or to each *item,* in all the various formats? How will you handle multiple copies? How will you make matches between the different formats?

---

i   For further discussion of numbering, see the description chapter.

the rest of your archival program.[8] Set priorities. It is almost always better to have ten collections described at the collection, series, and subseries levels than to ignore nine and give the tenth the royal treatment. Then again, if that tenth collection is truly the queen of all photographic collections, that may be warranted. If a good, but not great, collection already has captions for all the images on the old envelopes or in a typed inventory, it will be easier to accomplish item-level description, and it may be reasonable to place it ahead of a slightly better collection that demands more effort.

There are several reasons for describing photographs at the item level. Unlike general researchers who ask for materials relating to a topic, a person, or an event, but rarely for a specific letter, picture researchers often seek specific images. They need a photograph of the Asian gallery in the 1930s, and they may not need or want to leaf through all of your other gallery shots, wonderful as they are. The content of an image, as we discussed above, may go beyond its original purpose or even its caption. Item-level description allows you to enhance this intellectual access with name, subject, and geographical terms, and to create or add to captions. Defining and using standard descriptive elements and terminology are particularly important at this level. The photographs of individuals creating Kuba cloth in Africa that a curator collected while writing an exhibition catalog have many potential uses beyond documenting the exhibition research process. Though they are presumably described as a group in the exhibition series, item-level description brings these materials to the attention of a wide variety of researchers.

Description is not only an access tool for researchers, but also a management tool for archives staff. While a collection- or series-level description may provide reasonable access for researchers to identify a collection as relevant and begin to browse through images, more detailed systems are usually required for administrative tasks, particularly rights and reproductions requests. Once an image has been published, repeated requests for it are likely to follow. Knowing that it is in a particular collection is helpful, but finding the image efficiently requires a deeper level of description, to the folder at least, and possibly to the item.

Because of the need for item access and for matching the same image in different formats, an item identification or numbering system can be helpful in managing photographic materials. Consider first, however, whether you really need to number every image, or if you can achieve reasonable control at the folder level. Some collections may require a more detailed approach, others are less demanding.

Automation is an obvious tool when you are working with collections at the item level. A database can allow you to describe each image, link it to others that have the same provenance, identify where it is filed, and match images with their negatives and with derivative formats such as transparencies. Researchers can find disparate materials using a keyword or pull together all images in a single collection. Database access greatly simplifies rights and reproductions activities, allowing you to find particular images, identify whether a negative exists, and track their use. Images that have been separated from paper files or that form part of a museum object accession can be managed easily, and the critical intellectual link maintained.

As you plan the best way to accomplish item-level access to images, investigate the resources that are already available in your institution. Collections management databases are a possibility, as are library systems. Designing your own relational database may be a reasonable solution.[9] If your museum has a slide librarian, talk to him or her; slide libraries have very detailed cataloging systems, which may not be appropriate for archives but could be instructive.[10] The ideal system (which doesn't yet seem to exist off-the-shelf) would reflect both the hierarchical arrangement of the archives—collection, series, subseries, folder, item—and allow access to individual items. In the end, make sure that the system you select fits the need for *archival* management of photographs: never lose the connection between group and item.

Access and Use

If you have correctly matched your descriptive tools to the needs of researchers and staff, basic access requirements should be met. A query, either verbally or via a database, will result in either a single image or, more likely, a group of images that can be retrieved for the researcher to peruse. Minimizing handling and exposure to light is an important goal, so the more focused

---

8   Sarah Demb, for example, rekeyed an entire photograph index in a finding aid at the Peabody Museum "in order to truly reflect the work [the creator] had done and make available the information contained therein, which was crucial to identifying the 500+ photographs, with their original field numbers. The original cards are also fairly fragile, so replicating the data on them was useful from a preservation perspective." See <http://oasis.harvard.edu/html/pea00013frames.html>.

9   See the section on automation in the description chapter.

10   See the Visual Resources Association Web site at <www.vraweb.org>.

the retrieval, the better for the photographs. While browsing will still remain a legitimate way to gain access to a photographic collection, it causes undue wear and tear on the photographs and should never be the only—or even the preferred—method. Creating well-organized binders of photocopies as an "entrance portal" for browsers can be a useful way to satisfy both access and preservation needs.

Once a researcher has identified images that are of interest, another universe of tasks arises. Unlike textual materials, which can be easily photocopied and which can be used at some level under the "fair use" provisions of the copyright law, photographs are more difficult to copy and more demanding in terms of copyright.

Producing photographic reproductions and licensing their use can be both a drain on the archives budget in terms of staff time and a significant contribution to the museum's revenue stream. Though photocopies may be sufficient for some research use, you will also need to produce duplicate prints, copy negatives, transparencies, slides, and digital image files for both study and publication. If images are to be reproduced, a procedure must be in place to ensure that citations are correct, copyright is observed,[11] and costs recovered. These management tasks can be very demanding, so devise procedures that are as efficient as possible. Larger museums often have a photo studio and a rights department, so you may be able to delegate some tasks, or you may find that all of the responsibilities fall on archives staff. In some institutions, due to the distributed nature of photograph collections, you may have to reconcile inconsistencies in reproduction agreements and use fees among the departments that make photographs available for outside use when devising your own policies and procedures.

Photographs that are museum records present the least worry in terms of copyright: if they were produced by and for the museum, the museum most likely holds all rights. If outside photographers were used, research their contracts and see if rights were assigned. Intellectual property policies that determine the ownership of field photographs, along with the field notebooks and other working records of staff research should be explicit in the archives mission statement. Keep in mind that the museum does not hold rights to copies of photographs from other institutions that are found in files. You can certainly allow researchers to study these images, but you have no right to allow them to be reproduced.

Photographs that are *not* museum records—either special collections or original photographs found in various record series—present more complicated rights issues. In an ideal world, each image would be marked with the photographer's name and address, and it would be easy to trace the subsequent ownership. Larger firms may still exist or the photographer may still be alive, but in many cases you will be unable to locate the holder of copyright to an image. If an individual wishes to reproduce a photograph from your collection that falls into this category, you may require *them* to do this research and show you permission in writing. Photographs with no identifying information whatsoever present an even knottier problem and should probably be restricted to research use. As in any question with legal ramifications, consult your museum's legal counsel and, if necessary, a copyright expert.

POLICIES AND PROCEDURES CHECKLIST

- General archives access and restrictions policy.
- Access or restrictions statements specific to photographic collections, if needed.
- Reproduction policy, including price list and/or other receivables (i.e., a copy of a published work); requirements for print, on-line, and broadcast uses; citation or credit line requirements; definition of academic, institutional, and commercial users; licensing for commercial use vs. one-time publication; time frame, including provision (or not) for rush jobs.
- Request to reproduce form.
- Permission and approval procedures, including citation check, copyright clearance, quality control of reproduction.
- Reproduction contract.
- Order forms and procedures for making photographic prints, copy work, slides, transparencies, digital scans.
- Handling procedures, especially when an outside photo lab is used, including proper enclosures, approved transit.
- Labeling standards, including type of label, information included, and format.
- Administrative procedures: definition and management of all required steps, billing and accounting.

---

11 Links to many resources on copyright and intellectual property (including some full-text guides) may be found at <http://palimpsest.stanford.edu/bytopic/intprop>.

Your photograph reproduction policy must also articulate any restrictions beyond the broad area of copyright. Some images or collections may be off-limits to any use beyond research. Archaeological and anthropological collections, for example, often include images of sacred sites and objects that might best be covered by some level of restriction.[12] Views of archaeological sites can provide information that would lead illegal pot hunters to protected areas. Some building photographs could compromise museum security if released. Photographs of members of the public may require a model release.

No discussion of access to photographic collections would be complete without considering digitization.[13] A well-considered digitization program can ease and enhance researchers' work, bring your collections to a wider audience, minimize the handling of fragile collections, and simplify the reproduction process. These positive aspects also bring with them costs: planning and executing projects, creating an interface and search capabilities, preserving and migrating electronic files, and dealing with increased traffic in rights and reproductions work (which, of course, can potentially provide financial support).

Explore digital access thoughtfully. Develop selection criteria based on a clear policy and a long-range plan, not on an *ad hoc* basis. Follow and stay up-to-date with current standards, vendors, and software packages, since the field is still in its early stages. Look into joining a consortium to "deliver" or present your images on the Web. This can ease in-house efforts, give you access to more experienced technology staff and resources, enhance the value of your materials by placing them in a broader context, and increase your visibility by bringing your collections to the attention of a wider audience.

Preservation Basics

Photographs are the result of chemical and physical interactions between layers or surfaces: an emulsion, or image-bearing, layer is adhered to a base, or support, layer. Numerous technical innovations and the availability of a wide range of materials over time have resulted in photographic materials that are complex and diverse: emulsions of silver halides, platinum pigments, and dyes; in carriers such as gelatin, collodion, and albumen; on supports of metal,

glass, paper, and various forms of plastic.[14] As a result, these materials probably present the most complex preservation problems of anything in the archives, so this is truly an area in which to "know what you do not know." The guidelines below present the barest preservation basics—they will point you in the right direction in a general way, but do not purport to be the only resource you will need. The many detailed and scientific resources on photographs can take you farther,[15] and the final stop in any questionable case must be an expert, either a member of your museum's conservation staff or an experienced photograph conservator.

Identification

Ritzenthaler cites examination as the first of the three functions of conservation[16] and recommends that archivists learn to identify the most common types of photographs and understand their problems and storage requirements.[17] The majority of the photographs that you encounter in collections of institutional records will probably be standard silver-gelatin prints on a paper or resin-coated paper base. Negatives in your care may vary a bit more: glass and the various film types—cellulose nitrate, cellulose acetate,[18] and polyester. Positive transparencies include glass lantern slides, 35mm slides, and other transparencies of various sizes. You are probably already familiar with all of these. When you come face-to-face with something new and different—a lovely blue cyanotype, a cased image on a metal sup-

---

12 See the NAGPRA chapter.

13 See the electronic records chapter for a more detailed discussion of digitization.

---

14 Ritzenthaler et al., *Administration of Photographic Collections*, 95.

15 Ibid., see also James M. Reilly, *Care and Conservation of 19th-Century Photographic Prints* (Rochester, N.Y.: Kodak, 1986); Henry Wilhelm and Carol Brower, *The Permanence and Care of Color Photographs: Traditional and Digital Color Prints, Color Negatives, Slides, and Motion Pictures* (Grinnell, Iowa: Preservation Publishing, 1993); and Lawrence E. Keefe, Jr., and Dennis Inch, *The Life of a Photograph* (London: Focal Press, 1984). See also <www.solinet.net/emplibfile/photobib.pdf> and <www.nedcc.org/leaflets/phobib.htm>. The Image Permanence Institute at Rochester Institute of Technology (<www.rit.edu/~661www1>) is an excellent resource: see, for example, James M. Reilly's two booklets, *The IPI Storage Guide for Acetate Film* (Rochester, N.Y.: IPI, 1993) and *The Storage Guide for Color Photographic Materials* (Rochester, N.Y.: IPI, 1998). See also the sidebar on standards in the preservation chapter.

16 Along with preservation and restoration. Ritzenthaler et al., *Administration of Photographic Collections*, 94.

17 In addition to the various published sources, hands-on workshops are a particularly good way to learn how to identify the various types of photographic materials. The Visual Materials Section of SAA frequently offers a workshop at the annual meeting; George Eastman House and NEDCC also sponsor workshops on a regular basis. See <http://mlin.lib.ma.us:80/mblc/ldev/preservation_calendar.shtml> for current offerings.

18 See the audiovisual chapter for more information on film types.

port (daguerreotype? tintype?), a carte-de-visite, an album, a photograph mounted on board—take the time to do some research and talk to an expert. Your preservation research and decisions must be based on an accurate identification.

Handling

A few simple principles govern handling of photographic collections: less is better, don't let anything touch the emulsion, keep the area clean, wear clean cotton gloves, minimize exposure to light.

Environment and housing

Because of their layered composition and variety of components, photographs are highly sensitive to environmental conditions. Consider a simple analogy: if you glue a piece of paper to a piece of mat board and then dampen the package or place it on top of a radiator, many things can happen, depending on the characteristics of the board, the glue, and the paper. The paper may wrinkle and buckle, the glue may separate or spread, the board may bend or fracture. Similar reactions can happen to photographic materials when their layers respond differently to changes in humidity and temperature. While different specifications may be found in different resources,[19] and different materials should ideally be stored based on their own specific requirements, an acceptable compromise solution provides temperature that is relatively cool (68°F or less) and humidity on the dry side (35% RH).[20] Negatives and color materials can benefit from an even cooler environment.[21] As always, consult with conservation staff, especially if your collection includes materials that are especially fragile or valuable. Most importantly, maintain *stable* temperature and humidity levels, since fluctuations are highly damaging to photographic materials.

As with all archival collections, storage materials—shelving, boxes, folders, and enclosures—must be stable and nonreactive. Ideally, use lignin-free boxes (not the less-expensive boxes that are lined with acid-free paper), acid-neutral (pH 7.0) folders and paper enclosures ("buffered" materials with an alkaline reserve are *not* recommended for most types of photographic materials), and inert plastic enclosures or sleeves (polyester, polyethelene, polypropelene, cellulose acetate, Mylar). Make sure that plastic enclosures are not coated (i.e., matte or semi-opaque), since this type of sleeve may be abrasive.[22]

Match housing to use at all levels and for all types of materials, keeping preservation requirements in mind. Filing cabinets have often been used for visual

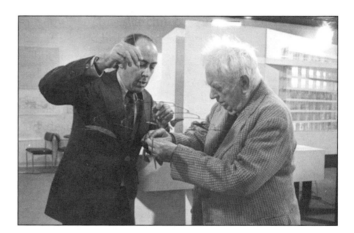

Alexander Calder (r) and Paul Matisse (l) with the maquette for Calder's *Mobile,* created for the East Building of the National Gallery of Art, 1976. NATIONAL GALLERY OF ART, WASHINGTON, D.C. GALLERY ARCHIVES.

materials storage—for ease of browsing—but they are certainly not ideal in terms of preservation: materials slump and curl; they are abraded as they are flipped through, removed, and refiled; drawers can jam, mangling items; damaging chemicals created as photographs deteriorate may be held in and concentrated, affecting a large number of images. Visual materials are best stored in boxes of appropriate size, segregated according to type and size, with, ideally, each item enclosed in its own paper or plastic sleeve. They may be stored either flat or upright, but with an eye toward potential damage, since each position has its advantages and disadvantages. Make sure upright boxes are comfortably full to avoid slumping. Never make heavy stacks or place other materials on top of curled items in flat boxes. If possible, don't mix different sizes; if you must, find a way to segregate and support them within each box. Consider the condition of what you are boxing, give it proper support, and protect it from the other materials in the box.

---

19 For example, Ritzenthaler recommends 68°F and 35%–40% RH (Ritzenthaler et al., *Administration of Photographic Collections,* 98) as a general guideline. Reilly quantifies the effect on longevity as temperature and humidity fall, stating, "make the temperature as low as you can and preferably make the average RH 20% to 30%," (*IPI Storage Guide,* 19).

20 Ritzenthaler et al., *Administration of Photographic Collections,* 98. If photographic materials must be stored with paper records, then 40% RH is acceptable, though not ideal.

21 Ritzenthaler recommends cold storage at 0°–10°F with 25%–30% RH for color materials, 0°F with 40% RH for nitrate negatives, noting that careful procedures must be observed when materials are removed from cold storage. Ritzenthaler et al., 116, 120.

22 Ritzenthaler et al., *Administration of Photographic Collections,* 100.

The choice of sleeve type depends on the anticipated use of the item as well as its type and condition. Clear sleeves allow easy viewing of images, but do not provide as much support as paper. Their static charge may lead to problems if the emulsion is flaking or if dirt and dust get into or on the enclosure. If humidity is a problem in your facility, the surface of the emulsion may ferrotype, causing shiny spots on the image, or stick to the enclosure. Labeling is difficult when using sleeves. If paper is chosen, four-flap enclosures are best, since they

The Children's Room, established in the Smithsonian Institution Building, c. 1901. Smithsonian Institution Archives, neg. 14738 (RU 95, Box 41, Folder 8).

allow you to label the image easily, have no seams to put uneven pressure on the item, contain no glue, and allow researchers to open and view the image without handling it. If you decide to use envelopes, make sure that they have a side seam, insert the photograph with emulsion away from the seam, and use care in inserting and removing materials.

Although we normally think of photographic

prints as "the collection," negatives are really the starting point for the image and must be protected with great care. If a negative is scratched, any subsequent prints will reflect that damage. Avoid using negatives as the "use" copy of an image—make reference prints or printouts from a quick scan. Minimize handling of negatives, use gloves, handle by the edges, and never touch or lay negatives down on the emulsion side. Four-flap enclosures are especially useful for larger negatives (4 x 5″, 5 x 7″, 8 x 10″); if you choose to use photograph envelopes, it is prudent to enclose the negatives in clear sleeves within the envelope to avoid abrasion damage. Special paper enclosures and clear sleeves are available for 35mm and other strip negatives. Store negatives separately from prints, not only because the recommended conditions for storage differ, but also as a security precaution: in case of a disaster, you could re-create a collection if you lost only the prints or only the negatives.

Be alert for "vinegar syndrome" in aging negative collections. The telltale smell of vinegar (acetic acid), a by-product of film deterioration, will announce this problem when you open a box.[23] The emulsion on negatives afflicted with vinegar syndrome eventually buckles and wrinkles as the base shrinks and distorts, making the negatives essentially unusable. You can slow the process with proper environment (colder is better, since it slows the chemical reaction), but it is inherent in the materials and will continue to progress. Archival supply vendors offer a barrier paper and boxes that absorb gases, which may be helpful. Be sure to isolate these negatives from other, more stable photographic materials, since the acid fumes are harmful. If the images are valuable, print them immediately and make copy negatives. Work with affected materials in a well-ventilated area.

Another risk in negative collections is the presence of cellulose nitrate film. Produced between 1889 and 1951, nitrate film is unstable, and the fumes it produces as it breaks down are damaging to other materials stored nearby. It is also highly flammable under certain conditions. If your collection includes film negatives that are not marked "safety" on the edge, it is important to ascertain whether you have nitrate negatives that need special

---

23 For a detailed discussion of vinegar syndrome and ways to slow its progress, see Reilly, *IPI Storage Guide*.

attention. As always, do some research, consult an expert, and take appropriate actions.[24]

Glass negatives also present some inherent problems. Glass can break, the emulsion has a tendency to flake, and they are exceptionally heavy. Store glass negatives upright in boxes and pad the box with acid-free board or ethafoam if it is not full, so that they do not lean. Place strong dividers of acid-free corrugated board or ethafoam between groups of negatives to provide additional support. If desired, you can purchase specialized glass negative boxes with slots for each item, but do not reuse old wooden negative boxes, which are not made of inert materials and are affected by changes in humidity, creating stresses on the materials they house. Never overload boxes: thirty 8-x-10″ glass negatives in a standard five-inch document box weigh about twenty pounds, probably the limit for safe and comfortable handling. Label boxes of glass negatives with a bold "Caution! Glass! Heavy!" message on bright paper to alert the person paging the box, so that he or she will not be surprised at the weight and drop the box. Place glass negatives flat on a table when working with them and never stack in-progress materials. Four-flap enclosures are again an excellent choice for the individual items. Always wear gloves when working with glass negatives, to protect both yourself and the negatives. Finally, consider making a print and copy negative so that glass negatives do not have to be used—and endangered—repeatedly.

Your collections certainly contain 35mm slides and may include black-and-white or hand-colored glass lantern slides, an earlier type of projected image. You probably also hold color transparencies, another positive transparent medium that is often used for publication purposes. Housing for color transparencies mirrors negatives: four-flap enclosures work well. Inert sleeves are also an option, but make sure that no dirt is introduced into the sleeve to scratch the transparency. Modern slides can be housed in clear sleeves—a good choice for easy access—or, if demand is low, in metal slide cabinets, which are probably more space efficient. If you have a small number of lantern slides, treat them like glass negatives and store in boxes; for a larger collection you may want to invest in metal slide cabinets designed for these materials. Though a light box is usually sufficient for research use, having a projector available can enhance study of these materials. However, the light is very damaging and causes more rapid fading, so use the projector rarely, briefly, and only in very special cases. Never leave slides or transparencies exposed to light or in a projector for extended periods of time.

Fading and discoloration—particularly toward pink or red tones—are problems commonly seen in aging slide collections. They are caused by the inherent instability of some color films and, in some cases, by the use of motion picture film from the 1960s through 1983[25] (the latter most commonly found in sets of published slides). Once this has occurred, there is nothing that can be done for the original, though it is possible to scan images and digitally correct the color balance.

Scrapbooks and albums

Composite works with incompatible media and supports, such as scrapbooks or photograph albums, may combine photographs with a variety of printed and manuscript text. Album papers are often highly acidic and crumbling, photographs on opposing pages may come in contact with and abrade one another, bindings may be of deteriorating leather. While it is possible—and may be desirable—to preserve such an artifact, the difficulties are immense. Although disassembly of the scrapbook or photograph album may be necessary if the individual components are to survive, removing the photographs from the albums may destroy the integrity of the original scrapbook and the context of the photographs and annotations.

Careful analysis of the problem, consultation with conservators and subject specialists, and a measured approach are critical: do not rush into actions that may be irreversible. You may decide to have a professional conservator treat the volume; you may create a surrogate, take some simple preservation measures (such as interleaving the pages, making sure that the interleaving paper doesn't place undue pressure on the binding), and then carefully store the volume away; or you may decide that it is important to preserve as many of the individual components as possible by removing them from the album. Precede any disassembly with detailed description and documentation, including (at the very least) photocopies of all pages, and perhaps creation of a photographic or digital surrogate. As we have observed above, context increases the value of archival materials, and, in the case of scrapbooks and albums, a great deal of the value—intellectual and monetary—may lie in the compilation.

---

24 Ritzenthaler et al, *Administration of Photographic Collections*, 116–19.

25 Wilhelm, *The Permanence and Care of Color Photographs*, 631.

Reformatting

There occasionally comes a time when a physical object has outlived its lifespan. If we recognize this in time, reformatting may allow the intellectual content of the object to continue on. Photographs that are badly torn and mounted on crumbling, acidic board with fragile, cracked supports or exhibiting flaking emulsion can be treated by conservators (at significant expense). Even after these actions, they may be too fragile for research use. They can also be reformatted: a high-quality copy negative and print can be produced, and the damaged original carefully supported, enclosed, and stored away. Make sure that you clearly identify the originals as reformatted, so that an underinformed staff member who is keen to save the images does not eventually repeat the effort.

Heavily used collections can also benefit from reformatting, to postpone that inevitable day when they are no longer fit for use. If negatives are on hand, new prints can be made and the original photographs retired for only occasional, special-permission use. Producing copy negatives and prints is costly, but may be worthwhile for a valuable collection. Continuous-tone microfilming produces a high-quality 35mm reproduction that is easily used and has the added benefit that reels can be copied and loaned to distant institutions. Digitization may also be a useful tool for creating surrogates for research use, although it comes with many immediate and long-range costs.[26] Photocopying is a low-cost (but low-quality) option that may also allow you to provide enhanced access by creating multiple copies for browsing under different headings.

When considering reformatting, make sure that your actions are part of an overall preservation management plan and that you have a clear-sighted view of the value and the current and potential use of the collection or items. If you have already undertaken a preservation survey, you know the scope of your collections' problems and can place concerns specific to photographic collections on an overall priority list. If not, take some time to evaluate before jumping into a large and potentially costly project.

---

26 See the discussion in the chapter on electronic records.

17

AUDIOVISUAL MATERIALS

Polly Darnell

While fundamental archival principles apply to all materials, some by their nature require special attention. Currently, the bulk of our collections consist of paper records and photographs produced by traditional methods, but myriad forms and combinations of still photographs, moving images, and sound recordings turn up in our archives. Some museums have major collections of these materials; for most of us, small and growing quantities and formats of audiovisual materials are found in the institutional archives, but are not the major component of it.

Sound recordings and moving images are found in all kinds of record groups. For instance, audio tours and slide/audio shows may be part of exhibition files. The education department may have recorded museum programs on audio- and videotape. Curators' files may include film and audiotape field recordings and oral histories. Administrative records may include audiotapes of meetings. The museum may publish videotapes for sale in the museum shop. Curators may have acquired microfiche and microfilm in the course of their research.

The main characteristic that separates these materials from the bulk of our records is the need for machines to access their contents. You can't hear what's on an audiotape without a tape player. And while you can see what's on slides and movie film without a projector, you get only some of the information they contain (on a small scale) without their intended effect. In addition to the need for equipment, the physical nature of the materials leads to different preservation problems and solutions than those for paper and photographic prints on paper.

This chapter provides an overview of a variety of audiovisual formats and issues in preserving and providing access to them, without attempting to define best practices. For further information, consult the sources listed in the bibliography and develop cooperative relationships with other organizations that have an interest in the medium. For instance, the Shelburne

Museum archives has gotten advice about and assistance with sound recordings from the Vermont Folklife Center and the Flanders Ballad Collection at Middlebury College, which have collections of archival recordings. Northeast Historic Film, an archives that collects moving images and has addressed the associated technical and preservation problems, shared advice and technology. Vermont Public Television loaned us seldom-used hand-operated equipment for viewing movie film. The Association of Moving Image Archivists has a film shrinkage guide—an expensive piece of equipment—that it lends to members.

Audiovisual materials enrich the museum archives immeasurably, making them well worth the extra effort they require. Besides helping researchers, making that effort can also bring us closer to the staff who create these records, as we share our knowledge about how long they can be expected to last. More than other formats, audiovisual records demand collaboration—among departments, organizations, and disciplines. They also require more resources. How do we confront the need for additional resources to preserve them? The same way we do for other records: by letting people know what we have that can be of use to them and knowing what it will take to keep them usable. True, some of our materials may not survive until a researcher wants them. But they have a better chance of survival if we take what steps we can by treating them as equals of the paper records and photographs with which we're more familiar.

Nature of the Materials

Sound recordings

Within ten years of Thomas Edison's historic first recording of a human voice in 1877 on a cylinder wrapped in tinfoil, there were two competing kinds of phonographs, each using a different medium to record sound: wax-coated cylinders and flat discs.

Within twenty years, inexpensive phonograph players and recordings were commercially available.

Over the years, three different recording techniques have used a variety of media. The earliest uses a stylus and groove on cylinders or discs. Even as discs replaced cylinders, they were not standardized. They were made of vulcanite (hardened rubber), shellac, acetate over a base of aluminum, and finally vinyl. Formulations and manufacturing processes changed with time. For instance, glass was used as the base for acetate discs during World War II, and cardboard was

Architect I. M. Pei, museum director J. Carter Brown, and donor Paul Mellon (l–r) in the atrium of the newly completed East Building of the National Gallery of Art, 1978. NATIONAL GALLERY OF ART, GALLERY ARCHIVES, WASHINGTON, D.C.

used as the base for home-recording discs. Recording and playback speeds changed from 78 to 33⅓ or 45 rpm (revolutions per minute). Variations in recording technique, first mechanical (i.e., acoustic) and later electrical, produced monophonic and then stereophonic recordings.

Magnetic tape recording was developed in Germany in the 1930s and brought to this country after World War II. Ferromagnetic particles in a thin binder on a base of cellulose acetate or polyester are aligned to copy sound waves during recording. Cellulose acetate was used for the base until the early 1960s, when polyester superseded it. Various additives are used during manufacturing.

With the introduction of a portable, self-contained tape recorder in 1951, sound recording became commonplace, with tapes on open reels in various sizes. Reel-to-reel tapes can have up to twenty-four tracks on them. Cassettes, in which tape is on reels enclosed in a case, were introduced in 1963. Eight-track stereo cartridges, in which the tape is on a continuous loop instead of reels, were introduced in 1966.

Specialized or proprietary formats, such as microcassettes or Dictaphone belts, were developed for office or commercial use, but they employed the same basic techniques and share the same preservation problems. A wire recorder, invented in 1939, was used by the military during World War II and by amateurs until the late 1950s.

Both the grooves on a disc and magnetic particles on a tape or wire physically reproduce the sound waves they record, hence the term *analog* recording. *Digital* recording, on the other hand, encodes the sound waves into binary digits—ones and zeros. The first digital audio compact discs came out in 1982. Digital audiotapes (DAT) were introduced in 1987. Digital formats require software and format-specific machines to interpret the code and translate it back into sound.

Optical discs

Optical discs, so called because they're read by a beam of light, were introduced in 1982. They are made of a core (composed of polycarbonate, metal, or etched glass), a reflective layer (usually aluminum, sometimes gold), and a protective lacquer coating, sometimes with ink on top. The information on them is encoded. On read-only CDs, such as commercial music, it is stamped as pits and flat areas on the disc. The metal alloy surface of writable CDs (WORM, CD-R, CD-RW) changes from amorphous to crystalline form when heated by the laser that writes information on them. They can be used to store encoded sound or images.

Motion pictures

In the hundred-plus years since motion pictures were developed in the 1890s, the media used have not varied quite as much as those for sound recording. Film producers have standardized somewhat on sizes: 35mm for professional motion pictures, 16mm or 8mm for home movies. At times, other sizes have been used by different manufacturers for special purposes, for example the Baby Pathé 9.5mm film introduced in 1922 and the 70mm film currently used in IMAX theaters. Film consists of a base and a layer of gelatin emulsion that contains either bits of silver or color dyes that react to exposure to light and to chemical changes during development. The film base has changed from cellulose nitrate (used as the base for commercial movie film until the early 1950s) to cellulose acetate (introduced in 1912 by the Edison Company in 28mm for special uses and in 1923 by Kodak for home movies) to polyester (about 1960). Originally black and white, movies have been made in color since the mid-1930s, using several different processes. Some involve a negative and intermediate film generations, before getting a final color print on film. In others,

upon development, the film used in the camera becomes the finished film.

Since 1956, when the first practical videotape recorder was developed, over fifty different video formats have been used, including 2″ Quad (the earliest) for professional use, ¾″ U-Matic (1971) for educational and individual use, Betamax (1975) and VHS (1976) for home use, Betacam (1982) for educational and professional use, and finally digital formats, beginning in the mid-1980s.

Combinations

Sound was added to movies first in a separate format, the Vitaphone phonograph disc, which played simultaneously with the film. Eventually the sound was added to a track on the film. Al Jolson's 1926 film *The Jazz Singer* was the first widely distributed, full-length feature film with some synchronized sound, using a

CELLULOSE NITRATE

The speed with which nitrate film deteriorates depends partly on its manufacture and largely on the environment in which it has been stored. As cellulose nitrate film deteriorates, it will fade, soften and become tacky, form bubbles and smell of nitric acid, congeal, and finally turn to brown powder. It should be isolated from other film, as the nitric acid will affect other films, but it should not be stored in airtight cans. According to the Library of Congress, in *Care, Handling and Storage of Motion Picture Film,* "cans of nitrate film that have remained closed for some time should be opened in unconfined, well-ventilated spaces. If gasses given off by decomposing nitrate-based film

are trapped in a confined space—such as in a sealed can—they can ignite at temperatures above 100°F. Nitrate film is highly flammable, ignites easily, and cannot be extinguished after burning has begun."[i] Insurance companies require that it be stored in accordance with local fire regulations, which are generally based on the National Fire Protection Association's recommendations.[ii]

---

i   See http://lcweb.loc.gov/preserv/care/film.html.
ii NFPA 40: Standard for the Storage and Handling of Cellulose Nitrate Motion Picture Film (Quincy, Mass.: National Fire Protection Association, 2001).

CELLULOSE ACETATE

Cellulose acetate (and later polyester) films are known—and were labeled—as "safety" films because they didn't burn as readily or rapidly as cellulose nitrate films. Although Kodak experimented with cellulose acetate as early as 1908, large-scale manufacture didn't start until the 1920s. All Kodak's 8mm and 16mm movie films were cellulose acetate.

Used in both sound recordings and film, cellulose acetate gives off acetic acid, with its distinctive vinegar smell, as it decomposes—hence the name *vinegar syndrome*. Cellulose diacetate was eventually replaced

by cellulose triacetate, but recent research has shown that the triacetate will also deteriorate. As part of the deterioration, the film base shrinks, causing the emulsion (which shrinks at a different rate) to buckle. Once it starts, the process speeds up as it goes along.

The Image Permanence Institute in Rochester, New York, has developed a simple test to tell if vinegar syndrome has started before you can smell the acetic acid, using strips of specially treated paper. The A-D Strips are available from the Institute.

technique that had been pioneered on short films. You can often tell whether a film has a sound track by visual examination. An optical sound track will appear as a squiggly line or one or two strands of small beads running down the space between the image and the sprocket holes. A magnetic sound track will appear as a narrow brown strip in the same area. Sound has also been combined with still images in filmstrips and slide presentations; special audiotapes trigger the projector, which then advances to the next image.

The square-rigged ship *Joseph Conrad,* built in 1882, as photographed in 1935 by Stanley Rosenfeld. Acquired by Mystic Seaport after World War II, the *Conrad* is one of the largest artifacts in the museum's collection and is home to several popular school and interpretive programs. Courtesy Mystic Seaport, Rosenfeld Collection, Mystic, CT.

Transparencies

Transparencies are positive images viewed by shining light through them. Lantern slides, an early form made on glass, were projected for popular entertainment and educational programs in the late nineteenth century. Kodak's Kodachrome was the first direct positive (i.e., no negative) transparency film. It came out in 35mm slide format in 1936. Today, positive transparencies come in other sizes as well. Many museums will have 2-x-2″ slides in their collections, as well as 4-x-5″ and larger transparencies that are used for high-quality printing. These are frequently referred to as "chromes" from the current industry practice of giving positive transparency film a name ending in "chrome" (e.g., Fujichrome, Kodachrome). Negative film names typically end in "color" (e.g., Kodacolor).

Different kinds of mounts have been used over the years, some of them made for use in specific projector trays. Cardboard and plastic mounts hold the film by the edges, while glass mounts sandwich the slide film to provide protection from fingerprints and to hold the film flat during projection for longer than the usual fifteen to thirty seconds. These glass mounts are often used in slide libraries.

Filmstrips are another type of transparency. Microfilm and microfiche, though projected, are actually negative or positive black-and-white film. Though their sizes and projection equipment vary, the media themselves present the same preservation and storage problems as those discussed above.

Appraisal

The appraisal of audiovisual materials in the museum archives will be guided, of course, by your collection policy. However, the answers to questions about your ability to preserve and make audiovisual materials available for use may be more complicated than they are for other materials. Besides preserving the materials, you must maintain (or obtain) machines to play them. Additionally, the inherent instability of some media means they will have to be copied, so you must also decide what medium and method to use. You may find that supporting a limited number of formats will meet your needs.

Having decided which formats you will routinely support, include that information in your collection policy to guide future appraisals. You may, for instance, decide that because slides were routinely used to document your exhibitions and are therefore a major component of exhibition files, you will make special efforts (such as installing cold storage) to preserve them. Conversely, transcripts of lectures given in museum programs could be kept, while deteriorating audiotapes of them may be discarded. Note all such decisions for future archivists.

Appraise audiovisual materials rigorously, carefully identifying their value to your institution and researchers and equally carefully identifying the steps necessary to ensure their continued accessibility. Your appraisal may be done a few items at a time during appraisal, accessioning, or processing of the record groups where they are found, or after a survey of all audiovisual materials in the archives. In either case, maintain a file with information about all audiovisual materials in the collection to help you manage them; keep this administrative file separate from the finding aids used by researchers.

Identify AV holdings by following the same routine you do with paper records. Use your knowledge of the institution, accession records, labels (typed, printed, or handwritten), and adjacent papers. Compile what you learn about which departments used what formats when for what purpose. Check published sources to learn which media were in common use at the time you think the item in question was made. Don't play it. Evaluate its condition by eye first.

Nontechnical criteria in appraising audiovisual materials include whether the material was published, the quality, its original purpose, the condition, and—always—the research value. Was it published by the museum (i.e., duplicated for sale or distribution)? Your collection policy probably addresses museum publications and other products made for sale. If it was commercially published, was it about the museum, or about people closely connected with the museum? Were museum collections used in making it? Answering yes to any of these doesn't automatically mean that you should keep something. Just as you don't necessarily keep every textbook that used an image from the museum, you don't have to keep every item that incorporates an image you own. A local television station's documentary about Vermont in the 1950s that incorporates some footage from a film the museum owns about moving the steamboat *Ticonderoga* to the museum (see sidebar) is at best a library resource and can be weeded out when it is no

CASE STUDY: AV VERSIONS

When the Shelburne Museum moved the last steamboat on Lake Champlain overland two miles to the museum, it hired a photographer to film the move. Partway through, it also hired a cinematographer. Afterward, a company was hired to produce a final, edited version called *Last Voyage of the* Ticonderoga. The film was shown on the boat. Through a distribution company, it was also loaned to television stations and to organizations like the Rotary Club, which showed it to members. Eventually, the museum switched from film to videotape to laser disc on the boat. A preliminary survey of film in the archives labeled "Ti" or "Last Voyage of the *Ticonderoga*" has turned up the following formats related to the museum's movie:

- 16mm film not used in the final version;
- a 35mm reel from the production company;
- two 16mm reels from the production company labeled A and B (possibly the original camera negatives);
- 30 copies (some black and white, some color) of the final film;
- U-Matic videotape copies;
- VHS copies (presumably of the U-Matics).

Still to be determined are whether there are two final versions of different lengths. In addition, there are

- home movies of the Ti move;
- film of the Ti when it was still running excursions on the lake;

- interviews on videotape with the former owner and pilot.

Many of these were not clearly labeled.

Moving the steamboat *Ticonderoga* two miles overland from Lake Champlain to the Shelburne Museum. SHELBURNE MUSEUM ARCHIVES, 4.20.6-45.

longer useful. On the other hand, Mystic Seaport would probably be happy to have movies such as *Java Head* and *Down to the Sea in Ships,* since both feature its ship, the *Charles W. Morgan.* The films were made in the 1920s, nearly two decades before the museum acquired the venerable whaler. The fact that she was used in movies after her career as a whaler ended is a significant part of her history, and the films show her in a way that she cannot be seen now.

In appraising productions in any format, it is essential to know what stage the material you have represents. Some movies, audio-, and videotapes are made in one step, with the film or tape in the camera or recorder becoming the final copy. In other cases, there is considerable editing, with some sections taken out and others added from different sources. Several versions may be made and multiple copies may exist. You need to figure out what elements of a production you have. Paper records are an integral part of a production, including proposals, release forms, contracts, scripts, logs, and promotional materials.

The quality of the material must be considered. Are audio recordings clear enough to hear what is being said?[1] Are images in focus? "Home" movies or videotape often suffer from too much movement. Instead of holding the camera still and panning slowly, amateurs are often too active, swinging the camera this way and that. Do they actually stay still long enough for you to see something of research value? If you have some film of the museum made by a local television station, do you need to keep home movies of someone's visit during the same era, showing the same exhibitions?

If what you have are video or audio field recordings, the quality is a less-important factor. Original research materials that help define objects in your collections— for example, records made during excavations or collecting trips, interviews with artists—are essential. An audio tour by the curator of an exhibition and associated slide shows and videos are important exhibition records. At the Shelburne Museum, a recording of Katharine Prentis Murphy, a collector who furnished one of the historic houses, is more valuable than a recording of a guide giving a tour thirty years later.

Quantity will also enter into your decisions. Slides, for instance, are often produced in great numbers,

whether for commercial sale or internal museum use. Do you need to keep them all?

Condition is often a consideration with audiovisual materials. If it's so bad you can't get a usable copy of it, do you really want to keep it? Is it worth the cost of stabilizing its condition, managing it, and storing it in hopes that technology will someday make it usable? Will anyone want to use it? Will you be able to afford the technology while the original still exists?

You may choose to store some materials of marginal or uncertain value after minimal processing against the day that demand for them justifies the cost of reformatting or their condition justifies discard. With this approach, researchers can learn of their exis-

---

ELEMENTS OF A PRODUCTION

- *Unedited ("raw") footage:* film as shot, before any editing takes place.
- *Camera negative:* film that goes through the camera. During editing it becomes the *cut negative,* with materials removed (*outtakes* and *trims*). Finally it is used to produce the *fine grain master* (or FGM).
- *Dailies:* low-quality positive prints on film of the camera negative for immediate viewing during the production process.
- *Outtakes:* scenes not used in the final version.
- *Trims:* unused portions of scenes that were used in the final version. Often discarded.
- *A & B negative:* cut negative used to create the fine grain master. During editing the camera negative is cut and spliced with blank film into two sequences on separate reels that, when put together, create the single complete film. Not to be confused with the *A & B wind* of the film on the reel (emulsion side in or out) or the *A & B roll* of TV news (A being the person interviewed and B the cutaways of the hands or room furnishings).
- *Fine grain master* (FGM): positive (if black and white) or interpositive (if color) of the cut negative, with titles and credits added, made on high-quality film stock, from which the dupe negative is made.
- *Dupe negative* (DN): negative (if black and white) or internegative (if color) that is used to print multiple copies for distribution.
- *Prints:* positive prints of film for distribution, projection, viewing.

---

1 Sound editing software (for example, Sound Forge or Cool Edit) is now readily available, inexpensive, and relatively easy to use. As a result, the value of poor-quality sound recordings may be increased. For example, noise can be reduced, making older recordings more useful for broadcast, exhibition programs, and research—though at a cost in time and effort.

tence, while the choices that must ultimately be made are delayed.

Preservation

The physical nature of audiovisual materials leads to different preservation problems and solutions than those applicable to paper. Film and magnetic tape are both composed of several layers:

- base (cellulose acetate, cellulose nitrate, polyester)
- binder (gelatin for film; often polyester polyurethane for audio- and video-tapes)
- information (ferromagnetic particles; silver particles for black-and-white photographs; color dyes on film)

Many disc recordings are also made of combinations of materials. Each has different physical characteristics that may cause them to react slightly differently to their environment and to age at different rates. One layer may shrink more than another, leading to distortions. Some components may be very unstable.

The preservation of audiovisual materials has received increasing attention in recent years, leading to the establishment of businesses that specialize in restoration and reformatting of audio- and videotape and film and, more recently, preservation labs with specialized equipment in institutions with major collections. Get professional help when needed. Just as you wouldn't have an amateur bookbinder tackle a binding on a unique volume, don't entrust your videotapes to the local video store.

As with other formats, the environment is of primary importance, as heat and humidity levels may speed up or slow down the chemical reactions causing deterioration. Stability is always a goal, with cooler and drier conditions preferred. Specific recommendations (which often vary from one reference source to another) are noted below, but a stable environment within the general range of 65°F–70°F and 40%–50% RH is considered an acceptable compromise for a range of materials and functions.

Cleanliness is of the utmost importance with any machine-readable material. Always wear clean white cotton gloves when handling audiovisual materials. Store and work with them only in a clean environment. Dirt—even dust or fingerprints—can interfere with the

playback or viewing and will be ground into the material by the machine playing it, multiplying the damage. Air-filtering equipment helps to minimize dust.

Maintain and use equipment based on instructions in the owner's manuals. If you don't have the manuals, contact the manufacturer or a dealer for copies. If you aren't certain of the condition of a machine, try using it first with a nonarchival item. Never put a valuable original into a machine that may not be operating correctly: that's asking for damage. Many originals—vinyl records, for example—lose a

First Lady Hillary Rodham Clinton discusses French paintings with children at the J. Paul Getty Museum in Los Angeles, November 22, 1997. PHOTOGRAPH BY CINDY ANDERSON. ©THE J. PAUL GETTY TRUST.

bit of clarity with each playing and should be played only to make a preservation copy.

Preservation often means creating a number of copies, which will allow you to preserve the original for as long as possible. Preservation copies should be the highest quality possible, made to archival standards using archival materials and stored under the best possible conditions. Identify one preservation copy as the duplication master; use it to make reference copies as needed and to fill requests from researchers for copies. Researchers should always work with use (or service) copies that are made from the duplication master. Label each item clearly, with information tying it to the original and identifying what type of copy it is.

Several formats may be used for copies to serve the various purposes. For instance, the preservation copy of a movie film can be made on film, since the polyester currently used as a film base is more stable than the older nitrate or acetate bases. A Betacam videotape may be made as a master for duplication, with VHS copies for use. DVDs may replace videotapes as the access copy. Many institutions with sound collections are making copies in both analog (either reel-to-reel or cassette tapes) and digital (CD) forms. (DAT tapes are not being used, as they are not as reliable.) Digital formats allow copying from generation to generation with minimal loss of sound quality, but the physical medium (tape, CD) is not necessarily long lasting. At this point, no digital formats are truly archival and all should be considered transitional storage media. Regardless of the estimated longevity of the medium itself, the software to interpret the copy and the hardware to play them may be even shorter-lived. There is no easy answer to the question of what format to use: format obsolescence is one of the most difficult issues media archivists face. Do the best you can with the resources you have and document what you did and why.

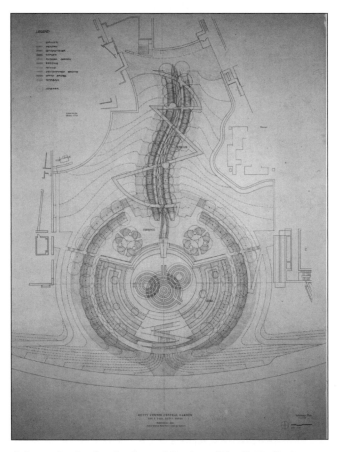

Schematic plan for the Central Garden of the Getty Center, Los Angeles, 1994. Robert Irwin, artist. Drawing by Andrew Spurlock. INSTITUTIONAL ARCHIVES, RESEARCH LIBRARY, THE GETTY RESEARCH INSTITUTE.

Arrangement, Description, and Reference

For safe and efficient storage and convenience of use, audiovisual materials are usually separated from paper-based collections and stored with similar materials. Keep a detailed paper trail linking them to related paper records and to their record group of origin. The paper records may both explain and enhance the value of the audiovisual records and vice versa. For instance, the contract with a video company to produce an orientation film for your museum, the outline, notes about sources, and the like would be found with the records of the department overseeing it, while the video itself would be stored with the audiovisual materials. A separation sheet kept with the paper materials and original location information recorded as part of the AV description maintains links in both directions.

Other papers that may provide critical information are the containers, which may have printed data about the format, as well as handwritten notes. During processing, if original containers are replaced, photocopy all sides on permanent paper to ensure that information is not lost. Keep any papers—logs showing the sequence of shots on a film, for example—found in or with the container, but store them separately, not in the container.

In some institutions (like mine) films, videos, sound recordings, and slides were all gathered together—regardless of their provenance—before an archives program was established. Rather than try to track down their origins, we now keep them as artificial collections.

Finding aids to audiovisual materials require more detail about the physical object than those for paper records. Some specific data elements are listed under the various formats described below. In addition to the creator, date, title, and subject content, your description should identify the format of both the original and any use copies, thus indicating what equipment is needed. In the background note, be sure to include whether the item was created for broadcast or public viewing and whether it was published. There are cataloging standards for both visual materials and sound recordings, just as there are for archives and manuscripts. Even if you store audiovisual materials separately, your finding aids must describe them in context with the related paper materials. Conversely, researchers should be able to find out what you have for audiovisual materials without having to wade through all record group descriptions. Good description will help researchers know whether they do indeed wish to use specific items and will help you know which are worth reformatting for use.

Providing reference service for audiovisual materials means making it possible to view or hear them. Do not use originals for reference. Provide use copies in a standard format for which you maintain equipment for researchers, for example VHS videotape copies of films and audiocassettes of sound recordings. Most of us won't have use copies of all the AV material in our collection ready to hand to the researcher when they are wanted. Your collection policy should address making use copies on request, including who will pay for them and who owns these copies.

Processing

Movie film

Materials: Problems with film stem from both the deterioration of the base and of the color dyes, which fade. Cellulose nitrate was used as the base for professional motion picture film until the early 1950s, while cellulose acetate was used for all of Kodak's home-movie film, starting with 16mm in 1923 and 8mm in 1932. Both will deteriorate, the nitrate more seriously (see sidebars). The next biggest danger to film, after inherent instability—which in many cases can be controlled by a good storage environment—is use and handling. If film has shrunk, for example, sprocket holes will tear in a projector. Film labs use a film shrinkage gauge to test for this.

Storage: Store movie film in a cool environment, 35°F–50°F, with relative humidity (RH) between 20% and 50%. Freezer storage is another alternative, but moisture-proof packaging is essential. Wind the film evenly, with the emulsion side out, on plastic cores (not on reels, which provide uneven support) and store it in undamaged containers made of metal, polypropylene, or archival quality board. Containers should pass the Photographic Activity Test (PAT) to make sure that they will not interact negatively and should usually be vented to allow gas to escape. (Special containers for acetate film that contain molecular sieves to absorb excess acetic acid must be sealed

COLD STORAGE

Slides, motion picture film, and cellulose acetate or nitrate negatives can all benefit from the lower temperatures and relative humidity of "cold storage." This is relatively easy to achieve for small collections.

You can use a conventional home freezer that will maintain a temperature between 0° and -8°F. "Frost-free" (not "cycle-defrost") freezers[iii] are acceptable, as the temperature only jumps for a minute or two a day when the coils are heated. The melted ice then runs to a pan and evaporates. Either upright or chest-style freezers can be used, but it's easier to access collections in an upright freezer. Dedicate the freezer to this use: a freezer that is used to store food is opened too often to maintain even temperatures.

Package collections in moisture-proof storage containers. One archival supply company sells a "freezer kit" with supplies and directions for packing photographs. When removed for use, the collections *must* remain in the closed packaging until they have come up to room temperature to avoid condensation problems. Allow several hours for this process.

When planning or packing for cold storage, consider the way the stored collections are used. Smaller containers with related materials are better than large containers with unrelated images. For fast retrieval, keep a record of what is in cold storage, including a diagram of where boxes are on the shelves and make sure that box labels face the door. Maintain a log of what is removed, when, for what purpose, and when it is returned, just as you do for materials retrieved from closed stacks. Set up a procedure to monitor the freezer temperature (you can use a thermometer with a remote sensor that allows you to check the inside temperature without opening the door) and an alert system for power outages. In the case of an extended power loss, you may want to remove the collections once the temperature rises above freezing, to avoid damage from elevated humidity levels.[iv]

For storage of nitrate movie film, see NFPA 40.[v]

---

iv For standards on preparing and handling cold-storage materials, see ANSI/NAPM I9.20-1996, *Imaging Material: Processed Silver-Gelatin Type Black-and-White Film, Specifications for Stability.*

v NFPA 40: *Standard for the Storage and Handling of Cellulose Nitrate Motion Picture Film* (Quincy, Mass.: National Fire Protection Association, 2001).

---

iii Henry Wilhelm, *The Permanence and Care of Color Photographs* (Grinnell, Iowa: Preservation Publishing Co., 1993), 666.

to work.) Stack uniformly sized containers horizontally no more than twelve inches (or six canisters) high. Nothing should be in the can with the film, not even papers. Photocopy the original container on permanent paper if the contents are rehoused and retain any printed or written information on it.

Description: Descriptive elements for basic identification of movie film include

- *Film gauge:* 8mm, Super 8mm, 16mm, 35mm
- *Film base:* Until you can have it tested, consider 35mm film nitrate unless it says "safety" on the edge of the film or you know it dates from after the mid-1950s.
- *Emulsion:* negative, positive, internegative, interpositive, separation, print
- *Length:* Running time in minutes (for video) or feet (for film)
- *Color or black and white*
- *Silent or sound*
- *Quantity:* number of reels
- *Condition:* Does it have tears, crinkles, sticky emulsion, brittleness, scratches, torn perforations, an odor? Has it shrunk?
- *Reference copy available?*

Special practices: To view film without running it through a projector, you can use hand-operated rewinds and a standing loupe or magnifying glass over a light box. If you know from external evidence that the film is something you'll want, just go ahead and have preservation and reference copies made.

Martin Johnson with camera in Africa. AMERICAN MUSEUM OF NATURAL HISTORY LIBRARY, NEG. #13153.

Audiodiscs (phonograph recordings)

Materials: Generally, among discs, vinyl is the most stable and acetate the least, though environmental conditions and manufacturing will affect how well they last.

Storage: Sound recordings should be stored in an environment of no higher than 59°F–68°F with a relative humidity of 25%–45% in soft polyethylene inner sleeves (not paper, cardboard, or PVC sleeves) inside appropriate boxes. Shelve discs vertically, like sizes together, with even support every four to six inches. Boxes designed for discs will provide this support.

Description: Your description of phonograph recordings should include as much of the following as you know:

- *Total playing time*
- *Playing speed*
- *Size of disc*
- *Type of sound:* mono, stereo, high fidelity
- *Material:* vinyl, acetate
- *Stylus:* size and shape

Special practices: Never touch the surface of a recording, even with white cotton gloves. Hold discs by the edges only. Do not wipe discs with a dust cloth. Do not stack them. In creating your preservation copy, especially using digital technology, you will have to address issues of how faithfully to duplicate the original. Generally, preservation copies should match the original as closely as possible: scratches, hiss, pops, and all. Any improvements to the sound or image can be made on another copy.

Magnetic media (video- and audio-tapes)

Materials: The best-known threat to polyester magnetic tape is sticky shed syndrome, the chemical deterioration of the binder that holds the magnetic particles. Acetate tape's base is threatened by vinegar syndrome. Humidity is the major contributor to both processes, and it should always be kept under control, but there are other threats as well, including dust, poor handling, and machines not working well.

Storage: Stable conditions in the range of 65°F–70°F and 40%–50% RH are necessary for all magnetic media, with cooler and drier conditions preferred.[2] In addition, keep them away from strong magnetic fields, though magnetic fields are more likely to affect older tapes than newer ones. Containers should be made of inert plastic. Wind or rewind tapes all the way through without stopping. Wind audiotapes at playing speeds (not fast forward or rewind) and store "tails out" (played, but not rewound), if the tape is recorded on a single side, to minimize the effects of print through. A smooth pack or wind is important; no tape edges should stick up above others. Store videotapes standing upright, with the full reel at the bottom.

Description: It may be useful in the long run to know what kind of machine a tape was recorded on. If you have such information, be sure to keep it. As with other formats, your description should include the duration (i.e., running time) of tapes, the size, the format, and the number of tapes in a title. A sample physical description might be "1 videocassette (1 of 1 in title) (Betamax) (30 minutes), sound, color, ½ inch." The context in which it was made may vary considerably with tapes. Were they made for broadcast, as a report, an interview, or on-the-spot? Were they for use by museum visitors, as part of an exhibition or as part of an audio tour of an exhibition?

Special practices:
- Never touch the tape.
- Always label the individual tape reel or cassette shell, as well as its container.
- Have copies made as soon as you notice deterioration.
- Punch out the erase tabs on video- and audiocassettes to prevent accidental reuse.
- Periodic rewinding has been commonly recommended, but is being reconsidered. Inspect your collection periodically, and if you see tapes that don't look evenly wound, rewind them.
- Handle reel-to-reel tapes by the hub (i.e., center) or the edges; never put pressure on the flanges.
- Don't use videotape rewinders as they don't maintain an even tension. Use a regular VCR instead.
- Remove the heads from a reel-to-reel tape recorder used exclusively for winding, but adjust the tension to compensate for the change.

---

2   For more detailed information about a range of storage and operating conditions, see Koichi Sadashige, "Storage Media Environmental Durability and Stability," *Data Storage Technology Assessment 2000*, Part 2 (St. Paul: National Media Laboratory) [text distributed on CD-ROM].

Slides

Materials: Slides are subject to color changes, as well as to deteriorating film base. The color stability of different slide films varies widely, both in dark storage and during exposure to light. Those on cellulose acetate film base (see sidebar) may develop vinegar syndrome as the base breaks down.

Storage: All color slides will fade, but the environment can make a big difference in the speed. Slides should be stored in the dark, in a stable environment between 60°F and 70°F, with a relative humidity of 30%–50%. Better yet, put them in cold storage or in a freezer (see sidebar). Choose storage containers based upon how they're used and how frequently. Slides are best stored either in individual sleeves in boxes or in heavy-duty polypropylene pages that can be put in notebooks, boxes, or specialized hanging slide files.

Description: Because slides exist in such quantity, they're rarely described individually, unless that is done when they are created. If you have any influence, try to have staff members who create slides label them with the photographer and date, at a minimum. Your collection description will include the subject matter. You may have, after all, fifty slides of one exhibition. Related records will tell what the various objects in the exhibition are. Include in the physical description the size of the slides and type of film, if known.

Special practices: Don't project valuable original slides or allow them to be exposed to light any longer than necessary. Light damage is cumulative; if someone working on a slide project is interrupted, return the slides to the dark. Make copies for use and keep a set of original slides for the archives, preferably in cold storage. Low-use slide collections may go into cold storage with duplication on demand, instead of wholesale duplication. You'll need advance notice when they are needed, since materials taken from cold storage must acclimate before their moisture-proof containers are opened.

Optical discs

Materials: The life expectancy of optical discs (most commonly, compact discs or CDs) depends on their manufacture and on storage conditions—it is estimated at anywhere from ten to two hundred years. The composition of CDs has varied in the years since their introduction in the early 1980s.

Some are less stable than others, as the reflective layer may oxidize and the layers may delaminate.

Storage: Store CDs vertically in rigid cases of inert plastic (such as their polystyrene "jewel cases"), in the dark. Never bend or put pressure on CDs. Maintain stable conditions in the range of 65°F–70°F and 40%–50% RH, with cooler and drier conditions preferred.

Description: The description of CDs should include notes about their physical characteristics, the software needed to decompress and interpret them, and the hardware necessary to play them.

Special practices: Never use adhesive labels on CDs intended for long-term storage. The label can throw the CD out of balance and the adhesive may damage the CD's protective coating. Try to avoid writing on CDs, but if you must, write only on the inner ring and use a water-based marker with a soft tip.

18

ARCHITECTURAL RECORDS

Maygene Daniels

Conceptual renderings, construction drawings, specifications, building photographs, landscape plans, and other architectural records have particular importance for museums. Museums are places. Their buildings protect collections, safeguard specimens, hold exhibitions. The availability and size of spaces such as auditoriums, classrooms, and laboratories shape museum programs. The buildings themselves are often landmark structures identified with the museum's creation and history. Buildings and landscape settings—whether natural or urban—are critical elements in day-to-day operations of museums and help shape their institutional character. For this reason, architectural and landscape records are among the most important documents in a museum's archives.

Architectural records have multiple values and uses for museums. They are an important source of information for the plumbers, electricians, masons, carpenters, and others who maintain heavily used museum facilities and keep complex systems operating efficiently. Architectural records are important tools when buildings are retrofitted to accommodate increased numbers of visitors, high-speed telecommunications, improved access for the handicapped, or special programs. They are often used by designers who adapt exhibition spaces and install new presentations.

In addition to these day-to-day uses, architectural records are important during renovation and expansion projects. Architects depend on information about the design and structure of existing buildings as they plan for major changes and additions. The location of structural supports, the capacity of mechanical systems, the materials and construction of the roof, and other architectural data can be important to plans for expansion and change. Architectural documents provide this information reliably and efficiently. Protecting and preserving architectural materials in a museum archives can save both time and money.

Beyond the practical, landmark museum buildings and landscapes are themselves subjects for research and historical study. No less than other records in a museum's archives, architectural documents can serve the needs of scholars and provide information of broad public interest. Architectural drawings, renderings, and photographs also are often beautiful objects in their own right, suitable for exhibition, for publication, and as inspiration for sales items. Architectural images and designs can be used as potent symbols of the museum's identity.

The Survey

The first step in developing an effective institutional approach for architectural records is to survey building and landscape documentation throughout the institution. As in any records survey, materials in every physical format should be identified and described by subject, quantity, organization, physical form, and date. Storage conditions and use also should be noted. Important types of architectural documents likely to be found in museums include:[1]

- Drawings documenting the architect's conception of building design, including preliminary sketches, design development drawings, and other materials that precede scale drawings. These materials may belong to the architect, but often are transferred to the museum under contract or by request.

- Architectural renderings, landscape drawings, and three-dimensional models. These are materials usually prepared by the architect or designer to present a concept for the proposed building project to the museum and its

---

1 *Envisioning Architecture: An Analysis of Drawing* by Iain Fraser and Rod Henmi (New York: Van Nostrand Reinhold, 1994) is very helpful in understanding types of architectural drawings that might be found in museums.

trustees. They may be found framed or on display and are likely to be of interest for future exhibitions.

- Construction files. These include subject or chronological files created and maintained by the museum during a building project. Reports concerning building requirements, correspondence with the architect, meeting memoranda, and other records documenting building progress, requirements, and changes are likely to be included. The museum's copies of building permits and inspection reports also may be part of the files.

- Construction or working drawings. These are drawings, drawn to scale, prepared by the architectural firm, and released to contractors for construction bids. They then are used—and often altered—during building construction. Construction drawings can include site plans, excavation diagrams, architectural and structural drawings, sections and floor plans, diagrams for mechanical and electrical systems, landscape designs, and other scale drawings. They are the most extensive documents generated during building construction and usually the most important for ongoing building work and structural maintenance.

- Specifications. These are written documents from the architect that give detailed technical instructions to the builder concerning such subjects as building materials and mechanical system requirements to supplement construction drawings.

- Photographs showing building progress including site clearing, excavation, and construction. Often construction photographs are taken from a fixed viewpoint at regular intervals, such as once a month, to provide a systematic view of building progress. Builders are commonly required by contract to supply construction photographs to document their work.

- Shop drawings, usually created by specialized subcontractors. These are scale drawings detailing specific aspects of building construction or finishing.

- Equipment manuals, building warranties, maintenance contracts, and operating instructions for building systems. These may be delivered to the museum by the building contractor or acquired over time as new equipment and systems are installed.

- Building operation records, including administrative correspondence, maintenance records, utilities information, repair records, and other materials relating to ongoing building management.

Documents found during the survey should be evaluated to determine which groups of materials should remain in active office files, which should be transferred to the archives, and which should eventually be discarded. Decisions should be made in consultation with administrative and building management staff.

Conceptually, archives seek to bring into their holdings only documents that are non-current and are no longer needed day-to-day for ongoing business. Yet valuable architectural records with information on museum buildings will continue to be consulted and used for building maintenance and renovation, irrespective of their age. Even though architectural records are used in the present, they will be needed in the future, as long as

Office of John Russell Pope, detail of interior architectural decoration for the West Building of the National Gallery of Art, 1939. Blueprint.
NATIONAL GALLERY OF ART, GALLERY ARCHIVES, WASHINGTON, D.C.

buildings remain in use. Building administrators and maintenance personnel, experts in their crafts and professions, are not necessarily reliable custodians of irreplaceable records. For this reason, there is an important ongoing role for museum archives.

Records that document fundamental building design and structure in particular have long-term value for the museum. Of these, construction drawings are probably the most common type of architectural document in the museum and the most important for ongoing facilities work and for long-term historical retention. Construction drawings are easily recognized. During the twentieth century, architects generally prepared construction drawings in systematic series, usually labeled with letter abbreviations to indicate the type of drawing: "A" for architectural, "E" for electrical, "M" for mechanical, and so on. Although practices (and letter identifications) have varied over time, the series usually are consistent and tightly organized. Drawings within a series are sequentially numbered and thus easily identified and distinguished from one another.

Each drawing may exist in many versions, reflecting changes, both large and small, made during construction. Each time it is revised, the architect redates the drawing. The various versions of each drawing thus are distinguished by the last revision date, noted in the title block. The later the date of the drawing, the more likely that it will be an accurate representation of building conditions.

After construction is complete, contracts often require builders to prepare final "as-built" drawings to record the work as performed. The information in as-built drawings generally supersedes all previous versions of the drawings.

The individual construction drawings are the building blocks of the museum's architectural collection. As museum offices and storerooms are surveyed, each drawing should be identified and listed by series and number (A-13, E-76) together with the most recent revision date or "as-built" notation. Because drawings often have been roughly used or heavily annotated, their condition and any additional notes written on a particular copy should be recorded. The latest revision of each construction drawing should be identified and saved. These should include all significant drawings showing the building's design, materials, and architectural characteristics. Mechanical, electrical, and other systems drawings also have long-term administrative value, although, in principle, these can be eliminated should they become superseded or obsolete.

While the archives, in principle, should hold key documents with long-term value, operating offices also need copies for immediate reference. Fortunately, multiple copies of drawings frequently already exist within the museum. Depending on the time period of the construction, drawings usually were created on a reproducible medium such as coated linen or transparent Mylar that can be repeatedly copied to create multiple inexpensive sepia, blueprint, blueline, or diazo prints. More recently, electronic files also have been used as the source for multiple printed copies.

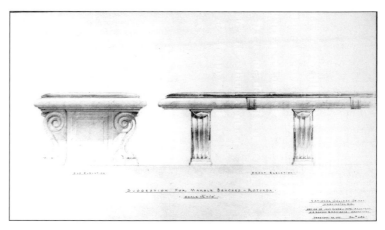

Office of John Russell Pope, suggestion for marble benches, rotunda, 1939. Graphite with gray wash and white gouache. NATIONAL GALLERY OF ART, GALLERY ARCHIVES, WASHINGTON, D.C.

When drawings needed for ongoing business are well organized and safely stored in building management or architectural offices, it may be appropriate to leave them in their existing location. Nonetheless, the archives should remain cooperatively involved and should be prepared to assume physical custody of the materials when they are no longer needed for regular use. The archives is the ideal storage location for any documents and drawings with long-term value, and archivists should seek to acquire valuable architectural documents to the greatest extent possible in keeping with practical museum management concerns.

While the primary goal of the survey of architectural records is to determine the nature of architectural documents as a guide for deciding which should be retained in operating offices and which transferred to the archives, a secondary purpose is to allow destruction of all of the unneeded extra and superseded copies of drawings, specifications, and other materials. The quantity of unneeded materials can be extraordinary. Disciplined housecleaning often brings unwieldy piles and rolls of confused materials down to a manageable size and serves both operating offices and the archives well.

Office of John Russell Pope, model of the proposed National Gallery of Art building, 1939. Plaster. NATIONAL GALLERY OF ART, GALLERY ARCHIVES, WASHINGTON, D.C.

In general, records that document continued building operation and maintenance are of little long-term value when no longer needed for building administration. These documents generally can be maintained in facilities management offices until they are replaced by more up-to-date information. Records schedules are useful tools to describe and track temporary records and to organize timely disposition.

Physical Management

Physical management and storage of architectural materials, especially drawings, is a particular challenge.[2] Construction drawings are large, unwieldy, and often tattered. They are difficult to store, burdensome to move, challenging to copy. Appropriate space and storage equipment are particularly important to manage them successfully.

Optimally, large drawings should be stored unfolded in large, flat, metal file cabinets (often known as "flat files" or "map cases") sized to accommodate the drawings. If space permits, the file cabinets can be stacked to tabletop height, creating important working space for organizing and examining the documents. Within each flat-file drawer, the drawings should be stored in large archival folders, no more than ten to fifteen drawings per folder. Protective folders should always be used when individual drawings are

removed from the drawers and transferred from place to place. Because of their size and weight, the folders may require two staff members to move safely.

Oversized drawings should be rolled on acid-free cardboard tubes and wrapped with archival paper for protection from dirt and light.

Architectural renderings should be placed in protective mats and should be stored flat in drawers or boxes.

Because of space limitations, storage compromises are often necessary to accommodate architectural drawings. Architects' offices maintain some less-used drawings, especially voluminous shop drawings, folded and filed in traditional file drawers, frequently with the title block on the outside of the folded drawing. In the archives, previously folded drawings can be stored folded in cubic-foot-sized acid-free boxes, as long as they are not heavily used.

If rolled or folded drawings are to be stored flat, they should be opened carefully and weighted with felt-covered bricks until they lie flat naturally. Torn or brittle items should be examined by conservators and possibly humidified prior to unrolling or flattening.

Drawings that are received flat should not be folded. If adequate drawer space is not available, the drawings should be rolled on the outside of acid-free tubes (as described above) and stored on large shelves. Although this option protects the drawings, it also makes them relatively difficult to retrieve and examine.

The museum's conservators may be an excellent source of advice concerning the impact of various storage options on materials with different physical characteristics and use requirements. Temperature, humidity, dust, and light controls should be the same for architectural documents as for other forms of archival materials on paper.

Arrangement

Intellectually, the arrangement of architectural materials in an archives is simple and straightforward. As with all archival materials, architectural records should be assigned to record groups, in principle based on the office that used and maintained them. Because some architectural materials are found repeatedly in different offices, however, in practice this can create extensive repetition and confusion. For practical efficiency, one record group can be designated to hold the master set of all construction drawings.

---

2   *A Guide to the Archival Care of Architectural Records, 19th and 20th Centuries,* prepared by the Architectural Records Section of the International Council on Archives (Paris: ICA, 2000), is the most comprehensive guide to the archival care of architectural records.

Beyond the record group, architectural documents, including files, photographs, specifications, and other materials, should be arranged following the same principles as other institutional records. This also is true of construction drawings, which, although usually the most extensive series of documents, also are the easiest to organize, even for the nonspecialist. As described above, architectural drawings usually are precisely identified in predetermined series with each drawing assigned an alphanumeric designation. Following this scheme, architectural drawings can easily be placed in numerical order, item-by-item. This ensures that the heavy, awkward drawings will be handled as little as possible when they are needed.

Large architectural drawings should be handled with particular care during the process of arrangement. Large, flat surfaces are important to accommodate the drawings comfortably so that they can be manipulated without damage.

Description

Just as other archival materials are managed primarily at the series level, architectural documents too should be understood and described as related groups of materials using the established tools of archival practice. In addition, many architectural records—particularly construction drawings—may need to be described at the item level. Architects and building managers use architectural drawings and other documents for specific and very practical reasons: to repair a leaking roof, to determine the square footage of the parking lot, to establish a floor load. Skimming through many drawings to find such detailed information would be impractical, if not impossible. A database with item-level information on each drawing is an ideal tool to ensure that enough information is available to locate a needed document.

In planning the description program, a database with flexibility and strong text search capabilities should be selected. It should have variable fields able to handle lengthy titles and extensive descriptive notes. Other capabilities, especially the ability to create attractive printed reports, are also valuable. The database should be planned carefully and tested before implementation. It should contain detailed data on each drawing, including at least the name of the architectural project or building, the drawing's alphanumerical designation, its title, latest revision date, medium, size, and scale. Administrative information,

including the number of copies, condition, and storage location, is extremely useful as well.

The goal of the archives should be to create an efficient, comprehensive system that can be realistically completed with available resources. In most cases, information in the database should be limited to data that can be obtained directly from the drawing. Extensive research on peripheral issues can take unnecessary time and, given limited resources, may make it far more difficult to provide basic information on all drawings in the archives.

Postcard of the Textile and Fine Arts Building in Fair Park, Dallas, Texas, ca. 1910. COURTESY OF THE ARCHIVES, DALLAS MUSEUM OF ART.

Several groups, including the Architectural Records Committee of the International Council on Archives and the Architectural Drawings Advisory Group of the Getty Research Program, have developed model forms and information elements to include in describing architectural records, especially at the item level.[3] These can provide useful ideas as you create new descriptive tools.

Use and Reproduction

Architectural records are likely to be used most frequently by museum administrators, especially for buildings and grounds projects. All architectural records, just as other materials in the archives, should be

3 *A Guide to the Description of Architectural Drawings,* developed by the Architectural Drawings Advisory Group of the Getty Art History Information Program (New York: G. K. Hall, 1994) contains detailed information concerning descriptive terms for architectural documents. Kelcy Shepherd and Waverly Lowell, *Standard Series for Architecture and Landscape Design Records: A Tool for the Arrangement and Description of Archival Collections* (Berkeley: University of California, ca. 2000) gives many useful examples of different types of architectural records and archival finding aids.

made fully available for these official uses. Ideally, museum staff members who need building information will study drawings in the archives to determine which ones may be needed for their work. Although extra copies of drawings may be loaned with strict controls, borrowing of unique items should not be permitted.

Much architectural, engineering, design, and construction is done by outside companies on contract, who are also likely to need the museum's construction drawings and other architectural materials for their work. These documents frequently include security-

Brooklyn Museum façade lit for the Hudson-Fulton Centennial, 1909.
BROOKLYN MUSEUM OF ART ARCHIVES, PHOTOGRAPH COLLECTION. MUSEUM EXTERIORS: HUDSON-FULTON CELEBRATION (NEG. #25).

restricted information that would not normally be made available to the public. The museum should establish an institutional policy that requires contract bidders or contractors to agree to use information they are provided only for the purpose of the museum's architectural project. They also should be required to transfer documents to the museum when the project is complete.

Museum staff members and contractors who consult architectural materials in the archives often need hard copies of selected drawings for detailed study, annotation, reference, and comparison to actual building conditions. Small drawings, specifications, and similar documents can be easily copied using readily available office copiers. Oversized drawings, however, can be difficult and expensive to reproduce, although document scanning technologies can now create high-quality products far more easily than in the past.

Although some museums have on-site copying facilities, typically drawings must be sent to reprographics vendors who provide copying services to

architects. If drawings are sent off-site for reproduction, the archives must ensure that the vendor's personnel are trained to handle unique materials with appropriate care. Fragile drawings or those with torn edges should be placed in clear polyester folders for protection while the drawings are scanned. Electronic files captured through the scanning process should be saved for later use. Almost every architect, engineer, or building manager will prefer to work with a printed copy, which can be produced most easily from the electronic file.

Microfilm copies or 135mm microfiche of architectural drawings have other important but distinct purposes. They are a reliable, proven technology for storing extensive information compactly. Microforms can be easily copied and can provide a quick reference to building information. Existing micrographic copies of architectural drawings should be preserved and used as much as possible to limit wear-and-tear on original drawings. Nonetheless, drawn-to-scale information is difficult to capture in micrographic form, and microfilm and microfiche lack some of the advantages of scanned drawings. Micrographics are gradually being supplanted by newer electronic technologies.

Reference Service

Museum buildings and their surroundings are often landmarks that are of interest in the study of architecture, landscape design, cultural history, and other subjects. For that reason, the archives access policy should provide that architectural records generally are available to researchers in accordance with the same rules that apply to public use of other museum records. At the same time, the physical characteristics and sensitive information in architectural documents may require special consideration and adjustments to general policies.

Because of the size and awkwardness of architectural drawings, special reference and research arrangements are usually needed. If surrogates of architectural drawings such as photographs or microfilm are available, researchers should be required to consult these as a first step. When researchers are permitted to consult original drawings, a large, clear tabletop space is needed. To avoid hazardous crowding, the number of researchers permitted to use drawings at one time can be limited. Tracing or writing on top of the documents should never be permitted.

Most important, in establishing an access policy for architectural records, the museum should be aware of the need to restrict access to certain information to protect museum security. Data on mechanical and electrical systems, collections storage areas, the security console, restricted building areas, and telecommunications installations, among other subjects, would be of little interest to scholars, but of significant value to thieves or terrorists. The policy should be established in cooperation with museum security personnel to ensure protection of sensitive information. If there seems to be a conflict between museum security and legitimate scholarly interest, it may be possible to eliminate sensitive information from copies of some documents for researcher use.

CAD Systems and Electronic Technologies

Architects, engineers, and landscape designers now use CAD (computer-aided design and drafting) systems in almost every architectural project. The electronic file is thus rapidly becoming the principal form of architectural drawing and is often one of the "deliverables" required by contract. This has many advantages, particularly in the ease with which electronic files can be copied and sent via the Internet for use off-site. Nonetheless, electronic architectural files, like all other forms of electronic records, are extremely fragile and impermanent. They must be actively maintained, usually through a strategic combination of creating multiple copies of electronic files on various media and periodically refreshing the data.

Even if the electronic files themselves are successfully preserved, however, their use is highly dependent on specific software. In all likelihood, current genera-

tions of CAD files will be illegible by computer systems of the future. If CAD system data is regularly used, maintained, and migrated to new systems, it may continue to be useful. This is, however, difficult to ensure. For that reason, for the present, archivists should plan to maintain redundant hard copies of key construction drawings and building information, at least until the ability to retain and retrieve electronic files for the long term has been demonstrated.

CAD systems also are being used increasingly to maintain and manipulate building information for day-to-day use. These graphic systems have the ability to store data about building structure in layers, making it possible to see separate systems, such as electrical, mechanical, or plumbing installations, grafted onto basic building data. CAD systems have great potential for recording and maintaining up-to-date information about museum buildings, even as systems change and repairs are made. They also are a ready source of data frequently needed for museum management.

Over time, as CAD and other electronic systems improve, it is likely that certain architectural documents in the archives that primarily are needed for museum management will become obsolete. At that point, these materials, probably relating to building systems, can be eliminated from archival holdings. No system, however, will ever supersede the essential historical information relating to the origin, the design, the character, and the construction of museum buildings and grounds. Design development materials, construction drawings and photographs, architectural renderings, and models will continue to be important for an understanding of the museum and its character and should remain a significant concern of every museum archivist.

19

ELECTRONIC RECORDS

Fynnette Eaton

Museums, like most institutions, employ computers to carry out many functions. Much of the information that used to be created by separate offices is now shared electronically through a network, increasing efficiency throughout the organization. This chapter addresses the ever-increasing use of electronic information, which can become electronic records[1] that archivists must deal with or lose. We will discuss the types of electronic records that are being created in a museum setting, the issues you must consider in planning for the long-term appraisal and preservation of electronic records, and the electronic systems that you might use to provide access to and manage your collections. We will also take a brief look at digitization, where archivists are beginning to create their own collections of a particular type of electronic record—the digital image. Electronic records and digitization are relatively new to archivists, and no firm answers or procedures are yet in place, but it is imperative to think about these issues, keep up with current research, and begin to work on implementing programs in our institutions.

---

1   For the purposes of this chapter, *records* are documents made or created in the course of carrying on the institution's business, in whatever format: paper, audiovisual—or electronic.

Types of Electronic Records

The electronic record systems used by your museum probably reflect the full range of its activities. Administrative functions yield the widest variety of computer applications: database systems to administer payroll, accounting, and personnel; e-mail; and document-sharing systems. One of the major innovations in the past five to ten years has been the consolidation of these administrative functions in software so that information can be shared and used for different activities. These Enterprise Resource Planning (ERP) systems are intended to reduce and simplify the amount of data entry required by administrative staff.

In the past, most offices had central files and administrators had secretaries responsible for maintaining the files. At some levels this may still exist, but with the introduction of the personal computer, secretaries and office assistants are less likely to perform this function and we are learning that this may mean the loss of key documentation for all types of offices and organizations. Most correspondence, internal and external, is now created electronically, as are reports, grant proposals, and all of the "paperwork" of an organization. These documents may be found on an individual's office computer or, at best, on a network drive. On a network or shared drive, information may be stored in a file folder, providing access to all accredited staff. Context, in the archival sense of a virtual "folder," may or may not be obvious.

E-mail is rapidly becoming the chosen method of communication. Many, if not most, institutions now send nearly all internal communications via e-mail, from critical policy decisions to daily meeting schedules. External correspondence depends heavily on e-mail as well; e-mail appears to be starting to replace the facsimile (fax) as the preferred solution for everyday business. Beyond simple e-mail messages, documents are often transmitted electronically as an attachment to an e-mail message, a link that may not remain active even if the message is saved. How to connect related electronic documents is a real concern.

Collections management systems (also called collection-information systems) are relational databases used by museums to catalog their collections. These complex databases, provided as turnkey systems by specialized vendors or developed in-house, collect and manage information about the museum's object collection, including descriptions of the items, conditions, creators, locations, rights and reproductions, and donor information. In many cases, digital images of the objects described in the database are linked to the description. Collections management systems are replacing the card catalogs long used by registrars to properly administer their collections. They are used for many other functions, as well. Among these ancillary functions—formerly documented in independent, dispersed, paper record systems—are loan administration; storage and movement tracking; exhibition planning and implementation; and accessioning and deaccessioning. Curators use the system to record detailed cataloging and research data. A public version of the database may be made available on a museum Web site for external use.

Scholars of all types serve on museum staffs and create a wide variety of research files—as noted earlier in this manual—in every imaginable electronic format. Field notes, research databases, spreadsheets, CAD drawings of archaeological sites all exist on researchers' computers at the museum, on the museum network, and on their laptops at home and as they travel. These electronic records develop over time and may exist in formats ranging from the most current to the most archaic. When an important staff member retires, the archives may have to attempt to re-create a life's work in a process akin to an archaeological dig.

Dealing with Electronic Records

Many records are now created electronically, and while the final copy of some documents may still be printed onto paper and filed at your institution, a significant portion of records remain electronic throughout their life cycle.[2] E-mail is replacing correspondence and memos; your museum probably uses administrative systems to deal with financial transactions, personnel actions, and payroll; a collections

management system tracks the museum's objects; documents are created with word processing software and stored electronically; and various types of research databases store and manipulate critical data. Within the archives, you could be using a database to track and describe the materials in your custody, receiving a majority of your reference inquiries by e-mail, and placing your finding aids on your Web site to encourage greater use of your holdings. Staff members need concrete advice on how to manage all electronic records, including e-mail, *as they are created*. Archives staff must also ensure the retention of inactive records that have long-term value, either as part of the archives program or in conjunction with other departments. Both of these actions are critical in documenting the museum's activities: a "wait-and-see" attitude at this point can lead to the loss of critical documentation.

As you begin to develop an electronic records program, look closely at your institution to determine the best ways to deal with all of the issues associated with electronic records, working with your technology staff to manage the records, deciding whether to hire an outside contractor, and working out an interdepartmental resource-sharing plan to perform the necessary tasks of storing and providing access to archival electronic records. If you decide to assume custody of electronic records in the archives, you will need to determine which types of records to accept, what the costs will be for performing this function, and whom you will need to assist you to succeed in this challenging task.

The first step is a technology survey—you may want to study and adapt the steps discussed in the surveys chapter earlier in this manual. Which word processing, spreadsheet, workflow, or database packages are in use? Are most staff members using one type of word processing software? If so, you only need to commit to providing access over time to one word processing system to accept documents, not three or four. Or, is technology decentralized, so that you will have to find a way to deal with a variety of software packages?

Identify what types of electronic files are important to your organization—and consider the *information* maintained in electronic formats. Do not be either frightened off or overly impressed by the unfamiliar format—archivists are expert at analyzing information. Carefully study what is worth preserving, considering costs, risk analysis, and (limited) resources. One of the fallacies that you will confront is the common view that because it is so cheap to store electronic information and it really does not take up much space, you can and should keep everything. (Keeping everything,

---

2   At the Smithsonian Institution, there has been a noticeable decline in the thickness of folders being transferred to the archives. In one example, the size of the transfer decreased to one-third of what they were five years ago.

of course, may mean that you can't find anything, particularly if it's not well organized.) Long-term care of electronic files is more than just storage: maintaining these types of records presents archivists with demanding preservation and access issues.

Review the appraisal criteria that you have developed for the paper records. Does an electronic format change your reasoning? Certain types of paper records had only temporary value—are they now worthy of long-term preservation in the new format? Conversely, are there things you can now conveniently save in electronic format that were too bulky or difficult to use in paper format?[3] For example, your institution's Web site may present information about exhibitions, events, hours of operation, images from the collections, and a virtual exhibition, to name just a few possibilities. Should you capture all of this information to document your museum, some of it, or none? How often is the Web site updated? Must you document every incremental change? What fits your appraisal criteria? Because all of this information is in one place, should you focus on the museum's Web site as one of the primary electronic records and give it immediate attention? Is Web information also available in other, less ephemeral formats? These are the types of questions that you need to ask yourself as more work is created and posted electronically, rather than published.

---

3   For example, in the past you might not have had space to save the raw data sheets from an audience survey—retaining only the final report—but can now maintain a database that contains all the survey data.

Find partners to help you in your effort to both provide guidance and make educated decisions about how to manage electronic records that are no longer active (that is, no longer needed by the organization for the reason that they were created), but have archival value. Information technology staff can help you learn about the information systems currently in use, manage the storage of the electronic records appraised as having permanent or archival value, and monitor the files so that they can migrate to newer systems as the media and technology change. You, on the other hand, have a stake in making sure that the records being stored are an exact copy and that critical metadata is created as part of the process, and you can assist technology staff in developing appropriate criteria.

If the museum moves to standardize software and hardware use, you, as the archivist, should be included in the discussions. In such meetings, stress adopting uniform software packages and adhering to common standards museumwide. This will increase your ability to provide access to electronic records over time: minimizing the variety of formats that you have to accept into the archives, lowering costs by restricting the number of different software packages you need to purchase and support, and diminishing the software and operating system dependencies that become *de facto* restrictions on gaining access to the files from these systems.

Once you have evaluated the creation, use, and management of electronic records in your institution, you may decide to initiate an electronic records program and accept electronic records into the archives.

ARCHIVING VS ARCHIVES

Agreeing on a common vocabulary with technology staff is one of the most important—and potentially frustrating—tasks that you will undertake. You will have to develop a method for explaining the difference between *archiving* and *archives,* knowing that this discussion will recur frequently, until all have a clear understanding of the meanings of the words you both use to describe very different functions. Computer technicians refer to automatically backing up files and compressing them as *archiving* the data. This process, however, does not adequately address *archival* requirements: providing access to electronic records after they are no longer in current use. When the software and hardware in use by the specific office change, those "archived" backups may not be easily accessible.

Reliance on proprietary software and compression goes against best practices for preserving electronic records and defeats the goals of using open systems to improve the availability of electronic files. Emphasize that while backing up onto tapes is a storage method that meets current requirements, such backups are inaccessible to archivists because the technology is dependent upon specific platforms. Information technology staff members strive to maintain a "clean server," sending inactive materials to secondary storage and may even use automatic deletion software, especially on e-mail servers. In essence, in archival terminology, *archives* connotes long-term access, which is not currently addressed by *archiving* technology.

After identifying the records that should be transferred to the archives, you must work closely with both program and technology staff to assure the proper transfer of *all* the information you need to provide future access to the records. For a successful transfer, you must receive records in a format and media that you can handle; a full technical description, including any hardware or software dependencies; and information on the volume (number of records and/or number of bytes). In addition, it is critical to collect documentation related to the records (record layouts, code books, methodology associated with the file, reports, and the structure of the records including the document type definitions for SGML or XML files). As in all archival work, data without context loses much of its value.

In planning electronic records storage, consider hardware, software, and storage media to determine how to keep costs within reason and provide timely access to records for reference by your institution or by outside researchers. Working with your technology staff, select the best method of storage based on your institution's systems and requirements. Consider the

advantages and disadvantages of storing these electronic records on-line (keeping them on a server), near-line, or off-line. If your museum has established standards for software, consider retaining the information in current formats—at least for the time being—until better models of long-term preservation are developed. If there are too many types of systems in place, the best choice for your institution may be a more difficult decision. Once again, involve technology personnel because they can assist you in determining the least costly model to use, and, if they understand your needs, will include your requirements in future planning for new systems.

If you accept the responsibility for preserving and providing access to records that are stored digitally, you will need to consider how to accomplish the archival functions associated with records in your custody. Many of these functions will reflect the practices that you have developed to deal with paper and other non-textual records, though you will have to make adjustments where they are warranted.

One of the first requirements is a proper storage area. Digital records stored off-line (on tapes or discs), require very specific storage conditions, different from other archival materials. Current practice recommends a stable environment at 65°F (±2°) and 35% relative humidity (±3%).[4] To protect against media deterioration, create two copies of electronic files and store one of the copies at even cooler temperatures (45°F and 40% relative humidity). A key point to remember is that the digital records should not be stored with paper records because of paper dust. The processing room where you copy digital media should be a clean room, with no eating, drinking, or smoking permitted. It is best to limit staff access, for both cleanliness and security purposes.

Choosing appropriate storage media for electronic records is also important. Current best practices recommend the following magnetic media: 3480 cartridge, 3590E cartridge, or digital linear tape (DLT)—but an important point to remember is that today's storage solutions will certainly change. Stay current with advances in the field and plan on migrating the files onto new media as necessary. Magnetic media are inherently fragile and the drives in common use will undoubtedly change. National Archives and Records Administration archivists copy electronic files every

THE DUTCH DIGITAL PRESERVATION TESTBED

For a point of view on the preservation of electronic records that differs significantly from what has become the conventional wisdom of vigilant migration, explore the preliminary findings of the Dutch Digital Preservation Testbed. The project is sponsored by ICTU, a nonprofit organization that supports developments in the Dutch government's electronic systems.[ii] The testbed is examining the effectiveness of three approaches—migration, emulation, and XML—on four common electronic record types: textual documents, e-mails, spreadsheets, and databases.[iii] Early results involving the migration approach indicate that "migration from MS® Word 95 directly into 2002 gives better results than migration step by step."[iv]

—*Lorraine Stuart*

---

ii   Jacqueline Slats, *Practical Experiences of the Digital Preservation Testbed*, DLM Forum, Barcelona, May 7, 2002, <www.digitaleduurzaamheid.nl/bibliotheek/docs/PracExp_DLM2002.pdf>, 1.

iii Maureen Potter, "*Researching Long Term Digital Preservation Approaches in the Dutch Digital Preservation Testbed (Testbed Digitale Bewaring)*," RLG *DigiNews* 6 (June 2002), <www.rlg.org/preserv/diginews/diginews6-3.html#feature2>.

iv   Slats, *Practical Experiences*, 2.

---

4   Hunter, *Preserving Digital Information*, 56. Specific recommendations vary from one reference source to another, but a stable environment within the general range of 65°F–70°F and 40%–50% RH is generally considered an acceptable compromise, with cooler and drier conditions, if possible, for an extended life.

ten years or any time they encounter read errors as they copy files for researchers.

Descriptive practices for electronic records should follow your institutional standards, particularly the procedures you have developed for other forms of nontextual records such as maps, photographs, sound

Olmsted Brothers, upper drafting room, ca. 1930. PHOTOGRAPH COURTESY OF THE NATIONAL PARK SERVICE, FREDERICK LAW OLMSTED NATIONAL HISTORIC SITE.

recordings, and motion pictures. One of the key elements to consider is the documentation that accompanied the electronic files, either in paper or electronic form. Review both the data and the documentation from a user's perspective and illuminate those areas that are not clearly identified in the documentation— a new type of "added value," but a familiar process to most archivists when dealing with textual records.

Finally, develop a plan for providing reference service. What level of service will you provide—will you retrieve particular data or simply provide an entire file? Should you try to recover costs? If you decide to copy files onto other storage media, how will you support the costs of the media, preparation time, and processing time? Or will you simply provide on-line access? If so, will it be at no cost, cost, or cost plus? Each of these decisions requires careful thought and planning.

As we noted earlier, the most important elements to consider are the resources that you have available to you at your institution. Know what is available, develop a plan, and begin to act.

Thus far, we have assumed that the archives will have the primary responsibility for electronic records. There are other options that you should consider, however, based on the technology support you have within the archives, the funding available to institute an electronic records program, and staffing support for this function. If you have a good working relationship with technology staff members, and they are willing to assist you in preserving electronic records that you appraise as worthy of long-term retention, you might negotiate with that department to store records and perform the basic preservation steps of recopying to new media or migrating to new software. You will, however, need to define the activities and performance requirements carefully.

ARTIFICIAL INTELLIGENCE

Although it may sound futuristic, strides in the development of artificial intelligence (AI) may render it a useful tool in the management of e-mail. The new AI programs are nonrules based, using instead statistical clustering and parallel co-occurrence frequencies. In the simplest layperson's terms, this means the systems are not programmed with "IF/THEN" rules (If A occurs, THEN do B), but rather are trained to recognize documents that belong together by their shared elements. Thus, an AI program that has been fed excerpts from both the Bible and *Moby Dick* will be able to distinguish to which publication subsequent excerpts belong. Government agencies that have pioneered the effort include the CIA and the National

Security Agency.[v] Two companies developing AI programs for the private as well as public sector are Autonomy Systems, Ltd., and Hummingbird. The latter has developed a product that analyzes e-mail messages and feeds those that are classified as permanent into an existing records and information management (RIM) system.[vi] It may not be long before "off-the-shelf" AI software is not an "off-the-wall" concept.

—Lorraine Stuart

v   R. Kirk Lubbes, *"Automatic Categorization: How Does It Work, Related Issues and Impacts on Records Management,"* paper presented at ARMA Houston Conference, April 2–3, 2002, Houston, Texas.

vi Donald B. Schewe, *"E-Mail: Don't Just Send It—Sort It and Save It!,"* paper presented at ARMA International Conference, September 29–October 2, 2002, New Orleans, Louisiana.

If the technology office is unwilling or unable to perform this task and you have neither the funds nor staffing to support a program in the archives, then you may have to seek more creative solutions. Perhaps other institutions with similar requirements would be interested in collaborating to share the burdens and costs. Contractors are an option, but, again, you will need to understand and define very clearly the tasks they are to perform and develop an evaluation method to judge their work. Look for other institutions that have used contractors successfully and use them as a model. In drawing up an agreement, be sure to address security, access, preservation methods, ownership of software and data, and what happens if you want to switch vendors or if the company goes out of business.

In the best of all possible worlds—which we can hope will develop over the next few years—an electronic recordkeeping system would manage both the paper and electronic records created or used in your museum. Unfortunately, while there are records management applications available, they have not been tested enough to earn the endorsement of the larger community, and their ability to provide the necessary degree of interoperability and flexibility is still questionable. And, of course, purchasing and implementing such a system is very costly.

If your institution is interested in purchasing a software system to manage electronic records, successful implementation requires the existence of a strong records management program, including policies and procedures that govern the use, retention, and disposition of records in all media; up-to-date retention schedules; and file plans. If your institution lacks these elements, then the implementation of software applications will not move forward smoothly or quickly. *Electronic document management systems* (EDMS) manage all single objects (i.e., individual files) as equal and independent entities, while *records management systems* manage single objects as part of "object groups" or "series" that are interrelated and of the same type, purpose, or location. For example, a report could be drafted, revised, published, stored, retrieved, and used as a single file or as a group of files containing different versions; data used in the report may be stored in a spreadsheet or database. EDMS software does not have functions to record these interrelationships among files, nor will it manage how long the report and its related components should be retained. A records management application, on the other hand, has EDMS functionalities but can also group items and apply retention periods for both items and groups.

If your institution decides to purchase an electronic record management system or document management system to better manage its records, there are certain critical steps to a sound decision. Define the scope and benefits of the project, assign sufficient resources (staff and fiscal), know and use existing records management policies and practices, and gather information on your information technology envi-

The Thomas Oyster Company building being towed to Mystic Seaport, 1970. The building has been restored and is now a waterfront exhibit. COURTESY MYSTIC SEAPORT, MYSTIC, CONNECTICUT.

ronment and requirements. Involve technology staff members from the beginning, because they will be key for ensuring proper technical implementation of the product you purchase. Additional steps include defining the requirements of the software you wish to purchase, setting evaluation criteria, contacting vendors, requesting product demonstrations, developing a request for proposal (RFP) for vendors, and evaluating vendor responses.

Finally, in addition to the study, planning, and decision making we have discussed above, it is well worth noting that there are some simple, common-sense measures that you can take to ensure that the electronic records are managed properly. For example, at the Smithsonian Institution we developed a brochure "Treating E-mail as Records," which specifically states that e-mail messages are records if they document Smithsonian activities or are needed for future reference. The brochure recommends that e-mail messages be placed in a recordkeeping system, paper or electronic. Although we do not yet have an electronic records management system, we strongly suggest that electronic documents be retained electronically, in a parallel system to the paper file system in use by that specific office. This is not a perfect answer, because at some point the files will have to migrate to another system and the related costs and technical problems may be greater than the value of the information in the files. However, it is essential that electronic documents and e-mail records be managed systemically to assure access by the institution, not just the individual.

Los Angeles book dealer Jake Zeitlin displays the illuminated Spanish manuscript *Vidal Mayor* (1290–1310), one of a 144-item collection acquired by the J. Paul Getty Museum in 1983 from collector Peter Ludwig. The collection was considered to be the finest in private hands. Zeitlin is flanked by New York book dealer H. P. Kraus (on the left) and Thomas Kren, the Getty's manuscript curator. INSTITUTIONAL ARCHIVES, RESEARCH LIBRARY, THE GETTY RESEARCH INSTITUTE.

As we noted at the beginning of this chapter, electronic records are a new concern. The research and study going on now in the archival community will eventually lead us to answers. Although the procedures we adopt now are certain to change, we are at least beginning to understand how to preserve this new record format. Keep reading, stay current with new developments, and begin to take some logical actions.

Digitization

Most cultural institutions view digitization as a method for increasing the visibility of their holdings. Museums often employ digitization to promote their collections, placing digital images on the Web. If your museum has an infrastructure in place for digitization, determine if it also meets the needs of archival projects:

ensure that you are working with systems that fit the requirements of the archives, which we will discuss in this section, as well as those of the institution. Among the topics that drive the implementation of digitization projects are priorities, processes, standards, and funding.

Digitization is not usually a one-person project. Consider creating a planning group to determine responsibility, develop projects, respond to questions as they arise, and ultimately produce digital products. The group should be composed of all the "stakeholders" in the final outcome: staff members who work with and understand reference and access, description, preservation, and technology. The most important first step is to establish a philosophy of digitization for the archives—a digitization mission statement. Do you want to make your holdings more accessible or to preserve fragile materials—or both? Which audience do you want to serve? Is it a priority to publicize your holdings in general, or to present a particular collection?

The digitization team must also consider a variety of procedural questions. Who initiates digitization projects? How are projects initiated? What is required for a collection to be selected for digitization? Who supervises digitization projects? How is work divided to ensure quality control, standards, accountability, and funding as the project moves through the various steps of digitization (physical preparation, establishing standards, cataloging, and making these images available)? What standards must be used? How will images be made available to the public—on a Web site or on-line databases? How will digital imaging projects be linked to finding aids and other reference tools?

Selection is a critical task. As you carefully consider what you should digitize from your archival collection, think broadly, beyond isolated projects. You might consider developing a theme to link your digital collections together. An on-line exhibition that includes an institutional history timeline, photographs, and important documents could provide context for the collections that you choose to digitize. You might want to provide a surrogate research collection, bringing together materials from a group of related collections or series. Look carefully at your holdings to determine what would work best as an image on a Web site. The types of materials the archives digitizes will be very different from museum objects, and their presentation may be complicated by the need to provide context and express hierarchical relationships. Costs and effective access must both be included in decision making. For example, digitizing pages of logbooks with scientific observations that could just as easily be entered into a searchable database might not be the best use of limited resources.[5]

Standards—both technical and descriptive—foster better use, access, and longevity. Adhering to recognized standards makes information universally available to users, facilitates sharing and interchange of information, and enhances the probability of long-term retention. The archival profession has made considerable progress in this area, and you may be able to serve a valuable role by encouraging the museum to adopt standards, such as Dublin Core,[6] for example. Important areas for standards include descriptive metadata, which places basic information into standard fields for consistent retrieval; authority control for index terms, to promote greater visibility; administrative metadata, for institutional management purposes; and structural data, to navigate though digitized text (chapters, boxes, folders, etc).

A cost-benefit discussion can also be valuable as part of the planning process. Clearly identify what can be gained from digitization and determine whether this is worth the price. Columbia University developed guidelines for digital conversion that included *added value* as a criterion for digital capture:[7]

- enhanced intellectual control through the creation of new finding aids, links to bibliographic records, and the development of indices and other tools;
- increased and enriched use through the ability to search widely, manipulating images and text, and to study disparate images in new contexts;

- the encouragement of new scholarly use through the provision of enhanced resources in the form of widespread dissemination of unique collections;
- enhanced use through improved quality of image, for example, improved legibility of faded or stained documents;
- creation of a "virtual collection" through the flexible integration and synthesis of a variety of formats, or of related materials scattered among many locations.

Aerial photograph of the construction of the Getty Center in Los Angeles, 1997. PHOTOGRAPH BY JOHN STEPHENS. ©THE J. PAUL GETTY TRUST.

The Archival Resources and Cultural Materials initiatives of the Research Libraries Group (RLG) are bringing together a critical mass of collections of related materials, allowing researchers to "cross search" EAD-encoded finding aids and archival and visual materials held by disparate institutions, in much the same way as RLG's Research Libraries Information Network (RLIN), an international bibliographic database, already allows for MARC records.

Resource allocation plays an important part in any project. In the case of digitization, there are some hidden costs that are very important to consider. The Smithsonian Institution is actively encouraging the digitization of its collections to highlight the relationships between collections and to make its enormous collection of artifacts more accessible to the American public. The Smithsonian Institution Archives,

---

5   In a recent project, the Smithsonian Archives determined that the value of a collection of logbooks lay in the information recorded and recommended that the information be placed into a searchable database, which could then be made available through a Web site. Providing visual images of the data was not cost effective: 200 logbooks, each with approximately 100 pages, was estimated to be $80,000 for a total of 20,000 images, far more than it would cost to input the data.

6   See the Dublin Core Metadata Initiative at <http://dublincore.org>.

7   Columbia University Libraries, "Selection Criteria for Digital Imaging," <www.columbia.edu/cu/libraries/digital/criteria.html>.

Libraries, and other institutional partners are studying the possibility of working together to link images and documents relating to past Smithsonian expeditions. Beyond the simple cost of scanning, we will also have to quantify the cost of standardized description; creating the metadata necessary for access is a large portion of a digitization project budget. In addition, maintaining the digital image files and providing a migration path to ensure their continued usability over the years will add an ongoing cost to departmental budgets long after the project is completed.

The benefits of making an underused collection more accessible must also be balanced against compatibility with other digital resources and the collection's intrinsic intellectual value. As the Society of American Archivists noted in a white paper on digitization, the "mere potential for increased access to a digitized collection does not add value to an underutilized collection."[8] An interesting observation made in a Library of Congress report on digitization refutes an assumption that I presume most archivists would make concerning the use of originals after images have been scanned: James Reilly and Franziska S. Frey report that they witnessed increased handling of original documents as soon as they became available in digital form.[9]

There are many good resources to assist you in developing effective digitization projects,[10] many of which are noted in this manual's Resource Guide. Online resources are extremely valuable in this quick-changing field: the Library of Congress and the National Archives and Records Administration Web sites on digitization are particularly useful. But perhaps most important is your own analysis as you define who your users are and will be, what the purposes of your digitization effort are, and where you will find the resources that you will need to find to support this worthwhile but demanding medium.

DIGITIZATION VS MICROFILMING

When deciding to reformat information, you have several options. In many cases, the choice will lie between digitization and microfilm. Carefully consider the reason for reformatting. If you are interested in making this part of your archives more widely accessible, then you should consider digitization. If the primary reason is to preserve the records, then microfilming would be the better choice.

Major research projects have looked at the costs for digitization, microfilm, and for combining both of these processes. Though the focus in these projects has centered on brittle books, museum archives can benefit from these experiences. Microfilm continues to be a viable alternative, particularly for massive amounts of records, such as minutes, reports, or case files, particularly if the purpose is long-term preservation of the records. As noted in a study comparing digital imaging and preservation microfilm,[vii] until digital preservation capabilities are more robust and shown to be cost-effective, microfilm remains the primary reformatting choice. In certain circumstances, computer output microfilm is even the recommended format for records that are created electronically, but pose too many technological problems to ensure long-term electronic access.

vii Anne R. Kenney, "Digital to Microfilming: A Demonstration Project, 1994–1996. Final Report to the National Endowment for the Humanities" (Ithaca, N.Y.: Cornell University, 1997), at <www.library.cornell.edu/preservation/com/comfin.html>.

---

8   Abby Smith, "The Preservation of Digitized Reproductions" (Chicago: Society of American Archivists, 1997) at <www.archivists.org/statements/digitize.asp>.

9   James Reilly and Franziska S. Frey, "Recommendations for the Evaluation of Digital Images Produced from Photographic, Microphotographic and Various Paper Formats" (Rochester, N.Y.: Image Permanence Institute, 1996), at <http://memory.loc/ammem/ipireprt.pdf>.

10 Anne R. Kenney and Oya Y. Rieger, editors and principal authors, *Moving Theory into Practice: Digital Imaging for Libraries and Archives* (Mountain View, Calif: Research Libraries Group, 2000), and Anne R. Kenney, "Digital to Microfilming: A Demonstration Project, 1994–1996. Final Report to the National Endowment for the Humanities" (Ithaca, N.Y.: Cornell University, 1997), at <www.library.cornell.edu/preservation/com/comfin.html>, are highly recommended.

20

OBJECTS IN THE ARCHIVES[1]

Anthony Reed

It's a fair assumption that, in any institution, at least one collection (and probably more) will have some number of nonstandard historical items in an otherwise standard manuscript collection. How these items—called objects, artwork, realia, 3-D collections, specimens, samples, and many other things—are treated, cataloged, processed, and stored are vital matters for archivists.

The challenge comes in the intersection of professions. Traditional registrars and curators in the museum world—while knowledgeable of museum artifacts—may not have the training or professional network to know how best to treat an archival collection in their care. In the archival world, the odd and occasional object in a paper-based collection may be a simple stumbling block in the archival process to professionals trained in processing, arrangement, and description. A complex collection rife with objects may flummox an archivist altogether.

The safe generalization for all instances is this: if you're unsure of how to proceed, then wait. Depending on the severity of the situation, bring in colleagues from your institution, connect with the network of experts in your field to determine how others have proceeded in similar situations, and reach out to experts who specialize in the field with which you're contending. Probably the greatest talent one can acquire is to know when you don't know enough to proceed. This becomes especially important when dealing with unique, irreplaceable materials. As with all conservation and preservation efforts, everything you do should be reversible.

Certainly, the ideas of reversibility and consulting with professional colleagues are givens. However, at the risk of not doing anything for fear of not doing something right, there are methods by which a curator should feel comfortable working with an archival collection and an archivist should be able to move for-

ward with non–paper-based materials. This chapter will briefly explore the basic concepts of preservation and intellectual access, the two primary guiding principles of any curatorial or archival work. How best to implement these principles will be illustrated in examples, both hypothetical and real.

First, a discussion of the range of materials may be in order. Given the many types of museums, museum archives are a rich territory for looking at objects in archival collections. By the very nature of these collections, there will almost always be a fair amount of non-paper materials in museum archival collections. How object collections in the archives interact with the curatorial collections (often depending on how the archives staff members interact with the curatorial staff) will depend on how these objects are thought of, a topic that we will consider toward the end of this chapter.

Individually, an archivist may feel that since his is a fine-arts collection, for example, discussions of medical "wet specimens" would have no relevance to his work. Similarly, a history of technology curator may feel that work done by textile historians is by nature outside the limits of her field. However, this chapter takes as broad a view as possible in these matters; it may be helpful to have an exposure to different areas, in case such materials ever make their way into your collections. (I'm thinking of a Pacific Northwest high-tech corporate museum/archives that maintains a substantial collection of *objets d'art* given to its well-known founder and president.) Moreover, a well-rounded professional never closes doors; you never know where your next area of interest (or career move!) may come from.

One factor to consider is the general scope of the collection. How an artifact in an archival collection is treated may depend on whether it's an occasional object or the rule. A work of art, a product sample, a roll of cash, a piece of food, an animal specimen, a book, an autograph, a pressed corsage, a computer disc, a piece of jewelry, a prayer shawl, a stone fetish, a box

---

1 Or: *What the hell is that and what do I do with it?*

of cremains: any of these in an otherwise paper-based collection would be treated specifically. It's another matter if you're dealing with a collection where every other item has a pressed plant specimen attached to it. These "items"—the rule rather than the exception—become an aggregate: a herbarium collection. One pencil sketch found in a correspondence collection is very different than sheaves of pencil sketches, at which point you're not really working with an archival collection, but an art collection. You find one autographed, annotated booklet in a set of artist's records, it's an artifact; boxes and boxes of booklets and you have yourself a pamphlet collection. (If they're autographed and annotated, then maybe you're back to dealing with an archival collection, albeit a special materials, or even ephemera, collection.)

The point is, an object as an oddity in an archival collection might become the bulk in another collection of like objects. All are items of intellectual capital. The corsage that you pull from a collection of letters must be maintained intellectually with its cohabitants, even when (especially when!) that item is removed and stored separately from its original provenance to preserve the corsage and the letters that surround it.[2]

To give this topic some focus, some broadly defined areas may be useful to begin with. Generalizations about and examples from art museums, scientific collections, and history collections will be used to help illustrate what issues may arise in these types of institutions. These comments, however, should be read broadly, as any of these issues may arise across genres of museums.

Art Museums

Even within a broad field made more narrow, the diversity of art museums within the larger group of museums makes this work a challenge. Archival materials will vary from institution to institution depending on the museums' curated artistic collections: contemporary, antiquities, fine arts, sculpture, pop culture, high-tech, textile, installation or performance pieces, and beyond. Luckily, as cultural resources professionals, our work is already idiosyncratic and many

of our efforts are already determined institution by institution. However—as always—there are enough commonalties that we, as a community of professionals, can reach across differences and find some generalities that work.

In any kind of art museum, the collection and curation of pieces (paintings, installations, outdoor sculpture) will generate records of many kinds: catalog records, accession records, conservation records, correspondence with artists and donors, curatorial files, and exhibition records, all of which are dealt with in various places throughout this volume. For the purposes of this chapter, any of those may contain items pertaining to the donation, curation, conservation, restoration, and exhibition of the piece concerned.

When accessioning an object, museum staff may decide to retain its original packaging, if those materials are relevant to the item's provenance. Identification tags or original documentation of the object or its installation such as photographs, models, material samples, or videos of a performance piece may also have been saved. Similar materials may be found in conservation or curation files. When conservators or outside contractors repair or restore fine-arts objects, textile swatches, paint chips, or documentation of the work in various formats may become potential inhabitants of correspondence, conservation, or resource-management records.

All of these records—whether held by the conservation lab, the curatorial division, the acquisitions department, or the sole person responsible for all of these duties—are vital to the collections' care. The nonpaper objects within these files are often just as important as the correspondence with art restorers: they are necessary to track changes to collections. Exhibition materials, such as graphics, didactic labels, planning documents with models, ephemera, audiovisual materials, and electronic files, all may be included in curators' exhibition folders. These ancillary items should be maintained with the same level of care as the paper records themselves.

Correspondence files with donors and, more significantly, the artists themselves, are of particular interest to art museum archivists. As straight correspondence files, there may be voluminous paper records that document that artist's creative process and the sometimes-delicate interactions among artists, donors, and museums, but there may be more. Included in those records may also be other examples of an artist's work (small sketches, spec sheets of an installation, materials samples, models of artworks), ephemera, and audiovisual materials documenting an

---

2   The strong research potential for objects in archival collections is not discussed here, but is examined thoroughly in a few other sources, most notably Jill Robin Severn's excellent paper from the 2001 SAA conference "Adventures in the Third Dimension: Reenvisioning Access to Artifacts in Archives" (Session no. 36); as well as Gloria Meraz, "Cultural Evidence: On the Common Ground Between Archivists and Museologists," *Provenance* XV (1997); and Hugh Taylor, "'Heritage' Revisited: Documents as Artifacts in the Context of Museums and Material Culture," *Archivaria* 40 (Fall 1995).

artist's career. For museums that collect the personal papers of artists themselves, this issue grows from a challenge to an outright project.

Occasionally, it may be that the line between archival material and curated art object blurs. Sketchbooks may be utilized in a retrospective exhibition showing an artist's earliest work right up through current creative work. Certainly, marginalia in books, informal doodles, or miniature models of works never carried out may all be found in archival collections, and all may be treated as individually cataloged, curated objects. Deciding whether these items are treated as supplemental items within an archival collection or as stand-alone art objects is a complex process incorporating provenance, context, and collections storage. This process—and the difficulties involved—will be treated a little later in the chapter.

Straddling the fence between curatorial files and artists' sketchbooks, art museum archives may contain "documentary art," materials created by museum staff members (sometimes professional artists themselves) while on collecting expeditions. Akin to a scientist's or archaeologist's field notes and sketches, a curator's or museum artist's records may contain valuable (intrinsic or informational) items that resemble art pieces more closely than archival records. As documents of the museum staff, these works may record the decision-making process of acquisitions, show a work *in situ* or document its place of creation, provide information on the earliest provenance of a particular object, or provide insight into how objects were installed in the museum.

Science and Technology Museums

While art museum professionals enjoy the challenges of how to deal with restoration documentation or an artist's sample, science museums and their staffs have slightly different matters to deal with. Obviously, scientific collections also have to deal with curatorial files, donor records, and accession documentation. Beyond that, however, there are potentially more research-oriented materials, especially if an institution's collecting policy intersects with areas of study by staff researchers and faculty themselves. Samples of John Singer Sargent's work—charcoal sketches, pencil studies—may be a challenge to manage within an archival setting; samples from the work of Marie Curie would yield a vastly different set of issues. Academic archives share similar issues when they are forced to deal with faculty research samples and biological specimens.

ANDY WARHOL[i]

"What you should do is get a box for a month, and drop everything in it and at the end of the month lock it up. Then date it and send it over to Jersey. You should try to keep track of it, but if you can't and you lose it, that's fine, because it's one less thing to think about, another load off your mind.

"I started off myself with trunks and the odd piece of furniture, but then I went around shopping for something better and now I just drop everything into the same-size brown cardboard boxes that have a color patch on the side for the month of the year. I really hate nostalgia, though, so deep down I hope they get lost and I never have to look at them again. That's another conflict. I want to throw things out the window as they're handed to me, but instead I say thank you and drop them into the box-of-the-month. But my outlook is that I really do want to save things so they can be used again someday."

---

i   Andy Warhol, *The Philosophy of Andy Warhol (From A to B and Back Again)*, (New York: Harcourt and Brace, 1975), 145.

ANDY WARHOL'S ARCHIVIST

John Smith, archivist at the Andy Warhol Museum, sends this list of "10 interesting and surprising things from the archives of the Andy Warhol Museum":

- Undocumented artwork from the 1950s and 1960s
- Desiccated pizza dough
- Piece of Caroline Kennedy's birthday cake
- Dress belonging to Jean Harlow
- Pair of Clark Gable's shoes given to Warhol by Gable's widow
- Calvin Klein underwear autographed by Calvin Klein
- Original musical manuscripts by Lou Reed composed for the Velvet Underground
- A mummified foot
- Illicit drugs
- $14,000 in cash

Clearly, one aspect of scientific collections that needs exploration is the possible presence of organic, hazardous, or contaminated materials. Once again, the best knowledge to cultivate is to know what you don't know. Important as this is in dealing with irreplaceable cultural collections, such wisdom takes on a more immediate importance when facing potentially life-threatening materials. Working with these materials safely often requires the intervention of skilled handlers specific to the type of material. Your conservation staff is trained in the sciences, wise to hazards, and well

Conservators, curators, and carpenters not only used archival records in researching the Stencil House before conserving the stencils and reinstalling the exhibit, they also created archival records documenting their work. SHELBURNE MUSEUM ARCHIVES.

connected with other specialists: talk to them first. You may never be called upon to actually handle these materials, but if a decision is made to process suspicious materials (a decision that should not be made lightly or without consultation), consider the following precautions:

- If you suspect that a collection may contain dangerous chemicals or samples, find a well-ventilated processing space that is separate from staff and collections.
- When handling any samples, wear protective gear (disposable apron, latex gloves, goggles, and/or mask with respirator, depending upon the materials). Keep these items on hand if there is any chance of handling collections containing wet specimens or contaminated or hazardous materials.
- After handling, clean all surfaces and instru-

ments with appropriate disinfectant or germicide and dispose of handling equipment safely.

As we will discuss later, separate and specialized storage for objects from archival collections is often the best approach for the sake of preservation. For scientific samples and specimens, removal—if not outright disposal or destruction—may be necessary. The inherently high value of a specimen and low possibility of contamination or physical harm might suggest simply separate storage. An item that is of dubious research or artifactual value and higher threat to collections and staff would be a likely candidate for permanent deaccession and appropriate disposal.[3]

A good pre-emptive effort before being faced with a "process it or don't process it?" dilemma is to confront these issues at the time of acquisition. Granted, some of these problems are legacy or "backlog" issues (for instance, those seventeen boxes of unprocessed materials from the curator of tropical diseases that have been around since before the entire current staff), and, since they're on-site, the boxes have to be dealt with somehow. However—as with any collection—incoming acquisitions need to be carefully scoped out *in situ* and careful negotiations with the donor undertaken before any materials are transferred to the archives. Preservation issues and health-and-safety matters should be discussed at the time. If your institution is not equipped to handle radioactive items from a now-defunct laboratory, your best option is to refer the donating body to appropriate repositories that can handle those historic collections. (Other options may include altering your institution's mission, facilities, and staffing, but that may be cost-prohibitive.)

Beyond the matters of life-and-death, scientific museum archives deal with nonlethal but still complex objects in their collections, as do other repositories. Due to the "specialness" of the associated fields, however, archivists in science museums may be charged with documenting and preserving technologies that

---

3   It should be noted that science and technology curators and archivists are not alone in their burden of hazardous materials in the collections. Materials such as lead paint or lead musket balls, arsenic and mercury salt preservatives, and some carcinogenic wood preservatives all create problems for historic collections caretakers. See Catherine Hawks and Kathryn Makos, "Inherent and Acquired Hazards in Museum Objects; Implications for Care and Use of Collections," *Cultural Resource Management* 23, no. 5 (2000) for a good survey of the topic.

have long ago outpaced the standard set of courses offered by even the most cutting-edge archives management graduate programs. Information management professionals (archivists, curators, and librarians) are currently struggling with the questions of electronic records, and there will be no easy answer soon.

It is worth noting that in science-related collections, you should probably be ready to deal with the hardware, software, and data files that may be used or generated by museum staff and researchers whose papers your institution collects.[4] Again, the museum archives of a prominent high-tech company may be charged with maintaining the voluminous paper records of product design and creation, but may also be asked to retain copies of record of any software product licensed by the company, in many release (and pre-release) versions.[5] All of these matters delve deeply into the problems of legacy data and migration of new systems; since these issues rise with a mercilessly sharp obsolescence curve, managers of museum archival collections with technological components are strongly encouraged to join the dialogue with other technology-collection professionals sooner rather than later.

History Museums

Of these three broad-brush categories—art, science, and history museums—all three are necessarily overgeneralized. Within history museum archives, types of materials and subject-content can range as widely as those in the art and the science museums. Whether a historic home (which may lean more closely toward the art museum) or a Plexiglas-case-and-didactic-label-based archaeology and anthropology museum (which sidles up closer to a science museum), anything falling into this category serves visitors and researchers by preserving, interpreting, exhibiting, and making accessible for research items of historic importance or interest. And, as with the previous two categories, the history museum archives also has its own special issues when dealing with objects in the archives.

Many times, at historic sites, archival collections may come directly from inside the historic cabinetry

and furnishings themselves. Groups of letters tied with ribbons and string may have been removed from a desk in the parlor. Business records may come from filing cabinets or sorting bins in the estate office. In cases like this, the effort is not so much about removing an object from the archival collection (and preserving its provenance), but removing the archives from the object (and *still* preserving the provenance). Understandably, you'd be hard-pressed to find a lignin-free, acid-neutral container into which you could place a four-drawer oak filing cabinet, so the

T-shirts from the Dallas Women's Gallery Records, 1980s. COURTESY OF THE ARCHIVES, DALLAS MUSEUM OF ART.

rehousing of these particular objects is less of an issue. If a large object is not serving as part of a historic display, place it alongside other historic objects in museum-quality storage. As will be discussed later, it is important to link historic records intellectually to the historic furniture from which they were removed.

Objects Found in All Types of Museums

In long-running institutions, there may be a significant portion of records relating to the administration of the site. These business records of the institution may see active growth, as more records are generated by the museum and transferred to the archives. Among these records you will probably find objects that are historically related to the institution, such as plaques, models of construction, ephemera, guest registration books, awards, or audiovisual records. Particularly during a construction project, an anniversary celebration, or a time-capsule ceremony, fragments of the site

---

4   Personally, I pity the poor grad student tasked with processing my collection when I've passed on, as I intend to donate my CPU along with the file folders, the CDs, my grandmother's costume jewelry and my comic book collection.

5   Venia T. Phillips and Maurice E. Phillips, *Guide to the Manuscript Collections* (Philadelphia: Academy of Natural Sciences, 1963), 36.

and fabric of the structure may make their way to the archives as documentation of any of these events. Since they relate to the history of the museum, these objects need to be intellectually linked with (if not necessarily stored near) the archival collection.

The "sets" used in gallery exhibits are another type of material often seen in museum collections. Backdrops, murals, diorama settings, and the like may have been integral to the museum's interpretive design, particularly in exhibits earlier in the twentieth century. As these exhibits changed or were removed, parts of the displays themselves may have been saved and may now reside in the archives as records of the history of the institution. Though they are similar to the didactic labeling and fabricated exhibition materials discussed above, these materials may be of a slightly different class: they were sometimes executed by known artists or by muralists of lesser general fame, but known within the museum field. The importance of these items may also lie in their function as full-color records of times otherwise documented only by black-and-white photography.

What about books? Are they archival materials? Historic objects? Research monographs? Bernadette Callery, museum librarian at the Carnegie Museum of Natural History, believes, as a librarian/archivist, that

books that come as part of archival collections—as when one receives the entire collection of a scientist, artist, or researcher—should stay with the archives, rather than go to the museum's library. This applies mostly to the odd volume that turns up in the papers of a donor, rather than the case of an entire personal library. One could make the argument that, regardless of whether a significant collection of materials is maintained as a smaller, "special" collection or distributed into the museum's library and properly book-plated as part of a donor's bequest, you would still want to design some scheme to be able to reconstruct the contents of the collection as received.

Processing Collections that Contain Objects

As with any other processing or cataloging project, there are two main objectives: preservation and access. These two ideals become even more important when dealing with oddities in a collection. When you come across some artifact, specimen, or artwork that belongs—intellectually—with the collection but definitely does not fit physically with folder after folder of manuscript pages, you'll need to make a decision about what to do with it. More often than not, the

---

ANNOTATED BOOKS

Documentary evidence can take the form of annotations and corrections made to an existing printed text. In nineteenth-century natural science collections, it is not uncommon to find private collectors using copies of published monographs on their subject to serve as checklists or catalogs of their own collections. The Carnegie Museum of Natural History owns the archives and specimen collection of B. Preston Clark, a private collector of hawkmoths who gave his 34,000-specimen collection, complete with its 507 museum cases and 15 file cabinet drawers of correspondence dating from 1916 to 1943. Like Darwin, he corresponded with everyone who might be expected to share his interest and actively solicited collections from missionaries and tradesmen. His collection contains an interleaved, annotated copy of the major nineteenth-century monograph, A. G. Butler's *Revision of the Heterocerous Lepidoptera of the Family Sphingidae* (The Transactions of the Zoological Society of London, 1877). The copy is marked with numbers corresponding to the specimen collection

and further amended with penciled notations of nomenclature changes. Clearly, Clark was using this monograph as a means to record his own collection.

The Academy of Natural Sciences (Philadelphia) archives holds an annotated copy of an 1846 letterpress catalog of the large collection of birds that Thomas B. Wilson purchased from the Duc de Rivoli. In this case, the annotations clearly related the collection to the specimens, as "the catalogs lay for years beside the bird specimens in the department of ornithology."[ii] In a less striking find, the library's copy of the 1940 printed catalog of the British Museum of Natural History's library is marked with arrows to indicate the museum library's holdings, with additional editions penciled in.[iii]

—*Bernadette Callery*

---

ii Venia T. Phillips and Maurice E. Phillips, *Guide to the Manuscript Collections* (Philadelphia: Academy of Natural Sciences, 1963), 36.

iii *Catalogue of the Books, Manuscripts, Maps and Drawings in the British Museum (Natural History)* (London: British Museum, 1903–1940).

item itself will have to be removed from the collection and stored appropriately.

Broadly, the idea is to keep all materials in a collection in the best storage conditions possible. The right temperature, humidity, and air circulation for papers may not be ideal for a potsherd, a plant sample, a wax figurine, a crayon drawing, a corsage, or a piece of woven metal. A small model of an artist's sculpture, if left in the document box with papers, may abrade the documents, rust, and might even tear materials.

Beyond physical conditions, there may be other security reasons to relocate an object. That suspicious biological or radioactive sample may need to be quarantined (or destroyed), or a very important, valuable item may need higher security than is afforded in the manuscripts storage shelves. (It would be a shame if that diamond Cartier brooch that came with the artist's papers got misfiled.)

The example of the corsage from above can be broken down this way:

- During processing, the corsage is removed from the folder, placed in an archivally sound storage container (an inert plastic envelope or an artifact box, perhaps), and described as clearly as possible on a separation sheet: "Item is a semipressed gardenia and baby's breath corsage, with white silk ribbon, white netting, and green florist tape around stem. A large stickpin remains pierced through the stem. Appears to be from MJH 1939 high school graduation."
- Duplicate separation sheets are created on acid-free paper; one copy remains in the original location cross-referencing the object's new location, while the other copy remains with the object in its new location (or in a catalog folder) referring to its original location.
- In the finding aid, a mention of unusual objects removed from the collection is made, possibly in the collection description narrative, and a footnote is added to the box/folder list describing the object.

Essential to these processes are, again, the preservation of the object (by keeping the corsage and the historic documents separate for fear of migration of destructive materials and physical damage to papers from three-dimensional objects, and damage to three-dimensional objects by improper storage) and the preservation of the original context—the original order—of the collection (by documenting the original location and manner in which the object was stored).

At this point, a question may come up about whether these objects removed from archival collections are then accessioned into the museum's collections. Much will depend on the internal structure of an institution; sometimes the line between curatorial and archival departments is hard, fast, and impermeable. If the mandate in such an organization is that all objects go to the museum collections, then so be it.

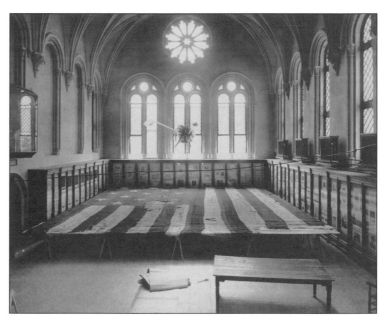

The Star Spangled Banner in the West Wing of the Smithsonian Institution building before it undergoes its 1914 restoration.
SMITHSONIAN INSTITUTION ARCHIVES, NEG. 27462 (RU 95, BOX 31A, FOLDER 25).

However, the provenance of that object must remain documented (as originating from a specific archival collection) and available to researchers and staff in both curatorial and archives departments. If the museum archives has storage space for objects available, the object should stay as close to the collection as possible, within the limits afforded by appropriate environmental conditions.

In other instances, it may be the opinion of an archivist working with a collection that an object most assuredly belongs with the museum's curatorial collection. Conversely, after a consultation with the curatorial staff, you may determine that a particular item should stay with the archives. Perhaps the item is deemed "unworthy" (especially in the case of fine-arts or "pure history" environments), because it is a piece of detritus or an extraneous appendix; perhaps it's not even integral to or associated with the museum object after all. Again, depending on the relationship between the two departments, and the players involved in these conversations, this interaction can be educational or rancorous. The collections of both areas are served best when collaborative work provides ideal care for and robust access to collections.

In an ideal world, the various information management professionals at an institution have an open, collegial working relationship; the lines between museum, archives, and library are permeable; and rigid lines are drawn less often and less severely. It may be that a particular piece from an archival collection dovetails nicely with a collection of similar pieces already in the museum's collections. Why not exhibit the one alongside the others, making the intimate connection between museum collections and archival holdings apparent to all (staff and visitors) and cross-promoting both divisions, perhaps even getting more organic research across disciplines?

For accountability's sake, it probably would not be a bad idea to catalog objects from archival collections and give them accession numbers, assuring their place in the institution's collections. In any collection documentation, those records must show where the item was originally located. This holds true as well for any storage cabinets or container furniture from which archival holdings were removed. Conversely, any archival documentation of objects removed to storage should include the museum's catalog number and documentation of the object's current whereabouts (although public documents should only give enough information without revealing specific secure locations).

In closing, I'd like to emphasize that, in a world that is complex and with a cluster of fields that are so similar to each other, yet so splintered from one another, these moments when an archivist, a curator, and a librarian all sit around a table with a thing in the center might provide the intersections where we make our collections most alive to our users (patrons, researchers, visitors, other staff). Each of those profes-sionals (assuming an institution can support at least one of each!) brings something to that table: public access cataloging; proper storage and handling standards; contextualized information systems based on historic documents; appreciation for the visitor experience; the ability to interpret materials and educate a lay public; professional reference assistance to deal with complex resources—and so on, and so on.

While that imaginary table with three attendees and an object in the center is purely a theoretical image, there are practical ways to bring museum, library, and archives staff together. Developing those relationships early and cross-training will help build the collegial connections that make it easier for, say, a librarian to cross the hall to the conservator's table to ask about repairing a spine on a nineteenth-century book. A registrar may want to know more about this EAD that's been talked about and see what similar projects may help the accessioning and cataloging work done at that desk. A new exhibition may be geared toward the user-base of an institution's library, require archival and library research, and incorporate materials—textual and nontextual—from the archival or library collections. Curators and registrars could help in identifying and advising on storage for objects from the archival collections. A major construction project may—most likely *will*—require some collaborative efforts by curatorial, archives, and library divisions, as well as maintenance, administration, groundskeeping, security, and all other offices. The availability of information on the Internet has changed the way we—as information professionals—work. As our fields draw nearer to unified information resource sharing, these conversations are becoming, if not necessary, then extremely useful. Museum archivists are in a special position to broker the relationship between object and textual resource; it's a rare opportunity and one we should look forward to.

21

FIELD RECORDS AND SCIENTIFIC NOTEBOOKS

Sarah R. Demb

Archivists in scientific and archaeological institutions face special challenges with records generated by staff members in the field and/or as a function of their scientific research. The line between a curator's museum responsibilities and his or her "personal" research can be exceptionally blurry, especially in institutions where original research is an important activity. In this chapter, we will consider several issues raised by these records: questions about intellectual property rights; worrisome physical condition problems; and access issues.

Original records containing curatorial and field research or scientific data can present difficult intellectual property issues. The very reasons archivists see these records as intrinsically valuable are often the same reasons potential donors give for not placing them in the archives.[1] The highly personal nature of research notes influences the extent to which their authors share that information and with whom they share it.[2] Museum archivists have a mandate to collect, preserve, and *provide access to* records relating to the work of the museum and often the research it supports. Thus, there is often an inherent tension between the museum archives' mission and the staff of curatorial departments, who may be inclined to restrict access to their research files—personal or departmental. This tension should be addressed in the archives mission statement and policies, in consultation with the museum administration and curatorial staff members. As one art museum archivist has noted, curatorial research is often indistinguishable from other records, particularly when it becomes embedded in departmental records such as exhibition files, where the research adds important knowledge about the museum's artifactual or object

holdings.[3] Whether the information was discovered as part of an external research project such as a dissertation or as part of a museum project does not make it any less useful to archival researchers and to the museum record of the artifact.

Much museum research, like other academic work, is ongoing, and some active scholars worry about protecting their field notes or data from the publishing projects of others in their field. Create a clear policy stating what constitutes an institutional record and what is a special collection, especially when dealing with curatorial research, field research, or scientific data that document artifact holdings and the museum's core activities. When acquiring and accessioning field notes or research files, limit access and use under clearly defined terms, either negotiated with the donor of a special collection or as part of your policy for institutional records.[4] Develop collections policies

---

3   Deborah Wythe, Brooklyn Museum of Art, personal communication, November 26, 2001.

4   Sarah R. Demb and Jill U. Jackson, *The Preservation of Anthropology Field Notes* (unpublished manuscript, 1996).

"Some sites are so inaccessible, remote, or so expensive to reach that the number of data gathering opportunities there are small. Any records, even incomplete or flawed records of expeditions to very remote areas may be worthy of retention."[i]

—*Deborah D. Day*
Scripps Institute of Oceanography,
UC San Diego

---

i   "Danger at Sea: Documentation of Oceanographic Expeditions," paper presented at the 2001 SAA annual meeting session, "Extreme Science: Pushing the Envelope on Land, on Sea, and in the Air." An abbreviated version of the text, from which this quotation is taken, may be found at <www.archivists.org/saagroups/sthc/aelements2002.html>.

---

1   Jean Jackson, "'I am a Fieldnote': Fieldnotes as a Symbol of Professional Identity" in *Fieldnotes: the Makings of Anthropology* (Ithaca, N.Y.: Cornell University Press, 1990), 10.

2   Ibid, 22.

that address the intellectual property issues. Who owns the data? Who can use it? For what purposes? At what point in time?

Note that research is often carried out by a group or team of investigators; be on the lookout for cross-institutional project data and other cooperative ventures to learn about other related materials and to ensure that all copyrights are transferred with the archival materials.

Deborah D. Day details several documentation concerns that might not immediately occur to archivists, noting the following issues relating to expeditions and their records. The normal distinction between professional and personal life that exists in most laboratories diminishes on hazardous field expeditions. Personal narratives reveal hierarchies and discipline and offer

Natural History curator Edward L. Morris with large crate and copious supplies of creosote bush used in packing cacti, pre-1913. BROOKLYN MUSEUM OF ART ARCHIVES, PHOTOGRAPH COLLECTION. MORRIS FIELD PHOTOGRAPHS.

"The large computers, with their ability to do something with literally millions of numbers, are revolutionizing physical oceanography. . . . A complete description of our object of study would fill so many rolls of magnetic tape that it would be larger than the object itself, and hence useless for human comprehension. The dilemma is constantly changing."
—*Roger Revelle*[ii]

ii Roger Revelle, Presidential Address to the International Association for the Physical Sciences of the Oceans, 14th General Assembly, 1967. International Association for the Physical Sciences of the Oceans, *IUGG Process-Verbaux* 10 (1967): 6.

excellent documentation of danger. Relationships among coworkers in the field are relevant to their work and consequently interpersonal communication is important. Records that might at first seem personal or trivial, such as personnel lists; bunk, tent, and mess assignments; menus; newsletters; and daily messages, can be important team documentation. These may reflect team cohesiveness, effectiveness, conflict, and hierarchies. There may be additional legal reasons for retaining scientific records. Expedition personnel may be required to sign contracts, swear oaths, or sign away certain rights when joining an expedition. Discipline and chain of command become manifest in some expedition records—documentation that is important to retain.[5]

Compounding the difficulty of preserving field and research data is the physical state of the materials: records are often created and housed in less than ideal conditions. Museum curators may work outside the museum environment or in laboratory settings that bring records into contact with debilitating environments or substances. For example, anthropologists have reported that the physical state of their field notes is frequently very poor even as they are generated in the field. They relate storing notebooks under mattresses, or in the eaves of thatch huts, and having to contend with extremes of heat and humidity, as well as the appetites and curiosity of bugs, rodents, and nonhuman primates.[6]

Records produced in the field and/or stored with artifacts collected in the field may be at high risk for infestations, mold, and, at the very least, dirt. Assess their condition in a "quarantine room" before bringing them into archival storage areas. Work with conservators to clean records safely before they are ready to be processed and made accessible for research. The dental vacuums used in conservation labs are a great help with loose particulates found on records. Notebook bindings and other covers that are permanently soiled or rusted can be removed from the text block and bagged to discourage dirt migration. Copy any information from the covers onto acid-free paper to store with the text block.

Consultation with curators and research in the archives may shed light on the types of compounds

5 Ibid., unpaginated (see "Collection Strategies: Areas of Documentation").

6 Demb and Jackson, *Preservation of Anthropology Field Notes*, 7.

used on art, ethnographic artifacts, or scientific specimens. Look at the accession records for your older archival collections to see where in the building they were stored before coming to the archives—it is very likely that they were housed in departmental storage areas along with objects. If notebooks are more than fifty years old, they may well have been stored with artifacts or specimens and exposed to pesticides.[7] Take appropriate precautions or explore microfilm and other reformatting options to prevent exposure to hazardous materials.

Notebooks are often ideal digitization projects. A digital version may prolong the life of the material by limiting its use; the digital image can be enhanced, making it easier to read than the original; and scholars can have intensive research access from a distance. Some materials may be good candidates for optical character recognition (OCR), yielding a searchable, full-text digital file. Note, however, that it may be necessary to disbind the notebook to obtain a usable image. Weigh access and preservation concerns against each other before embarking on an imaging project.

Providing access to field and scientific research materials can be challenging. Describing such research materials can often best be done in consultation with specialists in the field, so that the significance of the records is analyzed knowledgeably and they are described using the correct terminology. Experts can also alert you to potential problems—exposing information about archaeological sites to illegal pot hunters, for example. If the information in the notebooks goes beyond the research project and documents vital museum activities or key collections, consider indexing notebook sections within the finding aid rather than relying on summary cover descriptions to guide researchers. Both researchers and archivists may find related published reference works helpful when the notebooks contain standardized scientific notations.

One of the challenges—and rewards—of working in an institutional archives is the contact between records creator and archivist. Take advantage of this contact to gain as much knowledge about the researcher, the research, and the records as you can. Encourage curators to create metadata about their data (descriptions of the data elements), so that it will be more understandable to future researchers. Talk to curators about the research climate of their various fields: is it cooperative or competitive? Let them know that you understand their concerns about privacy and intellectual property, but create policies that are clearly defined and fair to all. Learn about all the research records that exist in your institution, even if they are likely to remain "active" for years. Keep in mind that waiting can be a useful tactic. The time between the institutional and personal collection of data and accessioning it into the archives can be very long due to the active usefulness of the data over the scientist's career. Schedule records accordingly and always consult with relevant staff members about the active life of data. Records that are firmly closed by the depart-

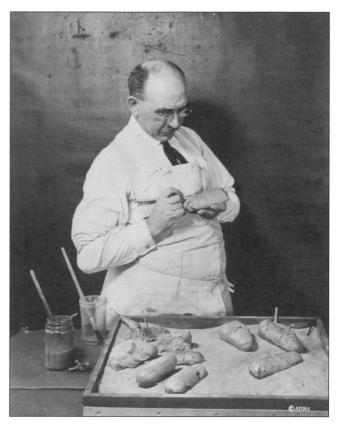

Mr. George Allen and dinosaur eggs, January 1924. PHOTOGRAPH BY H. S. RICE. AMERICAN MUSEUM OF NATURAL HISTORY LIBRARY, NEG. #310477.

ment now may eventually come to the archives and be opened when staff members retire.

And finally, learn everything you can about the physical characteristics of the records—where they were created, everything with which they may have come in contact, known hazards—and record this information for future archivists: remember when asbestos was considered a miracle material?

---

7   See the preservation chapter.

MUSEUM ARCHIVES ISSUES

22

NATIVE AMERICAN GRAVES PROTECTION AND REPATRIATION ACT (NAGPRA)

Sarah R. Demb

The Native American Graves Protection and Repatriation Act (NAGPRA) of 1990[1] mandates that all federal agencies and federally or partially federally funded museums return human remains, funerary objects, sacred objects, and objects of cultural patrimony (communal objects) to federally recognized Native American tribes. The National Park Service, the regulators of the law, required museums to submit collections summaries by November 16, 1994; museums then had until 1995 to attain "inventory completion" of all archaeological artifacts that fell into the above categories. Inventories were sent to tribal groups and a "notice of inventory completion" to the National Park Service; the latter was subsequently published in the *Federal Register*. Some of the largest museums were unable to complete inventories by 1995 and were first given extensions and, later, limited forbearances within which to complete the inventories. The Smithsonian Institution museums are exceptions to the law, but have their own repatriation regulations, which provide for return of the same types of materials cited in NAGPRA.

According to NAGPRA, once inventories are completed and published, tribes may claim artifacts. Museums are expected to work with tribes and their representatives to negotiate these repatriation claims. The entire process is based on meticulous research by all parties and can take many years to complete. The claims process will continue indefinitely, now that the initial inventories are complete. In addition, at the request of individual tribes, museums are required to inventory *ethnographic*[2] artifacts of cultural patrimony; no deadlines are specified for this aspect of the process.

The impact of NAGPRA on anthropology, archaeology, art, and natural history museums cannot be underestimated. Museums with large Native American collections have had to find additional funding to obtain the staff needed for such a large project. NAGPRA has provided these museums with an unprecedented opportunity to forge new relationships with Native American communities, even though these relationships grow within a framework that is often highly emotional and sensitive. This sensitivity must extend to the museum archives.

NAGPRA inventories are generated by museum staff members who work with archivists to use materials such as accession ledgers and files (the vital records of the institution), object records in both paper and electronic formats, museum correspondence, and field notes to document the artifacts. The NAGPRA process may lead to a number of issues that museum archivists must account for in planning repatriation activities.

The increased use of vital records by museum staff and outside researchers can damage or destroy fragile and older materials. Consider reformatting to make preservation copies of high-use items such as accession ledgers and field notes. Some museums have chosen to scan these materials to facilitate repatriation research and to encourage transparency within the process, by making the information easily accessible and portable.

Anticipate increased patron needs. Repatriation research often involves groups of on-site researchers. If your everyday patron service is usually restricted to one or two researchers at a time because of space or staff constraints, you will have to be resourceful. Small archives may be able to obtain grant funding to hire extra staff or to set up additional reading room space for NAGPRA consultation visits. One-person archival shops need to work closely with the museum administration to find creative solutions to the issues generated by

---

1 Public Law 101-601; 25 U.S.C. 3001–3013; 104 Stat. 3048–3058.

2 As opposed to the archaeological artifacts specified in the initial process.

increased demand for their services. Be on the lookout for tensions that may be created by competing demands for limited archival resources. It is important to remember that you must provide equal access to museum staff, tribal researchers, and other patrons in a reasonable, timely fashion.

Traditionally, only museum documents that contained donor or valuation information have been considered "sensitive." In the light of NAGPRA, you now need to look at repatriation-related records more carefully and flag other documents that may be identified as sensitive by patrons. Materials that contain archaic language derogatory to the visiting tribal members, genealogical or sacred information restricted to certain tribal members, or photographs of sacred objects not usually viewed by tribal members may require special treatment. Communicate with the repatriation staff and tribal consultants on NAGPRA to identify sensitive materials in advance of consultation visits. Verbal or written warning about sensitive materials enables a successful visit in what can be a stressful context.

Museum archivists have become used to developing access and privacy policies internally with perhaps some reference to state and federal law. During NAGPRA visits, tribal representatives may ask the museum to restrict access to certain materials—published and unpublished—considered private or sensitive by Native American users. Listening skills and a willingness to participate in this dialogue are essential to the NAGPRA process, as is creativity in devising workable solutions.

Depending on the extent of your collections, your museum's NAGPRA efforts may range from an office staffed by one or more specialists to a small project undertaken by a curator or registrar. Beyond the scope

NAGPRA IN BRIEF

Sec. 2 104 §3048–49 Definitions
(c) "sacred objects" shall mean specific ceremonial objects which are needed by traditional North American religious leaders for the practice of traditional Native American religions by their present–day adherents, and

(d) "cultural patrimony" shall mean an object having on-going historical, traditional, or cultural importance central to the Native American group or culture itself, rather than property owned by an individual Native American.

Sec. 5 104 §3003 Inventory
(2) Upon request by an Indian tribe or Native Hawaiian organization which receives, or should have received notice, a museum or federal agency shall supply additional available documentation to supplement the information required by subsection (2) of this section [list inventory of objects with geographical and cultural affiliation of each item]. The term "documentation" means a summary of existing museum or federal agency records, including inventories, catalogues, relevant studies or other pertinent data for the limited purpose of determining the geographical origin, cultural affiliation, and basic facts surrounding the acquisition and accession of Native American human remains and associate funerary or other objects subject to this section.

Sec. 5 104 §3004
The summary (written) after consultation with organization officials should contain the scope of the collection, kinds of objects, reference to geographical location, means and period of acquisition, where readily available.

Sec. 6 104 §3054 Summary
Upon request, Indian tribes and Native American organizations shall have access to records, relevant studies or other pertinent data for the limited purpose of determining the geographic origin, cultural affiliation, and basic facts surrounding the acquisition and accession of Native American objects subject to this section. Such information shall be provided in a reasonable manner to be agreed upon by all parties.

Sec. 7 104 §3054 Repatriation
(c) Sharing of information by federal agencies or museums. Any federal agency or museum shall share what information it does possess regarding the object in question with the known lineal descendant, Indian tribe, or Native Hawaiian organization to assist in making a claim under this section.

of the research and administrative work undertaken by these staff members, however, NAGPRA ultimately involves the expertise of people from several offices—curators, registrars, archivists, trustees, administrators—working with representatives from a broad cross-section of tribal groups. It is an opportunity to gain important knowledge and understanding for all participants.

POLICY AND PROCEDURES FOR SENSITIVE MATERIALS

"When materials have been identified as sensitive by tribal representatives, a statement detailing their concerns will be placed in the appropriate file(s) to alert researchers to the issues. . . . Requests to reproduce or cite materials identified as sensitive by tribal representatives or by Museum staff will undergo a more rigorous review, including involvement of appropriate curatorial staff. Commercial use of these research materials will be subject to closer scrutiny and may be refused if inappropriate. A letter of approval from tribal representatives may be required before permission to reproduce or cite is granted."

—*Guidelines: Native American Research Materials,* 1997
Brooklyn Museum of Art Archives

23

RESTITUTION OF NAZI-LOOTED ART

Catherine Herbert

The misappropriation of cultural objects is one of the many painful legacies of World War II. As museums have become increasingly aware of the extent of the Nazi art-looting problem, research into the ownership history of artworks and other cultural objects has become of paramount importance. This chapter will focus on Nazi-era provenance research in permanent museum collections, with examples and case studies from the Philadelphia Museum of Art (PMA). As we will see, the museum archives can play a key role in clarifying the often-murky history of objects in the collections.

Nazi Art Looting, 1933–1945

Throughout history, conquerors from King Nebuchadnezzar to Napoleon have seized art treasures from other nations as trophies or "spoils of war" to glorify their own empires.[1] However, the Nazi government's systematic campaign of art looting stands apart for its sheer vastness of scale and for the almost obsessive range of cultural objects stolen from private individuals, primarily Jews. The victims of this campaign lost hundreds of thousands of objects, from paintings, drawings, and sculpture, to tapestries, furniture, and other decorative art, even household linens and family archives, justifying the characterization of Hitler's regime as a "kleptocracy."

Hitler and his circle favored Old Master artists, particularly treasuring Northern European artists such as Rembrandt, Cranach, and Vermeer, whom they regarded as expressing the true "Aryan" spirit. Italian Renaissance and baroque art, as well as French eighteenth-century art and German nineteenth-century academic art were also collecting priorities. Although the Nazi regime despised all modernist art as "degenerate"—especially abstract, Cubist, Expressionist, and Surrealist art—such art was often looted and then exchanged with cooperative dealers for more desirable works. In other words, practically any type of art was subject to Nazi looting. Hitler planned to create a monumental museum of art in his childhood home of Linz in Austria, and by war's end some 8,000 artworks had been designated for Linz. The voracious Reichsmarschall Hermann Goering also amassed an enormous art collection at Carinhall, his country estate.[2] Such was his obsession with this cache of mostly looted art that at the end of the war in 1945, as the Soviet Red Army approached Carinhall, Goering evacuated his treasures by train to his villa in Berchtesgaden in Bavaria. Ironically, upon its arrival the train was looted by townspeople.

As early as 1933, soon after Hitler's rise to power, Nazi officials compelled Jewish families in Germany to relinquish artwork and other valuables in forced sales known as "Jew auctions." Some of the finest prewar art collections in Europe had been formed by Jewish families, among them the Bondy and Gutmann collections in Austria, which were plundered immediately after the German *Anschluss* (union) with Austria in 1938. In France, the Nazis looted the Schloss, David-Weill, Kann, and Paul Rosenberg collections soon after the invasion in 1940.[3] The opulent art collections and furnishings of the aristocratic Rothschild family, who had residences in both France and Austria, were

---

1 On this general topic, see Jeannette Greenfield, "The Spoils of War," in Elizabeth Simpson, ed., *The Spoils of War: World War II and Its Aftermath: The Loss, Reappearance, and Recovery of Cultural Property* (New York: H. N. Abrams in association with the Bard Graduate Center for Studies in the Decorative Arts, 1997), 34–38. Nor is the art restitution issue limited to Nazi activities: see for example the *New York Times* article concerning recent claims for art lost by Cuban families who fled Castro's government ("Reclaiming Art Caught in the Cuban Revolution," by Celestine Bohlen, June 6, 2002). Artwork seized by the Soviet Union from Nazi Germany as "spoils of war" and still held in Russian repositories represents another major aspect of the WWII looting issue, examined by Konstantin Akinsha in *Beautiful Loot: The Soviet Plunder of Europe's Art Treasures* (New York: Random House, 1995).

2 Jonathan Petropolous analyzes Nazi collecting policies in *Art as Politics in the Third Reich* (Chapel Hill: University of North Carolina Press, 1996).

3 Hector Feliciano discusses these major French collections and their fates in detail in his book *The Lost Museum* (New York: Basic Books, 1997).

particular targets. With the occupation of France, the Nazis established an elaborate art-looting task force, the Einsatzstab Reichsleiter Rosenberg (ERR), named after Nazi ideologue Alfred Rosenberg. In addition to obtaining cultural objects by outright coercion, when Jewish owners fled occupied France, fearing persecution, the Nazi government seized the artworks left behind as "abandoned property."

The ERR gathered the confiscated art at the Jeu de Paume in Paris, where it was meticulously cataloged and warehoused to await Hitler's or Goering's wishes.[4] Far from hiding the artworks' origins, Nazi officials took a perverse pride in identifying the prestigious Jewish collections from which they were looted. One of the paintings now in the collection of the PMA, Jean-Baptiste-Camille Corot's *Pensive Young Brunette,* was marked on the back with the ERR code "Ka 38," for the French collector Alphonse Kann from whom it was seized. Fortunately, in this case the painting was restituted to Kann after the war.[5] The ERR inventory cards, which were confiscated by the Allies and are now housed at the National Archives and Records Administration (NARA) in Washington, D.C., provide invaluable information about the origins and disposition of looted artwork.

Toward the end of the war, to protect the looted art from Allied bombs, the Nazis hastily gathered it in huge repositories, including a network of disused salt mines in Germany and Austria. There the Allied forces discovered the collections at war's end. To house and process these cultural objects, the U.S. military set up four central collecting points in the U.S. zone of Germany, the most famous of which, the Munich Central Collecting Point, specialized in objects to be restituted outside of Germany. The U.S. policy in general was to repatriate artwork to the national government of its country of origin (a painting by a French artist, for example, was returned to France). It was then up to the government of that country to restitute the work to its original owner. NARA also preserves the Allied records pertaining to the recovery and repatriation of Nazi-looted art.[6]

In the mid-1990s, several scholarly publications aimed at general audiences, including Lynn Nicholas' *Rape of Europa*[7] and Hector Feliciano's *The Lost Museum* drew attention to the subject of Nazi art looting and its contemporary repercussions. After a series of high-profile claims cases in the 1990s, museums in the U.S. belatedly discovered that, through no fault of their own, objects with dubious histories might have entered their collections through purchase or donation. While many looted artworks were restituted to their rightful owners after the war, many others found their way instead through various channels onto the international art market. Their movements during the Nazi era were either deliberately covered up or forgotten with the passage of time, so that later owners, despite purchasing an artwork in good faith, might find that in fact they did not have legal title to it. Recognizing this problem with regard to museums, the American Association of Museums (AAM) worked with the Presidential Advisory Commission on Holocaust Assets in the United States (PCHA) and the Association of Art Museum Directors (AAMD) to establish a standard for disclosure of collections information. In 1999, the AAM issued formal guidelines (amended April 2001) on the topic. AAM, AAMD, and PCHA also agreed that the initial focus of research should be European paintings and Judaica.

To fulfill the AAM's recommendation to make provenance information on their collections publicly accessible, most large museums in the United States now devote portions of their Web sites to their ongoing provenance research. Depending on the individual museum's resources, these sites may include lists of *all*

---

7   Lynn Nicholas, *The Rape of Europa: The Fate of Europe's Treasures in the Third Reich and the Second World War* (New York: Alfred A. Knopf, 1994).

TERMINOLOGY

Provenance: the history of ownership of a work of art from the time it left the artist's studio to its current owner.

Restitution: return of a cultural object or payment of compensation to the object's original owner or legal successor.

Repatriation: return of a cultural object to its country of origin.

---

4   In France alone, the ERR confiscated almost 17,000 objects from 200 families; see Nancy Yeide et al., *The AAM Guide to Provenance Research* (Washington, D.C.: American Association of Museums, 2001), 58.

5   The painting was donated to the Philadelphia Museum of Art in 1963 by Louis E. Stern (accession no. 1963-181-18). For a discussion and reproductions of the work, see the PMA's Web site, <www.phila museum.org/collections/provenance/objects1.shtml>.

6   The National Archives held a symposium, *Records and Research Related to Holocaust-era Assets,* in 1998. Papers from the symposium are available at <www.archives.gov/research_room/ holocaust_era_assets/research_conference_papers_reports/ papers_and_proceedings.html>.

paintings in their collections that could have been in Europe during the relevant time period, regardless of whether there are gaps in their provenance (the current AAM recommendation), or more narrowly, only those works with unresolved gaps.[8]

What Is Provenance Research?

The provenance researcher aims to track the movement of an art object from owner to owner and to document and date each transfer, whether by gift, inheritance, or sale, with the ultimate goal of demonstrating an unbroken chain of ownership from the artist to the work's current owner. Documentation is the watchword of provenance research. Ideally, every ownership transfer in an artwork's provenance will be

supported by some sort of written evidence. If a claim against an artwork is made, such documentation will be crucial in determining rightful ownership. This documentation can include published references such as early exhibition catalogs, auction catalogs, artist's monographs, artist's or dealer's memoirs, and so on, but often the supporting evidence will consist of unpublished records found in museum archives and registrar's files, such as dealer receipts and donor correspondence. As primary sources, these types of records are the most desirable for documenting transfers of ownership.

A complete provenance with every transfer fully documented is, however, a rare thing, and often gaps will remain despite the researcher's best efforts. Gaps do not necessarily indicate anything suspicious in the work's history. For example, paintings may have been passed down through a family for several generations with no record of sale. Records of dealers and auction houses active in the nineteenth and early twentieth centuries but no longer in business may have been lost or destroyed.[9] Additionally, private collectors often prefer to buy and sell works anonymously through dealers or auction houses, whose records therefore may hide their identity.

As mentioned above, the museum archivist's focus with regard to Nazi-era provenance research will be the permanent collections. Although the provenance of incoming loans and new acquisitions is also of major concern to museums, this research generally will not involve the archivist. Who will the provenance researcher be? Larger museums may have room in their budgets for one or more full-time provenance researchers; in smaller museums the task most often falls on the curators, who must pursue provenance research as time allows. In addition to a background in art history, provenance researchers are expected to have experience in using and interpreting a variety of historical sources, including archival sources, and to have proficiency in foreign languages. In general, provenance research is not as time sensitive as, for example, an exhibition project. The AAM guidelines recognize that provenance research is "an often lengthy and arduous process" whose results may remain inconclusive. However, museums *are* under considerable moral pressure to examine the history of their collections and make provenance information publicly available as soon as possible. Furthermore, it is to

---

8   For a list of these museums, with links to their Web sites, see the AAM site, <http://www.aam-us.org/initiatives/nazi-era/museum_nazi.cfm>.

MUSEUM RESPONSIBILITIES

In order to aid in the identification and discovery of unlawfully appropriated objects that may be in the custody of museums, the PCHA, AAMD, and AAM have agreed that museums should strive to:

1) identify all objects in their collections that were created before 1946 and acquired by the museum after 1932, that underwent a change of ownership between 1932 and 1946, and that were or might reasonably be thought to have been in continental Europe between those dates;

2) make currently available object and provenance (history of ownership) information on those objects accessible; and

3) give priority to continuing provenance research as resources allow.

From *Guidelines Concerning the Unlawful Appropriation of Objects during the Nazi Era,* American Association of Museums, 1999 (amended 2001).[i]

---

i   The guidelines are published in full on the AAM Web site, <http://www.aam-us.org/initiatives/nazi-era/procedures_nazi.cfm>.

---

9   The Smithsonian Institution's Archives of American Art has a searchable on-line catalog of its extensive holdings of dealer archives: <www.aaa.si.edu/catalog.htm>.

the museum's benefit to discover potential problems sooner rather than later, before a claim is submitted.

The bible of provenance researchers is the AAM *Guide to Provenance Research,* published in 2001 by the American Association of Museums. While its research principles are applicable to any type of provenance research, the guide is geared to Nazi-era provenance issues in particular. As a glance at the AAM *Guide* will show, provenance research encompasses a broad range of basic sources. The most important of these are the museum's own institutional files, *catalogues raisonnés,*[10] artists' monographs, exhibition catalogs, auction catalogs, and unpublished sources such as dealer records (whether belonging to an active dealer or housed in repositories), and other archival resources. On-line resources[11] include the Getty Provenance Index,[12] a group of searchable databases including provenance information on paintings gathered from museums throughout the United States, and auction catalog databases such as SCIPIO, part of the Research Libraries Group's Eureka system. The object itself can also provide important clues: paintings often have labels on the back indicating former owners, dealers, or exhibitions to which the work was lent.

More often than not, the provenance information with which the researcher is first presented is incomplete. The curatorial object files are the first place the researcher will look. These are active files that typically include basic "tombstone" information concerning each piece (artist, title, date, medium, date of acquisition, and donor, if any), and its known provenance. Curatorial object files also track published references and exhibitions, plus curatorial correspondence concerning the object, if any, and may include copies of conservation records (these last are usually restricted to museum personnel). Much of this information is now being entered into electronic museum databases such as TMS (The Museum System) by Gallery Systems, Argus by Questor, and other collections management systems.

The Role of the Museum Archives

Although much provenance research can be pursued in a library, the researcher will rely on the museum archivist to guide him or her to unpublished sources within the institution. After the curatorial files, the museum archives is one of the first resources the provenance researcher turns to for primary documentation. While each institution's organization of its collection files is idiosyncratic, certain basic groupings are typical, including the above-mentioned curatorial files, as well as registrar's files, donor files, and institutional archives.[13] In the case of the PMA, many of the objects falling within the AAM guidelines were not recent acquisitions purchased by the museum itself, but rather were acquired as collections formed by various donors in the early to mid-twentieth century and bequeathed to the museum in the 1950s and 1960s. Thus many of the relevant donor files are no longer active and have been deposited in the museum archives.

The archives can be a goldmine of provenance information: donor files, for example, may contain dealer receipts as well as correspondence with dealers and former owners. By the 1950s and 1960s, some collectors were even aware of the looting problem and made a special effort to record provenance information. Dealers sometimes provide a written provenance along with a receipt. The dealer's provenance may—or

---

13 AAM *Guide to Provenance Research,* 15–17.

COMPLETED PROVENANCE: MARC CHAGALL'S 1943 PAINTING *In the Night*

With Pierre Matisse Gallery, New York, from the artist, 1943 [1]; sold to Louis E. Stern (1882–1962), New York, November 22, 1943 [2]; bequeathed to the Philadelphia Museum of Art, 1963, accession number 1963-181-16.

(Note: if there were a gap in the provenance, the entries would be separated by a period rather than a semicolon.)

1. Matisse Gallery stockbook, purchases 1932–1947, purchased from Chagall November 27, 1943 (Pierre Matisse Gallery Archives, The Morgan Library, New York, Box 171, file 33).

2. Copy of dated receipt in curatorial file (original in Philadelphia Museum of Art Archives, Stern Collection files).

---

10 A *catalogue raisonné* is an exhaustive catalog of the artist's entire output, typically including for each work a provenance, exhibition, and publication history.

11 For an extensive annotated list of on-line resources relating to Nazi-era provenance research, see the Museum of Modern Art's Web site: <www.moma.org/provenance/provenance_online.html>.

12 <http://www.getty.edu/research/institute/provenance/index.html>.

may not—be entirely reliable, but at least serves as a place to start. Some donors were more conscientious than others about keeping receipts and correspondence with dealers; do not be surprised, therefore, if such documentation is entirely lacking. Biographical materials (including newspaper clippings, etc.) about donors are often found in the files and can provide clues to the donor's collecting habits: for example, when and where they traveled and what dealers they typically patronized; sometimes the files even include dated photographs of the collector's home with artworks installed. Largely because Nazi-era provenance issues have only recently become a major concern, copies of receipts and other valuable provenance information preserved in the archives may not have made their way into the curatorial files. For example, the personal papers of donors Louise and Walter Arensberg, who bequeathed their major collection of twentieth-century art to the PMA in 1950, provided a wealth of documentation in the form of original receipts and correspondence from dealers not recorded in the object files. Because of the vast size of the archives, the project archivist's knowledge of the material was crucial to locating relevant items.[14]

Be aware, too, that useful information about an object, such as dealer receipts, may sometimes be found with the registrar's records, because they pertain to the legal aspects of the artwork (its acquisition, valuation, and loan). Because of its sensitive nature, price and insurance valuation information is of course typically restricted to museum personnel, depending on the type of information and whether the donor is living or deceased, for example.[15] Information about whether an object was borrowed or loaned for exhibition will also be found in the registrar's files and can be very useful in pinning down the whereabouts of an artwork at specific times, as well as explaining labels found on the back of the piece. For example, if its pre-World War II ownership history is unknown, but it can be shown to have been exhibited consistently in the U.S. during the war years, then it is highly unlikely to have also been in Europe (and hence subject to looting) during that time.

If a donor's collection was extensive enough to warrant a separate published catalog, the curator in charge of cataloging may have conducted basic prove-

nance research, including sending letters of inquiry to dealers. These materials would then be preserved in the curator's records and may well contain more detailed information than the published catalog. In the case of the PMA's Louis E. Stern Collection, bequeathed to the museum in 1963, assistant curator of paintings Henry G. Gardiner conducted extensive provenance research for the collection catalog published in 1964. His research files are preserved in the museum archives, organized with the object files of the museum director of the time, Henri Marceau.

This archival documentation played a crucial role in resolving the problematic history of one of the museum's paintings, *Nude Reclining by the Sea* by Gustave Courbet.[16] Publications had simply noted that Paul Rosenberg & Co. sold the painting to Louis Stern on April 1, 1953, a fact confirmed by the original sales receipt preserved in the PMA archives. What was not commonly known was that the Nazi art-looting task force, the ERR, seized the painting in 1941 from the collection of Paris dealer Rosenberg. An ERR code on the back of the painting identifies it as one of 162 paintings taken from Rosenberg's bank vault in Bordeaux, where he sent part of his collection for safekeeping. Further, the ERR catalog card (now at NARA) is marked with the initials "HG," indicating that the painting was selected by Hermann Goering for his personal collection or exchange. When preparing the catalog of the Stern Collection in 1964, Gardiner wrote to the Paul Rosenberg firm to inquire about the Courbet's provenance. The reply from Rosenberg's son Alexandre, also in the museum archives, confirmed that *Nude Reclining by the Sea* had indeed been looted during the war, but noted that the Allies had restituted it to his father, then living in New York City, in the late 1940s.[17] The letter verified that the work had been restituted to its former owner and later legally sold to Stern, affirming the museum's good title to the painting. Interestingly, the published catalog made no mention of the painting's WWII history.

The story of the Courbet is but one example of the fundamental role of the museum archives in Nazi-era provenance research. Not every story will end as happily for the museum; however, it is essential that the museum community continue to strive to redress the wrongs committed more than half a century ago.

---

14 The Arensberg Archives is currently part of a project funded by a grant from the Andrew W. Mellon Foundation to enhance scholarly access to several historically significant manuscript and record collections through an integrated program of processing, database development, digitization, and encoding for Internet distribution. However, whether archives are accessed electronically or through old-fashioned finding aids, the museum archivist's expertise serves as the portal for the researcher's approach to the material.

15 See the chapter on research use.

---

16 The Louis E. Stern Collection, 1963; accession no. 1963-181-20.

17 Letter from Alexandre Rosenberg, Paul Rosenberg & Co., to Henry G. Gardiner, June 9, 1964, Philadelphia Museum of Art Archives, Marceau Object Files, Series 2; Stern, Louis E. (Collection), 1964; Research for Catalogue. For a full account of the painting's history, which was researched by Jennifer Thompson of the PMA, see the museum Web site, <www.philamuseum.org/collections/provenance/objects1.shtml>.

TOP Gustave Courbet, *Nude Reclining by the Sea,* 1868. Philadelphia Museum of Art, The Louis E. Stern Collection, 1963, no. 1963-181-20.

RIGHT Reverse of Courbet *Nude Reclining by the Sea,* with Nazi-era labels and markings. Philadelphia Museum of Art. Photo: Graydon Wood.

BOTTOM RIGHT Detail of reverse, with ERR code "Rosenberg Bordeaux" painted on stretcher. Philadelphia Museum of Art. Photo: Graydon Wood.

BOTTOM LEFT Detail of reverse, with Nazi cataloging label recording the title, "Reclining female nude," and the source from which the painting was looted, the Rosenberg Collection, Bordeaux. Philadelphia Museum of Art. Photo: Graydon Wood.

RESOURCE GUIDE

Laura Peimer

PROFESSIONAL ARCHIVAL ORGANIZATIONS

There are numerous local, state, regional, national, and international professional organizations for archivists. These organizations generally meet once or more during the year and provide an opportunity for archivists to congregate, discuss work issues, and network. As a member of a professional organization, you have the opportunity to attend seminars, workshops, or meetings sponsored by the organization and may receive publications, including directories and newsletters. Contact the specific professional organization for information on membership fees, the benefits of membership, and a schedule of events and meetings.

For complete, up-to-date lists for the United States and Canada see:
            <http://www.archivists.org/assoc-orgs/directory/index.asp>
            <http://sophia.smith.edu/~pnelson/regionals/>

For a list that includes organizations based abroad see:
            <http://www.archivesinfo.net/proassn.html#assc>

Information about selected organizations:

- **Society of American Archivists (SAA)**
  <http://www.archivists.org>
  527 S. Wells Street, 5th Floor, Chicago, IL 60607-3922
  phone: 312-922-0140, fax: 312-347-1452;
  The Society of American Archivists is the national organization for archives professionals. It coordinates an annual meeting for members consisting of lectures, panel discussions, and workshops on archival topics. Members receive the journal *American Archivist* and a newsletter, *Archival Outlook*. Among the many institutional and functional sections and roundtables within SAA is the Museum Archives Section. This section, open to all SAA members, meets at the SAA annual meeting and produces a newsletter, *Museum Archivist,* which is an excellent source of articles relating to museum archives.

- **Mid-Atlantic Regional Archives Conference**
  <http://www.itd.umd.edu/MARAC/archives.htm>

- **Midwest Archives Conference**
  <http://www.midwestarchives.org/>

- **New England Archivists**
  <http://nils.lib.tufts.edu/newengarch/>

- **Northwest Archivists**
  <http://www.lib.washington.edu/nwa/>

- **Society of California Archivists**
  <http://www.calarchivists.org/>

- **Society of Southwest Archivists**
  <http://southwestarchivists.org/>

- **Southern Archivists Conference**

- **Archivists Round Table of Metropolitan New York**
  <http://www.nycarchivists.org/>

- **International Council on Archives**
  <http://www.ica.org/>
  The mission of the ICA, the professional organization for the world archival community, is the advancement of archives through international cooperation. For information on the categories of membership and benefits, see the ICA Web site.

RELATED PROFESSIONAL ORGANIZATIONS

- **American Association of Museums (AAM)**
  <http://www.aam-us.org/>
  The American Association of Museums is the national organization for the museum community. The organization offers an annual meeting, seminars, workshops, and special interest groups, and it publishes *Museum News* and *Aviso*, a monthly newsletter with job listings. See the AAM Web site for more information about AAM's mission and the benefits of membership.

- **American Association for State and Local History (AASLH)**
  <http://www.aaslh.org/>
  AASLH sponsors an annual meeting, workshops, and seminars; the magazine, *History News;* and a newsletter, *Dispatch.* Its Technical Leaflet series is of great value to museum professionals.

- **New England Museum Association (NEMA)**
  <http://www.nemanet.org/>
  The New England Museum Association offers professional development opportunities such as conferences, seminars, workshops, and publications. NEMA publishes a quarterly journal, *NemaNews,* and a bimonthly job listing, *NemaJobs.*

- **Mid-Atlantic Association of Museums (MAAM)**
  <http://www.altrue.net/site/midatlantic/>
  The Mid-Atlantic Association of Museums coordinates an annual meeting, workshops, and publications, including a newsletter, *The Courier,* published quarterly.

- **Western Museums Association (WMA)**
  <http://www.westmuse.org/>
  The mission of the Western Museums Association includes the promotion and support of "the role of museums in bettering and enriching the diverse and dynamic cultural life of the Western United States." WMA organizes an annual meeting and provides scholarship opportunities.

- **Society for the Preservation of Natural History Collections (SPNHC)**
  <http://www.spnhc.org/>
  SPNHC is a multidisciplinary organization composed of individuals who are interested in the development and preservation of natural history collections. The organization supports a professional publication program, including the journal *Collection Forum,* and hosts an annual meeting and workshop.

- **National Initiative for a Networked Cultural Heritage (NINCH)**
  <http://www.ninch.org/>
  NINCH, a coalition of organizations created to assure leadership from the cultural community in the evolution of the digital environment, produces publications and educational programs to advance that mission.

- **Archives & Museum Informatics**
  <http://www.archimuse.com/>
  Archives & Museum Informatics organizes an annual international conference devoted exclusively to museums and the Web. Since the first Museums and the Web conference in 1997, the conference has grown to become the largest gathering of cultural heritage technology professionals worldwide.

- **The Association for Information Management Professionals (ARMA International)**
  <http://www.arma.org/>
  ARMA members include records managers, archivists, librarians, administrators, and educators.

- **First Archivists Circle**
  Pascua Yaqui Tribe, 7474 S. Camino De Oeste, Tucson, AZ 85746, 800-572-7282
  An organization, founded in 2002, for Native American archivists and archivists who deal with Native American records and tribal archives.

- **Council for the Preservation of the Anthropological Record (CoPAR)**
  <http://copar.asu.edu/>
  CoPAR's mission is the identification, support, and promotion of the use of anthropological records. To achieve this, CoPAR organizes workshops and conferences and initiates other special projects, as needed.

For a list of additional museum professional organizations and links to their Web sites, go to the AAM Web site or see:
  <http://dmoz.org/Reference/Museums/Museum_Resources/Organizations/>

CONTINUING ARCHIVAL EDUCATION OPPORTUNITIES

For information on educational programs and institutes, see the SAA *Directory of Archival Education in the United States and Canada* and *Continuing Education and Basic Institutes* at <http://www.archivists.org/prof-education>. For additional educational opportunities in your area, contact your state archives or local library and archives programs.

- **Society of American Archivists**
  SAA's Education Department offers continuing education workshops on a range of archival topics throughout the year at various locations around the country. See the SAA Web site for more information and a catalog of courses.

- **Museum & Library Archives Institute**
  Monson Free Library, 2 High Street, Monson, MA 01057; phone: 413-267-3866; fax: 413-267-5496
  This annual two-day institute is held each summer in New England. Designed for professionals in museums and libraries with limited training in archival methods and procedures, the institute covers all of the archival fundamentals on a two-year cycle and also offers a parallel track for more experienced archivists, focusing on a different special topic each year.

- **New York State Documentary Heritage Program**
  <http://www.archives.nysed.gov/a/nysaservices/nysaservices_training.shtml>
  The Documentary Heritage Program offers workshops on archival topics in New York State.

- **New York State Archives**
  <http://www.archives.nysed.gov/>
  New York State Archives, Training and Grants Support Services, 9A61 CEC, Albany, NY 12230; phone: 518-474-6926
  The New York State Archives provides training in records management and archival issues free of charge to local governments, state agencies, and historical repositories.

- **Modern Archives Institute**
  <http://www.archives.gov/preservation/modern_archives_institute.html>
  The Modern Archives Institute is a two-week course that provides instruction on the basic theory and practice of archival work. The program covers techniques for those who work with personal papers and institutional records and is designed for new archivists in the field.

- **Georgia Archives Institute**
  <http://www.soga.org/ce/gai.html>
  The Georgia Archives Institute is a twelve-day course designed for beginning archivists, covering basic archival theory, concepts, and practical application in archival administration and management. The institute is sponsored by the Georgia Department of Archives and History, the Jimmy Carter Library, and the Atlanta Regional Consortium for Higher Education. The institute also includes a practicum that allows students to try out their new skills at several local archival institutions.

- **Western Archives Institute**
  <http://www.ss.ca.gov/archives/level3_wai.html>
  The Western Archives Institute is a two-week program that focuses on archival fundamentals and is designed largely for individuals who have no previous archival education. The course includes site visits.

- **UCLA/Getty Museums, Libraries and Archives:**
  Summer Institute for Knowledge Sharing
  <http://www.dlis.gseis.ucla.edu/si>
  The Summer Institute for Knowledge Sharing is a four-day program of instruction for archivists, librarians, curators, and others working with electronic information in cultural heritage institutions. Participants discuss issues surrounding the acquisition, creation, management, and preservation of digital collections.

Selected Bibliography

The entries in this section, arranged topically from the general to the specific, include standard references on archives, museum archives, and museums. These suggestions should be a starting point to lead you to more in-depth research in a particular area.

Archival Theory and Practice

Bellardo, Lewis J., and Lynn Lady Bellardo, comps. *A Glossary for Archivists, Manuscript Curators, and Records Managers.* Chicago: Society of American Archivists, 1992.

Conway, Paul. "Perspective on Archival Resources: The 1985 Census of Archival Institutions." *American Archivist* 50, no. 2 (1987): 174–91.

Cox, Richard J. "Archivists and Professionalism in the U.S. Revisited: A Review Essay." *Midwestern Archivist* 15, no. 1 (1990): 5–15.

Daniels, Maygene, and Timothy Walch, eds. *A Modern Archives Reader: Basic Readings on Archival Theory and Practice.* Washington, D.C.: National Archives and Records Administration, 1984.

Hunter, Gregory S. *Developing and Maintaining Practical Archives: A How-To-Do-It Manual.* 2nd ed. How-To-Do-It Manuals for Librarians, no. 122. New York: Neal-Schuman Publishers, 2003.

Jimerson, Randall C., ed. *American Archival Studies: Readings in Theory and Practice.* Chicago: Society of American Archivists, 2000.

Murrah, D. J. "Employer Expectations for Archivists: A Review of a 'Hybrid Profession.'" *Journal of Library Administration* 11, nos. 3–4 (1989): 165–74.

O'Toole, James M. *Understanding Archives and Manuscripts.* Chicago: Society of American Archivists, 1990. (Revised edition forthcoming in 2005)

Pearce-Moses, Richard. *Glossary of Archival and Records Terminology.* Chicago: Society of American Archivists, forthcoming, 2005.

Sample Forms for Archival and Records Management Programs. Lenexa, Kans.: ARMA International and Chicago: Society of American Archivists, 2002.

Schellenberg, T. R. *The Management of Archives.* Washington, D.C.: National Archives and Records Administration, 1988.

Kurtz, Michael. *Managing Archival and Manuscript Repositories.* 2nd ed. Chicago: Society of American Archivists, 2004.

Yakel, Elizabeth. *Starting an Archives.* Metuchen, N.J.: Scarecrow Press, 1994.

Museum Archives

Abid, Ann. "Archives in Art Museums: A Preliminary Survey." *ARLIS/NA Newsletter* 8, no. 2 (February 1980): 42–43.

Bain, Alan L. "An Archivist's Perspective on Natural History Archives." *Association of Systematics Collections Newsletter* 18, no. 6 (December 1990): 86–87.

———. "The Muses' Memory," *Museum News* 70, no. 6 (November/December 1991): 36-39.

Barbour, Sheena, ed. "Museums Association Guidelines on Archives for Museums." *Museums Yearbook,* 1991–1992. London: The Museums Association, ca. 1991.

Baty, Laurie A. *Federal Funding for Museum Archives Development Programs: A Report to the Commission.* Washington, D.C.: NHPRC, 1988.

Bigclow, Susan. "Duels or Dialogues? The Relationship between Archivists and Conservators." *Archivaria* 29 (Winter 1989/90): 51–56.

Bolton, Robin. "Historical Records in Community Museums." *Museum Round-Up* 55 (July 1974): 24–28.

Bottomly, P. Michael. "Conservation and Storage: Archival Paper." In *Manual of Curatorship.* London: Butterworths, 1984: 39–52.

Breton, Arthur. "Professionals Join in Bemont [sic] Conference." *Registrar's Report* 1, no. 9 (1980).

Carlin, John. "Your Past Is Disappearing: What Museums Should Know about the 20th Century Archives Crisis." *Museum News* 78, no. 1 (January/February 1999): 46–49.

Cooper, Adrienne, and Mei-Lin Liu. "Salvaging the Past." *Museum News* 70, no. 6 (November/December 1991): 50–52.

Daniels, Maygene F. "Developing New Museum Archives." *Curator* 31, no. 2 (1988): 99–105.

Davis, George. "Unlocking Nature's Story: Archives and Archivists at the Academy of Natural Sciences, Philadelphia." *Museum News* 70, no. 6 (November/December 1991): 43–45.

Deiss, William. *Museum Archives, an Introduction.* Chicago: Society of American Archivists, 1984.

Eisloffel, Paul, and Lisa Gavin. "Archival Materials in the History Museum: A Strategy for Their Management." Technical Leaflet 179. *History News* 47, no. 3 (May/June 1992).

Fleckner, John A. "An Archivist Speaks to the Museum Profession." *Museum News* (October/November 1986): 17–25.

———. "Archives and Museums." *Midwestern Archivist* 15, no. 2 (1990): 67–76.

Fox-Pitt, Sarah. "The Tate Gallery Archives." AICARC *Bulletin* 10 (1983): 28.

Gartaganis, Arthur. "Archivists and Curators." *Occupational Outlook Quarterly* 29, no. 3 (Fall 1985): 18–22.

Geary, Christraud M., Melissa A. N. Keiser, and Joan Stahl, "Museum Image Banks." *Museum News* 70, no. 6 (November/December 1991): 53–57.

Glaser, Jane R., and Artemis A. Zenetous. *Museums: A Place to Work—Planning Museum Careers.* London: Routledge, 1996.

Gracy, David B., II. "Two Peas in a Pod: Archives for Museums." *Museumline* (Spring 2001): 11.

Greenaway, Frank, et al. "Research: Science Collections." In *Manual of Curatorship: A Guide to Museum Practice.* London: Butterworths, 1984: 142–91.

Haglund, Kristine. "Documenting Our Past." Colorado-Wyoming Association of Museums *Highlights* 2, no. 4 (Winter 1980): 4.

Hartt, Kathleen. "A Manifold Resource." *Museum News* 70, no. 6 (November/December 1991): 40–43.

Heacock, Walter J. "Business Archives and Museum Development." *American Archivist* 29, no. 1 (January 1966): 49–54.

Hommel, Claudia. "A Model Museum Archives." *Museum News* 58, no. 2 (November/December 1979): 62–69.

Johnson, Steven P. "Hornaday, Beeke, Crandall, and More: Archives at the New York Zoological Society." *Proceedings of the* AAZPA/CAZPA *Annual Conference* (September 1992): 13–17.

Jones, Matthew. "Archives and Museums: Threat or Opportunity." *Journal of the Society of Archivists* 18, no. 1 (1997): 27–35.

Kane, Katherine. "Bridging the Gap." *Museum News* 70, no. 6 (November/December 1991): 46–48.

Kelly, Michael. "In the Beginning . . . Some Thoughts on Starting a Museum Archives." Colorado-Wyoming Association of Museums *Highlights* 2, no. 4 (Winter 1980): 5.

Lytle, Richard. "Archival Information Exchange: A Report to the Museum Community." *Curator* 27 (1984): 265–73.

Melton, Maureen. "Preserving Love's Labors in the Museum Archives." *Art Documentation: Bulletin of the Art Libraries Society of North America* 15, no. 1 (1996): 7–9.

Museum Archives Guidelines. < http://www.archivists.org/governance/ guidelines/museum_guidelines.asp >

Museum Archivist. Newsletter of the Museum Archives Section, Society of American Archivists. For past issues, click on "Newsletters" and then scroll down until you reach "м" at < http://www.chin.gc.ca/English/News/index.html >.

Ormond, Richard L. "The National Portrait Gallery [Great Britain] Archives." *Journal of the Society of Archivists* 4 (October 1970): 130–36.

Ormond-Parker, Lyndon. "Access to Museum Archives: Whose Information Is it Anyway?" *Museum National* 7, no. 1 (August 1998): 9

Rydell, Robert W. "The Historical Researcher." *Museum News* 61 (April 1983): 39–42.

Schwartz, Carole, ed. "Keeping Our House in Order: The Importance of Museum Records." *Museum News* 61, no. 4 (April 1983): 38–48.

Smith, Bruce. "Archives in Museums." *Archives and Manuscripts* 23, no. 1 (May 1995): 38–47.

Stover, Catherine. "Museum Archives: Growth and Development." *Drexel Library Quarterly* 19, no. 3 (Summer 1983): 66–77.

Summerville, James. "Using, Managing, and Preserving the Records of Your Historical Organization." *Technical Report* 9. Nashville: American Association for State and Local History, 1986.

Swift, Michael. "Archival Research in Museums." *Proceedings of the Annual Conference, Association of Museums,* New Brunswick, Canada, October 1977. Fredericton, N.B.: Association of Museums, 1977.

Trudgeon, Roger, ed. "Do Documents and Objects Mix?" Symposium Proceedings, June 1993. Melbourne, Australia: Deakin University and Health and Medicine Museums Section of Museums Australia, 1994.

Whalley, Joyce. "The Archives of Art and Design in the Victoria and Albert Museum." *AICARC Bulletin* 16: 2–5.

Yoxall, Helen. "Collecting Archives: A Challenge to the Museum Community." *Museum National* 4, no. 1 (August 1995): 11–13.

_____. "Documenting Our Own Place: The Need for Archival Programs in Museums." *Museum National* 3, no. 4 (May 1995): 14–15.

Museum Studies

Bazin, Germain. *The Museum Age.* New York: Universe Books, 1967.

Bennett, Tony. *The Birth of the Museum: History, Theory, Politics.* New York: Routledge Press, 1995.

Bolton, Richard, ed. *Culture Wars: Documents from the Recent Controversies in the Arts.* New York: New Press, 1992.

Conn, Steven. *Museums and American Intellectual Life, 1876–1926.* Chicago: University of Chicago Press, 2000.

Crane, Susan A. *Museums and Memory.* Stanford: Stanford University Press, 2000.

Duncan, Carol. *Civilizing Rituals: Inside the Public Art Museum.* New York: Routledge Press, 1995.

Handler, Richard, and Eric Gable. *The New History in an Old Museum: Creating the Past at Colonial Williamsburg.* Durham, N.C.: Duke University Press, 1997.

Hooper-Greenhill, Eileen. *Museums and the Shaping of Knowledge.* New York: Routledge Press, 1992.

Karp, Ivan, Christine Mullen Kreamer, and Steven D. Lavine, eds. *Museums and Communities: The Politics of Public Culture.* Washington, D.C.: Smithsonian Institution Press, 1992.

Kirshenblatt-Gimblett, Barbara. *Destination Culture: Tourism, Museums, and Heritage.* Berkeley: University of California Press, 1998.

Kotler, Neil, and Philip Kotler. *Museum Strategy and Marketing: Designing Missions, Building Audiences, Generating Revenue and Resources.* San Francisco: Jossey-Bass, 1998.

Leon, Warren, and Roy Rosenzweig, eds. *History Museums in the United States: A Critical Assessment.* Urbana: University of Illinois Press, 1989.

MacDonald, Sharon, ed. *The Politics of Display: Museums, Science, Culture.* New York: Routledge Press, 1998.

Ripley, S. Dillon. *The Sacred Grove: Essays on Museums.* New York: Simon and Schuster, 1969.

Weill, Stephen E. *Making Museums Matter.* Washington, D.C.: Smithsonian Institution Press, 2002.

_____. *Rethinking the Museum and Other Meditations.* Washington, D.C.: Smithsonian Institution Press, 1990.

West, Patricia. *Domesticating History: The Political Origins of America's House Museums.* Washington, D.C.: Smithsonian Institution Press, 1999.

Appraisal

Appraisal of Local Government Records for Historical Value. Local Government Records Technical Information Series, 50. Albany, N.Y.: State Education Department, 1996.

Armstrong, John, and Stephanie Jones. *Business Documents: Their Origins, Sources, and Uses in Historical Research.* London: Mansell, 1987.

Densmore, Christopher. "Understanding and Using Early Nineteenth Century Account Books." *Midwestern Archivist* 5, no. 1 (1980). (Reprinted in *Archival Issues* 25, 2000.)

Ham, F. Gerald. *Selecting and Appraising Archives and Manuscripts.* Chicago: Society of American Archivists, 1993.

Meissner, Dennis. "The Evaluation of Modern Business Accounting Records." *Midwestern Archivist* 5, no 2 (1981).

Yates, Joanne. *Control through Communication: The Rise of System in American Management.* Baltimore: Johns Hopkins University Press, 1989.

Arrangement and Description

Fox, Michael J., and Peter L. Wilkerson; edited by Suzanne R. Warren. *Introduction to Archival Organization and Description: Access to Cultural Heritage.* Los Angeles: Getty Information Institute, 1999.

Matters, Marion. *Introduction to the USMARC Format for Archival and Manuscripts Control.* Chicago: Society of American Archivists, 1990.

Miller, Fredric M. *Arranging and Describing Archives and Manuscripts.* Chicago: Society of American Archivists, 1990.

Procter, Margaret, and Michael Cook. *Manual of Archival Description.* 3rd ed. Brookfield, Vt.: Gower, 2000.

Taylor, Arlene G. *The Organization of Information.* Englewood, Colo.: Libraries Unlimited, 1999.

Walch, Victoria Irons. *Standards for Archival Description.* Chicago: Society of American Archivists, 1994.

Wilstead, Thomas. *Computing the Total Cost of Archival Processing.* MARAC Technical Leaflet No. 2. Mid-Atlantic Regional Archives Conference, 1989.

Encoded Archival Description (EAD)

Encoded Archival Description Working Group of Society of American Archivists. *Encoded Archival Description: Application Guidelines, Version 1.0.* Chicago: Society of American Archivists, 1999.

Encoded Archival Description Working Group of Society of American Archivists and the Network Development and MARC Standards Office of the Library of Congress. *Encoded Archival Description: Tag Library, Version 2002.* Chicago: Society of American Archivists, 2002.

Research Libraries Group, EAD Advisory Group. *RLG Best Practices for Encoded Archival Description.* Mountain View, Calif.: Research Libraries Group, 2002. <http://www.rlg.org/rlgead/bpg.pdf>

Society of American Archivists. "EAD: Part 1—Context and Theory." *American Archivist* 60, no. 3 (1997).

Society of American Archivists. "EAD: Part 2—Case Studies." *American Archivist* 60, no. 4 (1997).

Society of American Archivists. *Encoded Archival Description Tag Library, Version 2002.* Chicago: Society of American Archivists, 2002.

Reference, Access, and Outreach

Benedict, Karen. "Archival Ethics." In *Managing Archives and Archival Institutions,* James Gregory Bradsher, ed. Chicago: University of Chicago Press, 1988.

Case, Barbara, and Ying Xu, "Access to Special Collections in the Humanities: Who's Guarding the Gates and Why?" *Reference Librarian* 47 (1994): 129-46.

College Art Association, *Code of Ethics,* 1995. <http://www.collegeart.org/caa/ethics/art_hist_ethics.html>

Danielson, Elena. "Ethics and Reference Services." *Reference Librarian* 56 (1994): 110-13.

_____. "The Ethics of Access." *American Archivist* 52, no. 1 (Winter 1989): 52-62.

Esterow, Milton. "Barnes Bars Barr," *ARTnews* 90, no. 10 (December 1991): 100-103.

Farr, Gail. *Archives and Manuscripts: Exhibits.* Chicago: Society of American Archivists, 1980.

Finch, Elsie Freeman, ed. *Advocating Archives: An Introduction to Public Relations for Archivists.* Chicago: Society of American Archivists and Scarecrow Press, 1994.

Greene, Mark. "Moderation in Everything, Access in Nothing?: Opinions About Access Restrictions on Private Papers." *Archival Issues* 18, no. 1 (1993): 31–38.

Hodson, Sara. "Private Lives: Confidentiality in Manuscripts Collections." *Rare Books and Manuscripts Librarianship* 6, no. 2 (1991): 108–18.

Lankford, Nancy. "Ethics and the Reference Archivist." *The Midwestern Archivist* 8, no. 1 (1983): 7–13.

Lennon, Donald. "Ethical Issues in Archival Management." *North Carolina Libraries* 51 (Spring 1993): 18–22.

Lord, Barry, and Gail Dexter Lord, eds. *The Manual of Museum Exhibitions.* Walnut Creek, Calif.: Altamira Press, 2002.

Museum Learning Collaborative. < http://www.museumlearning.com/default.html>

Pederson, Ann E., and Gail Farr. *Archives and Manuscripts: Public Programs.* Chicago: Society of American Archivists, 1982.

Peterson, Gary, and Trudy Huskamp Peterson. *Archives and Manuscripts: Law.* Chicago: Society of American Archivists, 1985.

Petropoulos, Jonathan. "Exposing 'Deep Files.'" *ARTnews* 98, no. 1 (January 1999): 143–44.

Pugh, Mary Jo. *Providing Reference Services for Archives and Manuscripts.* Chicago: Society of American Archivists, 1992.

Screven, C. G., ed. *Visitor Studies Bibliography and Abstracts,* 4th ed. Chicago: Screven and Associates, 1999.

Serrell, Beverly. *Exhibition Labels: An Interpretive Approach.* Walnut Creek, Calif.: Altamira Press, 1996.

Simmons, Ruth. "The Public's Right to Know and the Individual's Right to be Private." *Provenance* 1, no. 1 (Spring 1983): 3ff.

Society of American Archivists, *Code of Ethics for Archivists and Commentary.* Chicago: Society of American Archivists, 1992.

Society of American Archivists. *Standards for Access to Research Materials in Archival and Manuscripts Repositories.* Chicago: Society of American Archivists, 1973.

Witteborg, Lothar P. *Good Show! A Practical Guide for Temporary Exhibitions.* Washington, D.C.: Smithsonian Institution Traveling Exhibition Service, 1981.

Yoxall, Helen. "Privacy and Personal Papers." *Archives and Manuscripts* 12, no. 1 (May 1984): 38–44.

Oral History

Baum, Willa K. *Oral History for the Local Historical Society.* 3rd ed., revised. Nashville: American Association for State and Local History, 1995.

Ives, Edward D. *The Tape-Recorded Interview: A Manual for Field Workers in Folklore and Oral History.* 2nd ed. Knoxville: University of Tennessee Press, 1995.

Jackson, Bruce. *Fieldwork.* Urbana: University of Illinois Press, 1987.

Matters, Marion. *Oral History Cataloging Manual.* Chicago: Society of American Archivists, 1995.

Neuenschwander, John A. *Oral History and the Law.* 2nd ed., rev. and enlarged. Los Angeles: Oral History Association, 1993.

Ritchie, Donald A. *Doing Oral History.* New York: Twayne Publishers, 1994.

Ritchie, Donald A., ed. *Oral History Evaluation Guidelines*, rev. 2000, Oral History Association Pamphlet #3. Los Angeles: Oral History Association, 2000. <http://www.dickinson.edu/organizations/oha/EvaluationGuidelines.html>

Sadashige, Koichi. "Storage Media Environmental Durability and Stability." In *Data Storage Technology Assessment 2000*, Part 2. CD-ROM. St. Paul, Minn.: National Media Laboratory, 2000.

Stielow, Frederick. *The Management of Oral History Sound Archives.* New York: Greenwood Press, 1986.

Records Management, Surveys, and Security

Brown, Karen E., and Beth Lindblom Patkus. *Collection Security: Planning and Prevention for Libraries and Archives.* Technical Leaflet 12, Emergency Management. Sect. 3. Andover, Mass.: NEDCC, 1999. <http://www.nedcc.org/plam3/tleaf312.htm>

Fleckner, John A. *Archives and Manuscripts: Surveys.* Chicago: Society of American Archivists, 1977.

Guide to Record Retention Requirements in the Code of Federal Regulations. Washington, D.C.: Office of the Federal Register, National Archives and Records Administration, 1992.

Institute of Certified Records Managers Web site, <http://www.icrm.org/>

Oliva, Mary Lou et al. *Glossary of Records and Information Management Terms.* 2nd ed. Prairie Village, Kans.: ARMA International, 2000.

Robek, Mary F., Gerald F. Brown, and David O. Stephens. *Information and Records Management: Document-Based Information Systems.* 4th ed. New York: Glencoe/McGraw-Hill, Inc., 1995.

Skupsky, Donald S. *Recordkeeping Requirements.* Denver: Information Requirements Clearinghouse, 1991.

_____. *Records Retention Procedures.* Denver: Information Requirements Clearinghouse, 1994.

Trinkaus-Randall, Gregor. *Protecting Your Collections: A Manual of Archival Security.* Chicago: Society of American Archivists, 1995.

Preservation and Disaster Planning

(See specific formats for additional entries.)

American Institute for Conservation. *Basic Guidelines for the Care of Special Collections.* <http://aic.stanford.edu/treasure>

Conservation OnLine. *Disaster Planning Resources.* <http://palimpsest/stanford.edu/bytopic/disasters/>

Dorge, Valerie, and Sharon Jones, comps. *Building an Emergency Plan: A Guide for Museums and Other Cultural Institutions.* Los Angeles: Getty Conservation Institute, 1999.

Lindblom, Beth, and Karen Motylewski. *Disaster Planning for Cultural Institutions.* Technical Leaflet 183. Nashville: AASLH, 1993.

Nason, James D. "Repatriated Materials and Pesticides." *Registrar's Quarterly* (Fall 1998): 5.

Ogden, Sherelyn, ed. *Library and Archival Materials: A Manual.* 3rd ed. Andover, Mass.: Northeast Document Conservation Center, 1999. <http://www.nedcc.org/plam3/manhome.htm>

Patkus, Beth Lindblom. *Disaster Planning.* Technical Leaflet 3, Emergency Management, Sect. 3. Andover, Mass.: NEDCC, 1999. <http://www.nedcc.org/plam3/tleaf33.htm>

Ritzenthaler, Mary Lynn. *Preserving Archives and Manuscripts.* Chicago: Society of American Archivists, 1993.

Selwitz, Charles, and Shin Maekawa. *Inert Gases in the Control of Museum Insect Pests.* Marina del Rey, Calif.: Getty Conservation Institute, 1999.

Silverman, Sydel, and Nancy J. Parezo. *Preserving the Anthropological Record.* New York: Wenner-Gren Foundation for Anthropological Research, Inc., 1995. <http://www.wennergren.org>

Photographs and Audiovisual Materials

Betz, Elizabeth, comp. *Graphic Materials: Rules for Describing Original Items and Historical Collections.* Washington, D.C.: Library of Congress, 1982.

Bowser, Eileen, and John Kuiper. *A Handbook for Film Archives.* New York: Garland, 1991.

Grout, Catherine, Phil Purdy, and Janine Rymer. *Creating Digital Resources for the Visual Arts: Standards and Good Practice.* Oxford: Arts and Humanities Data Service, 2000.

Hsieh-Yee, Ingrid. *Organizing Audiovisual and Electronic Resources for Access: A Cataloging Guide.* Englewood, Colo.: Libraries Unlimited, 2000.

Keefe, Lawrence E., Jr., and Dennis Inch. *The Life of a Photograph.* London: Focal Press, 1984.

King, Gretchen. *Magnetic Wire Recordings: A Manual Including Historical Background, Approaches to Transfer and Storage, and Solutions to Common Problems.* <http://depts.washington.edu/ethmusic/wire1.html>

Library of Congress. *Care, Handling and Storage of Motion Picture Film.* <http://lcweb.loc.gov/preserv/care/film.html>

Lindner, Jim. *Confessions of a Videotape Restorer or How come these tapes all need to be cleaned differently?* <http://palimpsest.stanford.edu/byauth/lindner/lindner1.html>

_____. *Digitization Reconsidered.* <http://palimpsest.stanford.edu/byauth/lindner/digirecon.html>

_____. "Magnetic Tape Deterioration: Tidal Wave at Our Shores." *Video Magazine* (February 1996). <http://palimpsest.stanford.edu/byauth/lindner/tidal.html> (On-line version may differ from published article.)

_____. *The Proper Care and Feeding of Videotape.* <http://palimpsest.stanford.edu/byauth/lindner/lindner3.html>

_____. *Videotape Restoration—Where Do I Start?* <http://palimpsest.stanford.edu/byauth/lindner/lindner2.html>

Martin, Abigail Leab, ed. *AMIA Compendium of Moving Image Cataloging Practice.* Chicago: SAA and Association of Moving Image Archivists, 2001.

Milano, Mary, and IASA Editorial Group, eds. *IASA Cataloging Rules: A Manual for the Description of Sound Recordings and Related Audiovisual Media.* Stockholm: International Association of Sound and Audiovisual Archives, 1999. <http://www.iasa-web.org/icat/>

National Library of Canada. *The Preservation of Recorded Sound Materials.*
<http://www.nlc-bnc.ca/6/28/s28-1017-e.html>

Reilly, James M. *Care and Identification of 19th-Century Photographic Prints.*
Rochester, N.Y.: Eastman Kodak Company, 1986.

_____. *IPI Storage Guide for Acetate Film.* Rochester, N.Y.: Image Permanence
Institute, 1993.

_____. *Storage Guide for Color Photographic Materials.* Albany: The University
of the State of New York, New York State Education Department, New York
State Library, The New York State Program for the Conservation and
Preservation of Library Research Materials, 1998.

_____. *Film Decay and How to Slow It.* National Film Preservation Foundation.
<http://www.filmpreservation.org/preservation/film_decay.html>

Ritzenthaler, Mary Lynn, Gerald J. Munoff, and Margery S. Long. *Archives and
Manuscripts: Administration of Photographic Collections.* Chicago, Society of
American Archivists, 1984.

Schoenherr, Steve. *Recording Technology History Notes, 1999–2002.*
<http://www.history.acusd.edu/gen/recording/notes.html>

St-Laurent, Gilles. *The Care and Handling of Recorded Sound Materials.*
Washington, D.C.: Commission on Preservation and Access, 1991.

Vidipax Videotape Format Guide (poster). New York: Vidipax, The Magnetic
Media Restoration Co., 1997.

Wilhelm, Henry, and Carol Brower, contributing author. *The Permanence and
Care of Color Photographs: Traditional and Digital Color Prints, Color
Negatives, Slides, and Motion Pictures.* Grinnell, Iowa: Preservation
Publishing Co., 1993.

Zinkham, Helena, and Elizabeth Betz Parker. *Descriptive Terms for Graphic
Materials: Genre and Physical Characteristics Headings.* Washington, D.C.:
Library of Congress, 1986.

Architectural Records

Architectural Drawings Advisory Group of the Getty Art History Information
Program. *A Guide to the Description of Architectural Drawings.* New York:
G. K. Hall, 1994.

Architectural Records Section of the International Council on Archives. *A
Guide to the Archival Care of Architectural Records, 19th and 20th Centuries.*
Paris: ICA, 2000.

Ehrenberg, Ralph E. *Archives and Manuscripts: Maps and Architectural
Drawings.* Chicago: Society of American Archivists, 1982.

Fraser, Iain, and Rod Henmi. *Envisioning Architecture: An Analysis of Drawing.*
New York: Van Nostrand Reinhold, 1994.

Shepherd, Kelcy, and Waverly Lowell. *Standard Series for Architecture and
Landscape Design Records: A Tool for the Arrangement and Description of
Archival Collections.* Berkeley: University of California, 2000.

Electronic Records and Digitization

Bearman, David, ed. *Archival Management of Electronic Records.* Pittsburgh:
Archives and Museum Informatics, 1991.

_____. *Electronic Evidence: Strategies for Managing Records in Contemporary Organizations.* Pittsburgh: Archives and Museum Informatics, 1994.

Dollar, Charles M. *Authentic Electronic Records: Strategies for Long-Term Access.* Chicago: Cohasset Associates, 1999.

Hedstrom, Margaret, ed. *Electronic Records Management Program Strategies.* Pittsburgh: Archives and Museum Informatics, 1993.

Hunter, Gregory S. *Preserving Digital Information: A How-To-Do-It Manual.* How-To-Do-It Manuals for Librarians, no. 93. New York: Neal-Schuman Publishers, Inc., 2000.

Kenney, Anne R. *Digital to Microfilming: A Demonstration Project, 1994–1996.* Report to the National Endowment for the Humanities. Ithaca, N.Y.: Cornell University, 1997. <http://www.library.cornell.edu/preservation/com/comfin.html>

Kenney, Anne R., and Oya Y. Rieger. *Moving Theory into Practice: Digital Imaging for Libraries and Archives.* Mountain View, Calif.: Research Libraries Group, 2000.

National Initiative for a Networked Cultural Heritage. NINCH *Guide to Good Practice in the Digital Representation and Management of Cultural Heritage Materials.* Washington, D.C.: NINCH, 2002. <http://www.ninch.org/guide.html>

Reilly, James, and Franziska S. Frey. *Recommendations for the Evaluation of Digital Images Produced from Photographic, Microphotographic and Various Paper Formats.* Rochester, N.Y.: Image Permanence Institute, 1996. <http://www.memory.loc.gov/ammem/ipirpt.html>

Saffady, William. *Managing Electronic Records.* 2nd ed. Prairie Village, Kans.: ARMA International, 1998.

Smith, Abby. *The Preservation of Digitized Reproductions.* Chicago: Society of American Archivists, 1997. <http://www.archivists.org/statements/digitize.asp>

Objects in the Archives

Hawks, Catherine, and Kathryn Makos. "Inherent and Acquired Hazards in Museum Objects: Implications for Care and Use of Collections." *Cultural Resource Management* 23, no. 5 (2000): 31–37.

Meraz, Gloria. "Cultural Evidence: On the Common Ground Between Archivists and Museologists." *Provenance* 15, no. 1 (1997): 1–26.

Taylor, Hugh. "'Heritage' Revisited: Documents as Artifacts in the Context of Museums and Material Culture." *Archivaria* 40 (Fall 1995): 8–20.

Field Records and Scientific Notebooks

Cooperation on Archives and Science in Europe (CASE). <http://www.bath.ac.uk/ncuacs/case.html>

Day, Deborah D. "Danger at Sea: Documentation of Oceanographic Expeditions." Paper presented at the 2001 Society of American Archivists annual meeting session, "Extreme Science: Pushing the Envelope on Land, on Sea, and in the Air." <http://www.archivists.org/saagroups/sthc/aelements2002.html>

Demb, Sarah R., and Jill U. Jackson. *The Preservation of Anthropology Field Notes.* Unpublished manuscript, 1996.

Illinois State Geological Survey Library. *Field Notes.* <http://www.isgs.uiuc.edu/library/fieldnts.htm>

International Union of History and Philosophy of Science. *Resolution on Preserving the Records of Modern Science.* <http://www.aip.org/history/newsletter/fall2001/iuhps.htm>

Jackson, Jean. "'I Am a Fieldnote': Fieldnotes as a Symbol of Professional Identity." In *Fieldnotes: The Makings of Anthropology.* Ithaca, N.Y.: Cornell University Press, 1990.

Mandeville Special Collections Library, University of California, San Diego. *Register of the Roy Rappaport Papers 1942–1985.* San Diego: University of California, 2000. <http://www.orpheus.ucsd.edu/speccoll/testing/html/mss0516e.html>.

Mexican Archives Project, Benson Latin American Collection Rare Books and Manuscripts, University of Texas at Austin. *Campbell W. Pennington Papers: Indexes to the Manuscript Notebooks from the Parral Archives.* 1995. <http://www.lib.utexas.edu/Libs/Benson/Mex_Archives/Pennington_pt4.html>.

Riley, Martha. *A Guide to the Archives and Manuscripts of the Missouri Botanical Garden.* St. Louis, Mo.: Missouri Botanical Garden Library, 1995. <http://www.mobot.org/MOBOT/molib/part1.pdf>

Shankar, Kalpana. *Understanding the Record-keeping Practices of Scientists.* MARAC Technical Leaflet No. 10. Mid-Atlantic Regional Archives Conference, 1999.

Silverman, Sydel, and Nancy J. Parezo. *Preserving the Anthropological Record.* New York: Wenner-Green Foundation for Anthropological Research, Inc., 1995. <http://www.wennergren.org/>

University of Kent. *Anthropology Resources.* <http://lucy.ukc.ac.uk/>

Native American Graves Protection and Repatriation Act (NAGPRA)

Association of Canadian Archivists, Special Interest Section on Aboriginal Archives. *First Nation Record-Keeping Issues: A Brief Resource Guide.* Ottawa: Association of Canadian Archivists, 1999. <http://archivists.ca/home/>

NAGPRA primer. <http://www.cast.uark.edu/products/NAGPRA/nagpra.html>

Native American Archives Coalition, Society of American Archivists. <http://www.nativeculture.com/lisamitten/ailanewsW97_archives coalition.html>

Restitution

Akinsha, Konstantin, and Grigorii Kozlov, with Sylvia Hochfield. *Beautiful Loot: The Soviet Plunder of Europe's Art Treasures.* New York: Random House, 1995.

American Association of Museums. *Guidelines Concerning the Unlawful Appropriation of Objects During the Nazi Era.* Washington, D.C.: American Association for Museums, 1999, amended 2001. <http://www.aam-us.org/resources/ethics_guidelines/nazi_guidelines.cfm>

Feliciano, Hector. *The Lost Museum: The Nazi Conspiracy to Steal the World's Greatest Works of Art.* New York: Basic Books, 1997.

Museum of Modern Art. Online resources relating to Nazi-era provenance research. <http://www.moma.org/provenance/provenance_online.html>

Nicholas, Lynn. *The Rape of Europa: The Fate of Europe's Treasures in the Third Reich and the Second World War.* New York: Alfred A. Knopf, 1994.

Petropoulos, Jonathan. *Art as Politics in the Third Reich.* Chapel Hill: University of North Carolina Press, 1996.

_____. *The Faustian Bargain: The Art World in Nazi Germany.* New York: Oxford University Press, 2000.

Simpson, Elizabeth, ed. *The Spoils of War: World War II and Its Aftermath. The Loss, Reappearance, and Recovery of Cultural Property.* New York: H. N. Abrams in association with the Bard Graduate Center for Studies in the Decorative Arts, 1997.

Smithsonian Institution, Archives of American Art. Online catalog of dealer archives. <http://www.aaa.si.edu/catalog.htm>

Trienens, Howard J. *Landscape with Smokestacks: The Case of the Allegedly Plundered Degas.* Evanston, Ill.: Northwestern University Press, 2000.

Wechsler, Helen J., Teri Coate-Saal, and John Lukavic, comps. *Museum Policy and Procedures for Nazi-Era Issues.* Washington, D.C.: American Association of Museums, 2001.

Yeide, Nancy H. "Behind the Lines: Lessons in Nazi-Era Provenance Research." *Museum News* 79, no. 6 (November/December 2000): 50–53, 56–59.

Yeide, Nancy H., Konstantin Akinsha, and Amy L. Walsh. *The AAM Guide to Provenance Research.* Washington, D.C.: American Association of Museums, 2001. <http://www.museum-security.org/AAM-provenance.htm>

Sample Policies, Procedures, and Forms

The many possible statements, forms, and guidelines relating to the administration of archives include mission statements, acquisitions policies, accession forms, records survey forms, records schedules, processing guidelines, disaster recovery plans, and forms for researchers. Although each archivist must determine what should be included in these forms and guidelines, below are ideas and samples that may be useful as you develop your policies and procedures. See also *Sample Forms for Archival and Records Management Programs,* published by ARMA International and the Society of American Archivists in 2002. This useful resource contains nearly two hundred sample forms, including an appraisal worksheet, conservation survey, permission to publish, and records management policy statement.

Mission statements or statements of purpose

What is the mission of your archives? Consider your department's goal and purpose, what the archives collects and why, and how your mission relates to the larger institution. Included in your statement could be a collection development policy, acquisitions criteria, and access information. Below are sample mission statements and excerpts that vary in level of content.

• Newark Museum

The Newark Museum Archives

The Newark Museum Archives serve as the institution's permanent memory by preserving and making available approximately 3,100 linear feet of records, dating from 1900 to 2001. Documents relate to the Museum's collections and the physical products of employees' work, such as administrative files, exhibit and historic photographs, correspondence, and exhibition files. Holdings also consist of architectural drawings, scholarly

"Increasing the Usefulness of Museums," article by John Cotton Dana, 1916

articles written by the staff concerning the Museum's collections, and materials related to the Michael Graves renovation. Exhibition files include the research and development records of registrars, curators, and exhibition designers for programs dating from 1906 to 2001. The photo archives contain 10,000 items related to the history of the Museum, various programs and exhibitions, employees, and the city of Newark.

Washington Street facing North, ca. 1886

The Archives arranges and describes records so that they are accessible to the Museum's staff and visiting researchers. All documents are kept in their original order and according to provenance; this expedites internal usage and preserves the evidential value of departmental record series. Finding aids indicate available materials and specify confidential documents. Valid scholarly requests to use restricted records are evaluated on a case by case basis.

In order to inform potential researchers of available record series, the Archives disseminates finding aids to educational institutions and professional organizations, such as regional historical societies and museums, university and city libraries, and other archival organizations. In coordination with the Education and Educational Loan Departments, archival materials are accessible to elementary school teachers, high school students and educators, as well as college and university students and professors. The Museum's current website – www.newarkmuseum.org – will display updated finding aids and archival news beginning in Fall 2002.

The Museum of Modern Art Archives

MUSEUM ARCHIVES MISSION STATEMENT

The Museum of Modern Art Archives was established in 1989 by resolution of the Board of Trustees, under the authority of the General Counsel, to preserve and make accessible the Museum's historical records to Museum staff, outside scholars, and researchers, and to create and direct the Museum's Records Management Program. Additionally, the Museum Archives is the custodian of primary source material and other historical documentation related to Twentieth-Century art.

Purpose:	The purpose of the Museum of Modern Art Archives is to organize, preserve and make accessible records not in current use and to collect documentation relevant to the work of the institution, including: a) records relevant to the Museum's history (minutes, committee reports, departmental papers, photographs, sound recordings and video tapes); b) personal papers of curators and directors when relevant to Museum interests or history; c) papers of individuals related to Museum interests, such as Trustees, and former staff; d) oral histories; e) twentieth-century primary resource material, including papers, manuscripts and photographs. The Museum Archives provides necessary research support in order to enrich and enhance the Museum's curatorial and educational missions.
Structure:	The Museum Archives exists under the authority of the Museum's Deputy Director for Curatorial Affairs and is directed by a professional archivist who is also responsible for the Museum's Records Management Program. Sensitive data is protected, evidentiary values and provenance are observed, and copyright and privacy issues are respected; basic conservation methods are employed.
Access:	The Archives serves outside researchers as well as Museum staff. Users are informed of the Museum's archival resources through published guides, and through entries in the RLIN database and the Museum's DADABASE system (available via the Internet). Certain archival records have been (and will continue to be) microfilmed by the Archives of American Art and who makes them available internationally through inter-library loan.
Staff:	The Museum Archives staff includes a full-time professional Museum Archivist, Assistant Archivist, and Records Manager, and a grant-funded Project Archivist, Dedalus Fellow, and Administrative Assistant. Additional assistance is provided by interns.

Survey forms

An important first step in organizing your archives and familiarizing yourself with the records in your care is to survey the collections. Collection surveys can be a detailed evaluation or a brief overview.

• Newark Museum

Пↀ

Inventory Worksheet

Date: _____   Number: _____

Department	Author(s)
Records Series	Dates

Description and Notes:
➤ Special Requirements, Originals Elsewhere...

Volume	Restrictions
Records Medium/Size: Letter/Legal/Other	Associated Files/Items
Disposition/Transfer Rate	Office Location (Building, Rm #)

Arrangement:
❑ Alphabetic By   ❑ Numeric By   ❑ Other

Index or Finding Aids?

Inventory Taken By   **Date**

THE ARCHIVES OF THE PHILADELPHIA MUSEUM OF ART

Inventory Worksheet

Date:_____Accession number:_____

Inventoried by:_____Record group/subgroup title(s):_____

Creator:_____Provenance:_____

Dates (inclusive):_____Restrictions:_____

Types of records (note arrangement):_____

_____

Conditions/special aspects:_____

_____

Location in Archives:_____Quantity (cubic feet):_____

PRELIMINARY SERIES AND FOLDER LIST

_____

_____

_____

_____

_____

_____

_____

(attach additional sheets as needed)

DRAFT
V – 02
12/10/98

Accession Report

Accession # _____

Transferring Department and Contact

Type of Transfer (check one)   **Transfer Documents**

_____ **Department Records**   **Records Schedule #** _____
_____ **Non-Department Records**   **Date of Transfer** _____
_____ **Personal Papers**   **Received By** _____

Restrictions

Tentative Title

Approximate Inclusive Dates

Arrangements/Series List

Descriptive Entry

Finding Aids   **Temporary Index Terms**

PROCESSING GUIDELINES

<u>CARDINAL RULE</u> -- **ASK IF UNSURE IN ANY WAY !**

      Preserve
      Organize
      Describe

1. Survey the file and judiciously correct order of documents.
      First assume that order is correct, and look for the reason that a document seems out of order to you. Discuss possible changes with DW. If it really is in the wrong place, move it, and anything clipped to it, to the right place. Always keep things together that have been clipped together, even though you will remove the fastener.
      Nb: Many files will be in reverse chronological order.
      If file will be more than about 3/4" thick, divide at some logical point(s). The folder title will be the same, but with [01], [02], etc. added at end.

As you process, note types of materials, subjects, important respondents, inclusive dates. This will become the folder description.

2. Remove all foreign objects:
      Staples, paper clips, rubber bands, fasteners.

3. Unfold all folded pages and flatten.
      Remove legal-size pages to oversize folder, large sheets to map case folder. Lightly mark series & folder title in upper right corner. -- Insert separation sheet.
      Exceptions: documents such as invitations <u>may</u> be left folded if: back section is blank, no information runs across fold, and there are not so many that they will make a lump in the folder.

4. Orient pages in folder so that researcher can use them easily. For "landscape" format, bottom of page goes toward fold of folder.

5. Mark deteriorating pages with a sheet of scrap paper for later photocopying:
      Yellowed, brittle, torn more than minimally, glue, tape.
      Nb: some paper is naturally yellowish--check for an acid shadow on the next sheet to see if it is "safe" yellow or not. See "deteriorated samples" folder and ask if unsure.

6. Remove all photos to a separate folder.
      <u>Lightly</u> mark series, folder title in extreme upper right margin in soft pencil on back of photo. Insert separation sheet in original folder. Label photo folder with same title as original folder.
      Consider grouping photos from several folders into one "photos removed" folder. Discuss with DW.

7. Remove all publications for transfer to Library.
      Insert separation sheet in folder.

8. Remove 3x5 cards when more than approximately ¼" thick. Place in "Cards removed" box; identify source on oversized card and place it in front of cards. -- Insert separation sheet in folder.

9. Remove all duplicates. Keep one copy--the original, if possible, or the clearest carbon. Do not discard any that are annotated, corrected, or written on in any way without discussing with DW.

10. Neaten completed stack of documents--don't leave any hanging edges to get crumpled.

11. Make a new folder, creasing bottom to match thickness of records. **Neatly label in pencil**, as follows:
Folder title   **Series Inclusive dates**
      Folder title is copied from old folder, if possible. Format may be revised for effective computer sorting, if necessary (discuss with DW).
      For exhibitions, use formal title, not working title. Check catalog or ARL exhibition card catalog. Include exhibition dates in folder title. Inclusive dates reflect materials in folder.
      Any special instructions or information may be noted on front of folder (i.e. "Nb: Restricted file" or "See also 1958 Art in America exhibition").

12. Keep folders in original order, unless clearly out of place. Before moving anything, discuss with DW.

Deed of gift forms or gift agreements
A deed of gift or gift agreement is a signed contract between a donor and the institution that forms a permanent record of a donation of a collection and its intellectual content.

• National Air and Space Museum, Smithsonian Institution

DEED OF GIFT
NATIONAL AIR AND SPACE ARCHIVES
NATIONAL AIR AND SPACE MUSEUM
SMITHSONIAN INSTITUTION
WASHINGTON, D.C. 20560

1.	By these presents I, Donor's name (hereinafter referred to as donor), of City, State hereby irrevocably and unconditionally give, transfer, assign, and deliver to the National Air and Space Archives, National Air and Space Museum of the Smithsonian Institution by way of gift, all right, title, and interest in and to the materials (hereinafter referred to as the materials) described in Appendix A, attached hereto. I affirm that I own such material and that, to the best of my knowledge, I have good and complete right, title, and interest to give and that this transfer of material will not infringe the copy or other rights of others.

2.	The donor further grants to the National Air and Space Museum such literary rights and copyrights in these materials as he/she may possess.

3.	Title to the materials shall pass to the National Air and Space Museum upon the execution of this agreement.

4.	It is the donor's wish that all the materials be made available for research without restriction as soon as possible after their delivery to the National Air and Space Museum.

5.	The National Air and Space Museum may dispose of or transfer to another depository any of the materials which it determines to have no permanent value or historical interest or when it determines that it is in the interest of the National Air and Space Museum to do so, provided that prior to any such disposal or transfer reasonable efforts are made to notify the donor and offer return of the materials.

6.	In the event that the donor may from time to time hereafter give, donate, and convey to the Museum, for deposit in the archives, additional papers and other historical materials, title to such additional papers and other historical materials shall pass to the Museum upon their delivery, and all of the provisions of this instrument of gift shall be applicable to such additional papers and other historical materials. A description of the additional papers and historical materials so donated and delivered shall be prepared and attached hereto.

Dated this _____ day of _____, _____:

Donor_____
Donor's name

Accepted by the National Air and Space Museum, Smithsonian Institution this _____ day of _____, _____:

_____
Thomas Soapes, Chair of the Archives Division

THE ARCHIVES OF THE PHILADELPHIA MUSEUM OF ART

Deed of Gift Agreement

I (We),_____

hereby unconditionally give, donate, bestow and set over to the Archives of the Philadelphia Museum of Art the property described in this document and, if necessary, on attached sheets, to be used and/or stored by the Archives at its unrestricted discretion; and for myself, my distributees, and by personal representative, I waive all present or future rights in, to, or over said property, its use or disposition.

Signature:_____Date:_____

Witness:_____Date:_____

For the Archives of the Philadelphia Museum of Art:_____

Title:_____Date:_____

Description of material: provide details about the item(s), including but not limited to the creator, provenance, inclusive dates, media, condition, and special aspects. For multiple items such as personal papers, please provide a folder listing using the Inventory Worksheet (04).

_____

_____

_____

_____

_____

DRAFT
V – 05
12/10/98

Loan agreements

When the archives borrows materials, the transaction is documented with a legal agreement that includes basic information about the lender and the items loaned, along with more detailed terms and conditions such as the length of the loan and procedures for extending it, insurance coverage, storage/display conditions, indemnity, transportation and packing requirements, permission to photograph and reproduce, and how the loan is to be returned. An example of a loan cover sheet follows.

- Holocaust Museum Houston

Holocaust Museum Houston
5401 Caroline Street
Houston, Texas 77004
713/942-8000

Loan Agreement

Date:_____   Receipt No.:_____

As of the above date, the following described items are hereby transferred by their Owner into the custody of Holocaust Museum Houston:

Item Description   Owner Specified/Agreed Replacement Value

These objects are left in the custody of the Museum for the purpose of:

_____Consideration for acquisition by the Museum

_____Study, identification, duplication, photography, storage, other_____

_____Exhibition for the period beginning_____ending_____

Name of Owner_____

Address_____

City_____State_____ Zip_____

Phone (hm)_____ (wk)_____

Agreement and Acknowledgment of the Parties:

I **warrant that** I own the above artifact(s) and to the best of my knowledge I have good and complete right, title, and interest (including **but not limited to** all transferred copyright, trademark, and related interests) in the above mentioned property. **I agree to indemnify and hold harmless to the fullest extent permitted by law, the Holocaust Museum Houston, its directors, employees, and agents from all claims, demands, damages, causes of action, and expenses (including but not limited to reasonable attorneys' fees and court costs) arising out of or resulting from My breach of the warranty hereinabove.** I have read, understand, and agree to the terms and conditions of this contractural agreement. **I acknowledge that it is my right and sole decision whether to consult independent legal counsel before signing this Agreement.**

Owner Signature:_____

For Holocaust Museum Houston:_____

Oral history release and documentation worksheet

• Mystic Seaport Museum

MYSTIC SEAPORT®

75 Greenmanville Avenue
PO Box 6000
Mystic, CT 06355-0990
Voice 860.572.0711
TDD 860.572.5319
www.mysticseaport.org

ORAL HISTORY PROGRAM
SOUND ARCHIVES GIFT AGREEMENT & RELEASE FORM

In consideration of the commitment Mystic Seaport Museum, Inc. has made to preserving the maritime related heritage of America, I hereby donate in form and content any and all rights in and to the video and/or audio tape recorded interview(s) given on _____, together with any supplementary materials listed on this form (collectively, the "Material").

I represent and warrant that (i) I have the authority to grant the above rights to the Material; (ii) that this agreement does not conflict with or infringe upon the rights of any third party; and (iii) not rights to the material have been granted to any third party.

Mystic Seaport Museum, Inc. shall have the right to use, reproduce, distribute, and give access to this Material for any purpose whatsoever and may use my name and/or likeness in connection therewith.

INTERVIEWER

_____
signature   date

_____
print name

_____
address

NARRATOR

_____
signature   date

_____
print name

_____
address

THE MUSEUM OF AMERICA AND THE SEA

MYSTIC SEAPORT®

75 Greenmanville Avenue
PO Box 6000
Mystic, CT 06355-0990
Voice 860.572.0711
TDD 860.572.5319
www.mysticseaport.org

Oral History Interview Documentation Worksheet

INTERVIEW DETAILS
Date of Interview:
Location:
Narrator:
Birth Year & Place:
Address:
Telephone #:
Interviewer:
Date of Birth:
Department:

INTERVIEW CONTENT & PURPOSE
Key themes or subjects:

Purpose of interview:

Conducted for a specific project?

RECORDING DETAILS
Location details / Recording environment (others present; etc.) / Technical Notes

EXPLANATORY INFORMATION & ADDITIONAL NOTES (use extra sheets if needed)
Explanation of specialized terms; proper name spellings; etc.

Related material in other Mystic Seaport collections:

Related Source Material (books, articles, videos, etc.):

Prepared by: **Date:**

™

THE MUSEUM OF AMERICA AND THE SEA

Disaster recovery plans

Archives staff should have easy access to written procedures on how to handle emergencies such as water damage and fire in the archives. The National Air and Space Museum produced flow charts for what to do in case of infestation, mold and mildew damage, fire damage, power outages, and water damage. A sample follows.

• National Air and Space Museum, Smithsonian Institution

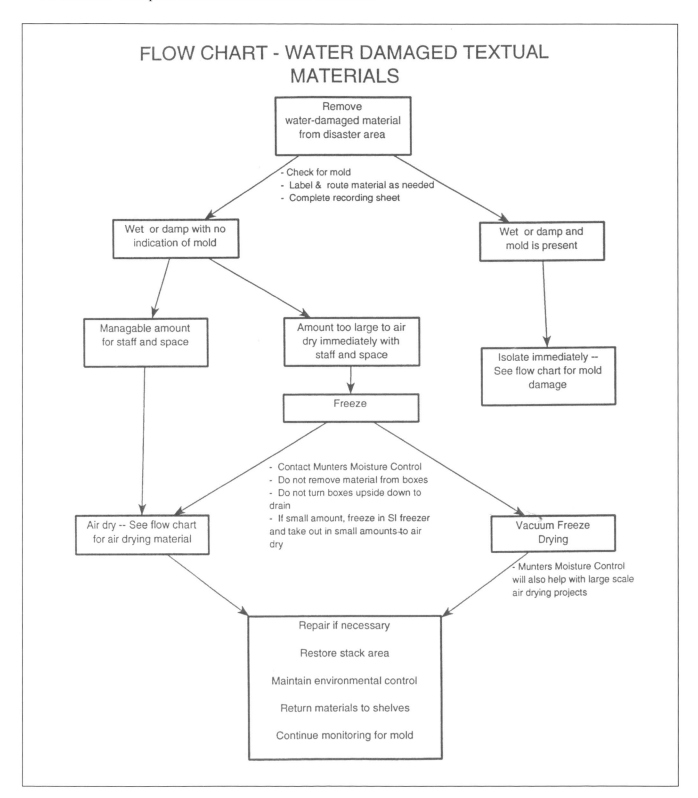

Records schedule (excerpt)

- Museum of Fine Arts, Houston

MUSEUM OF FINE ARTS, HOUSTON
RECORDS RETENTION AND DISPOSAL SCHEDULE

DEPARTMENT: Accounting, Payroll

Code	Record Title (Other Titles)	Description	Retain in Office	Retain in Archives	Total	Comments
ACC-10	Payroll Backup, Salaried (Authorizations)	Source documentation for the Check Register including new hire forms, personnel changes, and special events forms.	CY + 1	5	7	See ACC-4, ACC-13 and ACC-60 for permanent payroll records.
ACC-11	Timesheets, Salaried	Record of hours worked per pay period including requests for time-off.	A	7	A + 7	Transfer files of terminated employees annually. See ACC-4, 13 and 60 for permanent payroll records.
ACC-12	Timecards and Timesheets, Hourly	Report of hours worked per pay period including requests for time-off.	6 mos.	6.5	7	See ACC-4, ACC-13 and ACC-60 for permanent payroll records.
ACC-13	"W-2" Forms, Hourly and Salaried	Copies of original "W-2" forms sent to each employee recording each calendar year's earnings.	CY + 1	P	P	See ACC-4, ACC-13 and ACC-60 for permanent payroll records.
ACC-14	Cancelled Checks, Payroll	Cancelled payroll checks bundled in groups of 100.	CY + 1	5	7	See ACC-4, ACC-13 and ACC-60 for permanent payroll records.
ACC-15	Manual Check Copies, Payroll	Payroll checks issued manually due to unusual circumstances.	CY + 1	5	7	See ACC-4, ACC-13 and ACC-60 for permanent payroll records.

CY = CALENDAR YEAR   FY = FISCAL YEAR   A = ACTIVE (PROJECT OR ACTIVITY IS ONGOING)   P = PERMANENT

DEPARTMENTAL RETENTION AND DISPOSAL SCHEDULES TAKE PRECEDENCE OVER THE GENERAL RETENTION SCHEDULE.

05/13/94

Reading room and researcher forms

Archivists who have reference responsibilities should notify researchers of their legal and scholarly responsibilities when using and citing records. These obligations may vary depending on whether the user is a staff person or a member of the public. Terms and conditions for using the collections should be available to researchers and signed statements obtained, as appropriate.

Registration and material request form

- The Museum of Modern Art, New York

Last Name _____

The Museum of Modern Art Archives

APPLICATION FOR ACCESS TO THE MUSEUM OF MODERN ART ARCHIVES

Name _____ Occupation _____ Date _____

Address (Permanent/Home) _____

Address (Local/Office) _____

Telephone Number (Permanent/Home) _____ (Local/Office) _____

Institution _____

Research Subject _____

Purpose of Research _____

May we advise others of your research? _____

If research will be published, please give proposed title, publisher, and projected publication date:

_____

CONDITIONS FOR USE

1. Documents may not be removed from the reading room without permission.
2. Briefcases and coats may not be brought into the research area.
3. Smoking, eating or drinking is not permitted.
4. Pens are prohibited in the reading room; pencils may be used for note-taking.
5. Materials may not be leaned on, written on, folded, traced from, or handled in any way likely to damage them.
6. Materials must be kept in the folder and in their original order, even when this order does not seem meaningful.
7. The Museum of Modern Art reserves the right to set restrictions on access to and photocopying of archival materials.
8. Materials to be copied should not be removed from folders.
9. All references to materials in the collection should cite archival series and title and acknowledge "The Museum of Modern Art Archives, NY." When publication is intended, an application for publication rights for any material quoted from the Museum Archives collections must be submitted to the Museum. These stipulations also apply to dissertations and research theses.

APPLICATION AGREEMENT

I have read the above conditions for permission to use The Museum of Modern Art Archives. I agree to observe them and *understand that if I fail to do so*, permission for further access may be withdrawn.

Signature _____ Date _____

How did you learn about The Museum of Modern Art Archives? _____

Have you ever visited The Museum of Modern Art Archives Web site _____

THE ARCHIVES OF THE PHILADELPHIA MUSEUM OF ART

Researcher Registration Form

Name:_____

Permanent Address:_____

_____

Home Telephone:_____

Philadelphia Address:_____

_____

Philadelphia Telephone:_____

Institution:_____Title:_____

Nature of Material Sought:_____

_____

WARNING CONCERNING COPYRIGHT LAW

The copyright law of the United States (Title 17, United States Code) governs the making of photocopies or other reproductions of copyrighted materials. Under certain conditions specified in the law, libraries and archives are authorized to furnish a photocopy or other reproduction. One of these specified conditions is that the photocopy or reproduction is not be "used for any purposes other than private study, scholarship, or research." If a user makes a request for, or later uses, a photocopy or reproduction for purposes in excess of "fair use," that user may be liable for copyright infringement. This institution reserves the right to refuse to accept a copying order if, in its judgment, fulfillment of the order would involve violation of copyright law.

VIOLATORS OF THE ABOVE LAW ARE SUBJECT TO PENALTIES.

I have read the PMA Access Policy and the above copyright warning, and agree to follow the specified guidelines.

Signed:_____Date:_____

DRAFT
VII – 04
12/10/98

THE ARCHIVES OF THE PHILADELPHIA MUSEUM OF ART

Reference Interview Form

Researcher's name:_____

Date(s) for appointment:_____Reader hours:_____

Form of contact: Telephone___   Contact info:_____

                    Letter_____   _____

                    In person____   _____

                    E-mail_____   _____

Reference questions/research topic:_____

_____

_____

_____

_____

Search strategy/record groups to check:_____

_____

_____

_____

_____

Number of copies made:_____Charges:_____Paid:_____

DRAFT
VII – 05
12/10/98

Photograph order form

- Henry Ford Museum and Greenfield Village, Dearborn, Michigan

---

HENRY FORD MUSEUM & GREENFIELD VILLAGE *featuring* **IMAX THEATRE**

Research Center
20900 Oakwood Blvd
PO Box 1970
Dearborn, MI 48121-1970
Voice: 313.982.6070 x2517
Fax: 313.982.6244

PHOTOGRAPHIC ORDER FORM

INVOICE NO. _____

Sent to Photographic:
Due from Photographic:

THIS IS THE ONLY FORMAL INVOICE YOU WILL RECEIVE — **payment must be included with this invoice before processing will begin**

Please itemize each image. Include catalog number and brief description of each image, and/or the title, description, and number of minutes for audiovisual material. **Please attach an additional page if necessary**. Refer to fee schedule on p. 3 of this Agreement. **Use fees will not be refunded.**

Name:

NEG #	ID#	TITLE/CAPTION/DESCRIPTION	LOCATION		TYPE OF REPRO			FEE	OFFICE USE
			Used for:			B/W	Color		
			Acc# & Box		8x10 Print	35mm slide	Trans-parency		N e g / D E P / R P
					◆scan		◆scan		
1									
2									
3									
4									
5									

Henry Ford Museum & Greenfield Village Federal I.D. #: 38135951 3-N

Special Instructions:

Subtotal	
New Photography Fees	
6% MI sales tax◆	
Shipping Charges✛	
Rush Fees	
TOTAL	

✛No additional charge for items sent First Class US Mail w/in the US and Canada. Other shipping destinations and services available, charges vary by destination, service, and size of order. Please ask.

Or, provide your Shipping Acct #

◆If tax exempt, enter number here: _____

◆ **For scanned images, please choose:** FILE FORMAT: ( ) JPEG or ( ) TIFF
DELIVERY METHOD: ( ) CD-Rom or ( ) e-mail attachment

Method of payment (Payment must be made in U.S. dollars):
( ) Cash (for in-person orders only)
( ) Check or Money Order payable to "Henry Ford Museum & Greenfield Village"
Payment Company Name (if different from yours) : _____

( ) Credit Card (Mastercard, Visa, Discover, and American Express)

Name on Card _____

Credit Card # _____

Expiration Date _____

HFMGV Photo Reproduction Permission Forms

Protocol for handling records

What items can a researcher bring into the archives? What is prohibited (food or drink, pens, cell phones)? Researchers should be told how to handle fragile items and keep records in order and files in correct boxes.

- Brooklyn Museum of Art

R E S E A R C H E R S !

These materials are F R A G I L E -- please handle gently.

P L E A S E

Keep pages in order.

Keep pages in folder in book-like fashion:

Use only one folder at a time.

Do not fold, wrinkle, or otherwise mistreat papers.

Mark items to be photocopied with "identi-tabs."
See archivist for permission to photocopy.

When finished, please stack papers neatly (and gently) and return
folder to box in its original place.

Use pencil for note-taking.

Application to publish

If the researcher is allowed to publish from the materials in your archives, he or she must cite sources correctly and understand his or her responsibilities regarding obtaining copyright permission. The Denver Museum of Nature and Science (DMNS) Archives used the following language to clarify this point in its "Rules for Use of the Holdings By DMNS Personnel": "The Library/Archives staff will attempt to assist the user in locating authors or heirs, but the Library/Archives makes no representation that the DMNS is the owner of intellectual property rights (other than in its official records), unless such rights have been specifically and in writing transferred to the DMNS by the owner of those rights. As a condition of use, the researcher assumes full legal responsibility for any infringement of literary, copyright, or publication rights belonging to the author or his or her heirs or assigns."

• The Museum of Modern Art, New York

The Museum of Modern Art Archives

APPLICATION TO PUBLISH MATERIALS FROM THE MUSEUM ARCHIVES

Name (please print) _____ Date _____

Affiliation _____

Address _____

Telephone Number _____

I hereby request authorization to publish material from the Museum Archives of The Museum of Modern Art (the "Archival Materials"). Such authorization is subject to my warranting that I will not misrepresent the contents of the Archival Materials in any publication, and that I will include a citation to the correct source for the Archival Materials. This citation shall conform to the standards set forth in the *Format for Citations to Materials from The Museum of Modern Art Archives*, a copy of which is attached to this form.

I have attached to this signed form is a copy of the relevant citations and portions of the text to which they refer.

I acknowledge that the Museum is not responsible for the accuracy of Archival Materials or the contents thereof, or for verifying that I have used or represented the Archival Materials accurately. I further acknowledge that I am solely responsible for complying with all laws which may pertain to the publication of the contents of the Archival Materials, including, without limitation, the laws of libel, copyright and privacy. I agree to obtain any consents or permissions which may be necessary in connection with the publication of the intellectual property contained in the Archival Materials, including, without limitation, any necessary authorizations from the copyright holder thereof.

Bibliographic information on the planned publication is as follows:

_____

Signature _____ Date _____

The Museum of Modern Art Archives retains all rights in and to the Archival Materials, including the right to publish them itself or to grant permission to others to do so. If the Museum Archives grants permission to publish, such permission will be in writing. The Museum Archives requests a copy of any such publication.

Send completed application to: Museum Archives
                                   The Museum of Modern Art
                                   11 West 53rd Street
                                   New York, NY 10019

THE ARCHIVES OF THE PHILADELPHIA MUSEUM OF ART

Permission to Publish Materials Request Form

Name:_____

Institution and status:_____

Address:_____

_____

Telephone number/e-mail account (if applicable):_____

Description of materials used (attach additional sheets as needed):_____

_____

Title of work and publication date if known:_____

_____

Please carefully read the following policy and regulations concerning publication:

1)   The Philadelphia Museum of Art holds copyright to most of the materials housed in its archival collections. Potential publishers of written works based on reproductions of documents and/or substantial quotes from the Museum's archival collections must be granted permission to publish by a Museum representative. Dissertations are considered to be published works.

2)   In order to receive permission to publish from the Museum, a request should be addressed in writing to the Archivist or the Senior Curator overseeing the archival collection in question. Upon approval, a signed copy will be returned to the researcher for their records.

3)   In providing permission to publish materials obtained from its archival collections, the Museum does not assume any responsibility for infringement of copyright or of publication rights for materials that might be held by others. The publisher assumes all responsibility for obtaining permission from any additional copyright holders, and is subject to any claims under the Copyright Law or the laws of libel that could be made as the result of the publication.

4)   In giving permission to publish materials obtained from its archival collections, the Museum does not surrender its own rights to publish the material or grant permission to others to publish them.

5)   Permission to publish materials obtained through the Museum's archival collections is granted for a one-time use only. The responsibility for obtaining additional permission required for subsequent publication remains with the publisher of the material.

6)   Publishers should specify above which materials they plan to cite, plus the name of their publication and its publication date, if known. The publisher also agrees to provide a draft of the work to be published, with correct citations in the following form: (record group, series, item identification, and date), Philadelphia Museum of Art, Archives.

I have read the policy as stated above and agree to comply with its regulations.

Signature of Publisher:_____Date:_____

Signature of PMA Representative:_____Date:_____

DRAFT
VII – 07
3/26/99

Application to reproduce photographs

· National Air and Space Museum, Smithsonian Institution

Archives Division, Room 3100
National Air and Space Museum
Smithsonian Institution
Washington DC 20560-0322

Permission Number

APPLICATION FOR PERMISSION TO REPRODUCE NASM PHOTOGRAPHS
for use in BOOKS and PERIODICALS

Smithsonian Institution photographs may not by reproduced, resold, or commercially used without specific written permission from the Smithsonian Institution. This form must be completed if you anticipate publishing National Air and Space Museum (NASM) photographs in a **book or periodical**. If you anticipate using NASM photographs in some other application, please obtain the appropriate alternate permission application form (Film/Video, Electronic Media, Advertising, Museum or Miscellaneous) from the NASM Archives Division.

Submitted by: Name: _____   ☐ Author   ☐ Publisher

Organization: _____   ☐ Other: _____

PUBLICATION INFORMATION

BOOK	PERIODICAL
Title of Book:	Title of Article:
	Title of Periodical:
Type of Publication:	
Edition: Estimated Date of Publication:	Type of Publication:
Estimated Print Run:	Edition:
Estimated Cover Price:	Circulation: Cover Price:
AUTHOR:	**PUBLISHER:**
Address:	Address:
Telephone:	Telephone:

PLEASE LIST REQUESTED IMAGES ON OTHER SIDE OF THIS FORM

NOTE: COPY PHOTOGRAPHS MUST BE ORDERED SEPARATELY—THEY ARE NOT INCLUDED IN THE PERMISSION FEE.

If you already have a publisher:

Please complete the AUTHOR, PUBLISHER, and **ALL** the appropriate PUBLICATION INFORMATION section above (BOOK **or** PERIODICAL).

If you do NOT have a publisher:

Please complete the AUTHOR section above, and as much of the PUBLICATION INFORMATION section as possible (title, type of publication, etc.) The NASM Archives Division will review the copyright status of the images specified and issue a **Conditional Release** form listing those images which can be released by NASM as well as those images for which NASM cannot issue permission (RESTRICTED images). **This will NOT be a Permission to Publish.** The NASM Archives Division will hold your Application on file until you have a publisher for your book or article. At that time, please complete the PUBLICATION INFORMATION portion of your Conditional Release form and return it to the NASM Photo Archives so that we may complete the processing of your Permission Application.

NASM USE ONLY:

SI-OPPS Order Number: **NASM Letter Log No.**

Permission is requested to use the following materials from the National Air and Space Museum:

NASM Videodisc No.	SI Negative Number	Subject / Description of Image (File Location or Source if no Videodisc No.	Size (1/4 page, etc.)
2A-00353	A 26767-B-2	Wright 1903 Flyer, Kitty Hawk (First Flight)	EXAMPLE!!

If you have more than 14 items, you may attach additional sheets of paper to this form. Please use the same format as above.

NASM Archives Photograph Fee Schedule
(Send no fees with this form—You will be sent an invoice.)

For use in Books:

Print Run	½ Page or less	More than ½ Page	Cover
Under 5,000	$5	$10	$20
5,001-10,000	$15	$20	$40
10,001-20,000	$25	$40	$80
20,001-40,000	$30	$45	$90
Over 40,000	$35	$50	$100

For use in Periodicals:

Circulation	½ Page or less	More than ½ Page	Cover
Under 10,000	$5	$10	$20
10,001-100,000	$15	$25	$50
100,001-500,000	$25	$35	$75
Over 500,000	$40	$50	$100

RESTRICTIONS and REQUIREMENTS

COPYRIGHT DISCLAIMER. National Air and Space Museum photographs are obtained from many sources and are intended primarily for research and educational purposes. Certain works may be protected by copyright, trademark, or related interests not owned by the Smithsonian Institution. Permission will be granted only to the extent of the Smithsonian Institution's ownership of the rights relating to your particular request. **The responsibility for ascertaining whether any such rights exist, and for obtaining all necessary permissions remains with you, the applicant.**

PERMISSIONS. All permissions are issued for **ONE TIME USE ONLY,** for nonexclusive worldwide rights in all languages. Subsequent use of these photographs is restricted and requires additional permission authorization. This includes usage in a new edition or new format as well as usage in any promotional materials related to the book or periodical usage applied for above.

RESTRICTIONS AND LIMITATIONS. These photographs shall not be used to show or imply National Air and Space Museum or Smithsonian Institution endorsement of any commercial product or enterprise, or to indicate that the National Air and Space Museum or the Smithsonian Institution concurs with the opinions expressed in, or confirms the accuracy of any text used with these photographs.

COPY OF PUBLICATION. As part of the agreement to grant reproduction permission, the Smithsonian Institution requires that, immediately upon publication, **one copy** of the publication in which National Air and Space Museum photographs have been used be furnished at no cost to NASM for use in our library and division files. No new photo orders or permission requests submitted by the above author or publisher will be processed if this copy has not been received by NASM within **three months** of the stated release date. Publications should be sent to Archives Division, Room 3134, National Air and Space Museum, Smithsonian Institution, Washington, DC 20560-0322.

Signed: _____ Date: _____

Organization: _____ Title: _____

Address: _____ Telephone: _____

Revised by MANK & BDN 26 march 1999

INTERNET RESOURCES

Listservs

Listservs allow you to be involved in on-line discussions among archives professionals; they are a great resource for learning what's new and a useful place to pose questions. Below are some relevant listservs; the SAA Web site has links to these and other lists.

- The Archives and Archivists list serves the diverse archives community.
  listserv@muohio.edu

- The SAA Museum Archives Section list is designed specifically for museum archivists.
  listserv@sivm.si.edu (leave the subject line blank, and in the body of the e-mail, type: SAAMUS-L@SIVM.SI.EDU [First Name, Last Name])

- EAD (Encoded Archival Description) list
  Listserv@loc.gov

- Microsoft Access for Archivists list
  MSAccess4Archives-subscribe@topica.com

On-line Information on Archival Theory and Practice

- Conservation Online (COOL)
  <http://palimpsest.stanford.cdu>
  The Conservation Online Project (COOL) from the Preservation Department at Stanford University provides links to tools, resources, and information regarding conservation for a variety of record formats. The site also covers other important archival topics such as disaster planning, intellectual property, and copyright.

- The Archivist's Toolkit
  <http://aabc.bc.ca/aabc/toolkit.html> or
  <http://mayne.aabc.bc.ca/aabc/toolkit.html>
  Sponsored by the Archives Association of British Columbia, this site is designed for small and medium-sized archives. It includes sample forms, standards, and definitions for basic archival theory and terminology.

- *A Manual for Small Archives.* Archives Association of British Columbia, 1988, partially revised 1994.
  <http://aabc.bc.ca/aabc/msa/default.htm>

- National Park Service
  <http://www.cr.nps.gov/museum/publications/handbook.html>
  This site offers an on-line museum handbook. It includes disaster plans and a bibliography.

Finding Aids on the Web

Many institutions have encoded their finding aids and provide them for researchers on the Web. A few samples follow.

- Online Archive of California
  <http://www.oac.cdlib.org/dynaweb/ead/>
  This site contains finding aids from various institutions throughout California, including many museums.

- Smithsonian Institution
  <http://www.si.edu/archives/archives/2fatoc.htm>

- Japanese-American National Museum
  <http://www.janm.org/collection_guide/index.html>

- Peabody Museum of Archaeology and Ethnology, Harvard University
  <http://www.peabody.harvard.edu/archives/finding_aids_bak.html>

Funding Sources

There are myriad funding agencies, foundations, and donors that support archives. For information on funders, visit a Foundation Center office (in several major cities across the nation). Foundation Center resources and services are described on the Center's Web site at <http://www.fdncenter.org/>. Contact your state archives, as well. Some major funders of archival projects are listed below.

- Institute of Museum and Library Services (IMLS)
  <http://www.imls.gov/grants>
  The Institute of Museum and Library Services is a federal agency that supports the nation's museums and libraries. In addition to offering publications, conferences, and other resources, the IMLS provides National Leadership Grants for Library-Museum collaborations. These grants support projects to study how museums and libraries can more effectively serve the public through technological innovations and educational programs.

- National Endowment for the Humanities (NEH)
  <http://www.neh.fed.us/grants/guidelines/preservation.html>
  The Preservation and Access program of the National Endowment for the Humanities provides grants for projects to preserve and make available research materials of educational or historical value.

- National Historical Publications and Records Commission (NHPRC)
  <http://www.nara.gov/nhprc>
  The National Historical Publications and Records Commission provides grants for arrangement and description of archival materials and has a long history of providing seed money for new museum archives programs. The Commission also accepts applications each academic year from archival professionals for a fellowship in archival administration. The fellowship provides a stipend and benefits to archivists with two to five years experience who want to expand their knowledge and expertise in archives. The NHPRC chooses a host institution, and the grantee works at that organization, improving his or her knowledge and archival administrative experience.

SELECTED ARCHIVAL PRODUCT VENDORS

Below is a selection of major vendors of archival products. Many vendors exhibit their products at the SAA annual meeting; others may be found through advertisements in regional and national archival publications.

- Conservation Resources International
  <http://www.conservationresources.com>
  tel: 800-634-6932; 703-321-7730; fax: 703-321-0629

- Gaylord Archival Products
  <http://www.gaylord.com>
  tel: 800-634-6307; fax: 800-272-3412

- Hollinger Corporation
  <http://www.hollingercorp.com>
  tel: 800-634-0491

- Light Impressions
  <http://www.lightimpressionsdirect.com>
  tel: 800-828-6216 (U.S. and Canada);
  714-441-4539 (international); fax: 800-828-5539

- Metal Edge
  <http://www.metaledgeinc.com>
  tel: 800-862-2228; fax: 888-822-6937

- University Products
  <http://www.universityproducts.com>
  tel: 800-336-4847; fax: 800-532-9281

MUSEUM ARCHIVES GUIDELINES

The Museum Archives Section of the Society of American Archivists (SAA) is composed of individuals who are responsible for the organization and care of archival collections located in museums. The "Museum Archives Guidelines" have been created by the section to assist all types of museums—independent museums as well as museums contained within larger institutions—in the development and administration of archival programs. The guidelines outline the components of a successful museum archives program and should be used in conjunction with detailed information on the administration of archives that is available through SAA and from other professional sources.

Introduction

A museum's organizational records document the history and development of the museum, its collections, exhibitions, and programs as well as the contributions of individuals and groups associated with the museum. These records are unique and irreplaceable assets of the organization. A museum should maintain an active, professional archives program to systematically collect, organize, preserve, and provide access to its organizational records of enduring value and to recommend policies and procedures for the creation, maintenance, and ultimate retention or disposition of current museum records in all formats. By supporting an archives program a museum not only promotes its own history, but also ensures that its vital records are preserved and that information resources are readily available to support the work of its staff and meet the research needs of scholars and the general public. However, it should be noted that if a museum exists in a setting where a decision has been made to concentrate all institutional records in a central archives (e.g., university archives), it is the responsibility of the museum staff to work closely with the institutional archives staff to determine the appropriate setting for the archives of the museum.

1. Definitions and Scope

A museum's archives identifies, preserves and administers records of long-term and permanent administrative, legal, fiscal, and research value not in current use. Records may be in any form—including, but not limited to, paper, electronic, photographic, and magnetic media. A museum's archival records could include:

  a. Organizational records, in particular those which relate to administration at all levels. For example: correspondence, memoranda, minutes, financial records, reports, grant records, departmental files, architectural plans, documentary photographs and negatives, film, audio and videotapes, and publications created by the museum.

b. Collection records, such as object or specimen files and records of exhibitions and installations. These may be housed in the archives or, if actively used, in the curatorial, registration, or collections management offices.

c. Acquired materials, such as papers of individuals and organizations, which promote the museum's mission through their relation to subject areas of particular interest to the museum (e.g., science, anthropology, natural history, art, history) and which add value to the museum's collections and exhibition programs.

2. Mission Statement

The archives should have a mission statement, approved by the director of the museum or the institution and ratified by appropriate governing bodies of the museum or its parent institution, which defines the authority of the archivist within the museum and the parameters of the archival program. The statement should explicitly recognize the archivist's role in the museum and/or parent institution's records management program. All general policy statements concerning the archives should be in writing and approved by the appropriate authority.

3. Status of the Archives

The archives should be an entity within the museum's administrative structure, supervised by an individual having custodial and related authority delegated by the director of the museum or parent institution. When practical, the archives should be a separate department within the museum. The museum archives may be an administrative affiliate of a parent institution's archives.

4. Professional Archivist

The museum should have a professionally trained archivist. If resources do not permit this level of commitment, expert advice should be sought in the development of the museum's archives and archival training provided to the staff member made responsible for them. The functions of the archivist are to appraise, acquire, arrange, describe, preserve, and make available the records of the museum and collections of related materials acquired from outside the museum.

5. Museum Records and Personal Papers

The museum should have a statement of policy which clarifies the difference between the official records of the museum and documents which might be considered the personal property of curators, directors, members of governing bodies, and other relevant positions. This is to discourage such persons from taking, as their own property, records that belong to the parent institution or museum, and that may be an integral part of the museum's archives. Donation of personal papers to the museum's archives is strongly encouraged in order to promote the preservation of significant documents not created by the museum itself.

6. Acquisition Policy for Collected Materials

The museum should define and make public an archives acquisition policy, which delineates the collecting of materials other than those created within the museum itself. The collecting activities and acquisition policies of other entities in a parent institution or outside institutions should be taken into account to avoid unnecessary competition. The policy should describe the conditions and procedures for accessioning and deaccessioning documents and collections that are not official records of the museum, and address principles regarding the ownership, administration, and use of all acquired materials.

7. Criteria for Retention of Museum Records

The archivist must be involved in the determination of how long and under what conditions particular records are to be kept. The criteria for permanent retention include:

a. Evidence of the structure, development, mission and functions of the museum over time.

b. Documentation of the actions, decisions, policies, and fiscal and legal rights and responsibilities of the museum.

c. Research and informational value.

8. Current Records

The advice of the archivist should be sought on policies and guidelines pertaining to the creation, maintenance, disposition, and preservation of museum records (including electronic records and systems) with the aim of avoiding the unnecessary creation of duplicate records and the needless retention of nonpermanent records. The archivist should be consulted for recommendations on the protection of permanently active records of archival value in non-custodial situations (such as collection or accession records under the care of the registrar, collections manager, or curator and computer network backups under the control of the information technology staff). The archivist should also approve the appropriate disposition of records that do not have permanent value, or are required to be maintained by the archives of a parent institution.

9. Location and Conditions

a. The archives should be located in a separate and secure area with adequate protection against fire, flood, vermin, theft, and other hazards.

b. Temperature, light, and humidity should be controlled at appropriate and stable levels to ensure the preservation of materials. Certain records may have special environmental requirements.

c. To prevent flood damage, archives should not be placed below ground level.

d. If neither suitable accommodation nor adequate staff can be provided on-site for the archives, the institution should consider:

   i. Placing its records in the archives of its parent institution if applicable or in a nearby archival repository willing to administer them on a continuing basis.

ii. Forming or joining a consortium whereby several institutions cooperate to ensure that their archives receive adequate care.

iii. Contributing to cost in the above choices.

10. Arrangement, Description, and Preservation of the Records

a. The archivist organizes records in keeping with the professional principles of provenance and the sanctity of original order whenever possible.

b. The archivist produces written descriptive inventories, guides and other finding aids in accordance with accepted archival standards and makes them generally available.

c. The archivist implements basic preservation measures such as the use of archival-quality containers.

11. Access

Subject to reasonable restrictions on the grounds of fragility, security, or confidentiality, records should be available to staff members, scholars, and other persons demonstrating a need to consult the material for research purposes. Access policies and restrictions should be in writing and applied equally to all researchers. Reference service should be provided to both on-site researchers and those at a distance.

Adopted by SAA Council, August 19, 2003

CONTRIBUTORS

Susan K. Anderson comes from a visual arts background, which she initially channeled toward teaching and conservation after graduating with an MFA from Southern Illinois University. She discovered the archives profession while working as a conservation technician with Pennsylvania Hospital's Historic Collections. Doing archival work proved more enticing than book repair, so she enrolled in Drexel University's Information Science program, and became Archivist for the hospital in 1994. In 1998, she became Archivist of the Philadelphia Museum of Art, which allows her to keep in touch with her artistic "roots."

Marisa Bourgoin received a BA in the History of Art from Bryn Mawr College and began working at the Corcoran Gallery of Art, where she intended to pursue a museum career. She found that the archival profession combined her varied interests in curatorial work, museum education, and museum registration. She completed an MLS at the University of Maryland at College Park and has been the Corcoran's archivist since 1995.

Fred Calabretta is Associate Curator of Collections and Oral Historian at Mystic Seaport, where he formerly served as the Museum's Sound Archivist for nine years. He has conducted several hundred audio and video oral history interviews, is past president of the New England Association of Oral History, and past chair of the Oral History Section of the Society of American Archivists. He published the *Guide to the Oral History Collections* at Mystic Seaport Museum in 1992.

Bernadette Callery was initially attracted to botanical bibliography as one of the few scientific disciplines where descriptive bibliography really mattered. She has served the collections of the Hunt Botanical Library in Pittsburgh and the New York Botanical Garden Library, promoting those collections through exhibitions, lectures, articles, and an on-line catalog. Working as the museum librarian at the Carnegie Museum of Natural History in Pittsburgh, she was intrigued by the broader field of museum recordkeeping systems, particularly the various schemes used to capture documentary evidence of museum collections. She has been at the Carnegie since 1995 and began her involvement with the archives after she took an archival appraisal class from Richard Cox and had an epiphany about functional analysis as a means of analyzing organizational processes.

Maygene Daniels is the Chief of Archives at the National Gallery of Art, Washington, D.C.. She has served as the chair and as a member of the Architectural Records Committee of the International Council on Archives. She also is a past president of the Society of American Archivists and the Academy of Certified Archivists and has been involved in many other professional activities. Before joining the National Gallery of Art, she worked in a number of capacities at the National Archives and served as Director of the Modern Archives Institute.

Polly Darnell is the Archivist and Librarian at the Shelburne Museum in Shelburne, Vermont. She established the museum's first archives program under a grant from the Henry Luce Foundation, starting in 1995, shortly before the museum's fiftieth anniversary. Before that, she managed the research collections at the Sheldon Museum in Middlebury, Vermont, and spent a year in western New York visiting all kinds of historical records repositories as Regional Archivist for the Documentary Heritage Program.

Sarah R. Demb, of the International Records Management Trust in England, was formerly Assistant Archivist, Reference and Technical Services, at the National Museum of the American Indian, Smithsonian Institution. She holds a BA in anthropology from the University of British Columbia and an MLIS from the Graduate School of Library and Information Science at the University of Texas at Austin. Previously she was the Archivist for the Peabody Museum of Archaeology and Ethnology, Harvard University. Sarah's interest in museums began with an undergraduate summer job at the Far Eastern Department Library of the Royal Ontario Museum in Toronto, Canada.

Fynnette Eaton recently joined the Electronic Records Archives Program at the National Archives and Records Administration. From 1997 to 2002, she served as Director of the Technical Services Division within the Smithsonian Institution Archives, where she focused on preservation of archival materials and development of an electronic records program at the SI Archives. She has a BA and an MA in history from the University of Maryland. Previous experience included serving as Chief of the Technical Services Branch at the Center for Electronic Records at NARA and as an archivist in the Office of Presidential Libraries and Documentation Standards Staff. She has presented papers and is author of articles on the preservation of electronic records at the National Archives. She was selected as a Fellow of the Society of American Archivists in 1995 and received the IAC/IRM Technology Excellence Award in 1996 for designing the Archival Preservation System at NARA.

Catherine Herbert is the Provenance Researcher at the Philadelphia Museum of Art, where she is investigating works of art in a variety of curatorial departments. She received her Ph.D. in medieval art history from the University of Delaware in 1997. Although Nazi-era provenance research may seem far removed from her original focus of study, the work makes good use of her research skills and foreign language training, as well as being fascinating in its own right. Before joining the museum staff, she worked as a bibliographic specialist for the University of Pennsylvania's Biddle Law Library and in the Public Services Office of the Conservation Center for Art and Historic Artifacts, a regional paper conservation laboratory in Philadelphia.

Susan Klier Koutsky is the leader of the Brittle Materials, Reformatting, and Deacidification Team in the Preservation Production Group in the University of Maryland Libraries. Previously, she was the Archivist at the National Museum of Women in the Arts in Washington, D.C.. She began working in this position when the museum was only fifteen years old and as its first full-time archivist, she set up the archives and records management programs, wrote the policies and procedures manual, and processed museum records. Prior to this position, she was a music librarian/archivist for "The President's Own" United States Marine Band in Washington, D.C.. Koutsky is active in national and regional archives and library organizations and has presented workshops and training in disaster preparedness and preservation issues. She has also served as an archival records consultant to area music organizations. Koutsky earned her master's degree in library science from the Catholic University of America and her bachelor's degree in music education from the University of Illinois.

Peter C. Marzio is Director of the Museum of Fine Arts, Houston. Prior to accepting the directorship of the MFAH in 1982, he was CEO and Director of the Corcoran Gallery of Art. During his tenure there, from 1978 to 1982, he instituted the Corcoran's first archival program. Within two years of his appointment at the MFAH, he established the MFAH Archives, one of the oldest continuously operating art museum archives in the US and the first in Texas. Dr. Marzio has served as Director of the Association of Art Museum Directors (AAMD) and as Chairman of the Federal Council on the Arts and Humanities. He is active within the National Endowment of the Arts, the Institute of Museum Services, the National Endowment for the Humanities, and the Mayor's Art Advisory Committee for the City of Houston.

Laura Peimer received a master's degree in history with a certificate in archival management from New York University in January 1996. She has worked as a consulting archivist for The Winthrop Group, Inc. and as a photo archivist for the American Jewish Historical Society in Massachusetts and New York. She is currently the Mellon Project Archivist at the Brooklyn Museum of Art.

Ann Marie Przybyla received undergraduate degrees in English and History from SUNY at Buffalo and an MLS with a concentration in Archives Administration and Master's of Medieval History from the University of Maryland at College Park. She has held positions as archivist/records manager at national research institutions, including the National Archives, the Smithsonian Institution, and the National Gallery of Art, and was Archivist of the Cleveland Museum of Art from 1996 to 2000. She is currently a Regional Advisory Officer for the New York State Archives, where she provides advice and support to local governments throughout eleven counties in the Adirondack Region.

Anthony Reed was born and raised in Southern California and received his BA in Women's Studies and Sociology from the University of California, Santa Barbara, before earning his MLS from Simmons College in Boston in 1996. Having relocated to Seattle for a couple of years, Anthony spent some time working for Microsoft, Amazon.com, and the archives of the Catholic Archdiocese of Seattle. After returning to Boston, Anthony worked for Boston College, Boston Public Library, and the town of Burlington, Massachusetts, before finally landing a job with the National Park Service. He is currently an archivist at the Frederick Law Olmsted National Historic Site in Brookline, Massachusetts, and lives in Boston with his partner and their cat, Smokey Joe.

Paula Stewart, CA, CRM, began her association with the Amon Carter Museum as an intern in summer 1985 and was hired as a cataloger in the photography collection later that year. In 1992, she became the museum's first archivist. She graduated with an MA in history and a certificate in archives administration from the University of Texas at Arlington in 1987 and earned her Certified Records Manager designation in January 1999 and Certified Archivist designation in fall 2001.

Deborah Wythe has been Archivist of the Brooklyn Museum of Art since 1986, when she was hired under an NHPRC seed-money project. Her introduction to museum archives came as an intern at the Metropolitan Museum of Art, working on the records of the Musical Instrument Department, while she was pursuing doctoral studies in musicology at New York University. She also served as Curator of the Steinway Collection at the LaGuardia Archives, LaGuardia Community College, City University of New York.

ACKNOWLEDGMENTS

*T*he following paragraphs illustrate the depth of involvement of current museum archivists in this project: hardly a name is missing from among active members of the SAA Museum Archives Section, both experienced and new. We have learned from each other over the years, sharing our experiences and solving our problems together on the telephone, via the section listserv, in the newsletter, at section working groups, and at section meetings. We have also depended upon our colleagues in other museum professions—the curators, registrars, and librarians cited here and in the text—for input about the interactions between their work and our own. This manual, in which the authors share their expertise, is essentially a compilation of that cooperative learning process.

Many members of the Museum Archives Section enriched this project by contributing their thoughts and expertise during the section working groups at the 2000 and 2001 SAA annual meetings: Ann Abid, Cleveland Museum of Art; Susan Anderson, Philadelphia Museum of Art; Alan Bain, Smithsonian Institution; Marisa Bourgoin, Corcoran Gallery of Art; Maygene Daniels, National Gallery of Art; Polly Darnell, Shelburne Museum; Sarah Demb, Peabody Museum of Archaeology and Ethnology and National Museum of the American Indian, Smithsonian Institution; Fynnette Eaton, Smithsonian Institution, currently NARA; Michelle Elligott, The Museum of Modern Art; J. Todd Ellison, Center of Southwestern Studies, Fort Lewis College; Anne Foster, Montana Historical Society; Susan Koutsky, National Museum of Women in the Arts (currently University of Maryland); Andrew Martinez, Rhode Island School of Design; Susan McElrath, National Anthropological Archives, Smithsonian Institution; Lonna McKinley, United States Air Force Museum; Maureen Melton, Museum of Fine Arts, Boston; Fae Palmer, Museo de Arte de Puerto Rico; Judy Prosser-Armstrong, Museum of Western Colorado; Ann Marie Przybyla, Cleveland Museum of Art (currently New York State Archives); Paula Stewart, Amon Carter Museum; Lorraine Stuart, Museum of Fine Arts, Houston; Kate Theimer; Cassandra Volpe, University of Colorado, Boulder; Michele Wellck, California Academy of Sciences; Kathleen Williams, Smithsonian Institution; Deborah Wythe, Brooklyn Museum of Art.

As editor, I would like to thank the two other members of the editorial committee, Ann Marie Przybyla and Sarah Demb. Ann Marie acted as scribe for our Presidents' Day weekend planning meeting in 1999, organized our many thoughts, produced the prospectus, and submitted our proposal to the Society. Ann Marie also served as general editor during the early months of the project and chaired the two working groups. Sarah Demb contributed many excellent ideas, kept us on track in our discussions, and has been a great support during the entire project. In addition, heartfelt thanks to Susan Fox, Executive Director of the Society of American Archivists, for her support in providing funds for the 1999 planning meeting; to Diana Wythe Tyler and William Drinkuth, our Presidents' Day weekend hosts, for providing the perfect working-weekend hideaway in Vermont; and to Teresa Brinati, SAA's Director of Publications, for her assistance as we worked our way through the entire process.

All the participants owe a vote of thanks to our institutions for supporting our work during this project: Amon Carter Museum; Brooklyn Museum of Art; Carnegie Museum of Natural History; Cleveland Museum of Art; Corcoran Gallery of Art; Mystic Seaport Museum; National Gallery of Art; National Museum of the American Indian; National Museum of Women in the Arts; Frederick Law Olmsted Historic Site, National Park Service; Peabody Museum of Archaeology and Ethnology; Philadelphia Museum of Art; Shelburne Museum; Smithsonian Institution; and University of Maryland.

The editor and authors would like to thank the following individuals, whose help was invaluable, as well as all of our families, friends, and partners for supporting us during evenings and weekends of writing and editing.

Laura Peimer, the manual's able photo editor, sought out, organized, selected, and placed the many wonderful images that illustrate the richness of all of our collections. Our thanks to the following for their contributions: Susan K. Anderson, Laura Botts, Marisa Bourgoin, Fred Calabretta, Jeff Carr, Liz Clancy, Victoria Cranner, Maygene Daniels, Polly Darnell, Sarah Demb, Fynnette Eaton, Michelle Elligot, David Farneth, Duncan Ganley, Kristine A. Haglund, Michelle Harvey, Catherine Herbert, Mark Katzman, Raegen Kennett, Charles S. Klein, Barbara Mathé, Sammie Morris, Christine Nelson, Alex Pezzati, Anthony Reed, Susan Sacharski, Peggy Tate Smith, Lorraine A. Stuart, Kathleen Williams, Deborah Wythe, and Julie R. Yankowsky.

Laura was also assisted in the huge task of compiling the Resource Guide by many individuals, including Susan K. Anderson, Fred Calabretta, Mary K. Coffey, Polly Darnell, Sarah Demb, Fynnette Eaton, Michelle Elligott, Mark A. Greene, Kristine A. Haglund, Patricia A. Hamilton, Ann Hitchcock, staff of the Holocaust Museum Houston, Kristine L. Kaske, Robert Leopold, Melissa McGann, Jeffrey V. Moy, Ann Marie Przybyla, staff of the Rensselaer County Historical Society, Jennifer Trant, Kathleen Williams, Deborah Wythe, and Helen Yoxall.

Lorraine Stuart was responsible for obtaining our foreword from her director, Peter Marzio, and served as a reader for the final draft. Kathleen Williams helped outline the description chapter, provided guidance for the appraisal chapter, and read and commented on the entire volume. Thanks are due to the many Section members who contributed their experiences and ideas about appraisal during our two working groups on that topic. Susan Anderson, Laurie Baty, Polly Darnell, and Laura Peimer were kind enough to serve as readers and editors for the editor's own chapters. Laura Peimer and Michelle Harvey assisted in reading proofs.

Our thanks to the many museum archivists (beyond the authors) who supplied information for sidebars, including Alan Bain, Thelma Boeder, Alan Crookham, Douglas Doe, Michelle Elligott, Kristine Kaske, Nancy Kirkpatrick, Elizabeth Knowlton, Andrew Martinez, Melissa McGann, Miriam Meislik, Jeffrey Moy, Christine Nelson, Steve Ourada, Richard Pearce-Moses, Toniann Scime, John Smith, Lorraine Stuart, Kathleen Williams, and Matt Wrbican.

The *Museum Archives Guidelines*, accepted by SAA Council as a standard in August 2003, were drafted by the Guidelines Committee of the Museum Archives Section, published in several draft versions in *Museum Archivist*, and discussed at the annual section meetings, beginning in 1998. Committee members included Polly Darnell and Andrew Martinez, chairs, Sarah Demb, Mary Elizabeth Ruwell, Paula Stewart, and Deborah Wythe.

From Susan Anderson: For their informal advice and observations about restrictions and ethics, thanks are due to Bernadette Callery, Carnegie Museum of Natural History; Maygene Daniels, National Gallery of Art; Sarah Demb, National Museum of the American Indian; Michelle Elligott, The Museum of Modern Art; Charles Greifenstein, College of Physicians of Philadelphia; Kristine Kaske, National Air and Space Museum; Susan Koutsky, University of Maryland; Julie McMaster, Toledo Museum of Art; Maureen Melton, Museum of Fine Arts, Boston; Alessandro Pezzati, University of Pennsylvania; Ann Marie Przybyla, New York State Archives and Records Administration; Bart Ryckbosch and Mary Woolever, Art Institute of Chicago; Lorraine Stuart, Museum of Fine Arts, Houston; and Deborah Wythe, Brooklyn Museum of Art. A special thank-you goes to Clarisse Carnell, the Philadelphia Museum of Art's Registrar for the Collections, for starting the dialogue.

Marisa Bourgoin would like to thank her colleagues at the Corcoran, particularly Elizabeth Parr, Exhibitions Director.

Polly Darnell is grateful to Elizabeth Dow for patiently reading her truly terrible first drafts and finding something of value in them; to James Reilly of the Image Permanence Institute for corrections to the audiovisual chapter; to Alan F. Lewis of the National Archives and Records Administration for immeasurably improving the AV chapter and generously educating her about AV materials; and to Karan Sheldon and David Weiss of Northeast Historic Film for their reading of the AV chapter.

From Sarah Demb: Thanks to my colleagues at the Peabody Museum and the National Museum of the American Indian and to the SAA Museum Archives Section members, without whose vocal and consistent support my sections would not have been written. Special thanks to my co-contributors to the manual, to Dr. Viva Fisher for many thought-provoking conversations about the complexities of accessioning, and to Deborah Day, Archivist at the Scripps Oceanographic Institute.

Catherine Herbert notes: I am grateful for the guidance of Susan Anderson in compiling this chapter and for her assistance in my ongoing provenance research at the Philadelphia Museum of Art. I would also like to thank Jennifer Thompson and Katherine Luber of the PMA for their generous advice and encouragement.

Fynnette Eaton wishes to thank Kathleen Williams and Sarah Stauderman for their assistance in the development of her chapter.

Anthony Reed would like to thank the fine, hardworking archives staff of the Olmsted National Historic Site and in the broader National Park Service who make his job fun. He'd also like to thank the scores of professionals with whom it's his pleasure to work and socialize, day in and day out. Special thanks to Virginia Hunt at Harvard University's Countway Library of Medicine for insights into the specific challenges facing science museums, as well as John Smith at the Andy Warhol Museum in Pittsburgh, Bernadette Callery at the Carnegie Museum of Natural History, also in Pittsburgh, and Sarah Demb from the National Museum of the American Indian, for their help and contributions.

Paula Stewart thanks her colleagues at the Amon Carter Museum for their continuing support over the years. She also gives special thanks to Susan Hubbard, CRM, and Pamela A. Price, CRM, her mentors in the records and information-management field.

INDEX